T0311728

ROUTLEDGE LIBRARY EDITIONS: MODERN WORLD ECONOMY

Volume 2

THE CRUMBLING OF EMPIRE

THE CRUMBLING OF EMPIRE
The Disintegration of World Economy

M. J. BONN

Routledge
Taylor & Francis Group

LONDON AND NEW YORK

First published in 1938 by Allen & Unwin

This edition first published in 2017
by Routledge

4 Park Square, Milton Park, Abingdon, Oxon OX14 4RN

605 Third Avenue, New York, NY 10017

Routledge is an imprint of the Taylor & Francis Group, an informa business

© 1938 M. J. Bonn

British Library Cataloguing in Publication Data
A catalogue record for this book is available from the British Library

ISBN: 978-1-138-63020-8 (Set)
ISBN: 978-1-315-20964-7 (Set) (ebk)
ISBN: 978-1-138-63370-4 (Volume 2) (hbk)
ISBN: 978-1-138-63371-1 (Volume 2) (pbk)
ISBN: 978-1-315-20718-6 (Volume 2) (ebk)

Publisher's Note
The publisher has gone to great lengths to ensure the quality of this reprint but points out that some imperfections in the original copies may be apparent.

Disclaimer
The publisher has made every effort to trace copyright holders and would welcome correspondence from those they have been unable to trace.

The

CRUMBLING OF EMPIRE

The Disintegration of World Economy

by

M. J. BONN

LONDON

GEORGE ALLEN & UNWIN LTD

MUSEUM STREET

FIRST PUBLISHED IN 1938

To my friends
and colleagues of the
London School of Economics

PREFACE

THE scramble among the Powers for the remaining un-
claimed parts of the earth in the last quarter of the nineteenth century had blinded people's eyes to the fact that
the age of colonization was over. By that time all independent
empty regions, into which a stream of mass immigration
could be directed, had been occupied and settled. In
climatically favoured spots a few more composite colonies
could be formed by planting a smallish white upper stratum
as overlords over the natives, whose numbers precluded the
growth of new genuine daughter-states. Or some native
state could be conquered and superficially westernized by
white administrators and business men. But opportunities
for every sort of colonial expansion were contracting.

The Rising of the Nations, moreover, which the Declaration of Independence had set going, was spreading. It was
no longer confined to those overseas countries which were
held in subjection by foreign masters. The foundations of
ascendancy were shaking in nearly every composite state.
After the War three great vanquished empires had crumbled
under the impact of the forces of disintegrating nationalism,
which proceeded to attack victors and neutrals alike. The
long-drawn-out age of empire-making was passing; an age
of empire-breaking was dawning.

I have on various occasions given an outline of this great
transition, which I called "the age of counter-colonization";
I am now attempting to depict it on a larger canvas.

I may be told that I have chosen an inappropriate moment.
In Manchuria, in Abyssinia, and in the German demands,
colonial questions have come once again to the front. Are
they the main issue in the clash which threatens to involve
the world?

Neither Germany nor Italy has gone to Spain merely
in search of colonies. Japan may have looked upon the

seizure of Manchuria as a colonial venture. Her wars on China are attempts at empire-breaking. For though China is much more of a Have-not country than Japan, especially since the sacking of Manchuria, her great population outlet, she still holds dependencies of her own. Whatever the outcome of this struggle for supremacy between two peoples, neither of whom can be called colonial, it will mean the end of Western colonization in the Far East.

To Germany, Italy, and Japan, so-called Have-not countries, the control of dependencies is a symbol, not the substance, of equality. These nations have discarded "equality" at home as an antiquated democratic principle; they are making it the centre of their foreign policies.

No reshuffling of colonial possessions, however, will stop counter-colonization. The substitution of new, perhaps more efficient masters might bring about a semblance of peace and contentment among subject races; the fires will go on smouldering beneath the surface.

Such shiftings cannot result in real equality; nothing short of the breaking up of the major colonial empires could accomplish this. They would have to go far beyond the exchange or conquest of a few colonies and lead to large-scale territorial rearrangements of the map of the world— not merely of colonial possessions—were they to achieve something like genuine equality between states.

In the past less-favoured nations could rely on a fair measure of equality of opportunity for their inhabitants. As long as Great Britain stood for free trade and maintained the gold standard as the basis of her world-wide trade connections, a large part of the earth was open to the enterprise of every nation. Up to the 21st September, 1931, economic universalism, as a great British tradition, coincided with British economic nationalism. On that date they parted company. To-day there are no more important free trade areas, apart from a handful of tropical colonies. Everywhere else policies based on unlimited national economic sovereignty are ousting the concepts of world economy and economic universalism, which had survived tariffs, quotas, premiums, and preferences.

No doubt a return to free trade in the widest sense of the word could establish much greater economic equality among the peoples, if not among the states, than any feasible territorial rearrangements. It would lessen tension considerably and prepare the way to better political understanding. But this course is no longer possible.

The resumption of international economic co-operation and the limitation of that aggressive state individualism directed against fellow-states (recently censured in the Van Zeeland Report), which is far more ruthless than its prototype among men, may perhaps result in some self-denying ordinance by countries which have not yet plunged very deeply into economic regimentation. But even they cling tenaciously to a few miserable tariff positions rather than to principles of freedom and peace. No totalitarian Power can be expected to scrap its new plants, the cherished hopes for future self-sufficiency, in exchange for some grudgingly given trade concessions, which might make it a little richer, but which would not make it more powerful and more safe. Autarchy to it is not a mere policy; it is a creed based on the concept of the national state as a kind of living physical organism. Such a body may have contacts with other bodies politic; it cannot afford to get its organs tangled up with theirs nor have its vital functions dependent on their activities.

The egalitarian issue which has been raised can be settled neither by colonial concessions nor by free trade. It is not a mere principle of statecraft, such as the Balance of Power, but, like all egalitarian doctrines, the core of a passionate fanatic creed.

The ultimate solution must be found in federation. Peaceful federation depends on far-reaching like-mindedness between possible partners. It is limited to countries who

A*

share the same outlook on life; they cannot join others who deny their ideals. But these can line up with one another and by pressure force unwilling smaller states into their ranks. Societies representing antagonistic economic principles cannot be brought into a single federation. Just now there is no hope for what might be called social monism. The choice seems to lie between dualism and pluralism. The world of to-day and perhaps of to-morrow is likely to be split into economic blocs, animated by divergent economic ideals and pursuing opposite political ends. Not even federation, so it seems, can restore unity to the world and bring back that Western universalism which once pervaded it. "Pan-Europa" is a pale shadow; "Mittel-Europa" is a concrete policy.

I have dealt sparingly with statistical data, as they can be found, among other works, in great detail in Grover Clark's *The Balance Sheets of Imperialism* or in *The Colonial Problem*, published by the Royal Institute of International Affairs. The promised new edition of J. A. Hobson's *Imperialism*—without which Lenin's *Imperialism* could scarcely have been written—will no doubt bring its author's earlier statements up to date.

I have to thank Mr. Bernard Keeling for the great trouble he has taken in verifying my statistics. He and Professor Lionel Robbins have kindly read the proofs and have helped me to avoid some at least of those reiterations which are apt to arise from continued occupation with one's subject. Miss V. N. M. Evans has compiled the index.

It is but fitting that I dedicate this book to my friends and colleagues of the London School of Economics, in whose congenial atmosphere I have been able to ponder on some of the world's great problems.

M. J. BONN

March 1938

CONTENTS

PART I

COLONIZATION

CHAPTER   PAGE

        INTRODUCTION   13

   I. CONQUEST AND COLONIZATION   33
   II. VOLUNTARY COLONIZATION   54
   III. TYPES OF COLONIES   66
   IV. THE TRADE EMPIRE   84

PART II

DISINTEGRATION

   I. DEMOCRACY, NATIONALISM,
        LIBERALISM   102
   II. ECONOMIC SEPARATISM   120
   III. IMPERIALIST NATIONALISM   128
   IV. THE RISING OF THE NATIONS   145
   V. THE ECONOMIC REVOLT   159
   VI. AUTARCHY   185

PART III

EMPIRE MAKING OR EMPIRE BREAKING?

   I. INEQUALITY   199
   II. EQUALITY   227
   III. CHANGE   236
   IV. EQUALITY OF OPPORTUNITY   261
   V. THE VALUE OF COLONIES   289
   VI. CONQUEST AND COMMERCE   339
   VII. SUPER-STATE OR EMPIRE   367
   VIII. THE MAIN ISSUE: CONQUEST OR   396
        FEDERATION

        INDEX   425

INTRODUCTION

I

WESTERN civilization in the European middle ages had been universal in things essential. The State in the days of "Gothic barbarity", as radical reformers called them at a later date, was rather loosely knit; it permitted a good deal of regional and individual diversity to those strong enough to use their liberty. The colourful variety of this stratified, medieval hierarchy, tinged with mellow traditions, contrasts pleasantly with the drab uniformity of modern rational democracy. But the pivotal elements of this society were the same in all countries belonging to the Western world. There was the unity of faith, implying not only the universality of a dominant creed, but also of a dominant Church, which looked upon all Christian realms as her vassals. The same code of morals and the same code of law were in universal use, wherever the allegiance to the Church was recognized. A universal language linked the ruling classes of each principality to one another and preserved for those who mastered it, the intellectual, legal, and cultural legacy of Imperial Rome. There was similarity, not to say identity, of political and social institutions, for church and language had salvaged some part of her social mechanism for her successors. And though the feudal system and the guild organization of the medieval cities may not have descended in unbroken lines from Rome, they were universal in the Christian world, irrespective of the variations (and they were considerable) due to particular regional circumstances.

The rupture between the Eastern and the Western empire and, later on, the schism between the Eastern and the Western Church had tended to break unity as well as universality. But when Byzantium was ultimately engulfed in the victorious Ottoman Empire and when Mohammedan states

fringed the shores of the Mediterranean from the Lebanon
to the Pyrenees, the inner discordances of the Christian
world gradually lost some of their significance. During long
centuries it was engaged in a struggle for life and supremacy
against the Mohammedan invaders. It regained the West
and very nearly conquered the East, but its rule was ultimately confined within much narrower limits than those of
Imperial Rome. Within these narrower frontiers unity and
universality became much more strongly expressed. Along
a battle front which, at one time, reached from Spain and
even France, through Africa and Asia Minor, to the gates
of Vienna, the spiritual conceptions and the social institutions of the West had to meet the forces of Islam. Both
religious civilizations insisted on ascendancy and attempted
conformity; spiritual conciliation and even cultural co-
operation, was out of the question. In this respect Mohammedan civilization was perhaps more elastic than its Christian
counterpart. Even the fairly primitive and rigid Turks let
the subject Christian races live under their rule from the
conquest of Constantinople (1453) to the burning of Smyrna
(1922), whilst Spain, the great protagonist power in the
struggle against Islam, expelled the Jews (1492) and the
Moriscoes (1609). Her notions of unity and uniformity were
very much stricter than those of her Moorish rivals, who had
intermittently practised a kind of pluralist statecraft, whilst
she professed a kind of religious, racial, and political Monism.

Outside the religious field, the Christian West and
the Moslem East need not have been antagonistic to each
other, for institutionally, culturally, and even racially, they
had much in common, for example, feudalism and chivalry.
Their rulers approached problems of state administration
and army organization from a similar angle, drawing con-
sciously or half-consciously on the experience and the pre-
cedents both had inherited from Byzantium and Rome. And
in the more limited field of arts and sciences there was a
good deal of give and take on both sides. The East learned

from the West and the West was taught by the East. During lengthy intervals there was a spirited exchange between both halves of the Eurasian world on a basis of cultural reciprocity.

II

Long before the struggle between Moslem and Christian civilization had been finally decided, the unity of the Western Christian world was disintegrating. The use of vernacular languages was spreading and relegated Latin to the background; it became a mere technical instrument for the clerics of the Church and the clerks of the State. As the vernacular literature ousted Latin, people's minds were freed from some of their old fetters. They no longer visualized the ancient world in the venerable setting framed for them by scholastic formalists. They let their imagination take new flights into hitherto unexplored regions. The modern state, conscious of its own separate individuality, was no longer willing to be treated as a mere province of a Holy Roman Empire, which had become holy indeed, since it had almost completely lost its material substance. Even the newly formed Papal states, which were playing an important part in the political wrangles of the age, were assuming a separate Italian nationality and were no longer "Roman" in the universal sense of the word. True enough, spiritual unity survived; it permeated an administration which regulated the moral issues of the entire Western world. Side by side with the tribal, local, or State-made laws of the Western nations, which could be enforced in limited regions only, the Canon Law continued, distinct from them and universal in binding all nations. Its servants attempted to identify it with the law of nature, which, being of divine origin, was ordained to overrule mere man-made law in every land.

The makers of each modern sovereign state were conscious of its separate personality; they were building up an administration of their own, based on Roman and sometimes on Saracen foundations. They strongly emphasized its separateness from other states, even though they might greatly resemble one another. They insisted on strict conformity within their boundaries. There was no room within them for the almost joyous and motley laxity of earlier feudal agglomerations, which had occupied the place of the state for some time. The English who attempted to denationalize the Irish, and the Spaniards who expelled the Jews and the Moors, or the French who broke the back of the Huguenots and ultimately drove them from home by the revocation of the Edict of Nantes, were not so much incited by a fanatical spirit of persecution (though many of them felt in duty bound to burn heretics) as by the conviction that conformity must be imposed upon all subjects of the State, and that heretics could not be allowed to practise their separate forms of divine worship.

These modern states themselves strongly objected to the conformity and the uniformity imposed on them by Rome. Their conception of sovereignty was of recent growth, they felt humiliated and hampered by the fiscal dependency in which they were held by Rome. They objected quite as strongly to the freedom of the clergy from State taxation as to the contributions imposed on clergy and laity by her. They saw in Peter's pence a kind of tribute levied on vassals by a superior lord, who gave them very little in return for it, as they no longer needed his protection. They denounced it with arguments which resemble those used in present day controversies about the payments of tributes, indemnities, or foreign debts.

The growth of these separatist modern states and their self-centred, purely utilitarian statecraft accelerated the consummation of the religious schism, the Reformation. Its victory in many parts of the world completed the disintegration of the universal system which had dominated Western Christianity. To the rivalry of languages, each striving to

conquer cultural worlds of its own, and to the jealousies
of states, each attempting to elbow itself into greater
freedom and space, was added the bitter animosity of relig-
ous feuds. It ripped up universalism from top to bottom.
Rival states could settle their differences by exchange of land
and by more or less important frontier rectifications. But the
struggle between two religious creeds whose devotees are
sure that they alone hold the key to the door of eternal
salvation, which is rigorously closed to the others, cannot
be settled by quantitative compromise.

III

The complete disintegration of the Western world, which
seemed almost inevitable in the days of the Reformation,
did not take place. For whilst the old forces which had united
the world for so long were losing their strength, fresh forces
making for a new type of universalism were rising.

The Roman Catholic Church emerged from the struggle
with a purified faith and a vastly improved administration.
Its rulers, though still deeply immersed in territorial politics,
were losing weight as Italian sovereigns. But the less they
counted as local potentates, the greater became their power
as the spiritual heads of an ever-increasing number of
Christians and of a widely expanding Church. The Church's
earliest great enemy, the Reformation, had purified her
spiritual life; her latest foe, the Italian *risorgimento*, deprived
her of her last vestiges of territorial possessions and, by
freeing her from the impediments of mere political statecraft,
made her once more universal.

The outbreak of the great schism had almost coincided
with the discovery of new worlds. Ultimately a large part of
them was destined to fall into the hands of Protestant powers.
But their early opening up revived the missionary activities
of the Roman Church on a truly heroic scale. In South and
Central America, in Canada and in some parts of what are

now the United States, in Australia and India, in China and in many parts of Africa, the Roman Catholic Church annexed new spiritual provinces, which numbered many more inhabitants than her lost possessions. She had to compete with Protestant rivalries when carrying the Gospel to the natives; but the universality of her outlook and her ways of mellow understanding gave her a great advantage in approaching the mind of backward races.

The treasures of Greek and Roman civilization, which had been snowed under for centuries by avalanches of Barbarian invasions, were uncovered after Constantinople had fallen to the Turks, and expelled Greek scholars had to seek new homes. The "new learning" they brought with them soon became the common property of the entire Western world. Whoever aspired to cultural leadership, Papist or Puritan, Anglican or Lutheran, was trained in it. To some of these men the new learning meant the return to a joyful paganism; to others it offered the chance of reading the Bible in the original version, and of a better understanding of the texts of the early Fathers of the Church. The leading classes in every country became ingrained with it. As time went on, the most important social cleavage in many lands was not the age-long distinction between rich and poor, between gentle-born and common herd, but the rift between men and women who had been taught the humanities and those who stood outside their pale. The old Greek conception of universalism and cultural unity was revived in some measure. Once again the world was split up into Hellenes and Barbarians. National origins counted for little. Those who had drunk their fill from the well of the new learning belonged to the same nation, whatever their origins or their creed; the others, though co-nationals or co-religionists, were "barbarians." With the weakening of religious animosities these conceptions grew stronger, for people had learned by bitter experience the devastating results of fanatical creeds and religious wars. They filled not only the minds of the educated upper classes and of the professional, clerical, and lay scholars; they dominated the training of the servants of the State, who had been organizing the new monarchies in nearly every country. They found their clearest expression rather late in the day in "La République des Lettres," to which belonged the intellectual élite all over the world. Its several members were scattered over many fatherlands, but its spiritual unity was not severed by any frontier.

IV

From the new learning arose a new way of thinking. The philosophers who inaugurated it belonged to various nationalities; they devised different methods and arrived at different conclusions in their concepts of the world and of the causes moving it; their actions and interactions ultimately created a new Western philosophy, which became the joint possession of all Western nations. It gave birth in its turn to new conceptions of State and Society, which again, by their actions and reactions, furnished the basis of political science for all lands. Bacon, Descartes, Spinoza, and Leibnitz had raised the framework for all modern thought. Bodin, Machiavelli, Althusius, Hobbes, and Locke laid the foundations on which the theory of the modern State arose and provided the arguments by which its workings could be justified. Whether they described and defended the ruthless rational State of the absolute monarchy or the atomistic State of the social contract, they started from the same fundamental concepts; and the doctrines they created became the common property of all Western nations. To the medieval conception that states *grow* as do the lilies in the field, which had allowed for an endless variety of social units, they opposed the conclusion that states are *made* according to plan by the application of human reason, from highly standardized human material. They inaugurated the age of deliberate purposeful "social engineering." Long before democracy had come into its own, modern state-makers like Richelieu and Colbert and modern army organizers like Cromwell, were shaping parts of the State—if not the entire society—according to plan, to serve and to accomplish a deliberately chosen rational purpose. The planning of new "societies" was undertaken over and over again in the various Plantations schemes which were drafted in the sixteenth and seventeenth centuries for the settlement of Ireland or of the New World. Whilst Machiavelli, Bacon, or Harrington outlined the theory, statesmen, soldiers, and adventurers embodied it in large-scale practical experiments. As one country after another took over the rational institutions devised by its neighbours, the newly formed standardized types spread universally and uniformly. Nations draw neither their inspirations nor their institutions from a single source. There is a give and take amongst them, sometimes the one and sometimes the other leads in the inter-play of exchanging institutions or ideas and in making them "universal." A French Age had followed a Spanish Age, which on its part had derived many of its notions from Italy; in the middle of the eighteenth century, English institutions, idealized by French *frondeurs*, began their conquering journey round the world. They, in their turn, were challenged and ultimately supplemented by ideas and institutions conceived in the British Civil War, brought to life in the American Revolution and universalized by the French Revolution. As long as the sun was rising in Versailles, the courts of the entire world reflected its glory. French culture was spreading everywhere. And as its greatest exponents viewed their own epoch as a glorious rebirth of the classic age, the uninterrupted continuity of universalism was apparently established.

Such transfers are not mere imitations of fashions. The organization of the Prussian Army, and especially the designation of the officers' ranks, bear the traces of French derivations. Terms and concepts of business life all the world over even to-day smack of their British homeland, though in commerce proper, words coined in the great mercantile republics of Italy are still in use. And the philosophical jargon, the terminology as well as the posing of problems, reminds the world of times long passed, when Germans had the right to call their people the nation of poets and thinkers.

The advent of modern democracy heralded the beginning of standardization all round; it made movements towards a new universalism fairly easy. Standardization was not created by modern industry. It originated with the standing armies of the modern absolutist state, whose "uniformed men" were drilled by recruiting sergeants to perform repetitive machine-like actions. The halting steps of the British Guards are older than the running-belt. This standardization was limited to the smallish group which made up the standing armies. When French democracy resorted to the *levée en masse* in its hour of extreme danger, and when Prussian absolutism democratized itself, by extending not the rights of suffrage but the duties of conscription, it became nationwide. Universal suffrage assumed a kind of cultural, spiritual, and economic equality amongst the voters. Universal compulsory military service *created* a kind of equality of action and outlook amongst those subjected to its standardizing procedure during the most formative period of their lives. It presupposed a nation-wide system of compulsory primary education, in the absence of which successful training could not go beyond a very limited stage. It greatly facilitated, on the other hand, the disciplinarian tendencies of modern industrial mass-production, the processes of which made subjection to standardization, industrial as well as military, comparatively easy.

The ancient philosophers may have been the spiritual fathers of modern democracy; but its actual growth was far more strongly influenced by absolute kingship and deep religious faith. Whilst kings by divine right derived their own kingly status directly from God, they did not admit the claims of their nobles to an equally elevated origin. They had been raised far above their entire people, nobles or commoners. They were the divinely appointed shepherds entrusted by divine grace with the task of tending the flocks. And they insisted on handling sheep as well as goats, both being subject to their arbitrary unlimited God-given authority. They paved the way for the march of those notions of equality which modern democracy has put on the Statute Book. Their worldly aspirations and ambitions ran parallel to some dominant religious conceptions, which perhaps were most strongly embedded in Calvinism. There is an arbitrary almighty God-Dictator in the Calvinist scheme of the universe, before whom all creatures are equal. His is the power to discriminate freely between those He has chosen for salvation and those He has branded for eternal damnation. He is the Lord of the Universe, who may exercise His power arbitrarily and indiscriminately in His unfathomable wisdom without respecting rights, equal or unequal, over those subject to His unchallenged authority. But He does not concede to those under His will the privilege of arbitrary discrimination against one another. Democracy's deepest roots go down to this mystical conviction of an absolute equality of all human beings before the Almighty. Each human being is possessed of an immortal soul, and though there are distinctions in the human form, in colour, shape, or functional qualities, there is an absolute equality of souls and of reason, as man's distinctive attribute. Churchmen have been willing to compromise with the powers that be over their treatment of men and women. They have often condoned injustice and discrimination, as long as they merely affected men's bodies, their material, physical shapes, the hull of their souls. But Christian denominations worthy of their name have always insisted on absolute spiritual equality as a cardinal point of their faith. Over and over again courageous missionaries have stood up against arrogant conquerors whenever they dared to deny this spiritual equality to native races.

Modern political science has, to a considerable extent, accepted these religious tenets as a starting-point for its own social speculations. The several "Declarations of the Rights of Man", when harping on the equality of man as ordained by nature and nature's God, have merely substituted scientific-sounding terms for old religious wordings. By exchanging impersonal Nature for a personal God, they have scarcely strengthened their case. For Nature, conceived as a great impulse which has created man can hardly be supposed to have exhausted her efforts on the inner man— the soul; she has created outer man as well, with differences of colour, shape, and of various grades of reactions to intellectual or emotional shocks. It is much easier to assert the religious doctrine that God has made a Bushman a Boer's equal by endowing them both with an immortal soul, than to base this principle on anthropological findings by considering them both products of nature. The anthropologist may evade the issue by declining to include the study of souls within his activities. But the Boers, who were a very religious people, got over the theoretical difficulties of their otherwise egalitarian creed by the practical expedient of not considering Bushmen and Hottentots as human beings at all, but as mere creatures (schepsels).

Religious individualism, intent on saving men's souls, set the pace of modern democracy by sharply demarcating the sacred precincts of the individual's inalienable rights. The atomistic concepts of early rationalism considerably strengthened this new individualism. The application of mathematical-mechanical principles to the outer universe had led to those epoch-making discoveries from which modern science started on its royal road. Nationals of various countries collaborated in this work; they exchanged their methods as well as their results with citizens of other nations. Until lately the findings of natural science were far more universally and unquestionably accepted than the body of doctrines in the medieval church.

The methods of natural science were applied to social science. Though natural science and religion were at logger-heads for a long time, some of their fundamental tenets could easily be fused. The religious conception of the individual soul as the fountain of all human activities and the materialistic views of the individual as an atom, on whose actions and interactions the structure and function of the commonwealth depended, could easily be made to fit each other. The newly discovered social doctrines spread quickly. From the days of the Physiocrats to Karl Marx and his followers, men became more and more convinced that all human societies are composed of more or less identical units, are controlled by the same social laws, are moved by more or less identical motives, and are bound to expand in a more or less pre-ordained evolution.

The economic development which resulted from the Industrial Revolution greatly strengthened these views. The Industrial Revolution was an indirect outcome of the New Learning. It had freed man's aspirations from the trammels of rigid ethical traditions. He was allowed to centre his mind and his actions on this earth and to apply the powers of reason with which Providence had endowed him, and in-crease the measure of satisfaction he desired. This was the spiritual side. The developments of natural science, on the other hand, made possible modern technique which put machine-power and technical invention at his disposal and enabled him to satisfy those wants. This was the materialist side. Modern capitalism came into being.

Capitalism and democracy have been the twin sources of the new universalism which has been capturing the world. Their functioning depended, on the one hand, on the acceptance of standardized units as elements of production and consumption (in the political field of voting) and, on the other hand, on the assumption that the human raw material for such units can be found everywhere and can, with requisite knowledge, be pressed into proper shape nearly everywhere.

V

The struggle for colonial possessions, in which the European Powers had been engaged since the sixteenth century, had accelerated the collapse of the universal conception of European civilization which had been a main feature of the Middle Ages. The new nationalism of the Renaissance and the Reformation had resulted in the formation of national states, who were founding national empires in opposition to one another. Whilst breaking up the previous universalism of the Christian world, each of them succeeded in giving a wider scope to its own special brand of Western civilization. They annexed new lands, which they either filled up with their own people or which they made subservient to their own purposes by transforming native societies to their way of living. Each of them had colonized part of the world by plantation, assimilation, and finally by the transformation of those native societies which came under their political or cultural influence.

The forces which had broken up the old universalist European world had been very strong. Schism, friction, and seemingly irreconcilable national antagonism, often followed by political disintegration, were on the increase all the time. Animosities were growing in intensity with the narrowing of the areas within which the striving forces could expand.

But appearances were misleading. There was a good deal of similarity between the several systems of economic and social structure which the European Powers were transferring to all parts of the globe. And the political regimes under which they lived had the same roots; they grew at varying speeds as varying conditions helped or hindered their development. The monarchial system in Germany or Austria differed greatly from the English political system at the end of the nineteenth century, but this was a difference of development rather than of fundamentals. The economic changes which were going on in the politically less advanced European countries were ultimately certain to bring about everywhere a kind of constitutional assimilation. Parliamentary government was the fashion all the world over. Germany, it is true, had not accepted it; her very union, not only her constitution, had been the work of its greatest enemy. But even Turkey and Japan were adopting it. And the economic system which functioned from Vladivostock to Lisbon, from Hammerfest to Cape Matapan, from Hudson Bay to Cape Horn and from Perth to Brisbane revolved everywhere round identical principles. In some of these countries this capitalist system was in its infancy, in others it had grown to maturity. In some it was mixed up with strong feudal elements, in others it had shed these ingredients or had never possessed them. The external aspect of the gold-fields of the Witwatersrand differed considerably from that of the coal-mines of Durham and Northumberland, and the textile mills round Mexico City worked in another atmosphere from that prevailing in Alsace-Lorraine or Lancashire. But these were minor external discrepancies. The system as such was the same all the world over, wherever Western civilization had outgrown the age of feudalism and where assimilating or imitating natives were following its lead.

The spread of Western economic institutions and of Western political conceptions was giving the entire world a new sense of unity. It replaced the oneness which Western Europe had lost by the breakdown of universalism, and in which the East and the new West had never participated. Now transportation had conquered space and colonization was transforming men.

This new world unity, which transplantation, assimilation, imitation, and trade had prepared, was heralded as the beginning of an age of deadening uniformity, in which a standardized universalism would ruthlessly annihilate the last traces of particularized national individualism. The churches and their propaganda had spread their creeds, the schools their knowledge; democracy had carried parliamentary institutions to the ends of the earth; trade and transportation had transferred the capitalist system. Last but not least, the structure of the European state, its centralized bureaucracy, its armies and its navies were imitated everywhere. Fascist Italy and Communist Russia are living on this legacy. And behind it all, there was a new scientific conception of the world as a universe, which was not ruled by the whimsical acts of a more or less arbitrary personal deity, but was obeying immanent laws, which natural and social science had successfully unravelled.

Liberals and Socialists differed sharply about their significance; nobody denied their existence. The clash of doctrines, which had originated from the same fundamental conceptions, divided the world amongst their adherents.

VI

Colonization by the Western powers has been going on uninterruptedly for at least eight hundred years. The Anglo-Norman knights who landed on the shores of Ireland in May 1169 were but the forerunners of those adventurers, explorers, conquerors, and traders who made half the world Anglo-Saxon. The Crusades saw the rise and fall of the first "New France," and the founding of the great Venetian maritime empire. The age of discoveries widened and accelerated these movements in all directions. European settlements spread over the entire world, to which two new continents had been added. A temporary setback followed the revolt of the Americas. But after a short interval the movement was resumed with new vigour. The great migration in the wake of the Industrial Revolution was beginning. Colonization along the shores of the Pacific replaced colonization across the Atlantic.

England and France extended the borders of their empires and the spheres of their influence unceasingly; they led in the partition of Africa, which, at the turn of the century, was almost complete, and added large areas to their possessions.

Very few countries remained independent or quasi-independent: in Africa, Abyssinia, and, to some degree, Liberia. In Asia the progressive partition of China opened up possibilities hitherto undreamed of, though sometimes not very attractive. The annexation of Afghanistan was not yet consummated; the dissection of Persia was well under way. In Europe the Ottoman Empire seemed to approach its long-expected dissolution. Schemes for its partition were entertained on all sides.

Germany and Italy, late-comers among the Powers, had entered the colonial field. They succeeded in getting a portion of empire from 1884 onwards, when the final scramble for Africa started. Even a small neutral country like Belgium founded a tropical empire, by becoming (indirectly) the ruler of the Congo Free State. Of the six Powers which formed the European Concert before the war, only Austria-Hungary held aloof from oversea conquest, partly on account of her continental situation and partly on account of her peculiar political structure. She formed, so to speak, a miniature empire of her own, in which several less advanced European races were concentrated round the remnant of the German people which had remained under the rule of the Habsburgs. But even she felt the urge for territorial expansion and acquired a large slice of the decaying Ottoman Empire, when the Powers entrusted to her the administration of Bosnia and Herzogovina; later on she turned this perfunctory title of occupation into one of legal possession by a unilateral act which very nearly started the Great War.

Russia, meanwhile, had spread all over the Northern and Eastern part of Asia. Whilst her spiritual and political leaders were dreaming of Constantinople and the Straits, her trappers had wandered over Siberia and her peasants were forging ahead. She had conquered Central Asia and was pushing her advance posts forward through spheres of interest via Persia towards Afghanistan, and ultimately towards the Indian frontier. She had become a great Pacific Power. Her occupation of the Port Arthur peninsula brought to the notice of the world her claims, as chief heir to the crumbling Chinese Empire. Her expansionist pretensions clashed with those of Japan, who had laid the foundations of a colonial empire of her own by wrenching Formosa and Korea from China. Russia looked upon the Balkan nations, which had been liberated from Turkey, as her "little brothers," whom for racial and religious reasons she was bound to protect, though they might block her road to Constantinople.

Some of the newly acquired dependencies and provinces were merely changing hands. They were torn from tottering empires by stronger rivals. China, Turkey, and Spain were disintegrating. More vigorous neighbours were entering their inheritance. Russia had wrested large tracts of what had been Armenia from Turkey; England had occupied Cyprus and Egypt; France had conquered Algeria and incorporated Tunis. Later on Italy despoiled her of Tripoli (Libya) and the Dodecanese. Similar developments were impending in the Far East, where France, Japan and Russia, Germany and England were preparing for the demise of China by mapping out spheres of interest.

Even the United States were willing to join in the finish, at least in the sphere of commercial enterprise. Dollar diplomacy was temporarily displacing the policy of the open door. Overland colonization had come to an end. The grant of statehood to the New Mexico territory marked the last stage in the winning of the West. But the expansionist spirit of the people of the United States was very much alive. They were ready to shoulder the colonial burdens Spain could no longer carry in Cuba, Porto Rico, and in the Philippines—the last remnants of the old Spanish world-empire; they had filched the Canal Zone from the Republic of Columbia by putting the independent Republic of Panama on the map.

Portugal was permitted to keep her oversea dominions, but plans for dividing them had been agreed upon between England and Germany in case she collapsed or decided to relinquish them. The only colonial empire which seemed relatively stable and changing very little was that of the Netherlands.

Signs of revolt amongst subject nationalities and of a breaking up of empires were not wanting—the Irish question had been very much alive all through the nineteenth century. The Austrian Empire was torn by nationalist strife. But outside the Balkans disintegration had not yet led to separation or independence; it merely brought about a re-shuffling of dependencies amongst several imperial masters.

The greatest colonial Power, England, was saturated. She had frequently objected to further partitions. She preferred the independence and the integrity of Turkey, China, or Persia, based on international agreements, to any scheme of partition. She was strongly supported in this respect by the United States, who had devised the system of the "open door," in order to make the incorporation of China commercially unprofitable to the despoilers.

Germany sometimes followed suit; she strained hard to prop up Turkey and Morocco as independent powers. But these principles frequently degenerated into mere diplomatic moves; they did not form the base of an unalterable policy. The same Power which insisted on the integrity of China or Morocco might be very eager for expansion in other places. And when it could not accomplish its objects, when independence and integrity became difficult to maintain, it quickly veered round and demanded a share of the spoils, as England did in Persia and China, and Germany in Morocco.

PART I

COLONIZATION

CHAPTER I

CONQUEST AND COLONIZATION

I

THE period preceding the war has been called "The Age of Imperialism" on account of the last-hour scramble for the few unappropriated slices of hitherto independent backward countries and for the remainder of the once mighty, now crumbling, empires, Turkey and China. It did not initiate a new policy, nor herald a new age; it was terminating rather an era which had begun with the Crusades and had reached its natural time limit with the Declaration of Independence. Once mankind accepted the doctrine that "men were created equal," the physical, as well as the moral, basis of Imperialism collapsed—the right of the stronger to rule the weaker.

Imperialism is a creed as well as a policy. As such, it sees in force, mainly physical force, the chief instrument for shaping human destinies. By the relentless use of this weapon scattered tribes had been compressed into compact states and states had been expanded into empires. This process has gone on without interruption since the dawn of history. But empire building is only one phase of a never-ending cycle, for empire makers are succeeded by empire breakers, who sometimes smash mighty existing structures into crumbling fragments, and sometimes, with a turn of the wheel, fuse these splinters into new empires. That the great Powers of the West as well as of the East were once again pursuing a policy of creating, organizing, maintaining and expanding empires merely showed that once again force had come into its own.

An Empire is a state of vast size, composed of various more or less distinct national units, but subject to a single

B

centralized will.[1] This conception of a super-state,[2] composed of many nations leading diverse lives, but united under a common ruler, is at least as old as Alexander the Great's dream of a European-Asiatic union, ruled by a monarch indifferent to the distinctions between Greeks and Barbarians, who would be looked upon by both Persians and Macedonians as their own king. In building this empire out of highly heterogeneous nationalities, Alexander was merely following the example of his Persian predecessors. They too had assembled various nationalities under a centralized rule. They had allowed them complete cultural independence and had tried to unite them, not by imposing compulsory national uniformity upon them but by securing common loyalty to a central head. National diversity, not national uniformity, has been the distinctive feature of empires. They were not held together by conscious racial unity, common origin, identity of language and of institutions, but by the personality of a deified emperor, by a universal faith (as in the Church after Constantine), or by the knowledge of a common past and the desire for a common future, which often included the consciousness of a spiritual mission. The snapping of a common spiritual link has often led to the break up of empires.

The growth of modern communications, which reduced distances and permitted the transportation of bulky commodities on a large scale, added an economic note to the concept of "empire"; it raised the vision of a self-sufficient super-state which is capable of living in splendid isolation from the rest of the world. It represents a combination of diverse nations and countries, each possessing a distinct economic character of its own and each contributing its particular natural resources to a common end and helping to accomplish complete economic independence of other

[1] Ernest Barker, "Empire" in *Encyclopaedia Britannica*.

[2] An empire is a super-state, but a super-state need not be an empire. See below, pp. 369–70.

nations and complete economic security, such as no mere state could achieve, either by territorial aggrandizement or by international commerce.

On its economic side, Imperialism represents a particular type of "predatory economics"—in contrast to mere "exchange economics." Since every age has its own method of widening the territorial base of national wealth and of winning domination or additional external resources by one or the other method of coercive pressure, it has its own brand of Imperialism. Coercion is either physical (military), spiritual (fear or intimidation) or economic (supply or denial of goods or services). Frequently enough Imperialist policy has used all three of them severally or collectively.[1]

[1] Lenin's definition, *"Imperialism is the monopoly stage of capitalism"* (*Imperialism*, p. 84), is arbitrary, too narrow, and unhistoric. Some of the greatest colonial empires of modern times were conquered in pre-capitalist days. None of the late-comers, like Germany, Italy, or Japan, whose claims accelerated the resumption of empire-making, had reached "the monopolist stage of capitalism" when they acquired their colonial possessions. They were—and Japan is to-day—economically semi-feudal.

Since *"capitalism only became capitalist Imperialism at a definite and very high stage of its development"* (p. 84), Lenin's definition can evidently not be applied to Czarist Imperialism. As Russia had certainly not reached this stage (p. 92), she cannot have been "imperialist," notwithstanding the uncontested *fact* that she was. To fit this and other cases, the definition might be inverted and read, "But Imperialism only became capitalist at a definite and very high stage of its development."

Scarcity of available objects for colonization, not the monopolistic structure of the capitalist world, accounts for the particular revival of the monopolist element in Imperialism.

Ernest Seillière sees the driving force of Imperialism in "desire or lust of power" (*"volonté vers la puissance ou volonté de puissance."* Philosophie de l'Impérialisme, vol. iii, pp. 7 and 16). This definition of Imperialism is too wide. But it furnishes a better demarcation of Imperialist policies than the attempts to limit Imperialism to the Capitalist Age. The main economic object of expansion is the acquisition and exploitation of additional natural resources, not the exploitation of additional labour. The nationalization of the means of production in a Communist state might eliminate the *individualist profit-motive*; in countries like Russia, which possess huge undeveloped resources, the *collectivist profit-motive*— the desire to acquire additional external resources—is at present absent. It would be very strong were the Soviets in the position of Japan. The

The Imperialism of the Feudal Ages relied on conquest and land grabbing as appropriate means for widening and enriching society. Its methods were resumed in the nineteenth century, when the backwoodsmen spread over the prairies in the United States, and the Voortrekkers over the South African veldt, or when Russian peasants wedged themselves into Siberia, between Mongols, Tartars, and Kalmuks.

The Imperialism of the Mercantile Ages, on the other hand, did not go after territorial possessions; its objects were goods, particularly precious metals and rare spices. Where it could not get them by regular reciprocal exchange-operations, it resorted to monopolist control of trade-settlements and oversea routes; it became "quasi-territorial" only when the normal flow of these goods from trade or piracy was no longer sufficient, and when it had to apply pressure to native governments to make them turn out an adequate supply. This brand of mercantile Imperialism was shot with a very strong streak of military or naval coercion.

Some of these methods survived the Mercantilist Age—witness the attempts to expand exports by opening up the Chinese and Japanese ports through war or naval demonstrations, or the diplomatic pressure used by rival Powers to force loans upon reluctant foreign governments, or the collection of debts from them by blockades and naval threats.

Imperialism can be tribal, feudal, mercantile, capitalist, and even communist. Its main feature is not expansion, but expansion by force. Regular trade expansion in foreign

power-motive, on the other hand, the desire to rule men, is very much in evidence in Stalin's State. As long as the power-motive is active, Imperialist policies will be pursued whenever the men animated by it deem it advisable. Feudal and capitalist Imperialism have often persuaded themselves that they were acting for the ultimate benefit of those they coerced. And they believed quite as fervently as the Soviet administrators to-day that the end justifies the means. These ends may have changed, but the means, *force*, have essentially remained the same. A gun is a gun, whoever fires it, irrespective of the kind of enemy on which it is trained.

countries, be they independent or dependent, is not imperialist; it becomes so only by the application of force.

Economic exploitation by capitalists may be quite as ruthless as military exactions at the point of the sword; but it is different. Capitalism has been imperialist whenever it has accomplished its objects by conquest; it has been semi-imperialist at other times, when it has raised profits by coercion (forced labour); the application of military coercion for gainful purposes by way of expansion, not the profits or the expansion as such, is imperialist.

Imperialism does not constitute the last stage in capitalist development; it is much older than capitalism in most countries and will probably outlive it. Its place in the capitalist structure is mainly due to the survival of feudal and militarist groups in capitalist societies, who cling to their old traditions. Any national or social system in need of territorial or economic aggrandizement becomes imperialist when it resorts to military or semi-military coercion against its neighbours. There is no reason whatsoever why a Communist state, placed in such a situation, should refrain from doing it.

Communism is not a pacifist creed. Its devotees advocate the ruthless use of force for missionary purposes. They have employed violence, terror, and fear against their internal opponents; they cannot be expected to refrain from using them externally, if and when economic or political necessities may demand it. The Bolshevist creed is strongly imbued with missionary Imperialism. And the Soviet policy in Chinese Turkestan or Outer Mongolia differs little from capitalist interventionism. It ignores nationality in the same way as Rome and Byzantium ignored it: all nations were equally subject to the Emperor. Russian absolutism took over this concept from Byzantium and bequeathed it to its Soviet successors: they put the party and its tenets in Caesar's place.[1]

[1] L. Trotsky, *The Revolution Betrayed*, p. 167.

Imperialist methods might fall into disuse in a world federation of Communist states; they might be equally well dispensed with in a world-federation of Capitalist states. As long as diversity of social systems, of cultural standards, of wealth and of power prevail among nations, missionary Imperialism is likely to survive.

Irrespective of its social structure, a state will seek relief by more or less aggressive methods at the cost of its richer neighbours whenever it feels cramped, provided it sees a chance of easing the pressure successfully. A Communist state may denounce predatory methods at home; there is ample room for them in its relations with foreign non-Communist bodies.

II

Empires have been created either by voluntary association or by forcible annexation. In rare instances a nation, threatened by foreign attack, has chosen to throw in its lot with an alien neighbour who was strong enough to defend it. Such was the origin of the Hungarian connection with the House of Habsburg, under whose wings the Magyars sought protection against the onslaught of the Turks. Otherwise only political groups related to each other by race, origin, language, and social institutions, have been federated in a peaceful way, and then nearly always at the end of a long period of internecine war.

The faith in peaceful voluntary confederation as a substitute for war is of recent origin. The great success of federation in the United States has made this powerful commonwealth the advocate of a more or less hazy doctrine of voluntary confederation between several nations, not merely between the fragments of one nation which have splintered into several states. Their spokesmen have frequently enunciated it in glowing language. "The way of force is not the way to achieve the union of mankind." "We are fighting to end the Roman method of world consolidation and to substitute in its place the method of agreement. We are fighting not necessarily to beat Germany, certainly not to crush Germany . . . but to make it clear to anyone who reads history hereafter that the Roman method no longer pays."[1] These views, which seemed to be oblivious of the fact that the United States had not accomplished their present unity without conquest and civil war, lay at the root of President Wilson's conception of a League of Nations.

Most empires have been founded by conquest and annexation. Countries of superior military, economic, or cultural strength have conquered other countries and incorporated them in their dominions. But when fresh expansion beyond the established borders is no longer desirable, and when the consolidation of the divergent parts into a more closely-knit imperial unit is of prime importance, Imperialism has frequently adopted peaceful methods. British Imperialism was distinctly aggressive when it conquered India or wrested South Africa from the Dutch or Canada from the French. It can scarcely be called so at present when it is attempting the establishment of a commonwealth of free and kindred nations within the framework of the existing British family of nations.

The advocates of Imperialism sought to justify the use of force or intimidation by a philosophy which stressed its moral qualities: Power to them is a blessing, it is of divine origin, and those who wield it are instruments of Providence, who carry out its decrees. Starting from a fixed belief in the natural right of the stronger to exterminate or enslave the weaker, Imperialism frequently assumed a missionary character. Nations or groups who are endowed with superior strength must use it at the behest of Providence, in order to transfer to the conquered the creeds and institutions with which they have been blessed. Conquest has often been naïve and spontaneous. Lust of wealth, love of power, and

[1] Dwight Morrow, July 11, 1918, in Harold Nicolson, *Dwight Morrow*, p. 233.

war have made a master-nation fall upon weaker neighbours and ruthlessly enslave them. But, on the other hand, its passions have often been fanned to white heat by a call arising from some mystical depth, which told of a great vocation and of manifest destiny. "If the empire of a common-wealth be an occasion to ask whether it be lawful for a commonwealth to aspire to the empire of the world, it is to ask whether it is lawful for it to do its duty, or to put the world into a better condition than it was before,"[1] queried one of the great writers of the Commonwealth.

This type of missionary Imperialism may well become a greater trial to subject races than a more primitive and not self-conscious form of exploitation. The latter may be satis-fied with the annexation of foreign territory and the tributes of conquered nations. They will be permitted to live their own lives and to preserve their own language, their own institutions and even their own gods, so long as their loyalty can be depended upon—provided they do not fall under the rule of a chosen people. For a chosen people whose national-ism flows from mystical tribal emotions, rather than from arrogant theories of its unique position, must not mix with the race it has conquered, or its blood would be defiled. The only way in which it can spread its culture and fulfil its mission is by ruthless extermination. It cannot confer on the conquered the blessings of its own ways, for these are the inheritance of the chosen. Its superiority is exclusive, not communicative. Less arrogant conquerors, who are not enjoined by the divine power to spread "like the sand of the sea" have been more gentle. They would not prevent the conversion of their subjects to their way of living, but they would not compel them to it. They would rely on the "infectious quality" of their victorious civilization and not force it upon the conquered.[2] Such was the attitude of the Greeks in the Alexandrian Empire, whose highly civilized

---

[1] James Harrington, *Oceana* (Morley's Universal Library), p. 241.

[2] M. Rostovtzeff, *A History of the Ancient World*, vol. i, pp. 378, 381-2.

city settlements spread Greek culture among the barbarians. They offered it to them as the highest reward for voluntary spiritual effort. And the Romans, under the Republic as well as under the Empire, latinized the world, not by compelling subject nations to accept Roman civilization, but by generously admitting them to its blessings when they had proved worthy of them. This "tolerant" nationalism of the conqueror was met half way by an "imitative" nationalism on the part of the conquered.

But when the temporal power was the exponent of an exclusive spiritual creed, as the Roman Emperors after the conversion of Constantine or some great Moslem rulers, Imperialism became exclusive and missionary. It was no longer content with the uncontested political domination of subject nations. As it represented a unique and exclusive faith, on the acceptance of which depended loyalty in this world and salvation in the next, it demanded the religious assimilation of its subjects. It desired spiritual uniformity and insisted on conformity; it uprooted ideas and destroyed institutions which stood in the way, or might be thought to stand in the way, of attaining this goal. As most native religions were closely interwoven with the cultural and institutional life of the country, a process of compulsory assimilation followed; had it succeeded completely, it would have transformed the agglomerations of disconnected, diversified, and composite elements, hitherto called "Empires," into unified and uniformed super-states. The advent of the great monotheistic religions with their creed of exclusiveness changed the nature of Imperialism: it became propagandist. Recalcitrant peoples, who objected to being converted, were either exterminated or expelled. The easy-going pluralism of the classical heathen world was succeeded by the rigid monism of Christianity or Islam. Such toleration as was shown in particular instances was not so much the result of a spirit of tolerance, as of a statesmanlike appreciation of political difficulties and economic losses compulsory conversion would entail, were it to involve the extermination or expulsion of non-conforming elements.

III

Some empires have grown laterally by *horizontal incorporation*. They are combinations of political groups which have reached the same level of economic, institutional, and cultural advancement. Others, including the colonial empires of the nineteenth century, were composed of political units whose levels of social attainments ranged from those of primitive races living under tribal chiefs on the outer fringes of the empire to the highly complex societies of motherland and dominions. These have expanded downwards by *vertical incorporation*. Their rulers represent more and less advanced civilizations; the gap between the social achievements of the metropolis and those of its lowest dependency is often very wide.

Social advancement may be measured by different gauges. As the Western Powers have been the great empire makers in the last five hundred years, the results of expansion must be appraised by their standards. The objects they strove for may not have been worth while pursuing; they may compare unfavourably with the ideals of other civilizations. This final issue cannot be decided until the question whether these objects have been attained and whether the means employed have been appropriate to the purpose has first been answered.

Western empire builders were not alone in the field. At one time Moslem Powers very nearly dominated the Mediterranean, and until the fall of Granada put an end to Arab domination in Western Europe, Spain might easily be described as a rebel province seceding from a world-wide Arab Empire. And only two or three centuries ago the Ottoman Empire was ruling within its wide confines many a Christian nation, once under the sway of Rome or Byzantium, and was pushing its frontiers to the gates of Vienna. Though the Chinese and the Mogul Empires never controlled any part of Europe and began to crumble when brought into contact with the Western Powers, both of them bore the unmistakable hallmarks of empire.

IV

Lateral expansion—the conquest and incorporation of countries which have reached the same, or nearly the same, degree of social efficiency—is an arduous task. It is nearly always the result of a major war. It presents grave problems of administration. The conquered nations cannot be kept permanently in subjugation. To give them freedom without being sure of their readiness for co-operation may be dangerous; and it is rarely possible to assimilate them without giving them freedom. The Habsburg Empire foundered on this rock; British imperialist statesmanship—successful with French Canadians and South African Boers—failed as conspicuously in Ireland as the Germans did in Alsace-Lorraine.

On the other hand, *vertical* expansion, the conquest and incorporation of more or less backward societies, is a fairly simple military enterprise. Until recently, bands of conquistadores and tiny expeditionary forces easily overran native empires. When victory had been won, control was assured, though it implied complex problems of colonization.

The peculiar character of the modern European world is due to the alternate subjugation of one European nation by another and to the political, social, economic, and cultural interplay following upon it. Though the cultural levels of colonizing and colonized nations did not differ very much, the dominating races were conscious of their superiority; they were not satisfied with mere lateral extension and insisted upon some sort of assimilation downwards such as is implied in colonization. The Venetians who had founded an empire in the Adriatic and in the eastern part of the Mediterranean sent out colonists to lord over Illyrians, Slavs, and Greeks; even now some cities on the Dalmatian coast are tiny replicas of the "Queen of the Adriatic," with a square of San Marco, a small dome in imitation of its famous namesake, and a graceful column from the top of which the winged lion of Venice keeps watch over the conquered lands. They are as much symbols of political and cultural colonization as the huge Plaza de la Constitucion in Mexico City. In the old world as in the new a ruling race had enslaved a native population and impressed upon it the external forms of its civilization. That the subject race in one case consisted of fellow Europeans and fellow Christians and in the other of heathen natives, did not make much difference to the social system. In both hemispheres the conquerors' day is gone; their sway has passed. The rising tide of nationalism has swept away the overlords; the southern Slavs have extirpated "La piccola Venezia" more thoroughly than the Mexican Indians have swept away "La nueva España."

Community of faith, colour, and culture has never prevented wars; it has scarcely ever made them more human. Nor has it stopped annexation and colonization. But it has frequently made them more hazardous. It is harder to defeat a nation which lives on the same plane of civilization than a less advanced race, however brave it may be. World conscience is shocked by the extermination of a Christian brother nation, whilst it may be willing to condone —nay even to praise—the extirpation of some heathen barbarians. Morals apart, such a policy of extermination is less profitable when applied to economically efficient workers than to natives who do not want to adjust themselves to their masters' economic methods, and who are looked upon as slackers and loafers. The greater the cultural gap between colonists and natives, the easier it is to coerce and control them by brute force. The Spaniards had fewer difficulties in winning and holding Mexico and Peru, many thousands of miles away, than the English experienced when attempting the permanent subjugation of the neighbouring Irish Celts. The nearer in colour, creed, and culture the natives are to their colonizing masters, the harder it is to keep them under control and to make them accept the laws and languages of their lords. The late Habsburg Empire was confronted by much greater difficulties than colonial empires with non-European populations, for it consisted of a medley of races nearly all of European stock and nearly all Christians. An imperial bureaucracy, imbued with German traditions of centralization, had to rule a collection of non-German races, who greatly outnumbered the comparatively narrow German fringe on which the original Habsburg power was founded. They differed in outlook and attitude amongst themselves, and their cultural level was distinctly lower than that of the Germans, but not low enough to make them accept permanently their unquestioned leadership.

Colonization indicates some sort of power, ownership, or domination. The establishment of purely political control might be called *primary colonization*. The government of one country or of a group of people is exercised or supervised by the government of another country; the interests of the governed country are openly subordinated to those of the governing country. Colonization has frequently begun by the annexation of vacant lands; this leads to *the formation of a new society*. The invaders colonize them by settling members of their own race upon them; they become a dependency of the conquering motherland.

The annexation of countries inhabited by native populations results in a more or less complete *transformation of existing native societies*. The adventurers who conquer a native state make themselves the masters of its lands and of the people inhabiting them. They colonize it by transforming the existing native society. This transformation can go very far, when the invaders are strong or numerous enough to overthrow the native social structure, as the Spaniards did in Mexico and Peru. It is comparatively slight where climatic, social, or political causes permit of but a small inflow of alien invaders and prevent them from making their permanent home in the conquered territory. They come to it as soldiers, civil servants, and merchants and spend in it only the active period of their lives.

In the preliminary stages, the structure of native society is not much affected; the new masters are quite content with financial spoils, commercial privileges, and political allegiance. By and by genuine "transformation" sets in. This has been the experience of the British in India.

Colonization always leads to the incorporation of social units, which remain politically dependent on the conquering state. But primary political colonization (vertical expansion) is but the first stage in the process of colonization, which comprises both the creation of new societies and the transformation of old societies, by the transfer of men and of goods, of institutions, and of ideas. Incorporation and annexation, as such, are not colonization. For the annexation of territories inhabited by people who share the civilization of their conquerors results neither in the formation nor in the transformation of societies. The essential elements in colonization are (1) the formation of a new society or the transformation of an existing society and the political control of this society by the power which organized it—*primary colonization*; (2) the continued transfer of men and of goods, of institutions and of ideas from an old society to a new one—*secondary colonization*.

V

Some conquerors who have transferred themselves, their families, and their belongings to the conquered land have cut the political connection with the home from which they came before colonization was complete. After the Norman Conquest the centre of gravity shifted very quickly from

Tours and Rouen to Canterbury and London. England did not long remain dependent on the Duchy of Normandy. And though the Normans transferred many of their institutions to England and transformed many Saxon institutions by infiltrating their own, England did not become a colony of the Duchy of Normandy; her interests did not remain subordinate to those of the home of her conquerors. Similarly the Latin Kingdom of Jerusalem (1099–1291), which the Crusaders had founded, became immediately independent of the French Motherland, though it acknowledged a shadowy dependence on the Holy See. Cultural colonization, however, went on for a long time afterwards, for "the laws and language, the manners and titles of the French nation and the Latin Church were introduced into these transmarine colonies,"[1] which called themselves "la nouvelle France."

In other cases political independence has been of slow growth. It is bound to come in all "plantation" colonies in the old sense of the word, i.e. settlements which are, more or less exclusively, composed of members of the ruling race, who carry with them the political and cultural traditions of the country from which they sprang. Ultimately they either secede from the metropolis or become her partners. But the separation of a colony from the mother country does not terminate the process of colonization, for the transfer of men and of goods, of institutions and of ideas may go on. Long after the United States had politically become independent of England, their rapid expansion depended on help from European, predominantly Anglo-Irish, immigration and on the influx of European, mostly British, capital. For half a century the Monroe Doctrine would scarcely have been respected by France and Spain, but for its acceptance by the British government and for the supremacy of the British Navy. And long after the United States had become

[1] Gibbon, *Decline and Fall of the Roman Empire*, J. B. Bury, ed., vol. vi, chap. 53, p. 315.

materially independent of the mother country, and frequently politically antagonistic to it, traces of cultural and spiritual dependence remained.

VI

A colony is not a province or part of an empire, ruled from the capital like other provinces, but a separate political unit with a subordinate government of its own, formed by a plantation settlement or by a transformed native state. As long as it remains a colony it occupies a lower political, social, and cultural status than the metropolis. The mother country must either keep it on its inferior, national level or raise it to her own superior standards by assimilation. This may be justified where the controlling power clearly represents higher institutional, cultural, social, or spiritual values, which it wants to transmit to the dependent parts of the empire. In an empire in which complete cultural equality between all members prevails there is no room for colonization; any attempt at compulsory assimilation is a denial of equality. But a policy of assimilation implies the need of partial colonization; it has sometimes destroyed highly developed institutions and superior spiritual conceptions to the detriment of the entire world. But though brute force has often succeeded in the political field, it has nearly always failed in its cultural ambitions. Many a ruling race has been submerged in the civilization of subject nationalities, whose independence it wrecked, but whose charm it could not withstand, whose plasticity it could not crush, and whose tenacity it could not break. The Chinese have assimilated their Manchurian overlords. Greece became Rome's cultural tyrant after she lost her independence to her.

Frequently, too, a ruling class of alien origin has been pulled down from its assumed political, economical, and cultural pedestal by intimate cohabitation with its subjects. The plaint that the sons and daughters of Norman lords,

Elizabethan adventurers, and Cromwellian Ironsides, who had been planted as trustworthy garrisons on the soil of that elusive and enchanted island, had become more Irish than the Irish themselves runs through the never-ceasing efforts of the English to force their civilization on the Irish Celts.

VII

The dazzling results of modern colonization by the white race in America, Australia, Africa, and Asia have obliterated the memory of earlier movements in Europe and Asia. And since most recent colonies were oversea dependencies, colonization was regarded as a more or less transoceanic long-distance adventure.

There is no fundamental difference between overland and oversea colonization. The German colonization, which settled the north-eastern fringe of Central Europe, moved partly oversea and partly overland. Its methods in both directions were closely akin to those used later on by the French in Canada and the Spaniards in South America. The Germans sometimes expelled the natives and founded closed settlement-colonies; they sometimes let the natives remain and turned them into tributaries. The "Locatores" who laid out the German villages in Brandenburg in the twelfth century, after the Slavs had been driven away, closely resembled the Elizabethan undertakers in Munster, or the surveyors founding an American town, or the Seigneurs settling a Canadian côte; the latter, in fact, looks very much like one of those long-drawn-out German "street" villages (Fadendorf).

The Crusades were a huge colonial venture, an experiment in "collective Imperialism." The rulers of the temporal Christian states joined with their spiritual head in a series of expeditions, which were to widen the spiritual empire of the Pope and to add dependent colonies to the conquering states. Thus the Latin Empire, "New France," built in

1204 by French knights after the fourth Crusade, was rightly styled a "colony." Imperialism in those days was feudal and commercial on the one hand, the knights wanting land and the merchants profits from trade in rare commodities: it was missionary on the other. It did not set out to extirpate the infidels in order to get their lands and goods, though sometimes it succeeded in doing it to a certain extent. It wanted to redeem them and make them share by force in eternal salvation. It was not the last time that emotional spiritualism and rational materialism combined in a Gran Conquista Ultramar.

The colonization of the New World started as an oversea venture; after some time, overland expansion took its place and ultimately prevailed. The vast inland areas opened up by overland colonization have become much more important than the original relatively narrow coastal settlements. The pioneers who moved in the prairie schooners across the great American desert were quite as adventurous as the Pilgrim Fathers who crossed the sea in the *Mayflower*. And the toll of human suffering paid by them in the winning of the West was probably heavier than the sacrifice involved in the founding of the seaboard colonies. The constitution of the United States provided for the regular growth of overland colonies. The settlements formed by groups of early comers, who had drifted across the borders of the established states, were made into a "Territory"—a colony dependent on the federal government, which was almost automatically converted into a sovereign state when it had reached maturity.

Overland colonization of a similar kind transformed the seaboard settlements of South Africa, Australia, and Canada into continental dominions. It made the Russian Empire a giant state, for after having filled its European regions, it flowed over the North Asiatic continent, until it reached the China Sea. In the early years of the twentieth century, the numbers of land-seeking Russian peasants who crossed the eastern frontiers of European Russia ran overseas immigration to the United States pretty closely. It rose from 200,000 a year in 1906 to 750,000 in 1908. It soon fell back to 225,000 when the supply of settlement land seemed exhausted and when it met a counter-movement in the overland migration from China into Manchuria.[1]

The same motives animated the colonists in Europe and in the New World. The song of the Flemings who rode eastward eager for land and adventure is but a prelude to the hymn of the American pioneers who turned their faces to the golden West. It would equally well have suited the Boers on their Great Trek northwards over the Orange and the Vaal River, or the Kossacks riding into the boundless steppe.[2] Nor can the modernity of the following prospectus be questioned:

"These heathens are the very worst, but their country is the best for meat, honey, flour, and poultry, and if properly worked, for all products of the soil. So say those who know it. Saxons, Franks, Lotharingians, Flemings! Emperors of the world, worthy of glory, here is your chance to provide for the eternal salvation of your souls, and, if you like, to acquire the most fertile land to settle upon. May He, whose powerful hand made the Gauls, starting from the remotest West, triumph over his enemies in the farthest East, give you will and strength to subject these inhuman heathens living close

---

[1] A. und E. Kulischer, *Kriegs- und Wanderzüge. Weltgeschichte als Völkerbewegung*. Berlin und Leipzig, 1932, pp. 120, 190–4.

[2]   "Naer Oostland willen wy ryden,
      Naer Oostland willen wy mêe,
      Al over die groene heiden,
      Frisch over die heiden!
      Daer isser en betere stêe."
    (A. Rein, *Die europäische Ausbreitung über die Erde*, p. 42.)

And the marching song of the pioneers:
      "When we've wood and prairie land
      Won by our toil,
      We'll reign like kings in fairy land,
      Lords of the soil!"
    (Hamlin Garland, *A Son of the Middle Border*, p. 46.)

by, and let you thrive in all your ways."[1] It is an invitation, issued probably about A.D. 1108 in the See of Magdeburg, to recruit crusaders against the heathen Slavs.

VIII

Conquest has sometimes preceded and sometimes followed colonization. The early Western trading communities in the East were "tolerated" settlements under the control of native rulers. They established contact between Western and Eastern civilizations. But they did not exercise political power in these dependencies for quite a long time. They were frequently at great pains to avoid political commitments. Cultural colonization preceded political colonization. Political control came much later, sometimes against the wish of the great merchant companies, who were interested in a profitable trade, but not in colonial government. They became the rulers of Eastern dependencies almost against their will, when they had to step into the shoes of their native hosts. They did not wish to take over their administration and to reorganize it, they were content with making it a little more efficient and a little less arbitrary. They let their native subjects continue in their own native ways and were by no means eager to introduce startling reforms along Western lines. Neither the early English nor the early Dutch trading companies in the Indies can be accused of an ardent desire to transplant Western civilization to Eastern shores. Even after they had assumed political control, they minimized rather than maximized intervention, restricting it to what was essential to their own commercial purposes; they carefully avoided anything which might be called institutional colonization and felt no missionary urge to civilize the natives.

In the settlement colonies, on the other hand, political colonization (occupation or conquest) and cultural coloniza-

---

[1] A. Rein, op. cit., p. 42.

tion coincided from the first, but they did not do so indefinitely. Independence brought political colonization to an
end, whilst economic and cultural colonization continued.
As long as the former colonies imported men they needed
and goods they could not manufacture themselves, they were
economically dependent and looked to the old country's
institutions and traditions for inspiration and guidance.
Dependent countries take over political institutions from
their masters, not always of their own free will; independent
countries borrow technical skill and economic ways and
means from their creditors, and are eager to copy them. No
political and no economic system has ever been transferred
without some transfusion of the spirit which had engendered
it, as well as of the forms in which it is embodied.

This transfer of social systems and economic instruments,
of cultural, institutional, and spiritual values, of religious
creeds, philosophies, and educational methods has made for
a fairly universal spread of institutions and a world-wide
assimilation of spiritual attitudes. It has nowhere and at no
time resulted in a complete universalism. For national
character, as well as diverse natural and cultural surroundings, is bound to cause important variations. Parliamentary
government on a democratic basis and the capitalist system
may have become fairly universal all the world over; they
work differently in every country which has adopted them.
Structural similiarity is accompanied everywhere by functional diversity. The daughter-states of Great Britain and the
Western states of the American Union differ from one another
as well as from their parent state. And even the Catholic
Church, the most universal of all known institutions, has
had to adjust herself to the uneven cultural level of her followers in many parts of the world. She could never have
expanded over the entire globe, but for the spiritual colonization her missionaries carried over every continent, and she
would never have succeeded but for her great plasticity in
all things not essential.

CHAPTER II

VOLUNTARY COLONIZATION

I

In a few cases where colonization is *complete*, conquest or armed occupation has been followed by the transplantation of economic, legal, and cultural institutions. This happened in the daughter-states which were modelled on the image of the mother country. The development of these newly formed colonial societies has led them either to separation from the motherland, like the thirteen colonies, or into some sort of partnership, like the British Dominions to-day. In either case, a kind of *partial* (secondary) colonization in the economic, institutional, or spiritual field may go on after the political tie has snapped.

Whilst *complete colonization* must begin with coercion, *partial colonization* may be voluntary. The compulsory economic dependence of the American colonies ended with their successful revolution against the Old Empire, whose component parts they had been. But voluntary economic dependence went on for a long time. Notwithstanding the stimulus given to their infant industries by a protective tariff, England's conversion to Free Trade lengthened this phase of economic colonial dependence considerably. Some former colonies, like Brazil and Chile, relied almost entirely on the sale of a single product (coffee and nitrate), with the proceeds of which they could buy what they needed and could pay interest on the vast sums of money they had borrowed abroad. Partial colonization is not limited to countries which have outgrown political (primary) colonization. Economic, institutional, and spiritual colonization, severally or combined, has been carried on in many a country which has never been subject to the will of a foreign colonizing power. In this case colonization is voluntary, not compulsory.

Some rulers who had been brought into contact with foreign traders recognized the benefit they could derive from peaceful voluntary colonization. They invited representatives of economically more advanced nations to settle in their midst, so that their own subjects should learn skilled processes of handicraft or better methods of agriculture. From the middle of the eleventh century the Hungarian kings planted German colonies in the Hungarian marches and the kings of Bohemia granted charters to German settlers, who built their towns. And as late as the eighteenth century, the Russian Czars invited German colonists to Russia to settle and to develop important districts.[1]

When the East was brought into contact with the West, native despots willingly (and sometimes under coercion) granted settlement rights to enterprising Western traders. They were allowed to live in colonies of their own (concessions) under their own laws. The rulers did not let their native subjects come into too close a contact with these foreigners, as they wanted to keep them under their own control. But they were very anxious for the profits which could be drawn from a development of trade and exchange and they quickly recognized the expediency of letting these "infidels" run their own affairs in the interests of profitable commerce. Originally both races were intended to keep apart; but points of contact were established.

From them some sort of economic, institutional, and cultural colonization has radiated in many parts of the world. In the beginning this was a bilateral process. The white traders lived in a milieu created by and fitted for natives; they adopted some native ways and brought them home when they retired. They taught the West the use of Eastern goods and transformed the habits of the Western consumer.

[1] Friedrich List negotiated a scheme for the immigration of German peasants into Hungary as late as 1844.

Cotton and silk, tea and coffee, sugar and spices, have profoundly affected Western ways of living. And even the comparatively backward peoples of the American continent have taken a hand in remodelling the tastes of the colonizing nations by giving them potatoes and Indian corn, chocolate, quinine, and tobacco.

The direct influence of the East on Western institutions was comparatively slight and purely temporary. Returned Eastern nabobs may have corrupted English parliamentary life in the eighteenth century, but nobody can charge them with originating bribery. And though some faint traces of Red Indian habits or Negro customs have permeated American life, and some Spanish-American institutions have survived beneath American forms in the American South-West, they are merely like old lavender in a carefully kept linen closet—a faint scent, which in no way affects the texture of the sheets.

Purely spiritual influences, on the other hand, have been much stronger. Eastern philosophy and Eastern views of life have undoubtedly infiltrated into Western concepts. But they gained influence only after the cultural colonization of the East by the West had been of long standing. They are the outcome of a tardy reaction of the subject culture against the claims of supremacy by the colonizing power. Thus the Celtic revival did not burst forth in the sixteenth, seventeenth, or eighteenth centuries, when the English invaders were deliberately destroying Celtic institutions and the Irish language. It began towards the end of the nineteenth century as part of a world-wide counter-colonization movement, when the revolt against political and institutional dependence was already in full swing. And the Hindu claims to superiority over Western civilization were not launched when England imposed the Anglo-Saxon educational system on India, but after it had borne fruit, and had converted and educated India to the political ideals of Anglo-Saxon democracy.

The impact of the West on the social structure of the East has been very strong, even where contact was restricted to mere commercial intercourse. From the day when Suliman the Great granted capitulations to the French (1536) to the latest concession of settlements in Morocco or China, an almost uninterrupted line of "open ports agreements" gave the privileged foreigners the right to use certain ports and to live in them under the jurisdiction of their own officials, but restricted them from more intimate intercourse with the natives. In nearly every case these limitations broke down. Boundaries were widened, intercourse was amplified. "Connubium" of some sort followed "commercium"; race interbreeding has nowhere been completely prevented. The West taught the East not merely how to use Western goods, but how to apply Western methods of trade, production, finance, and government. And even where the East maintained its political independence (sometimes not by its own strength, but as a result of the jealousies amongst the various Western Powers) it had to take over an increasing number of Western institutions in order to withstand the onslaught of the West. Turkey, China, Persia, and Egypt, while maintaining a sometimes rather spurious independence, accepted Western advisers for the reorganization of their finances, their laws, their customs, their banks, their police, their army, their navy, and their schools. They had either to go under and become politically dependent or accept voluntarily a far-reaching measure of cultural and institutional colonization from the West.

II

Voluntary colonization has gone farthest in Russia and Japan. When Peter the Great westernized Russia as an independent despotic ruler, he insisted on ramming alien institutions down his subjects' throats. He meant to make his country equal, if not superior, to the Western Powers. And ever since his day, Russia has gone on taking over Western ideas and Western institutions. Her rulers did so of their own free will, being entirely independent of foreign governments, by using compulsion against their own people in order to make them accept these Western forms. They planted German colonists in the Black Sea regions to teach the peasants how to farm, they drafted craftsmen and entrepreneurs from abroad to start an industry which was ultimately protected by high tariffs; they have borrowed foreign minds as well as foreign money. Soviet Russia is continuing this old-established procedure of voluntary colonization. She rebelled successfully against the imitation of Western democracy and of Western capitalism, which her intelligentsia had attempted to introduce. But the social system she is building up is based on the socialist theories of the West conceived by Marx and Engels. The aggressive atheism and the communistic social tenets she is forcing upon her people have sprung from the brains of Western doctrinaires. There is nothing Russian in them, apart from their ruthless application, which is indeed a reincarnation of the methods of Peter the Great. The Soviet government would even have been quite willing to accept large loans from the West and, by paying interest upon them, become a tributary colony, had the Westerners been willing to let her have these means for accelerating her development. Owing to their refusal, she had to undertake the Five Year Plan and rely mainly on her own resources; she could never have carried it out, had she not borrowed the technique of the West for laying down the plans and its organizing skill for their execution by hiring American, English, and German engineers. The reorganization of Russia by the Soviets under the Five Year Plan is probably the greatest institutional loan-operation which has ever been carried out between several countries. It is the greatest large-scale experiment in voluntary technical colonization ever undertaken. For Russia is attempting to crowd into a short decade the industrialization of an extremely backward agricultural country, in the greater part of which colonial conditions prevail. She is seeking to jump some phases of evolution, and hopes to reach a stage of social development far ahead of the colonizing West, which the latter may follow up later on. She has, moreover, succeeded in completely inverting her cultural balance sheet. Instead of acknowledging her cultural indebtedness for ideas and institutions to her Western creditors, she has set up her own claims as the originator of a new system, the success of which depends on loans of capital and personnel.

Japan, on the other hand, tenaciously preserved the feudal background of her traditional social life, when she grafted modern alien institutions on the framework of her indigenous society. She has organized constitution and administration, army and navy, law and education, as well as business, on Western patterns, but she has seasoned them all with her particular national tradition. She has taken from the West the outer shell of its thoughts and is endeavouring to fill it with her own concepts; her voluntary colonization has been institutional and not spiritual.

Turkey and Persia are following her lead in a somewhat different way. While strongly stressing her nationality, Turkey and, to a lesser degree, Persia, is transplanting the technical, economic, and cultural institutions of the West into her soil. She is discarding at the same time essential parts of her national, spiritual inheritance by effacing the cultural influence of Arab and Persian domination, without, however, replacing it by European notions.

III

Some governments who had entered upon voluntary colonization floundered in the attempt. It was easy enough to borrow money for the reorganization of their state; but not quite as easy to spend it intelligently. Having wasted the greater part, and having overburdened their country with debts in order to pay the interest, they went bankrupt and had to appeal to their creditors. They preserved their political independence, at least in those cases in which the jealousy of rival European Powers made annexation or partition difficult; but they became economically dependent; they were made a dependency, not of foreign governments, but of foreign creditors. A council of foreign bondholders was established, to whom certain revenues, especially customs, excise, and certain monopolies were handed over, from which the charges of the loans were paid. Foreign advisers were appointed, who organized the honest and efficient collection of the alienated revenues and, by preventing waste and extravagance, made the budget balance. The old debts were pared down and new loans were issued, the proceeds of which were spent under foreign surveillance. In Turkey, in Egypt, and in a few smaller states, a group of foreign bondholders, who represented the various creditor-nations, was entrusted with the financial administration of the country; in China, part of the revenue was managed by foreigners. But for this partial control, the political independence of these countries could not have been maintained, for they could neither have met their foreign obligations nor have raised the revenue on which their existence depended. They would not have been permitted to default on their foreign debts and would have fallen under political tutelage. The bondholders transformed themselves from a body of mere money-lending capitalists, who wanted to develop a backward country's latent resources with an eye to profit, into an international agency which had to exercise some of the functions of a colonizing government.[1] They became the exponents of a policy of quasi-voluntary colonization. Sometimes this capitalist colonization ended in political colonization (as in Tunis), when rival powers withdrew their objections against annexation by a predominant state. But Turkey, Egypt and, to a lesser degree, China managed to maintain

---

[1] In some smaller American States this financial control was monopolized by the U.S.A. on account of the Monroe Doctrine.

a separate political existence, by accepting, under pressure, a sort of semi-voluntary colonization. It implied a good deal of cultural colonization. The productive spending of loans and the repayment of debts presuppose financial skill and a certain amount of technical training. Most of the posts in financial departments or in railway management were entrusted to native employees, for (quite apart from political considerations) an exclusively foreign staff would have been far too expensive. Natives had to be recruited and trained for these services. Their work in counting-houses and in factories, on harbour boards and on railways was bound to change their outlook completely and to revolutionize their education. Employment of this sort is the most powerful instrument of economic, cultural, nay even spiritual colonization, more powerful perhaps than schools or churches; for this imported foreign mechanism will not work without far-reaching psychological adjustment.

In countries subject to financial control capitalist colonization is quasi-governmental and direct. It is non-governmental and indirect in independent new countries which offer fairly safe opportunities to foreign investors. Foreign capital has always been attracted by the exploitation of natural resources, mines, forests, oilfields, water-power, the construction of transportation systems and of harbours, the establishment of banks and factories, the laying-out of municipalities and the provision of public utilities for them. It can get higher rates of interest than at home and secure cheap native labour to help it in the development of this virgin wealth. Capitalist colonization may assume very large proportions where the government of a new country can keep order and guarantee a minimum of security. Its representatives are quite willing to run considerable risks if there is but a chance of exceptional profits. Strong indigenous rulers of the type of Porfirio Diaz have frequently worked hand in hand with capitalist colonization of this sort. They deliberately protected it and gave valuable concessions to

American and European entrepreneurs, whose success in tapping the wealth of the country strengthened their own government. These types of colonizers meddle with native politics. They do not act in the interest of their own government, which refrains from using them for its home political objects. But they use its strength for their private business purposes. They do not care for the business of empire, but they do care very much for the empire of business. They are allowed to exploit, nay even to plunder the country. But they have to pay a heavy price for it: they must bribe the government which supports them, and at least provide it with tax-revenue. And they have frequently been tempted to interfere in the country's affairs by keeping in power a government which, but for their help, would have been overthrown, or by assisting (and financing) an opposition which offered them greater latitude. They have sometimes succeeded in enlisting the support of their own government for these ventures, under whose pressure the foreign government collapsed. But frequently too, these intrigues and machinations in local affairs have greatly embarrassed their own administration, as they interfered with its official policy.

IV

Quasi-voluntary colonization on a gigantic scale has been carried on in the spiritual sphere. The polytheist religions of the ancient world were not keen on missionary work. They saw no sense in wasting energy on converting barbarians to civilization. Civilization, as they understood it, could very well stand by itself. It was a boon to its possessors which did not need advertisement or propaganda. They did not withhold it from barbarians, provided they were willing, so to speak, to qualify for it. The advent of Christianity and Islam changed this completely. Its adherents held a faith which guaranteed them eternal salvation, whilst non-believers were eternally damned. This great spiritual boon of salvation could not be monopolized; it must be imparted to others; if they refused to be saved, because darkness clouded their minds, the light must be forced upon them, if needs be at the point of the sword. A vast propaganda started in the Moslem, as well as in the Christian world; it ruthlessly destroyed men's bodies in order to save their souls. Religious propaganda was one of the motives which drove the Spaniards to the discovery of the New World. The missionary fanaticism, the desire to spread the true faith, was for centuries closely linked with Moslem, as well as with Christian, expansion. It revived at the turn of the twentieth century in the form of mystical national or racial Imperialism, which forced empire-builders to shoulder the white man's burden in order to benefit the natives with the blessings of an alien civilization.

But though the transmission of institutional and spiritual values was frequently implemented by force, with the support and in the interest of expansionist governments, this was not always so. The missionaries of all churches have frequently gone into the wilderness to preach the gospel to the heathen, regardless of the wishes of their governments. Their success in winning members of the non-European races to a belief in and an appreciation of European civilization has been very impressive. It might have been even greater had rivalry amongst the churches in the political, as well as in the religious, field not lessened the strength of their appeal to the native mind, and had not the actions of European governments and of European settlers laid bare to the heathens the fundamental discrepancies between the moral principles of the faith of the white race and their application to life, private as well as public. Notwithstanding these grave obstacles, spiritual colonization on a purely voluntary base has been successful in many lands. It may be difficult to separate the results due to coercion from those due to persuasion (sometimes bribery too) in the countries which were dominated by European masters. "If colonists and conquerors seized trade and territory and felt no compunctions, it is not perhaps surprising if those whose interest was in religion should express the imperialism of the period in that field as well."[1] The spiritual triumph of American missionary activities in Turkey and, to a much greater degree, in China, was, however, not due to political support or pressure, but to the "infectious charm" of Western ways and knowledge. And the Chinese scholars trained in American ways of thinking helped to lay the foundations of modern China. On returning to their country they "live usually in groups together, their social life, on the whole, within the group, although this may be subdivided into smaller cliques, these being dependent on the countries where the members were educated. But the entire group forms a bridge between East and West."[2]

The secularization of the modern mind has greatly accelerated non-religious voluntary colonization in the spiritual and intellectual sphere. The war showed the native peoples all the world over the discrepancy between Western civilization and Christianity. The West was no longer united and Christianity was not an all-embracing creed, each Christian nation having, so it seemed, its own separate Christian god. Its faith was no longer superior, but its knowledge and institutions were.[3]

Concepts and ideas trickle from one country to another, sometimes spontaneously, sometimes in an organized way. The political institutions of the Western world have been eagerly imitated by many nations all the world over. The parliamentary system of Great Britain has been transferred to many a land, and has not always been an unmitigated blessing. Some political trouble in South-American republics would never have arisen, if their institutions had not been modelled on those of the United States. Political philosophies,

---

[1] Pearl Buck, "Missionaries of Empire" in Joseph Barnes's *Empire of the East*, p. 252. [2] Pearl Buck, op. cit., p. 264.
[3] Pearl Buck, op. cit., pp. 256 and 263.

Liberalism and Socialism, Fascism and Communism, flit over continents like electric sparks. They sometimes are mere fashions borrowed from abroad, which are discarded with the change of seasons; they sometimes are assimilated and become an integral part of a nation's way of life. From the transmitting towers of the entire world cultural, political, and commercial waves permeate the air, enabling men and women to take up voluntarily, if they choose to, particles of a foreign civilization and incorporate them into their own. The new creeds of the West—Communism and Fascism—are affecting the East. Atheistic science has invaded Japan on a scale the missionaries might well covet.[1]

There is an opposite, inverted current of voluntary cultural colonization. The opening of the New World resulted in mass migrations of millions of people, who forsook their old homes in order to share the opportunities offered them in new lands. In most cases, they had to submit to alien governments, who imposed upon them a frame of life which greatly differed from that under which they had grown up. They were thrown into a kind of melting-pot and though they frequently resented this assimilation, forced upon them by conditions of living rather than by governments, they underwent more or less voluntarily this process of "cultural colonization." But in doing so, they infused elements of their own national life into that of their hosts.

[1] Pearl Buck, op. cit., p. 258.

CHAPTER III

TYPES OF COLONIES

POLITICAL colonization has produced three distinct types of colonies: settlement colonies, native dependencies, composite colonies.

I

Settlement colonies arose through the peopling of uninhabited or quasi-uninhabited lands. These settlements were originally more or less faithful replicas of the homeland which had established them, and from which the bulk of the colonial population had been drawn. They owed their particular character to the transplantation of more or less homogeneous groups from a mother country, who carried their national institutions—religion, language, law, social order, and government—along with them.

In this way the North American colonies, Australia and South Africa were founded. None of these territories were vacant in the strict sense of the word, but they comprised large areas, roamed over by native races, who were too weak in number to offer lasting resistance. They were either expelled or exterminated or, to some degree, absorbed by the invaders. Thus a kind of reproduction of English society was accomplished. France in Canada, Portugal and Spain in Central and South America, and Russia in Siberia have planted similar settlements. But their people have not filled them up in sufficient numbers and their governments could not hold them. In the nineteenth century England alone retained her daughter-states, a fact which roused the envy and admiration of many nations, to whom colonial expansion had been denied. The formation of a new society, wholly composed of one's own kith and kin, seemed to them the greatest achievement which nations can strive after.

They saw in the rise of England's dominions the working of a deliberately planned national policy, and concentrated a good deal of their national energies on the acquisition of suitable territories, into which they too could direct mass immigration, and where they could "plant," as England had done, mighty daughter-states with people of their own flesh and blood.

Some of the early British settlements had indeed been carefully planned. Bacon's *Essay on Plantation* had laid down the general principles of colonization. Some colonial charters and land settlement schemes were based on deliberately conceived plans, which were frequently much sounder than many loudly-advertised planning programmes of to-day. The plantation of Munster and the Cromwellian settlement of Ireland, the peopling of South Australia and New Zealand in pursuance of Wakefield's theories resulted from such plans. They aimed at a more or less faithful reproduction of the stratified society of the homeland. There was nothing exclusively British about such plans, for the military settlements of the French on the banks of the St. Lawrence and its tributaries had followed similar lines.

The classless society which modern democracy established later on in the United States of America, in Canada and in Australia, was not in the minds of the early empire builders. It grew, so to speak, against their will. For in a new country in which there is no servile native population, a hierarchically stratified society cannot last long. Feudalism disappeared fairly quickly in the British settlement colonies, though the slave trade established it on a colour basis in the Southern States, where it was preserved until the end of the Civil War. After the Middle West had been thrown open to mass immigration by a policy of cheap land settlement, a kind of classless society arose in the United States, which very nearly fulfilled the boldest dreams of egalitarian philosophers. These experiments were almost as interesting to an earlier generation as Russian planning is to-day.

There was a good deal of deliberate construction in these new societies. The American township, cut into standardized quadrangles and reproduced endlessly on both sides of the borderline for hundreds of miles, and the self-adjusting mechanism which was to work the Wakefield settlements, were products of "social engineering," to use an appropriate American phrase. They afforded a strong contrast to the traditional ways which European development had taken. And the repercussions of these thoroughly rational man-made societies, composed of standardized egalitarian units, have affected the entire world. Though the roots of democracy and applied rationalism go back to the English and the French Revolutions, the American Revolution and the opening of the West put them on the map. But social planning of this sort would never have succeeded but for the dauntless individualist faith of the early Puritans, and the equally dauntless courage of the Frontiersmen.

Opportunities for the foundation of daughter-states were limited. The great Asiatic plain, over which Russian hunters and peasants wandered as far as the China Sea, was a Russian possession where it was not encroached upon by Chinese migration. It was not accessible to the Western powers. In the remaining parts of the world, success partly depended on climatic or biological conditions. No race can thrive and multiply in physical circumstances not conducive to its well-being. But mere physical conditions can be changed by the application of scientific methods (hygiene). Races can acclimatize themselves to mere external conditions and, by following reasonable ways of living, can maintain their hardihood for a few generations at least. The white people have never yet been properly subjected to this biological test, certainly not over a series of generations. Numbers of them have settled in the tropics; they have conceived and born healthy offspring, but they have nowhere had a chance of proving their mettle in the struggle for life. For in the West Indies, in Mauritius and in a few other selected tropical regions, whose history goes back sufficiently far, the whites were an aristocracy. Their successes, as well as their failures, were indissolubly bound up with the presence of a servile coloured race. Where their vigour has deteriorated, it may be the result of their socially sheltered lives; where their physical strength has been maintained, it may be due to their privileged position. No definite conclusion can be drawn from their social experiences, even when all pertinent facts have been carefully collected and critically sifted. But one conclusion can be safely drawn from these instances:

No settlement colony can flourish, whose members rely on native labour to any great extent. As long as indigenous labour is very much cheaper than imported labour, it will be used for the development of the colony, whatever its climatic conditions, or whatever the fertility of the soil. Its mere presence will make for a kind of superiority complex in the white immigrants; they will not care to compete for work with natives, even if by reason of their greater efficiency they could earn a very much higher wage. And their industrial superiority is rarely sufficient to offset the great difference in standards of living. The immigrants in a new country want to rise in the social scale; they did not come over to sink to the level of a native population, which is accustomed to the prevailing climatic conditions and is satisfied with very few comforts.

Countries inhabited by a native population, which can be easily pressed into the service of a white ruling class, offer ideal opportunities for the rapid rise of a kind of "white" aristocracy; they attract men with capital and with a gift for managing natives. They appeal to the aristocratic remnants in European countries, to impoverished owners of large estates or to younger sons, who want to lead the life of a country squire. But they attract business men too, who will sink mines where there are paying ores and establish plantations which can be run efficiently, if labour costs are low. But they offer no prospects to impecunious settlers who have to earn the small working capital needed even before settling on a homestead. And a tiny homestead in a native country is not large enough to maintain a white family in fairly decent comfort. Impecunious immigrant farmers will either sink to the level of the poor whites or take native women and become fathers of a coloured progeny. There is no scope for mass immigration in those countries. A modern democracy may be formed where land is cheap and labour expensive; where land is cheap but labour even cheaper, no genuine daughter-state will arise.

The presence of large vacant regions which native tribes never settled upon, but used only as grazing or hunting grounds or as shelter belts against aggressive invaders, can greatly speed up the development of a colony. These plains need not be taken away from the natives, who have no title to them; there need be no extermination and no struggle for land. But they cannot be quickly settled by the exclusive use of white labour. The moneyed settlers who come to take up their farms must not be prevented from employing native labour. Development would otherwise be far too slow. They will hire native workers even if these have to travel long distances. For white people can always offer goods which make it worth the natives' while to work for them at very low wages. Their government has ended tribal wars and will ultimately stop cattle-stealing. Under its sway the natives enjoy peace and security, and quickly multiply. Sooner or later they must go to work.

No region on the African continent is inhabited by a compact white society. Even very healthy fringes in the north and in the south, which originally maintained comparatively few native inhabitants, are "composite colonies." And they are surrounded by huge native reserves, the inmates of which multiply under white control until they are ready to spate forth any amount of workers, which the white planters, farmers, or capitalists may need as soon as new desires have been awakened by more or less intimate contact with them. No settlement colonies can be established within an easy reach of native populations; even if there are no railways, mere distance is no obstacle—as long as coloured labour in any form may be employed. If its use were prohibited, development would be very slow. The extermination of a sparse native population like the Red Indians and the Australian Negroids made settlement colonies in the American north and in Australia possible. Their rise forms a unique chapter in modern history; it could only be rewritten if the circumstances which brought it about could be repeated. To-day no vacant continents are left, and no government could undertake the extirpation or expulsion of natives on the scale needed for founding settlement colonies in Africa. The experiment would ruin the financial prospects of the new "settlement colony" and shake the foundations of all neighbouring African possessions.[1]

II

The Spaniards sailing westwards, began the planting of settlement colonies in the New World; the Portuguese, turning southwards and eastwards, laid the foundation of Europe's great native dependencies. The division of the oceans between the two Iberian powers by the Treaty of Tordesillas (June 1494)[2] almost coincided with a line of demarcation between two types of colonies.

Native states, which are inhabited by comparatively dense populations possessing a fairly advanced civilization of their own, cannot be "colonized" by "plantation." There is no room for planning a new commonwealth. They must be conquered and the conquerors are rarely driven by an overwhelming desire to present their institutions to the natives. They want privileges for the exchange of goods and rights

[1] Mrs. Elspeth Huxley's *White Man's Country* (London, 1935) contains many facts which show quite clearly why no part of Africa is really a white man's country. See below, pp. 276–84.

[2] A. Rein, op. cit., p. 89.

for the traders to live under their own laws in licensed settlements or concessions. Even in the heyday of religious fervour very few of the colonizing Christian governments encouraged enthusiastic missionaries to spread the gospel indiscriminately amongst the natives. They preferred to let the natives live in their own ways. They throttled immigration and restricted it to officials and traders, who did not make their permanent home in the colony, and blocked the way to genuine immigrants from home. The residence of members of the ruling race in the dependency was "functional" not "personal"; their task was not to transform native society, but to exercise such administrative and economic duties as were essential to the proper ruling or the exploitation of the colony. Sooner or later these alien governments had to interfere in native affairs, in order to accomplish these objects. They had to start institutional colonization bit by bit, very much against their wishes. They had to overhaul the financial system; they had to see that justice was done in a rough way, and they had to insist on a minimum of order and efficiency. After the Industrial Revolution had changed the economic system of Europe, they had to organize, or at least tolerate, some sort of capitalist colonization. Ports and railways had to be built. Factories were established, banks were founded, and monetary systems had to be devised. None of these things could be done without more or less violent changes in the natives' minds. The missionaries need not be given a free hand, but the counting-house and the factory could not be run without a certain amount of Western education. Native clerks and native civil servants had to be trained to do the work of the Western masters fairly efficiently and comparatively cheaply. This technical education could not be given to those conversant with native culture only; it had to be based on Western educational foundations. Western education became the key which opened doors to "clerical" employment to the natives. It revolutionized native society; the lowly-born brain-worker became more important than the blue-blooded warrior.

The transformation of a native economic system, steeped in traditions of war, and frequently based on war, into some sort of native capitalism was advocated by the master democracies in Europe. They no longer wanted to rule the dependency by force, but they did not want to hand it over to the old native warrior class. The movement for transformation gathered speed at the hands of native business interests. The old-fashioned native rulers and their bureaucratic overlords would have preferred the continuation of a somewhat purified patriarchal rule, but their educated subjects were becoming the apostles of democracy and demanded self-government and democratic institutions. Cultural colonization was becoming quasi-voluntary. The natives, not the invaders, insisted on complete institutional assimilation. Whilst European political institutions are being questioned to-day all over the West, and whilst the capitalist system is severely criticized, the leaders in dependencies such as British India and in independent countries like China are pressing for their adoption. They see in their possession a mark of "equality" and a means for successful national self-expression.

Native societies which have not yet reached a high standard of development, and where climatic conditions discourage mass influx of European settlers, present different problems. Their governments have to transform a more or less self-contained tribal society into a community, the members of which regularly produce goods for markets and for profit. This cannot be done by copying a few institutions. To make peace and business attractive, new motives have to be set going, as substitutes for the older impulses. A new business civilization has to be developed, which will replace the old order based on raids and forays. This is a lengthy process: it took the English several centuries to accomplish it in Scotland and Ireland. And even to-day the pace of healthy

c*

development cannot be forced, whether it be on the Gold Coast or in Basutoland, though modern transport and up-to-date technical equipment have greatly accelerated it. It can apparently be speeded up by ruthless exploitation, such as the rubber atrocities formerly perpetrated in the Congo Free State. But this does not solve the social problems involved, though it may yield very great profits for a short period. For the natives are not easily converted to a belief in the "dignity of labour", when "labour" means slaving for rapacious masters.

Colonial trade was originally carried on by barter; stocks in the possession of the natives were exchanged against European commodities, if they were not looted. As these stocks were inadequate, native production had to be speeded up. This was done in various ways: in the Western world the European conquerors ran mines or plantations by introducing coercive feudalism. The natives had to work for their European masters or task-masters. When native labour proved insufficient, negro slaves were imported. The slave trade became the backbone of the plantation system. (The meaning of this term was completely altered; it was originally applied to the settlement of a daughter society in "a pure soil", where there were no natives; later on it came to designate a peculiar form of exploiting a composite colony.)

Cultivation in the East was stimulated in a different way. The native rulers were forced to furnish quantities of valuable products, by way of tribute or taxation, or against payment. They forced their subjects to raise these crops, sometimes to the detriment of the country's general wealth and the natives' welfare. The stronger the native system of government, the easier this could be put through.

Compulsory cultivation could be imposed on primitive tribes too. Chiefs were compelled to furnish certain quantities of goods (rubber) under pressure from the administration, or else private "concessionaires" were entrusted with the exploitation of certain areas. As they could rely on the support of the government, the chiefs had to comply with their demands and put men at their disposal.

Both methods were fairly successful for the time being, but they led to a destruction of material resources and of man-power quite out of proportion to the ultimate profits. They could not be maintained in the face of the humanitarian opposition encountered at home. Coercive cultivation had to give way to voluntary or semi-voluntary production.

Individual planters or plantation companies represented by managers were allowed to lease or purchase land. Native labour frequently flocked to such plantations of its own free will in return for the money wages and the goods they could buy with them. But frequently, too, indirect compulsion was resorted to. The natives were made to pay heavy taxes, which they somehow had to earn. Even in well-managed colonics the pressure on natives to go to work was sometimes very formidable.

Native landowners or coloured (Chinese) immigrants have frequently taken up capitalist cultivation in the same way as Europeans; they benefited from it to a much greater degree, since their costs of production were much lower.

Again small indigenous landowners were turning their attention to "cash crops" and were becoming more or less successful rivals of those native, European, or Chinese capitalist entrepreneurs.[1]

The native dependencies under the control of European Powers represent a great variety of different social types; transitions between tribal, feudal, and capitalist institutions are frequent.

The outcome of colonization in such primitive countries has been an extremely superficial Westernization. A kind of mock-capitalism is established, which is run either for absentee European plantation corporations, by frequently changing resident managers, or by European planters, who return home when they have made their pile, and later

[1] I. C. Greaves, *Modern Production among Backward Peoples*, p. 67 seq.

on by native capitalists. It is often accompanied by a mock-democractic movement. The advent of Bolshevism in Russia and the evolution of a new sort of nationalism clamouring for a return to native pre-conquest institutions is undermining this form of colonization.

III

Conquerors have frequently invaded countries which were inhabited by a healthy native population; it was too weak to resist their settlement, but vigorous enough to hold its own after the first onslaught was over. Here the colonists had to form a new society and incorporate the natives in its framework. A "composite colony" arose on the basis of unfree coloured labour. It reproduced the forms of life of the mother country, a stratified feudal society, in which all manual work was done by natives. Where the natives could not stand the strain, the colonists imported coloured labour, negro slaves or coolies.

Here again planning and drifting went on side by side. Cortez had no elaborate schemes for "social engineering" when he conquered and organized Mexico. The reconquest of Ireland, on the other hand, led to endless discussions and many elaborate plans. The questions whether the new colony was to be a "settlement colony," from which the natives were to be ousted, or a "composite colony" depending on their work, was argued over and over again. The conquered country could be run by a bureaucracy and defended by an army of occupation. As the cost of this sort of administration would be prohibitive, the land was given to settlers, who would rule the country, defend their estates against the natives and garrison it without much expense to the taxpayer. The advice which Machiavelli had given was followed: "The other and better means to govern a subject-state is to plant a colony in one or two pivotal places of the country concerned; in such a colony the Prince incurs small expense and, without great expense (sometimes with none at all) he can rule it and control it."

In the ancient world, closed urban settlements or military camps, the garrisons of which remained permanently in the country, formed the prevailing type of "composite colonies." Under the feudal system the centre shifted to the rural areas. The natives were deprived of their estates, which the members of the tribe had frequently held in common. The conquerors expropriated them, but let them remain as tenants, serfs, or labourers on the land they had taken from them. The English reconquests of Ireland, the Spanish conquests in Mexico and Peru, the spread of the Boer commandos over South Africa, and the Turkish subjection of the Rajahs in the Balkans resulted in some sort of colonial feudalism. The main features of a South American encomienda and a Boer farm, of a Baltic estate of the Teutonic knights or a Turkish fief are very much alike.

Urban centres were interspersed between the estates by settling skilled artisans and professional men, all members of the invading race, in walled cities which dominated the open country.

The planting of composite colonies has gone on all over the inhabited world. It has resulted in splendid achievements and in terrible failures. A small band of Spanish conquistadores successfully "hispanized" half a continent by the forced labour of subject native races. They built, in a comparatively short time, mighty castles, cities, and cathedrals in a vast new land, whilst the English settlers in America, having no such labour supply at their beck and call, had to be content with wooden churches and small stockaded villages.

Most composite colonies are "tripartite." A comparatively narrow layer at the top is composed of colonists of pure extraction. At the bottom are the native masses, pure-blooded themselves, who live in their own time-honoured native ways, and cling fast to their customs and traditions, even where they have been converted to the conquerors' religion. The Indians of Mexico and even the Pueblo Indians of the United States may be fervent Roman Catholics; many of their religious practices do not differ much from those of their pre-conquest heathen ancestors.

The middle group is frequently composed of half-breeds of various shades. Inter-marriage with the leading native families at the beginning of the conquest is frequent enough, and the offspring of these unions often rank as white. Later on, when women arrive in greater numbers, racial attitudes harden. Inter-marriage is prohibited, but illicit intercourse has nowhere been stopped. However strong racial prejudice may be, it has nowhere prevented the growth of a mixed race; the presence of coloured women, not the absence of white women, is responsible for it. The mixed breeds passionately desire complete assimilation. They wish to enjoy the status of their white fathers and despise their mothers' race, despite the fact that their white masters frequently try to keep them at the level of the "mere natives."

The pure-blooded colonists own the land, they occupy the government posts, they monopolize the skilled trades and fill the learned professions. The heads of the Church and the chief servants of the State come from their ranks; they control and monopolize education. The natives and, to a lesser degree, the half-breeds, are tillers of the soil or unskilled labourers. Their profound ignorance would have precluded them from rising in the social scale, even if there had been no oppression.

The cleavage which originated in racial and cultural disparities was often deepened by legal discrimination. Colonists and natives were kept apart; they lived under separate codes of law. And antagonistic religious creeds frequently gave additional strength to the forces making for social disruption, until two more or less alien, and even hostile, nations faced each other within a single body politic. The English colonization in Ireland and the Spanish conquest of Mexico have produced such a type of society.

Composite colonies covered the eastern and south-eastern fringes of central Europe. In some of these regions the German colonists had expelled the original Slav inhabitants and established exclusive German settlements—somewhat in the manner in which the North Americans drove back the Red Indians. But there were other territories in which German colonists from the West, or Hungarian and Turkish invaders from the East, had established a kind of feudalism; they controlled the land, the government, the Church, and the towns, whilst native tributaries tilled the soil.

Societies of this type are originating at present in many parts of Africa. In the Union of South Africa and in Rhodesia, in Kenya and in Tanganyika, a loose sort of feudalism is growing up in mining areas and in farming districts, wherever white owners run their properties with black labourers and tenants. The white invaders frequently have settled on the healthy highland areas, where there were no permanent native habitations, for the natives preferred the low-lying valleys and merely roamed over the empty steppes and grazing grounds. The bulk of the natives is concentrated in reservations, where they can live in tribal ways. The whites no longer desire their complete assimilation, for "the white people in South Africa are haunted by a double fear—fear of miscegenation and fear of black domination. . . . Although in the past the whites have felt it their duty to advance the interest of the natives, they have held back because they had felt that every forward step of the natives was another threat to white superiority."[1] But the natives do not remain within their reservations, for the whites rely on their services and attract them by high wages. In this way even districts which never had any native inhabitants grow into composite colonies; there is no room for the mass

[1] General Hertzog in Debate on Cape Native Franchise. February 25th (*The Times*, February 26, 1936).

immigration which founded the American and Australian daughter-states. There are merely "white fringes" surrounded by densely populated territories in which the natives live on *reservations* under a more or less modified tribal law. Increased transport facilities, the lure of industry, the attraction of wages appeals to the natives, and to the whites, the chances of trading with the natives; they are slowly dissolving the tribal system and will ultimately widen the areas inhabited by mixed populations.

The old slave-holding plantations were such composite colonies. The masters of the plantations aspired to the position of a true aristocracy, whatever their origin may have been, surrounding themselves with the pomp and splendour which cheap servile labour can easily provide. Below them was a dense mass of black humanity deprived not only of opportunities for, but even of the desire for social advancement. Round them lived a large number of poor whites who conducted themselves towards the negroes as behoved freemen of the blood, but whose low standards of life earned for them the contempt of well-fed plantation hands. And there was a crowd of half-breeds of all shades whom their black mothers, as well as their white fathers, despised. Some of the harshest features of this society survived its downfall. The lot of the peon or of the share cropper was often not much better than that of the negro slave. He might enjoy more liberty; he had fewer comforts and no security.

IV

The early conquerors did not interfere with native habits, as long as their subjects were willing to serve as hewers of wood and drawers of water. They preferred indolence and ignorance to ambition and eager imitation. They did not object to some smattering of religion being taught them, provided this did not imply spiritual and, what was much more important, social or economic equality, and they often insisted on some sort of superficial external conformity. The English in the sixteenth century ordered the Irish to shave their ferocious-looking moustaches, and the Boers insisted that Kaffirs working in a white settlement must wear a pair of trousers and a shirt.

The rise of the absolutist modern state terminated the sway of tolerant Imperialism. A "pluralistic" conception of subject races was incompatible with the ways of a centralizing bureaucracy. Nor could the Christian Churches, filled with fervent missionary zeal, tolerate the exercise of native religions. They had to convert the natives in order to save their souls from perdition. They burned them on the stake, if they were not willing to serve the new God. But they saved them from extermination and tried to protect them against the oppression of cruel masters. They might be backward and they might be slaves, but their souls were immortal and, as such, of equal value to those of their masters. Where racial distinctions resulted from language only, assimilation and unification could easily be accomplished by education, supported by pressure if necessary. The attempt promised well in such composite colonies where racial, cultural, and religious discrepancies were not too wide. The English tried fairly successfully to assimilate the Irish by forcing on them their language and, with it, their customs. And the German-speaking bureaucracy of the Habsburg Empire very nearly succeeded in germanizing the Slavs by making German the official language.

Outside Europe the gap between the civilization of the natives and of the colonists was often too wide and too deep to be easily bridged. The attempt to make a negro in all essentials not only a French citizen, but a Frenchman as well, could never have been undertaken, but for the egalitarian fanaticism of the French Revolution.

The white masters who lived in the midst of a numerous coloured population, on whose subservience they had to rely, might be willing enough to recognize (with considerable reservations) the equality of the negro's soul, as a theoretical proposition insisted upon by the Church, which might entitle him to full rights in Kingdom Come. But in this world, the white people, the *Gente de Razon* of the Spaniards, were distinct and had to be kept separate from the native masses, who were bereft of the divine spark of reason. Imperialism became exclusive. The ruling race objected to assimilation; they not only thought it undesirable, but impossible, and they strongly objected to cultural colonization. For a long time the natives were themselves far too backward and too depressed to aspire to equality with their masters. Occasionally a half-breed revolted. As he might become a dangerous enemy, the Spanish government granted him the status of a "white man."

The advent of modern capitalism, which wanted to speed up native labour, made education inevitable. The demand for egalitarian cultural colonization revived with it. Democracy was beginning to modify the attitude of the ruling class of the metropolis, though not yet of the colony. Radical reformers at home advocated complete assimilation; they insisted on equal status for the natives and disregarded the violent opposition of the colonists. The colonists demanded equal rights with the inhabitants of the mother country. They revolted in Mexico and Ireland against the motherland, in the wake of the American Revolution, but they overlooked the difference between a settlement country and a composite colony, where there is but a small minority of alien colonists, who rule numerous natives, and thus prepared their own downfall.

The nationalism of subject races is apt to run through various stages. It may at first be fiercely *recalcitrant*; it may, with a better knowledge of the invading civilization, become *accommodating*. And it may turn passionately *imitative* when egalitarian desires have been awakened. But there is a final stage: when the claim for complete equality of a former subject race has been recognized, when assimilation is accepted, a revulsion in feeling will take place. The natives are no longer satisfied with equality. They claim "Ascendancy." The yearning for complete assimilation is satisfied; it is turned into a strong and passionate demand for a resumption of the old native ways—and assimilation becomes anathema. Cultural colonization is reversed when the former subject race has learned to value its own spiritual inheritance. Their nationalism becomes *arrogant* and *exclusive*, where before it has been *subservient* and *imitative*. The problems of the composite colony are not solved; they are merely inverted.

CHAPTER IV

THE TRADE EMPIRE

I

THE New World had been reserved for a limited part of Spain; only for the kingdoms of Castille and Leon Columbus had discovered it. It was to give the Spanish government access to the precious commodities of the East. And it offered an opportunity to the nations' missionary zeal for the prolongation of the "Reconquista" among the heathens of the new world, after the fall of Granada had deprived it of the last European outlet for its spiritual energies. Spain did not look for lands to settle a superabundant population; she had none to spare. Her government, moreover, early recognized the dangers in which these far-distant settlements ruled by ruthless conquerors might involve the metropolis. Its original economic concepts were commercial. So were those of the Portuguese, who had founded a mercantile empire by the conquest of Asiatic trading posts and by sweeping Arab merchant fleets from the Indian Ocean, but who did not want to found a territorial colonial empire. "Pepper and souls" were the objects of the Portuguese crusaders,[1] who were quickly transformed into conquering traders; "silver and souls" was the Spaniards' equivalent. Their government spent the precious metals on the armies and navies who were fighting for the world empire of the Habsburg Dynasty and for the supremacy of the Catholic faith. Charles V bore the crowns of a united Spain, of the Holy Roman Empire of the German nation and of its possessions and claims in Italy. For a fleeting moment the conception of "World Empire" arose once more on a genuine worldwide scale. The conquest of the New World, west of the

[1] A. Rein, op. cit., p. 117.

great line, stretched the territorial limits of his empire beyond the dreams even of the great Alexander. This new Imperialism was Spanish, Catholic, and Universal; it was to give to the Emperor the control of the world, the *Imperium mundi*. "Neither day nor night limit it, the setting sun looks upon it and the sun looks upon it when it rises in the New World."

The rich soil of the West Indies, the transformation of the Conquistadores into a landed aristocracy in Mexico and Peru on the pattern of an expanding European feudalism, and the exploitation of the silver mines turned those trading ventures into settlements.[1] Composite colonies were arising in the place of missions and commercial enterprises originally planned. The entire New World was divided between Spain and Portugal by the Treaty of Tordesillas (June 7, 1494), the Spanish running the Western Hemisphere and the Portuguese the Eastern.[2] Both parties claimed for their respective empires the exclusive rights to old as well as to new discoveries and denied the rights of other nations to found empires of their own by independent discoveries; both prohibited foreign traders from direct intercourse with their dependencies. They did not withhold their products from them; they offered them the surplus accumulating in Seville and in Lisbon. But they wanted to monopolize the wholesale trade, in which great profits could be made, and merely let other nations retail the residue amongst themselves. The Union of Spain and Portugal (1580) simplified the issue. The New Worlds, on both sides of the line, were held under a single control, which was animated by a Catholic spirit. An Imperial Power had arisen whose territorial exclusiveness and whose spiritual universalism forced the other nations to break the Spanish colonial

[1] By 1570, there were about 4,000 large estates (encomienda) and 32,000 Spanish households in the New World, who ruled and exploited an Indian population of $1\frac{1}{2}$ million families.—A. Rein, op. cit., p. 133.

[2] A. Supan, *Die territoriale Entwicklung der Europäischen Kolonien*, pp. 14 seq.

monopoly. The problem of the Haves and the Have-nots was posed.

II

It was solved in a twofold way. The excluded countries, France, Holland and England, broke through the barriers which the Iberian Powers had erected round their preserves. Their sea-dogs, corsairs, filibusters, and buccaneers crossed forbidden seas, smuggled cargoes into ports sealed to them, traded with native princes, wherever they found a chance of doing so, and chased and robbed the silver fleets or the spice-laden caravels. The Iberians had laid down a kind of colonial Monroe doctrine; they closed the seas by treaties amongst themselves, fortified by the blessings of the Holy See. They asked after each war for the recognition of their exclusive rights by the other parties.[1]

But they never succeeded in getting a settlement which guaranteed peace beyond the "lines," as well as peace in Europe. The inroads into the colonial empire never ceased; they reached a dramatic culmination in Morgan's sack of old Panama. The ruins of this once throbbing centre of the silver trade bear testimony to the ruthlessness of the attack which the heretic outsiders directed against the empire.

No naval and military strength could have kept it closed for ever. For though it was *closed*, it was not *self-sufficient*. It was, in fact, never intended to be so. The silver from Potosi or the spices from the Moluccas provided Spain and Portugal with colonial goods. They could neither consume the surplus nor pay for their imports with Iberian goods and services. They had to settle them by foreign imports

---

[1] In the negotiations of 1535 and 1538 the Imperial Commissioners were asked to make the French king renounce in the most solemn way any intention ever to start shipping or commerce towards the Indies or to undertake any enterprise in that direction. This proposal Francis I indignantly refused: "The sun shines for me as it shines for the other; I should like to see the clause in Adam's will, by which I am excluded from the partition of the world."—A. Rein, op. cit., p. 169.

into Spain, from where they could be diverted to the colonies. The trade of the dependencies with the non-Iberian Powers was organized compulsorily as "triangular trade"; goods converged from both directions on the metropolis from where they were distributed. The excluded Powers attempted to avoid this corner. They ultimately succeeded. When Portugal and its dependencies were separated from Spain and had fallen under British control (Methuen Treaty, 1703), and when Spanish sea-power was no longer capable of closing the seas, the Spanish government had to grant a limited amount of direct (free) trade to its rising rivals. The Asiento Treaty, as part of the Treaty of Utrecht, gave the British South Sea Company the exclusive right to furnish the Spanish colonies with slaves (4,800 a year for thirty years) and to send a ship every year to the port of Porto Bello. A kind of "free trade" was imposed upon the Spanish colonies by force of arms.[1]

The inroads into the colonial preserves of the Iberian Powers by the French, the Dutch, and the English had begun as trade ventures; the Have-nots desired to share the silver treasure of the Indies, which gave the Spanish Monarchy the wealth with which to fight the world. They had found out that foreign trade was as good a method for getting it as colonial conquest. They coveted the commerce in luxury goods from the New World, partly because they did not want to pay tribute to their enemies, Spain and Portugal, and partly because they wanted the carrying trade to strengthen their national navies. The commerce they aspired to was a closed commerce and the trade they practised was first cousin, if not brother, to war. They tried to establish monopolies. The present-day national and international monopolies are not the children of capitalist commercialism, but the great-grandchildren—a throw-back

[1] "El pacto del Asiento de Negros" had been given to the French Guinea Company in 1701. It had been unable to furnish more than one thousand negroes a year.—A. Rein, op. cit., p. 263.

—of that quasi-militarist mercantilism which, following Portuguese examples, built trading stations in East and West. These trading stations had to be protected from native attacks and were made strong enough to hold off European rivals. Ambitions did not go beyond this. "Missionary zeal was quite alien to Directors and shareholders of the East India Company. They took Asia as she was, merely looking out for business advantages."[1]

The conception of wealth underlying early European Imperialism had been "territorial": public and private wealth grew by the conquest of foreign countries, the annexation of their lands and the enslaving of their inhabitants.[2]

The countries which, at that time, did not control colonies formulated a new doctrine. "The ordinary means therefore to increase our wealth and treasure is by Forraign Trade."[3] The fate of Spanish commercial Imperialism had taught them the futility of closed empires, for the Spaniards

[1] A. Rein, op. cit., p. 194.

[2] The feudal conception of wealth revived in the days of the Physiocrats. They objected to the commercial theory of wealth of the Mercantilists on theoretical grounds, for wealth to them was objective, identical with the material, physical product it represented, whilst the Mercantilist theory of trade contained the germs of a subjective non-physical theory of value. But their best arguments were derived from France's political experience, which had shown them that trade, and the desire for trade, had been one of the main causes of costly wars. These strictures on eighteenth-century politics were quite correct as far as they went; the trade wars of the Mercantilist period are an outstanding fact of history, but they were not so much due to an inextricable connection between trade and war, as to the survival amongst early merchant adventurers and absolutist statesmen of the militarist notions of feudal conquerors and pirates, which had infused certain militarist and feudal elements into their philosophy of trade. This combination survived until Adam Smith destroyed the theory underlying it; its practice continued until the advent of the Manchester School. It revived again in the second half of the nineteenth century, when the iron and steel industries had become the basis of modern warfare and contributed a militarist, non-capitalist note to business life.

[3] Thomas Mun, *England's Treasure by Forraign Trade*. Reprint, 1895, p. 7.

had to utilize their silver surplus in exchange for other countries' goods. They merely impoverished themselves by restricting its free outflow. But their rivals enlarged their production, increased their exports and secured their share of the wealth of the new Spanish world; they bought its treasures with goods, at much smaller expense than the Spaniards, who had to shoulder the heavy military burdens caused by the conquest and the defence of empire. In this new non-territorial conception of wealth trade was no longer a camouflaged form of piracy, by which one either deprived a rich rival of his accumulated treasures or cheated him by fraudulent exchange. Wealth could be drawn from the exchange of goods and services. A nation need no longer filch land from another people and either exploit them through colonists or enslave its native inhabitants in order to get rich.

This mercantile concept of wealth originally assumed a natural division of labour and a particular specialization of production ordained by Providence for various countries. Its objects could be attained either by the commercial intercourse of various independent states with one another or by a union of dependent states within an empire. Since inter-imperial trade evidently had not achieved this purpose, international trade might do so. The foundations of a kind of "trade empire" were laid, the boundaries of which were invisible on political maps.

III

The enemies of Spain were by no means willing to resign themselves permanently to the position of colonial Havenots. While trying to crash the gates of an empire closed against free trade, they endeavoured, at the same time, to raise privileged empires of their own, which were to be quite as much closed to others as those of Spain and Portugal. Though trade did create wealth, it did not do so

automatically. Its direction and its volume had to be controlled. Its very existence depended on sea-power. Without
sufficient sea-power, the Dutch could not enforce the freedom of the seas against the Spaniards. When they possessed
it, the means for establishing an oversea empire of their
own were available. And if England could maintain the
doctrine of the open sea (*mare liberum*) against the Spaniards,
she might be strong enough to close the sea surrounding
her shores (*mare clausum*) and bar it to all outsiders.[1]

The great trading companies valued territorial possessions
as bases for exclusive trade monopolies. Could they have
relied on the native princes to keep away all foreign rivals,
they might have preferred exclusive trading rights, guaranteed by treaties and subsidies, to territorial control, which
had to be exercised by costly military and administrative
establishments. They closed their empires quite as rigidly
as the Spaniards, and as their economic structure was
far more elastic and their trade methods less cumbersome,
they might have continued to do so for a long time, but
for their struggles with one another.

England emerged from them as the owner of a colonial
empire, which possessed a dual nature; in the West it was
a "plantation empire," in the East, a mere commercial
venture. The oversea plantations were but the continuation
of a similar development in Europe, which had resulted in
the plantations of Munster and Ulster, and finally in the
ruthless Cromwellian settlement of Ireland. These plantation-
settlements provided an opportunity for organized production
in place of a mere exchange of existing stocks and stores.

The British Empire was not only a closed empire—the
Navigation Act saw to it that foreign shipping was excluded
from British, continental, and colonial trade—it was to be
a self-sufficient empire. The plantations enjoyed a great
deal of political self-government. But their commercial
intercourse with one another, with the metropolis and with

[1] Grotius, *Mare liberum*, 1609. Selden, *Mare clausum*, 1636.

foreign countries was regulated, and a statutory division of labour was imposed upon them, each section being restricted to some specialized product of which it enjoyed a monopoly. The empire was a seaboard empire. Transportation between the coasts and the islands composing it was easy. The seas which united these possessions were looked upon as a kind of closed area, which the mercantile marine monopolized, and which the navy had to defend against foreign interlopers. Similar conceptions of a self-sufficient empire prevailed in France. The so-called "pacte colonial" gave substance to the doctrine of imperial self-sufficiency, which saw in each colony an economic province, the *raison d'être* of which was the satisfaction of the metropolis' wants and the exportation of metropolitan products. Shipping, being the backbone of sea-power, was, of course, reserved to the mother country, which transported the colonial surplus she could not consume, to outside markets and, provided she saw fit to do so, brought to the colonies such foreign goods as she could not furnish herself.

But even under these circumstances, inter-imperial autarchy could not be accomplished. The surplus product of the colonies had to go to other markets than those of the metropolis. The metropolis, moreover, never meant to adjust her output to the limited demands of the colonies; she was unable to consume all their wares either qualitatively or quantitatively, nor was she prepared to pay as much as the foreigners. Sea-power had opened the Spanish possessions to foreign trade; it could prevent the crashing of the gates of an insular empire, but it did not stop smuggling on a colossal scale. Insistence on trade control by the metropolis contributed to the feeling of dissatisfaction from which the American Revolution drew its strength.

IV

The master minds of the eighteenth century had foreseen the doom of closed colonial empires. They advocated a system of "free trade" which was not dependent on domination but on exchange. "The consequence" (of the American Revolution), Turgot had noted as early as April 6, 1776, "will be the complete revolution in the political and commercial relations between Europe and America, and I am thoroughly convinced that every empire will be forced to relinquish its political domination over its colonies and let them have complete freedom of commerce with all nations; it must be content to share this freedom with others and to maintain with its colonies ties of friendship and brotherhood." Empires attempting to oppose this development "will see their colonies slip away from them anyhow and become their enemies instead of their allies." As one cannot control the colonies by force of arms, "one must look upon them, not as subject provinces, but as friendly states, protected perhaps, but foreign and separate."

The statesmen followed slowly. The trading monopoly of the East India Company in India was withdrawn 1813, and in China, 1833. But as late as 1837 the British government asserted that "with respect to trade it has always been admitted that an imperial legislature has the right to compel a colony to receive the produce of the mother-country and a right to restrict that colony in its commerce with other nations."[1]

Since the Industrial Revolution, foreign trade was no longer, as the Physiocrats had phrased it, *un pis aller*, a way of living by which incomplete splinter states had to eke out a precarious existence, but which a complete nation used only as a spillway for the disposal of superabundant crops. The importance of concrete natural features in the producing areas, on which the God-ordained division

[1] Lord John Russell's speech on Canada, January 16, 1837.

of labour depended, diminished; their place was taken by the abstract, artificial item of costs. Goods flowed from countries which could produce them cheaply—whether low costs were due to land, labour, or capital was immaterial—to countries which had higher costs. They were exchanged at their relative cost values. Mechanized production had raised output far beyond the purchasing power of purely national markets. Foreign trade was no longer a secondary function of the economic system; it determined its structure; it no longer disposed of a fortuitous surplus of output, it decided the scale of production. Political frontiers reduced the fluidity of labour and capital considerably and fixed them to the soil; within these limits the division of labour the entire world over was determined by costs. The same country might import foreign coal in some of its ports and export coal from others. The relative price of coal, not only its quality, was the decisive factor.

The spread of manufactures to many countries greatly enhanced the importance of this "artificial element" in economics. The production of many goods ceased to be regional and tended to become universal. Nature's niggardliness could be overcome by the application of science to industry. The control and exploitation of natural monopolies and of exclusive sources of supply became less attractive and less profitable. The main economic object in the early age of expansion had been the control of sources of supply; now the opening of markets was becoming much more important. Scarcity had brought power and riches; now cheapness was to bring wealth and peace.

Commercial policy henceforth looked to the widening of markets. It sometimes used military force in order to break down unreasonable obstacles, as in China or in Japan. It preferred profitable exports to costly domination. The British Empire became "an open Empire." Its statesmen endeavoured honestly to widen the area of this trade empire, by making other independent nations follow their example and by maintaining the integrity of "independent" states like Turkey or China, and bound them by international agreements to keep their markets open.

The republics which had separated from the old empires, chief amongst them the United States, had turned toward protection, but they accepted free immigration and the import of capital on a colossal scale; their purchasing power for goods and men soon exceeded many times that of the old closed colonial empires. The trade to these countries was far more important than commerce with the newly founded colonial possessions.

The "trade empire" was intersected by customs barriers. But these barriers did not prohibit the flow of goods; they merely deflected it. Changes in tariffs, in export bounties, premiums, subsidies, and subventions stimulated the production of certain national commodities and greatly disturbed prices and the output of particular goods; they forced producers and consumers to shift their ground over and over again. Trade itself, apart from a few cases of genuine prohibition, was never suppressed; it was merely driven from one channel into another. A system of commercial treaties kept tariffs stable for a number of years and made frequent arbitrary changes difficult. They normally contained the most-favoured-nation clause, which blocked the way to policies of international and interimperial discrimination. A fair amount of international "equality" and a good deal of stability existed. The world was held together by a huge network of trade relations; its meshes were continually being tightened or loosened at some particular point.

V

Territories remained "national," but commodities were being "internationalized." Types or qualities were becoming universal; national goods competed with one another on the markets of the world, irrespective of their origin. The standardization of manufactured goods which the machine age had brought about had spread to agricultural commodities; they were dealt with in graded types. Wants were satisfied not according to national desires, but according to typified standards.

The economic activities of the entire world were in process of being reduced to a common denominator. Most important commodities had a world price; the margins between the various national markets were just sufficient to cover freight. The adoption of stable currencies, especially of the gold standard, on an almost universal scale, connected the price-levels of the various countries. They differed from one another considerably, but the fluctuations which occurred in one country were quickly imparted to other countries by the almost automatic working of gold movements, which were controlled by various central banks. They observed fairly identical rules. Since fluctuations of the exchanges were strictly limited by the gold points, a sure method for restoring the equilibrium between the price-levels of the member countries was available, whenever it had been disturbed by national changes in costs, by overtrading, or by credit operations. Discrepancies could not go very far before they were corrected either by the outflow of gold and credit contraction, or by discount policy which attracted foreign money. National prices did not suffer as great a depression as they otherwise might have done; thanks to timely intervention, some reduction and some contraction did take place, but violent disturbances of the internal and the external price-level could be avoided. If the afflicted country had lowered its own price-level severely, lessened its purchasing power for foreign goods and increased its own supply of cheapened goods to foreign markets, other countries would have been compelled to follow suit and to depress their own price-levels correspondingly. A kind of violent international competitive price reduction (which has been such a familiar feature under the régime of manipulated currencies) would have set in. The gold standard, properly managed, tempered some of these consequences. It greatly facilitated easy short-term lending operations, which normally restored equilibrium between different international price-levels in a short time. The local fall of prices was lessened by being spread over many countries. Serious regional disturbances occurred occasionally, when a country had gone off the gold standard, or when it was on the point of doing so. They were easily localized when they affected minor economic Powers; in the case of major Powers, they were mainly due to a political catastrophe, such as war or revolution which had upset their budgets. A return to peace and order was quickly followed by a return to monetary stability.

The gold standard united the countries which had adopted it, in a sort of open-trade area. They formed a kind of Economic World Federation. No universal price-level existed; tariffs and other trade obstacles prevented the formation of an even international price surface: but a system of connected national price-levels, which automatically adjusted themselves to one another, functioned fairly well.

The currency of one country had a stable price in other countries. Purchases of goods either in national or in foreign currencies represented a definite obligation; they were not subject to violent appreciation or depreciation. This stability facilitated international trade and international lending. It did not matter very much in which currency loans were contracted—whether creditors or debtors had to shoulder the risk of currency fluctuations. As long as they were limited by gold points, risks were reasonably low, even for the more backward countries, whose currencies were not yet stable, but who aspired to stability through the help of foreign loans. As their national currency was bound to rise, the weight of foreign obligations was sure to decline.

Domination and federation bound many states and sub-states to one another. Beyond these national empires an international trade empire had arisen, of which they were important members. It was held together by economic ties: by the exchange of goods, of men, of services, and of loans.

PART II

DISINTEGRATION

A DOUBLE set of circumstances, the one mainly factual, the other spiritual, as well as factual, is determining the present-day world situation. On the one hand, *primary colonization*, the acquisition of external lands or the subjugation of alien, more backward populations, resulting in the formation of a new, or the transformation of an existing, society, has come to a standstill; no new colonial areas are anywhere available.

Even before the war, every inch of African soil had its master—with the exceptions of Abyssinia and the Republic of Liberia. The passing of the former from the ranks of independent countries has removed from the map the last object for colonization.

There is ample room for *secondary colonization* within the limits of existing colonies, or former colonies, who have reached independence or Dominion status. No new colonial societies can be formed. Colonies cannot be won any longer by comparatively cheap raids against weak native states; they must be taken from other possessory powers on European battlefields or at European council tables.

On the other hand, a decolonization movement is sweeping over the continents. An age of empire-breaking is following an age of empire-making.

CHAPTER I

DEMOCRACY, NATIONALISM, LIBERALISM

I

THE Declaration of Independence informed the world that the American colonies held it as self-evident that "men are created equal" and had the right, when they so desired, to "assume amongst the powers of the earth the separate and equal station to which the Laws of Nature and Nature's God entitle them." The modern counter-colonization movement had begun. It was the outcome of a new political philosophy, not a more or less spontaneous outbreak against repression, such as had frequently taken place when subject nations had risen against foreign oppressors who had burdened them with tributes, taken their lands, or interfered with their accustomed ways. It resulted from the actions of a self-conscious democracy, which deliberately applied the fundamental principles of Anglo-Saxon self-government to inter-imperial relations. The American colonies, who objected to the Stamp Act, took their stand on the old English principle: "No taxation without representation," which, in their opinion, should govern the relations between a dependency and a mother-country. "They are not represented in the House of Commons," the resolutions on the Stamp Act explained, "but only in their own assemblies, which therefore have the sole right to tax them."[1]

This modern movement, which broke up the colonial empires at the turn of the nineteenth century, took its stand on the right to self-determination to which every nation

[1] The Stamp Act itself was a well-constructed measure and eminently fair as an act of taxation; the sole objection to it was the way in which it was passed. It offended a generation steeped in Locke's theories of the original Government contract. Channing, *History of the United States*, vol. iii, pp. 50 and 57.

and every homogeneous group was entitled. It spread in
many directions. The English garrison in Ireland, ruling
over the natives, adopted the arguments of the Declaration
of Independence and revolted against imperial domination.
As it depended on British backing in case of native risings,
it accepted a kind of partnership in the form of a union,
the link of which was the king, whilst American democracy
drifted into separation.

Neither the French nor the Spanish colonies had enjoyed
local self-government; they were both ruled by alien bureaucrats. The American Revolution stirred them deeply. The
French settlers in the West Indies demanded complete
self-government, though they were but a small white
minority, like the settlers of Kenya to-day, but under slightly
different circumstances. They clamoured for the "rights of
man" to be given to the Planter Aristocracy, but not to
coloured people and slaves. They might have held out
successfully against the latter—at least for a time—could
they have secured the help of the coloured people and the
support of the motherland. The egalitarian French Republic,
however, was not willing to grant what is now called "Home
Rule" to a small feudal class who construed "Liberté,
Égalité, Fraternité" in a racially exclusive sense. It favoured
the emancipation of the entire subject race and broke the
planters' resistance. But it could not control its newly-made
citizens, who expelled the planters and founded the independent negro republic of Haiti. The former slaves on this
island were the pioneers of the "Agrarian Revolt," which
was to become a conspicuous feature of many decolonization
movements later on.

The disintegration of the Spanish Empire was heralded
by an agitation for independence amongst the educated
Spaniards born in the colonies. It came to a head
during the Napoleonic rule in Spain, when the imposition of an alien king had severed the ties of allegiance
between the Crown and the colonists. A medley of diverse,

sometimes antagonistic, forces was working for the same end. Traditionalism, which later on inspired the European Restoration, combined with revolutionary French Rationalism. The hatred against the foreign rulers of Spain fused with the colonial-born Spaniards' (Criollos') loathing of the Spanish-born bureaucracy (Peninsulares) and its control of trade in the interest of the Spanish merchants. Liberals who hated the prerogatives of the Church joined hands with colonial Catholics who disliked the favours shown to Spanish-born prelates, who enjoyed its great endowments. A few Indian risings, especially in Mexico, had taken place, but the strength of the movement lay with colonial-born Spaniards and half-breeds.

The return of the Bourbon Dynasty after the fall of Napoleon made the rupture permanent. It endeavoured to enforce the restoration of the old order against a generation which had learnt by heart the Declaration of Independence. And when Spain, supported by France, was preparing to reconquer the colonies, the United States launched their great manifesto of counter-colonization—the Monroe Doctrine.

By proclaiming "that the American continents, by the free and independent condition which they have assumed and maintain, are henceforth not to be considered as subjects for future colonization by any European Powers," they put the American continent outside the sphere of colonization. They did not dispute the rights to existing colonies. For the original Monroe Doctrine was not a platform for aggression, but a manifesto of fear. It was conceived for the defence of the American democratic system against attacks from the despotic European Powers.[1] And it was

[1] Later on the Monroe Doctrine became aggressive. "I should myself like to shape our foreign policy with a purpose ultimately of driving off this continent every European power. I would begin with Spain, and in the end would take all other European nations, including England."— Theodore Roosevelt to F. C. Moore, February 9, 1898. J. B. Bishop, *Theodore Roosevelt and his Time*, vol. i, p. 79.

no more successful in putting a stop to colonization on the American continent, than the Declaration of Independence had been. It merely made colonization in the Americas the monopoly of the American Powers. The Louisiana purchase, and the purchase of Alaska, decolonized the American continent from French and Russian influences. It opened the way to American colonization on an imperial scale. Its final triumph was assured by the Mexican war, which tore large remnants of the Spanish Empire from its Mexican heirs and substituted American for Spanish colonization. When Cuba rebelled against Spanish maladministration, the United States interfered repeatedly; they wanted to break another link in the chain which bound American dependencies to European masters, but powerful groups desired the annexation of the island.

II

The people of the thirteen colonies who had rebelled against the mother country were overseas Britons, from whom the traditional rights of British citizenship had been withheld—at this time over 80 per cent of the population were of British or Irish extraction; they did not become a separate American nation because they were an alien race oppressed by a foreign government.

The advent of nationalism added a new passionate note to the problem of self-determination. There have always been nationalities, i.e. groups "of persons who speak a common language, who cherish common historical traditions, and who constitute, or think they constitute, a distinct cultural society, in which, among other factors, religion and politics may have played important, though not necessarily continuous rôles."[1]

Nationalism is born when such nationalities become conscious of their distinctiveness from one another. The

[1] Hayes, *Essays on Nationalism*, p. 21.

D*

members of each national group pretend to be like-minded, if not like-featured; they sense a subtle distinctiveness in the make-up of their members, which those belonging to other groups do not seem to possess, at least not in the same degree. They attribute to them values which lift their possessors high above others and, in doing so, they convert external objective marks of classification into internal subjective attitudes, which become highly charged motive-forces in political life. These distinctive qualities may be transferred by inheritance; but there is a possibility, too, of acquiring them from surroundings, by living with others, by the voluntary acceptance of their habits, and by a voluntary surrender of one's own ways. Nationalism rests on a double basis; it herein resembles the concept of "blood brotherhood" which dominates the life of primitive tribes, and in which adoption, accompanied by the proper rites, is equivalent to blood-relationship through inheritance. In modern society the place of such adoption is taken by assimilation or nationalization, both depending on the working of external influences. Nationalism is not separateness or distinctiveness as such; its essence is the awareness of such distinctions and the importance given to them. In this respect Chinese nationalism, which is based on the conception of a common cultural inheritance, in which the barbarians invading the Empire on land or the "foreign devils" attacking it from the sea have naturally no part, does not differ much from Judaism, which is founded on the inheritance of blood and faith.

III

The modern states, whose founders were aware of their distinctiveness and were bent on developing ideas and institutions of their own within the territories they ruled, had destroyed the unity of the medieval world and the universalism of its outlook—though they did not differ very much from one another. The transformation of these absolute States into democratic nations released new power-ful forces. And the clash of modern democracies with the forces of absolutism and feudal traditionalism gave a fresh turn to nationalism. It bifurcated it, so to speak. Egalitarian democracy, on the one hand, flatly denied all distinctiveness; it truculently demanded, on the other hand, the rights of minorities to a separate existence. The fundamental equality of all men, regardless of frontiers, origin, colour, creed, race, and station in life, implied a "sameness" of the many peoples inhabiting the world. It made them self-governing national bodies, whose absolute *volonté générale* must control their ad-ministration. This being the case, all nations were entitled to democratic institutions. Nationalism was "institutional"; but it was spiritual and emotional too. Revolutionary France was successfully defending her newly-won egalitarian in-stitutions against foreign invaders. When she had driven the adherents of a stratified social system back across their frontiers, she felt called upon to embark on a spiritual crusade, in which her armies were to carry the gospel of democracy into the lands of heathen rulers, who withheld its blessings from their subjects. It was the sacred duty of the French Republic not only to defend these principles at home against foreign invasion, but also to help their neigh-bours and brothers who desired to adopt them.[1]

This egalitarian institutional Nationalism, which, in

[1] An almost mystical fervour rings through the various declarations of America's world mission: "God . . . has made us the master organizers of the world, to establish system where chaos reigns," said Senator Beveridge in the debate on the Philippines on January 9, 1900. "God has marked us as His chosen people to lead in the regeneration of the world. . . . He has made us adepts in government that we may adminis-ter government among savages and servile peoples." And a month before the outbreak of the war, Woodrow Wilson declared: "I do not know that there will ever be a declaration of independence and of grievances for mankind, but I believe that if any such document is ever drawn, it will be drawn in the spirit of the American Declaration of Independence, and that America has lifted high the light which will shine unto all generations and guide the feet of mankind to the goal of justice and liberty and peace."

many ways, was but the legitimate successor of the absolutist régime, had established egalitarian standards at home by imposing the national language on the provinces, with the help of a system of nation-wide elementary education, administration, and military service. The Industrial Revolution, which, in point of time, almost coincided with it, provided the technical moulds from which all men and their ways of living could be turned out in serial types.

A new wave of universalism swept over mankind. French ideas, French ways, French institutions were eagerly greeted as the proper equipment for all nations in an age of Reason. In some countries (Alsace-Lorraine and Savoy) the social changes which the Republic brought along with it led to voluntary association and assimilation; in others (Poland and Illyria) the Napoleonic creation of "national states" enlisted the sentiments of the subject-races on the side of France. But her offensive universalist nationalism aroused a defensive separatist nationalism amongst those nations who had to suffer from the plunder of liberating armies, the exploitations of republican commissioners, and later on from Napoleonic conquests and contributions.[1]

IV

The Spanish outbreak, a spontaneous reaction of outraged national instincts, was emotional and very little influenced by philosophical notions. The German movement, on the other hand, was strongly tinged with theoretical concepts of the rights of distinct national individualities and the superior values of particular national, social, and cultural systems. It rationalized the cultural, spiritual, and emotional anti-French nationalism, which had been growing up in the literary field, and transformed it into an anti-revolutionary institutional system.

The revolt against institutional conformity was due partly

[1] J. Holland Rose, *Nationality in Modern History*, passim.

to a hatred of tryanny and coercion and partly to antagonism to any sort of universalism. It objected to the identification of French notions, absolutist as well as democratic, with world-wide classical tradition. It assumed the existence of distinct individual national personalities, which, having been created separate by Providence, must be kept separate. "Where Nature has separated nationalities by language, customs, and character, one must not attempt to change them into one unity by artefacta and chemical operations."[1] It disapproved quite as strongly of voluntary assimilation, which infectious cultures are apt to bring about, as of coercive adaptation.

National individuality was determined by language. "Has a people anything dearer than the speech of its fathers? In its speech resides its whole thought-domain, its traditional history, religion, and basis of life, all its heart and soul."[2]

Nationalism had been *linguistic*—almost in a philological sense of the word—and vaguely cultural even before it had become, institutional.

The Slavonic nations, under the rule of the German-speaking Austrian bureaucracy, had raised claims to literary independence as early as the eighteenth century. The Romantic school of literature had turned away in disgust from the artificial, sophisticated monotony of imitative classicism to the natural, naïve, particular folk-lore and had paved the way for many a linguistic revival. It not only objected to the deadening levelling tendencies of assimilation, which deprived individual nations of their spiritual birthright; it attributed particular spiritual values to spontaneous national creation. In many parts of the world subject nations had been quite willing to acknowledge the superiority of their masters' culture. They were eager to adopt it of their own free will, whenever they were not ill-treated politically or

---

[1] Herder, *Briefe zur Beförderung der Humanität*. Sämmtliche Werke, ed. Suphan, vol. xviii, p. 206.   [2] Ibid., vol. xvii, p. 58.

exploited financially. The natives' desire for assimilation had accounted for the great success of the Hellenization which the ancient world had voluntarily undergone, and, though perhaps less voluntarily, for its later Romanization. It explains, too, the absence of national opposition to policy which forced English standards of culture on Indian education and on ambitious young India. Even the leaders of the Young Ireland movement of the eighteen-forties, though deeply conscious of Ireland's separate nationality, did not attempt to make her an Irish-speaking nation, but were content with rousing an "Irish spirit" magnificently garbed in the borrowed garments of the English language. "Dark Rosaleen" passionately yearned for freedom, but not yet for freedom from the tyranny of the English tongue.

The centralizing bureaucracy of absolutist governments had insisted on an assimilation of languages mainly for practical reasons: it would greatly facilitate their work. The preservation of language, on the other hand, meant everything to creative minds, who drew their inspiration from the myths and the folk-songs of their nation's glorious past. When they looked back on these grandiose achievements, somewhat dimmed perhaps by the lapse of time, they could forget an often rather humiliating present and were filled with hopes for a splendid future. Poets and philologists were reviving the soul of many a nation, which seemed buried for ever, deep under the rubble of a deadening alien civilization. There was something to be said for the universal use of Latin; it had survived in Hungary as official language until 1839–40. But since its supremacy had been destroyed by the growth of vernacular idioms, and since the universality of understanding was broken anyhow, there was no reason why any one of the upstart languages which had taken its place should have a better right than any other.

And there was a practical side to this demand for the revival of a dying language. If business in schools, law courts, and administrative offices had to be done in the language of the ruling race, its members would enjoy a great advantage when competing for appointments; if the vernacular language were the medium of such transactions, the native had a better chance than the foreigner. Since the great bureaucratic countries of Central and Eastern Europe were offering a multiplicity of small posts—and their numbers increased with the extension of State activities in the Post Office and the railway services—the demand for the equality, or even for the exclusive use, of the native language appealed very strongly to an army of small place-hunters, whom the literary claims of the national language might have left quite unmoved. The intellectuals, the poets, the writers, and the philologists had recognized the opportunities which the use of their own idiom would offer them. From mere translators, they would, so to speak, advance to the rank of creative writers. So they advocated, purified, and developed the native language; they unearthed its forgotten literary treasures, and whilst proclaiming its archaic beauties, tried hard to adapt it to the needs of modern life. Some of them were even quite willing to reconstruct a new literary language from a few philological morsels and the remnants of a popular patois which had gone out of use long ago.

Language expressed institutions as well as aspirations. The German Romanticists substituted a hierarchal "State," formed on the pattern of an idealized Middle Ages, for the egalitarian commonwealth which had arisen in France. They preferred the time-made society of the past to the man-made "artefacta" of the present and the schemes for the future.[1] They outlined an ideal of a nationalist, socialist, autarchic State, bound by no economic ties to the outer world. Whilst the classical writers of political economy had applied the spirit of reason to the construction of a world-wide system of international economic relations, based on

---

[1] The modern Corporative State is a kind of man-made medieval State.

a universal monetary system, they outlined a closed economic State, which had no international intercourse and manipulated a national currency of its own. This territorial nationalism was destined to attract men's minds in the days after the Great War.

V

The growth of natural science, and especially the application of Darwinism to social questions, shifted the problems of nationalism to quite a new ground.

The concept of nationalism, so far, had been spiritual. It looked to language, habits, institutions, creeds, and ideas as tests of that "separateness" which distinguished one nationality from another. A nation had been a group held together by ways of living. The Romantic school had turned it into a group speaking the same language. It now became the equivalent of an ethnical group, a race. None of the cultural and linguistic features which constitute a nationality were constant, none of them were indissolubly connected with physical features, and certainly none of them were mere mechanical functions of a definite physical structure.

After a short prelude, in which the phrenologists located the various functions of the mind in corresponding bumps of the skull, the cheap materialism which found expression in the works of Moleschott, Büchner, Karl Vogt, and, later on, Ernst Haeckel, emerged as a kind of popular philosophy. "Force" (living force) was a mere function of "matter"; concepts, ideas, sentiments, were mere secretions of glands —as the liver secretes bile, so the brain secreted ideas. Body and soul were one. The age-long conflict between them was bridged by a new Monist creed which made spiritual functions dependent on physical factors.

The ruling nations, the "top dogs," as well as the ruled nations, the "bottom dogs," could derive much comfort from these new theories. If the struggle for life and natural selection was accepted as the basis of social as well as physical existence, certain groups of people, and even entire nations, could lay claim to particular fitness by pointing to the position they actually held. Their survival at the top was a sure proof of their superior value. National or social groups, which were in control over other national or social groups, need no longer ascribe their success to accidental external causes; they owed it to the natural laws of selection, by which they had been singled out to fill the places which really mattered, on account of their inherent superior qualities. An aristocracy of vested interests could base their claim for the preservation of their privileged position on the recognition of these newly discovered laws of evolution; its members had got to the top because they had been fit, being the bearers of superior hereditary values; they need no longer justify themselves by showing their usefulness to the commonwealth. The mere fact of their being at the top was sufficient proof of their fitness, and as long as they did not throw it away by debasing their stock through interbreeding with inferior strains, their position was safe.

But as the process of selection was going on without interruption, bringing out strains and qualities which so far had been hidden, the patient striving masses might hope for an early reversal and their ultimate arrival at the top in course of time. They saw in their personal yearnings evidence of such selective qualities; they strongly felt that they were in no way inferior to those who had got there ahead of them. They had not yet reached the same stage of development. To use the technical terms of modern eugenics, the "genes" embedded in the chromosomes of proletarian individuals did contain those very qualities which make the leaders of a new age. They were merely younger, more vigorous, and (implicitly) morally superior to those who had preceded them, and who soon must show signs of decrepitude. Such conceptions brought wonderful consolation to the struggling masses which were surging upwards in many a country, but which had found the road barred by earlier arrivals. And they acted like a powerful stimulant, as well as a compensation, to those nations who were conscious of their own vigour and valour, but who had not yet succeeded in finding a place in the sun equal to their aspirations and ambitions. All through the nineteenth century, the Germans, being late-comers among the great nations of the world, felt thwarted; their urge for expansion pressed against immovable obstacles; they consoled themselves by prophesying the impending doom of the French and the English, who, they thought, were blocking their road upwards.

Early nationalist physiology had been rather romantic, even when it was based on more or less accurate observation of physical facts. Blue eyes and golden hair constituted the Nordic race, which was supposed to be pure. As long as the individuals possessing such external marks of divine grace, which had been extended to a particular nation, kept their blood undiluted—or rather that of their progeny—their biological properties could be handed on intact and constant to posterity. And as these biological properties closely corresponded to spiritual and intellectual qualities, a great race could be preserved. Ideas and institutions were mere functions. They depended on those permanent physical features which resulted from "genes" and had to be transmitted through inheritance; otherwise they could be acquired and transferred to anybody. Language could be taught (voluntarily or compulsorily) to other nations; it was a mere external accomplishment without inner significance. A Hottentot did not become a Dutchman by talking Taal. An Irish Celt or a Hindu was not turned into an Englishman because he had taken up English political ideas and was clamouring for British institutions in a more or less alien tongue. Nationality might be camouflaged in various ways. Its essentials could neither be altered by force, nor even voluntarily surrendered. They consisted in certain physical properties due to various "genes," which must be preserved by inheritance, i.e. by physical transmission from individuals possessing those invaluable and imperishable qualities. It could be lost by interbreeding with peoples of other groups, who were devoid of these "genes." The doctrine of the Nordic race was originally not much more than an effort on the part of a romantically minded, embattled aristocracy to assert its privileges against a rampant, egalitarian democracy, by basing its claims on the immanent and immovable laws of nature which protect pure lineage. It has been converted into a doctrine of nationalism by an egalitarian democracy, opposed to other nationalities, to whom—as well as to itself—it wants to prove the divine foundations of its own aspirations. It explains the physical properties of the members of some externally more or less homogeneous political group by their common descent from common ancestors; they share the same blood and draw their strength from the same soil. The naïve tribalism of primitive races is placed on a territorial basis; it is supported by a would-be scientific structure.

Biological nationalism is self-sufficient and exclusive. As national qualities cannot in any way be transferred to alien groups or persons, a policy of assimilation is senseless. It can only lead to more or less superficial imitation, to a kind of mimicry, as it were. No subject nation can ever acquire the superior qualities which are functions, as well as attributes, of the ruling nation's peculiar composition. This composition cannot be altered by change of environment or by cultural loans from other nations; it can only be developed along its own immanent lines. But it can deteriorate by mixing with inferior races. Self-preservation compels a nation to fight against the deterioration which is bound to result from a mixture with foreign elements. It should renounce the right to rule other nations, to mix with them, and to inflict its own ways upon them, rather than undergo miscegenation. But it must grow in numbers, for it must maintain the valuable strain with which it is endowed, and multiply in the interest of mankind. Fertility, as such, is a sign of vigour and superiority. So it may have to invade the demesnes of other nations and either exterminate them or expel them.

VI

Since business methods had been applied to plantation work in the colonies, slavery had become more profitable and much more terrible; it could no longer be described as a happy patriarchal state of existence, which sheltered merry black folk from the vicissitudes of life. The quicker the turnover of the capital invested in a slave, the bigger was the profit. The great agitation of the "Amis des Noirs" and of the Anti-Slavery Society originated, partly at least, in that arrogant intellectualism of the "Age of Reason," which would not recognize any distinction between men, whatever their colour or kind; but it owed a great deal of its strength, too, to the deep humanitarian humility, which saw in the suffering lowly-born slaves, objects of pity and commiseration, which the Christian Church could no longer neglect.

Great Britain suppressed the slave trade almost simultaneously with the United States; she impressed upon the Powers the need for patrolling the seas. She freed the slaves in her colonies. The doctrine that one half of mankind was born to be the chattels of the other half lapsed. One of the main props of ascendancy was crumbling. The primitive Christian doctrine that force in itself was wicked revived, and, with it, the abhorrence of using it against weak races. The superiority of a race of conquering invaders was no longer extolled; the spiritual purity of the native races was becoming the object of perhaps equally unjustified dithyrambic incantations.

The evangelical party and its associates began to denounce

the colonists who coveted the land, as well as the services of gentle savages, whose subjugation a wicked government either condoned, or, worse, actively engineered. Empire building was becoming anathema. The good Christians whose conscience was burdened by such exploits and the taxpayers whose pockets were rifled by paying for them, combined in an anti-colonial movement, which later on turned against the killing of "noble Zulus" and demanded the restitution of freedom to "brave Boers."

Empires were certain to break up anyhow, and the more rapidly this happened, the better it was for everyone concerned, since it would open the way to Free Trade. The place of several more or less monopolistic national empires would then be taken by an undivided trade empire, the component parts of which were kept together not by political coercion and economic preference, but by the free flow of men, goods, money, and services from one part of the world to the other.

Peaceful disintegration would safeguard natural economic development. It would neither retard a colony's progress as the old colonial system had done, nor accelerate artificially by a protective tariff the growth of its manufactures. The colonies would grow fast, but not faster than the utilization of their natural resources would permit. As they were very much greater than those of the older European states, the absence of any artificial speeding up would check their tendency to outgrow the parent states before they were even properly matured. And the old countries would not be forced to expand their industries feverishly in order to fit the colonies with manufacturing plants ultimately destined to displace their own products.

Free Trade was to end predatory economics. For, if empires were not worth keeping, they were scarcely worth acquiring. It made for peace and security in so far as it would equalize the strength of the various states. If empires were dissolved into their component parts, they would no longer overshadow other states which had been unable to form empires of their own. A democracy of states with equal rights would be established. The master states, shorn of their colonial possessions, would no longer menace the smaller independent states, and the smaller states would no longer be driven to defensive alliances, or tempted into efforts of empire-building of their own. The former colonial dependencies would join the family of nations not as subservient members, but as complete equals. With the disappearance of trade restrictions the "impertinent badges of slavery imposed upon them, without any sufficient reason, by the groundless jealousy of the merchants and manufacturers of the mother country"[1] would disappear.

A system of free and equal states, neither fearing nor threatening one another, linked together by a policy of Free Trade, would offer greater stability, greater equality, and greater security than a series of rival national empires.

Free Trade was not a mere device for keeping down costs of production by lowering wages and expanding markets through cheaper competition, as has often been suggested by the opponents of Cobden and Bright. It was the first blow aimed at power-politics, taking the control of policy from the classes whose political domination was passing, but whose economic domination was prolonged by monopolies. It meant to break the land monopoly of an aggressive landlord class at home, and to stop the expansion and domination of this acquisitive aristocracy over foreign countries, whose population they had enslaved as monopolist landlords (Ireland) or as monopolist traders (India). The Free Traders objected to colonies because they were acquired by force and had to be defended by expensive armies against movements of counter-colonization. They advocated the freedom

[1] *Wealth of Nations*, Cannan's edition, bk. iv, chap. 7, part ii, p. 84.

of the seas, for the right to confiscate private property on the high seas seemed to them the worst remnant of those predatory economics they desired to destroy. They were pacifists and opposed armaments, because the New Society, which had risen in the Industrial Revolution, must be based on the peaceful exchange of goods.

CHAPTER II

ECONOMIC SEPARATISM

I

THE British Empire had become Janus-faced; its widest areas, the growing daughter states, were becoming partners; its densest populations were ruled by proconsuls. In this controlled half of the Empire, Free Trade was maintained until nationalism became all-powerful. In the free empire, colonial nationalism rose in revolt against the régime of Free Trade which the motherland had imposed upon it, on the lines on which Alexander Hamilton had advocated economic decolonization in the U.S.A. His main motive had been fear. A young independent country, without industries of its own, would be menaced by war, which would not only stop trade between belligerents but, under the rules of British naval warfare, with neutrals as well. The independence and security of a newly liberated country depended on the prosperity of manufactures. "Every nation with a view to those great objects, ought to endeavor to possess within itself all the essentials of national supply . . . The possession of these is necessary to the perfection of the body politic; to the safety as well as to the welfare of the society. The want of either is the want of an important organ of political life and motion; and in the various crises which await a state, it must severely feel the effects of any such deficiency."[1] The protection of infant industries was to accomplish the system of complete national independence, which political separation had inaugurated.

[1] Alexander Hamilton, *Report on Manufactures*, from *Papers on Public Credit, Commerce and Finance*, pp. 227–8. Columbia University Press Reprint.

The grant of colonial (afterwards dominion) self-government to the colony, which had arrested political revolt in Canada, and prevented separatist movements elsewhere, made economic separatism inevitable.

Tradition might justify the Imperial authorities when claiming control over the colonies' commercial policy in the interest of the motherland. But responsible government included fiscal autonomy and the right to raise revenue from import duties, fiscal or protectionist. To the Imperial remonstrances against its first protectionist measures (1859), the Canadian government replied: "Self-government would be utterly annihilated if the views of the Imperial Government were to be preferred to those of the people of Canada. It is, therefore, the duty of the present government distinctly to affirm the right of the Canadian legislature to adjust the taxation of the people in the way they deem best, even if it should unfortunately happen to meet the disapproval of the Imperial Ministry." A few years later colonial claims to a nationalist economic policy went much farther. "The welfare of Canada requires the adoption of a national policy, which, by a judicious readjustment of the tariff, will benefit and foster the agricultural, the mining, the manufacturing and other interests of the Dominion; that such a policy will retain in Canada thousands of our fellow-countrymen now obliged to expatriate themselves in search of employment denied to them at home." "Protection is a matter of necessity for a young nation in order that it may obtain the full development of its own resources."

This doctrine was ultimately accepted by all self-governing British colonies. They had given up separation by political revolution. They relentlessly pressed on with their economic revolt against the mother country. They adopted protective tariffs, not for military, but for economic reasons, in order to develop a colonial nationalism of their own on a thoroughly materialist basis. They did not want to remain economic provinces. They aspired to a "balanced economy," in which a manufacturing industry would take its place by the side of a prosperous agriculture. They yearned for equality: a nation which bought manufactured goods with its agricultural staple produce represented an inferior type of society. Industry stood for skill, progress, and a higher brand of civilization; its development would kill the germs of feudalism, which were present in those new countries where huge, early land grants had been given to comparatively few settlers, who ultimately might form a squatter aristocracy. As long as the new countries relied exclusively on agriculture, the growth of population would be rather slow. The rapid influx of men and capital had depended on the development of highly profitable extractive industries, such as gold mining. The rush following the gold discoveries in Australia had led to a rapid inflow of population, much of which became unemployed when the mines began to peter out. Infant industries protected by a tariff were to absorb these unemployed and to attract immigrants and foreign capital. In these new countries Free Trade was rural, frequently feudal, and aristocratic; protection was urban, democratic, and egalitarian.

II

Continental nationalism joined hands with colonial nationalism in revolting against the empire of Free Trade which England was trying to establish. The rise of an industrial society had led to Free Trade in England, where the beneficiaries of the feudal system continued to exploit a fully developed industrial order by taxes on foodstuffs and raw materials. In the United States, on the other hand, the Slave Power, representing a crude feudalism, stood for Free Trade. The victory of the North was a victory for protection as well as for democracy. And on the continent, the industrial classes clamoured for protection against British manufactures. Under the shelter of the Great Blockade, continental industries had developed in rather a modest way.[1] The downfall of Napoleon established England's economic supremacy. She was flooding the continent with cheap manufactured goods. The success of her industrial class thus threatened the rise, nay even the existence, of similar classes abroad. In France, they were strong enough to drive public opinion towards the traditional policy of protection. Rising manufacturers and recently liberated farmers demanded a continuation of the halcyon days of war scarcity. "Prohibition," said the Chamber of Commerce of Rouen in 1814, "is the outcome of political and social rights. From the manufacturer who has made use of all his financial resources in order to establish a factory, down to the workman who finds there the means of existence for himself and his family —all demand, with perfect reason, the right to be the sole source of supplies for home consumption."[2]

The Congress of Vienna had denied national unity and constitutional self-government to the German people. But its rulers were willing to offer the rising bourgeois class an economic solace for its political disappointments. The Zollverein (1834) swept away the customs barriers which had cut Germany into separate units—there were nearly thirty State tariffs in force in the country. To German nationalists the Zollverein was a means for uniting the German nation economically at a time when political union

[1] Friedrich List assumed that the wars of 1790–1815 gave England a monopoly of overseas trade and a plethora of capital from trade profits, war industries, and flight capital from other countries, which put her far ahead of her competitors (1845, Friedrich List's *Werke*, vol. vii, p. 477). In other writings, *Der internationale Handel, die Handelspolitik, und der Deutsche Zollverein*, 1844, he insists on the great advantage which Continental and especially German industries derived from the Continental blockade. Ibid., vol. vi, p. 131. J. L. and B. Hammond, *The Rise of Modern Industry*, pp. 43–9, suggest that some of them may have declined on account of the difficulty of getting raw materials from overseas.

[2] P. Ashley, *Modern Tariff History*, p. 274.

was beyond their reach.[1] It originally favoured in a moderate way, the interests of the more advanced manufacturing regions. It gave industry a chance of growth. It adopted a moderate protective tariff and aimed at rather modest practical ends, though its theorists meant to use it against England's commercial supremacy. To them England was the "predominant nation," whose political and economic development had enabled her "to get hold of the greatest part of the markets in less advanced and less rich countries, open to free competition."[2] "All nations have a common interest to safeguard themselves against the drawbacks and arbitrary dangers, which British supremacy could inflict upon their industries"[3]; as England was leaning towards Free Trade, her rivals must take to Protection. To a nation held back by unfavourable circumstances rather than by intellectual, moral, or cultural deficiencies, the Customs Union held out the hope of its becoming the equal of the other great nations of the world. In England the rise of the middle class, progress, and anti-feudalism had depended on Free Trade; in Germany and in many other countries, it was based on industrial protection. Free Trade enabled England, in their eyes, to transfer the badge of slavery from

[1] "Es war endlich das erwachte Bewusstsein der Nation und das dadurch gewonnene Selbstvertrauen, sich durch eigene Kraft auf die Höhe der reichsten und mächtigsten Nationen der Erde emporschwingen und ihre Existenz für alle Zeiten sicherstellen zu können, wenn sie nur ihre kommerzielle, industrielle, und maritime Zersplitterung aufgeben, ihre Separatzolllinien niederbrechen und zusammenhalten wollte, wie ein Mann—zu See und Land,—wenn sie endlich nur einmal dieselben einfachen Mittel gemeinschaftlich anwenden wollte, die anderen Nationen zu Grösse und Macht verholfen. . . . Das war's, was die Sehnsucht der Deutschen nach einer *handgreiflichen* Nationalität erzeugte, und das ist es auch, was ihre enthusiastischen Wünsche nach einem wahrhaften Schutzsystem, nach einer tüchtigen auswärtigen Handelspolitik und nach zweckmässigen Navigationsgesetzen erzeugt, was allgemeine Erbitterung gegen die trügerischen Grundsätze der Freihandelstheorie verursacht." (F. List, *Die politisch-ökonomische Nationaleinheit der Deutschen*, 1845, *Werke*, vol. vii, p. 450.)

[2] F. List, *Le Système National d'Économie Politique* (written in French, 1837), *Werke*, vol. iv, chap. vi, pp. 222–3.   [3] *Ibid.*, pp. 224–5.

the emancipated colonies to the other nations of the world, who had to bow to her industrial supremacy. She was trying to consolidate this supremacy by preaching the gospel of Free Trade all over the world. The industrially less advanced nations had to defend their independence by protecting their infant industries, in order to emancipate themselves from British economic ascendancy.

The raising of infant industries by a protective tariff in colonies and in continental countries was an economic revolt, directed mainly against Great Britain. It was quite as much an act of separatism and economic world disintegration as the American Revolution had been. Alexander Hamilton's spiritual heir, Friedrich List, not only fathered the German Customs Union, he also consolidated Hamilton's stray suggestions in his "System of National Economy."

Henceforth emotional nationalism and rational industrialism became close allies in many countries on the basis of a "scientific system." Industrialism stood for political liberalism of various shades in countries like Germany or, later on, Australia, where a well-organized labour movement forced protection on a trading community, which was supporting the landed interest. In politically dismembered nations Protection became the handmaid of economic unity. It gave a united economic life to territories cut up among separate governments; it provided a material body for their spiritual yearnings, which would, one day, enforce political unity. In new settlement countries, on the other hand, deliberate economic separation from the mother country led to a distinct colonial nationalism. In the one case it brought together in an economic federation the fragments of a nation split by political division; in the other case it disintegrated a politically united empire into separate nations.

III

The Napoleonic wars had impressed upon the continent the usefulness and, at the same time, the limitations of economic self-sufficiency. Some observers had ascribed these wars to the commercial and colonial rivalries of the great nations. In their view, a complete cessation of international trade was needed to eliminate these frictions and to prevent future wars. They advocated the establishment of closed commercial states by a combination of peaceful exchange of territory, scientific discoveries, which provided substitutes for imported goods, and centralized planned economics. Such a state, closed to foreign commerce, would no longer need gold; the aggressive commercial policy which had endeavoured to get gold by forcing exports would become superfluous. International trade had been the proper policy before the rise of modern states, when the Christian world had constituted a politically united society. Since it had broken up politically, it must be dissolved economically, too, by the complete cessation of foreign trade and all attempts at colonial expansion. Neither trade nor colonial exploitation could proceed without war. Once nations had withdrawn within their national demesnes, a properly balanced economic system could be established in every country; agriculture and industry would equilibrate one another. The citizens of each country would be bound to one another by a system of home exchanges, effectuated by a national currency. The national money was paper money, issued by the government in appropriate quantities. No gold was needed, and no policy of expansion required to obtain it. Genuine economic nationalism was politically peaceful and socially just. Goods and services would be exchanged only between nationals; they would be paid for with national money. This national money would be of no use and of no value abroad. All separate empires would be broken into independent nations, and the world empire of international trade would cease to exist. Each nation would form a separate economic unit, whose members were united by national money. They were thoroughly cut off from the members of other nations. Nationalism was complete. It implied a system of State Socialism, for the necessary rearrangements depended on the control of all economic activities by the Government. It conscripted the property, as well as the lives, of its subjects. Leviathan was arising, no longer a hazy philosophical outline, but a living social organism, whose structure and functions were carefully planned.[1]

[1] J. G. Fichte, *Der geschlossne Handelsstaat.* Tübingen, 1800.

CHAPTER III

IMPERIALIST NATIONALISM

I

THE nationalism of oppressed subject races supplied the strongest force in the breaking up of empires, while the nationalism of ambitious ruling races gave the most powerful impetus to the revival of Imperialism.

In the first half of the nineteenth century, nationalism concentrated almost exclusively on suppressed peoples; it was a creed of freedom held by all liberals. The Greeks' rising against the Turks was hailed by Europe as the resurrection of Hellenism and the return of its glories to the modern world. The Poles, who fought hopeless battles against Russian despotism, were the darlings of emotional Western democrats. The hearts of all men who strove for self-determination and yearned for national freedom went out to them. The Italian conspirators, who plotted against the same Austrian domination which had just swallowed the last morsel of Polish independence, hailed them as brothers and heroes. And so did the Germans. Their sympathies for the Poles were the reflex of their hatred of the despotism which ruled Prussia, Russia, and Austria. They rose against it in 1848, in company with the Hungarians, whose nationalism, even in those glorious days, was defensive when directed against Habsburg domination and oppressive when dealing with the Southern Slavs. Democracy and nationalism seemed identical.[1]

But nationalism was not a pacifist creed. Though loathing the oppression of racial minorities, it did not fight it by passive resistance; though allied to Liberalism, it was rarely liberal; it was frequently militant and finally militarist.

[1] V. Valentin, *Geschichte der Deutschen Revolution*, vol. i, pp. 329–32.

Bismarck's policy of "blood and iron" established German unity on the battlefields of Düppel, Königgrätz, and Sedan, which German democracy had failed to win, either on the barricades of Berlin and Vienna or in the endless debates in St. Paul's Church in the old imperial free city of Frankfort-on-Main. Italy's road lay through the defeats of Novara, Lissa, and Custozza to the triumphal entry into Rome; but it had been blasted by the victories of Louis Napoleon and Bismarck, her allies. Cavour and Victor Emmanuel, not Mazzini and Garibaldi, had won through with the help of Bismarck, who had prepared and organized wars and armies in the face of a Liberal opposition.

By accomplishing the unification of Germany, and indirectly of Italy, on the battlefield, Bismarck had, so to speak, made war respectable. It was no longer a weapon of conquest and spoliation, directed by lust of power, from which men were beginning to recoil in disgust; nor was it a dangerous plaything in the hands of tricky diplomats, who wanted to maintain a precarious balance of power. It was the supreme effort of a great people for welding into a mighty nation its hitherto powerless fragments. A few years earlier, war had preserved the unity of the United States and had cut out the canker of slavery, which philanthropic reformers had been unable to remove.

Henceforth the motto, "Peace, free trade and goodwill amongst nations" was somewhat discredited. "The days of Cobden and Henri Richard are gone," said Visconti Venosta. "Their ideas, which assumed peace-loving, reasonable human beings are exploded."[1]

II

The Industrial Revolution, perhaps even more than the French Revolution, had changed the nature of war. Science and industry had once served the peace-loving citizens in

[1] Benedetto Croce, *Geschichte Italiens*, p. 115.

E

their struggles against the despotic state; they were fast becoming the allies of warlike governments. They had not only provided them with arguments justifying the divine nature of power; they furnished them with mechanical means for imposing their will on their subjects and on their enemies to the farthest ends of the earth. Science no longer supported liberty, but power; born in peace, and meant for peace, it went over to war. It ultimately made a gigantic scientific enterprise of it, a huge machine for destruction on a titanic scale, the workings of which depended on technique and organization: Minerva had sold herself to Mars.

The American Civil War had shown the importance of engineering industries for military purposes. The war-trained, war-minded soldiers of the South had been beaten by the farmers, business men, and engineers of the North. Manufacturing skill, not mere military value, had decided the issue. The dramatic appearance in action of the iron-clad heralded the advent of a new age of destructive engineering. The United States were bent on economic expansion; they did not care much for military affairs. Adventure beckoned to their people from the vast Wild West; it attracted restless spirits much more strongly than a career in a small professional army, which led an isolated life in lonely army posts. When the armies were disbanded and peace restored, nobody thought any longer of organizing the country's economic forces for purposes of war. Nor was there any need for this, for nobody threatened the United States.

Germany, on the other hand, was surrounded by un-friendly nations, who grudged her arrival amongst the first-class Powers. She had risen by force and she could not hope to maintain her position if her armour weakened. The needle gun of the Prussian infantry and the Krupp steel breech-loading guns had played a decisive part in Bismarck's great military triumphs. Since war was no longer the pastime of landed gentlemen, but the work of organizers, scientists, and engineers, industries had to be fostered. And ironmasters were more useful than cotton-spinners. Whilst England's economic policy was dictated by the cotton industry which needed the world's market, the influence of the heavy industry prevailed over others in modern Germany. It ranked next to agriculture, which fed the nation and provided the best recruits. Its representatives established close relations, socially and professionally, with the military and civil authorities, on the one hand, and the agrarian squire-archy on the other, their allies under the new system of Protection. For the plight of both groups in the crisis of the late 'seventies had made Germany turn from a policy of Free Trade to one of Protection. And the heavy industries developed the type of authoritarian capitalism somewhat peculiar to Germany, with a natural bent towards monopoly at home and to power politics abroad; it fitted in very well with the German theory of the State and with the traditional ways of bureaucratic control.

A genuine national army had won German national unity. At Jena, the standing army, formed after the traditions of the Great Frederick by recalcitrant peasants and hired mercenary riff-raff, and commanded by an exclusive officer caste, had broken down ignominiously; Prussia was replacing it by the system of universal conscription, under which each citizen was a soldier and each soldier "must be a citizen," which had transformed the French Armies[1] and saved France in the struggle against the Powers of the old world. After the Napoleonic Wars German nationalists had hated Rome, despotism, and the hired standing army with equal fervour. But they were not pacifists; their ideal was an armed nation, which would unite the country and defeat the despots. The great Prussian army reformers, Scharnhorst and Gneisenau, deliberately organized the new forces as an army of free citizens, in which everyone had to

[1] Taine, *Le régime moderne*, vol. i, bk. iii, chap. ii, pp. 258–96.

serve, and which did not recognize the privileges of a feudal class. They objected to the brutal drill of the old system, by which the army had been trained, and through which it had lost the war: "No soldier has ever been whipped so miserably as the Prussian, and no army has achieved less," wrote Scharnhorst in 1806.[1] They wanted "to nationalize the armies and to militarize the nation."[2] The people in arms, not the professionals, had won the war of liberation. The territorials and the volunteers had beaten Napoleon's army at the Katzbach. National conscription of all men was Prussia's contribution to democracy; it preceded manhood suffrage by nearly three-quarters of a century. The reform put in the hands of the ruling *élite*, headed by the king, an army in which all classes were represented, and in which people attaining certain educational accomplishments (in a country where education was made compulsory) could automatically rise to officer rank. Appointments as "officer" of the reserves conciliated the sons of the bourgeoisie with the privileges of the feudal aristocracy and the preponderance of the military. Whilst German romantic metaphysicians saw in this perfect military organization a combination of the valour of Sparta with the learning of Athens, the reserve officers linked the rising middle class closely and intimately to the army. By joining it—even on sufferance—they adopted its outlook. Compulsory education and universal military service administered by a professional (upper) officer class, produced a drilled democracy in Germany, which believed in discipline and authority, and which differed from other societies, where military duties were but the complement of political rights.

[1] Max Lehmann, *Freiherr vom Stein*, vol. iii, pp. 234, 241; vol. ii, pp. 542–7.

[2] Rühle von Lilienstern, *Vom Kriege*, quoted in H. von Treitschke, *Deutsche Geschichte*, bk. ii, chap. 3, part iii, p. 104.

III

German and Italian nationalists were opposed to absolutist rule, whether native or foreign. They wanted to unite under a popular government of their own. They were, economically, far behind England and France. They were politically backward too. But their cultural and spiritual position was not challenged. Their language and their literature held their own and rivalled those of the other great nations. They did not have to prove their merits and ask for recognition in order to get posts and appointments for their people. Their political, not their cultural, status was unsatisfactory. Dante and Goethe, Michelangelo and Beethoven, Galileo and Kant, testified to their standing in the Western world. Though the German nation was divided and powerless, two German states were among the ruling Powers. Prussia controlled a Polish dependency of her own with about four million subjects, whom she was most of the time engaged in germanizing.[1] Austria numbered sixteen million aliens outside her empire proper; she was, in the words of Prince Metternich, "an empire embracing under its sovereignty, people of various nationalities, but as an empire, she has only one nationality. This is the German—it is so on account of history, it is so as the centre of its provinces, it is so by its civilization."[2] German-speaking officials administrated the various Slavonic races under the Habsburg sway; they tried hard to wean Hungary from feudalism. Upper Italy was under Austrian domination and several of the principalities were owned by rulers closely related to the Imperial family. Lombardy and Venetia were governed in the same absolutist way as the German parts of Austria. But they were not regarded as colonies; Austria never desired to germanize them or to force German ways upon them. Italy had once been the master nation of the world; she remained so in the spiritual sphere. The Papacy was univer-

[1] V. Valentin, op. cit., vol. i, p. 89 seq.   [2] Ibid., p. 5.

sal, as well as Italian; its influence in Austria was immense. Austrian rule all along the Eastern Adriatic was based on Italian traditions which survived in scattered city settlements in Dalmatia from the days of Venetian greatness. Whilst persecuting Italian patriots in Lombardy and Venetia, Austria leaned heavily on her Italian subjects for the control of her Slavonic populations. Italian was the trade language of Austrian foreign commerce and the service language of the navy, which was manned by Venetians and Dalmatians.[1] Poles, Czechs, and Southern Slavs would have been satisfied had they but been recognized once again as living nations. The German and Italian nationalists wanted a united Germany and a united Italy, who would take their places amongst the leading nations of the world. Their statehood was established and recognized anyhow, but their nations were divided and lacked power. Until unity was accomplished, their national movement ran on parallel lines with that of the Poles, the Czechs, the Southern Slavs, and the Hungarians. They fraternized with other subject nationalities; they rose against the same despotic governments. But these governments were German. They did not want to get rid of them, but to control them. And they were by no means willing to renounce the cultural leadership which the German nation, as such, had assumed towards the non-German races subject to their rule. Only a few German liberals, democrats, or republicans desired a federation of free and equal nations. The others stood for "Ascendancy." As the non-German nationalities resented the German claims, the united front of democratic nationalism was easily broken. The Hungarians revolted against the absolutism of the Habsburgs; but they preferred it to a democratic Germanic Austria, which would exercise cultural preponderance over them. The Slavs, Czechs as well as

[1] Heinrich Friedjung, *Der Kampf um die Vorherrschaft in Deutschland*, vol. ii, pp. 446, 459. Most of the naval officers, being of Venetian extraction, had resigned their commissions in 1848-9.

Southern Slavs, feared German democracy far more than they did despotism. They hated Hungarian nationalist feudalism more bitterly than a German-speaking imperial bureaucracy. They flocked to the Imperial standards and gave to the tottering absolutist régime the armies which stormed Vienna and helped to lay low Hungary. And the Germans inside and outside Austria hailed Radetzky, the victorious Czech field-marshal, of Hungarian extraction, who subdued Lombardy and reconquered Milan, as the saviour of the State.[1]

IV

Russia's Slavophile creed had originally been purely defensive. It proclaimed the superiority of the Russian soul,

[1] V. Valentin, op. cit., i, p. 550; ii, p. 187.

Franz Grillparzer, Austria's greatest poet, celebrated Radetzky's achievement in the famous lines:

> "Glück auf, mein Feldherr, führe den Streich!
> Nicht bloss um des Ruhmes Schimmer
> In deinem Lager ist Österreich,
> Wir andern sind einzelne Trümmer."

Magyar nationalism was the nationalism of a compact, smallish, isolated race which had forced its rule on neighbouring regions, the inhabitants of which were closely related to alien, far more numerous peoples beyond the border. It differed, in this respect, greatly from its German, Italian, or even Slav counterparts. The Magyars were a proud and brave people, who rightly prided themselves on their historical achievements in the days when they had endeavoured to stem the Ottoman invasion. They were politically shrewd and ambitious, their ways of living were daring and attractive, but they were not given to wide statesmanlike views. They had evolved a particular civilization of their own, the value of which could scarcely compensate their alien subjects for the renunciation of their own national ways, which they demanded of them, for it was a regional civilization with no close affiliations anywhere else. Superficially their institutions resembled those of the progressive West; they were spiritually less a part of it than many nations whom they ruled. They were an embattled minority. Even their language isolated them, and could not connect them, or their subjects, with any one of the great civilizations. This feeling of almost hopeless isolation gave Magyar nationalism a particularly strident note after they had gained ascendancy, and drove its representatives to a policy of radical compulsory assimilation of the with its unlimited capacity for infinite sorrow and suffering over Western reason with its restricted shallow cleverness. Western society was rotten to the core, its decay imminent, for it had been poisoned by the Renaissance, split by the Revolution, and torn by class warfare in the Industrial Revolution. Russia was a land of peasants who lived in communistic co-operation. Capitalism and its ways were alien to the Russian soul; by refusing its adoption, Russia could be saved from the fate of the West.[1]

This mystical emotional nationalism very soon allied itself to economics. Russia's task was the destruction of individualism and the spread of a true form of civilization, based on the economic security of the masses and founded on the common possession of the land by the people.[2] The abnegation of European values depended on the prohibition of foreign goods; highly protected tariffs were needed for saving the Russian soul and for filling the pockets of the Moscow manufacturers, who became the staunchest supporters of this new—or rather—old creed.[3]

These particular Russian qualities were inherent in those of Russian extraction; they depended on a national faith, which itself was closely bound up with ethnical origins. "The more we consider the distinctive ethnical features of

peoples under their sway. Magyar nationalism in 1848 had been the nationalism of an oppressed race, but even then it was intolerant of the aspirations of its non-Hungarian subjects. The victory of the Prussian armies over Austria had finally given the Magyars the chance to acquire power by sharing it with German Austrians. They were still a minority. To remain in power they had to oppress the other, far more numerous nationalities, which the Vienna Government had to leave under their control when its purely German base had become too narrow for the ruling of the polyglot Habsburg Empire. With amazing rapidity, nationalism in Hungary shed its Liberal principles and adopted a policy of racial oppression.

[1] Schultze-Gävernitz, *Volkswirtschaftlichen Studien aus Russland*, pp. 176–86. The quotations are translated by Geoffrey Drage, *Russian Affairs*, pp. 44–6.

[2] Ibid., pp. 175–8 and 193. Drage, pp. 44, 45 and 49.

[3] Ibid., pp. 197–8. Drage, p. 49.

religion, the more firmly we are convinced how unattainable is a union of creeds. . . . The essential elements are so involved with the psychical nature of the race, and with the principles of their moral philosophy, that it is futile to separate one from the other."[1] Russia shared those elements with the Slavs in the Balkans and in Austria, though Poles, Czechs, and Croats had fallen away from her in the religious field. She would ultimately liberate them from the Austrian and Turkish yoke and free them from the shackles of an imported Church. This missionary nationalism was one of the main causes of the Crimean War, when Russia desired to extend her protection over the twelve million orthodox subjects of the Sultan;[2] it justified her in her own eyes in russifying Poland, Finland, and the Baltic provinces—solemn promises and constitutional guarantees notwithstanding—and in embarking upon a series of wars against Turkey for the liberation of the Slav brethren as well as for the aggrandizement of Russia. The Ottoman power in the East had protected the Slavonic peoples from Western domination: it was tottering. It had to be overthrown; the cross was to stand once again on the mosques of Constantinople, and the scattered Slavonic people, now under foreign domination, were to find themselves under the protection of Russia as their only anchor and refuge. Wars, even wars of conquest, were sacred instruments for accomplishing a holy cause. As war has made, and is making, nations strong and free, nationalism has sanctified it. German philosophy and Italian literature, Russian mysticism and Japanese traditionalism, agree on this conception, which is by no means alien to the Anglo-Saxon mind.

[1] M. Pobiedonostseff, *Reflections of a Russian Statesman*, quoted by Drage, pp. 53-4. The Russian ethnical totalitarian state has in this respect anticipated modern Nazi doctrines: the Church as a community of believers cannot and must not detach itself from the State as a society united by a civil bond.

[2] Nesselrode's interpretation of the so-called Vienna Note of August 1853 in Harold Temperley, *The Crimea*, p. 349.

Mine eyes have seen the glory of the coming of the Lord:
He is trampling out the vintage where the grapes of wrath are
    stored;
He has loosed the fateful lightning of his terrible swift sword:
His truth is marching on.

*   *   *

In the beauty of the lilies Christ was born across the sea,
With a glory in his bosom that transfigures you and me:
As he died to make men holy, let us die to make men free,
While God is marching on.

So runs the battle hymn of the Grand Army of the Republic, which was attempting to make America safe for democracy by forcing the institutions of the free North on the
slave-owning South by fire, sword, and devastation.

A few years earlier the outbreak of the Crimean War,
the most senseless war of modern times, had been greeted
with an outburst of dithyrambic passion:

The cannons are God's preachers when the time is ripe for war.

V

Notwithstanding the teaching of the American Revolution,
that colonies were decorative, rather costly remainders of
a policy of senseless plunder, pillars of an empire bound
to crumble in a very short time, empire making went on.
The glamour of adventure and wealth to soldiers, traders,
and restless spirits was not to be dimmed by the calculation
of utilitarian accountants; it lured them to action whenever
opportunities occurred. The growth of population in the
wake of the industrial revolution had lifted the colonial
problem on to a new plane. Colonies were providing a
receptacle for the surplus population, which otherwise would
depress wages at home; their vacant lands would check the
law of diminishing returns—for some time at least. The
pessimism of the Malthus–Ricardian economic system was
tempered and converted into a short-lived optimism by
Wakefield's theory of colonization.

Neither national unity nor increasing economic prosperity had completely satisfied Germany. Millions of the German race were living in foreign countries. There was an unredeemed Germany in Austria as well as in Russia, not to speak of the millions of Germans who had gone overseas. Prince Bismarck did not share the nation's ambitious sentimentality. His political conceptions were territorial, not racial. He never uttered a word against the russification of the Baltic Germans—though they belonged to the Junker class, nor did he look upon the plight of the Austrian Germans with the eyes of a redeemer. He held no exaggerated views of the value of colonies. They were, at best, useful trading centres, where Hanseatic merchants could run their affairs unhampered by foreign bureaucrats. He disliked new frontiers, over which friction with colonial powers, otherwise friendly to Germany, might arise. Germany's geographical situation made her, in his eyes, a continental power who was surrounded on all sides by possible enemies. Her strength should not be scattered by garrisoning outposts, which were neither profitable nor safe; he did not fancy the responsibilities of safeguarding maritime communications by building a navy which would have to be strong enough to challenge the sea Powers with whom Germany had no quarrel. And it did not seem worth while taking a great national risk for the two hundred thousand emigrants who were leaving the country year after year. A protectionist tariff might keep them at home; it would, in any case, provide revenue and split political parties into hostile economic groups. Log-rolling and lobbying might not be very elevating processes—they were an excellent antidote against the clamour of political parties who demanded parliamentary government. Prince Bismarck successfully turned constitutional aspirations into economic channels. But even he could not satisfy national emotions with iron and cotton duties or with a free grant to rural distillers who made spirits from potatoes. He had to make a bid for national sentiment, which he was weaning from its political hopes; the offer of a colonial empire is not a bad substitute for a vanishing dream of responsible government.

VI

Even in England the empire-breaking forces, though pretty strong, were unable to stem the tide. The Free Traders had succeeded at home and had broken the back of feudal England; but they had failed to shape England's foreign policy in accordance with their principles. They had managed to hamper their adversaries temporarily, when the Little Englanders were in power. They defended Majuba Hill and the fall of Khartoum, and they sympathetically approached Home Rule for Ireland. But the British Empire remained; it was in close contact with other aggressive, as well as dependent, Powers. They had not been able to prevent the Crimean War, nor expansion on the Indian borders, in South Africa, or in Egypt.

And after the manufacturing and, later on, the working classes had risen to power, their outlook on empire began to change. They were no longer held down by an imperialist government; they had become the partners of its strength and profited by its rule. They might not approve of the aggressive methods in China and Japan, by which trade barriers had been forced down, or of a foreign policy which maintained the integrity of Turkey for egotistical purposes, and with it Turkish maladministration. They were more than willing to accept the benefits to their widening trade which seemed to flow from a return to earlier methods of colonial expansion. Aggressive Free Trade might be worse than peaceful Free Trade, but it was very much better than trade hampered by idiosyncrasies of Oriental despots. They were getting reconciled to the old ways of governments.[1]

[1] Cobden wrote in 1863: "Nay, feudalism is every day more and more in the ascendant in political and social life. . . . Manufacturers and

New purchasers were needed to keep people employed. Native dependencies were conquered and developed as markets and sources of supply. Colonization was reverting to its original aims: trade and domination. Once more, Power was dressed up by poets and philosophers in the shining garments of their own imagination. To Benjamin Disraeli, Empire was a magnificent Oriental dream, a rebirth of Alexandrian conceptions. Democracy was drab and dull; it could trade and fraternize with sister democracies and daughter states of similar temperament; it could not govern native races who had enjoyed a proud civilization of their own, without going back on its principles. But a Queen-Empress could rule a widespread, many-coloured empire by that personal mysticism which derives power from God Almighty, and which easily blends with Asiatic ideas. Thus a new period of empire-making set in.

Trade was once more becoming militant. The tottering Oriental Empires in the Near, the Middle, and the Far East were propped up—as they could not yet be cut up. Their independence depended on the rivalry of the Powers. To maintain it they needed guns and ships, railways and ports. Their governments could grant concessions, contracts, and licences. Here were new opportunities which did not depend on territorial possession. The Great Powers ruthlessly fought for them. They used political pressure and turned their ambassadors into salesmen for their great national industries. Vickers, Krupp, Schneider, and Skoda had to be backed up, in the interest of national trade, as well as of national defence; loans were pressed upon impecunious governments by banks acting at the beck and call of their governments, if they would but consent to spend the cash received on orders to national industries. Low interest rates and docile investors became a great asset in this struggle;

merchants as a rule seem only to desire riches that they may be enabled to prostrate themselves at the feet of feudalism."—John Morley, *Life of Richard Cobden*, vol. ii, p. 489.

what could be saved on the cost of a loan might be added to prices.[1]

The spirit of the business community was no longer that of the peace-loving "Manchester Men," who had set their faces against an aggressive feudal aristocracy or a militarist bureaucracy. It reverted to the ways of the old mercantilist traders who had been the first organizers of aggressive monopolies. Capitalism had not succeeded in industrializing feudalism; feudalism and militarism were capturing capitalism. War, a glorious crusade, was coming into its own again. An armed nation which was willing to sacrifice its life in a national war was a free nation. Continental wars had united Germany and Italy. Colonial wars in Africa and Indo-China had given back to France her self-respect. Though war, unknown to the poets, was becoming a kind of business enterprise, which depended on mechanized mass production, rather than on personal heroism, it was regaining its glamour. It was inspired coercion, a weapon which the Almighty had put into the hands of heroes, who were to shape the world according to His pre-ordained plan, by arbitrary force and compulsion. Thomas Carlyle's Calvinist concept of a world ruled by an arbitrary God, whose ways could neither be spied out by human reason nor deflected from their purpose by human action, could easily be transferred from a spiritual to a political sphere. The ranting Scotch seer who prided himself on his spiritual affinity with Goethe, whose detached Humanism and pellucid Hellenism had nothing in common with his own dark and stark fear of Hell, became the intellectual father of modern dictatorship, the herald of force and compulsion, long before Nietzsche had deified the Superman; he left its transformation into collective tribalism to later successors.

These ideas flourished freely on the outskirts of civilization, where new empires were created by a handful of white men. Here war was still a great adventure, and the

[1] W. Hallgarten, *Vorkriegs Imperialismus*.

men who faithfully followed it found their singers. Rudyard Kipling rescued the British Tommy from the contempt in which the Victorian bourgeoisie had held him. He sang of the glory of empire and empire making, of the disinterested service of white men, who were shouldering the burden of winning and running an empire.[1] Ernest Psichari found in the wide sunlit expanses of the African desert, where France was building a new empire, a cure for the evils of the sophisticated modern world. "In my native land we adore war and secretly we are yearning for it. We have always made war, not to conquer a province, not to destroy another nation, not to settle a contest of conflicting interests. . . . We really make war in order to make war, without any other thought."[2] The German racialists saw in the relation of white masters to coloured people the realization of their dream of the superman, and the missionary fanaticism of the United States discovered in the conquest of the Philippines another proof of the manifest destiny by which God "has made us the master organizers of the world to establish system where chaos reigns."

"The blood of our soldiers and sailors, which has wetted the sands of Homs, of Sidi Messeri and of Ain Zara, has rejuvenated and elated us: young, valuable blood. The storm cannot cleanse the air, without uprooting trees and flooding the spring meadows. What is the value of the Djebel, the Fezzan, the Cyrenaica? I don't know. But I know they have given us this marvellous resurrection, this unity of the people, which in all her long history Italy never

---

[1] The following criticism by Professor Gilbert Murray was made at that time. "If ever it were my fate to administer a Press Law . . . I should first of all lock up my old friend Rudyard Kipling, because in several stories he has used his great powers to stir up in the minds of hundreds and thousands of Englishmen a blind and savage contempt for the Bengali nation." *Nationality and Subject Races, Report of Conference*, June 28–30, 1910 (London, 1911), p. 9.

[2] Ernest Psichari, *Terres de Soleil et de Sommeil*, p. 233.

He was a grandson of Ernest Renan, born 1883, and was killed in action, 1914.

had before." These were not the words of D'Annunzio whose flamboyant frigid passion saw in empire making but an opportunity of giving one's senses wider experience, but of a great Liberal, Ferdinando Martini, who was a poet as well as a statesman, and heir to everything best in the *Risorgimento*.[1]

---

[1] Speech on November 28, 1911, in Florence at the memorial service for the Tuscan officers who died in Libya, quoted in Croce, *Geschichte Italiens*, pp. 333–4.

CHAPTER IV

THE RISING OF THE NATIONS

I

THE forces of nationalism were thus working in opposite directions: subject nations were gaining strength and organizing resistance against their masters; ruling nations were expanding their boundaries; they tried to liberate their unredeemed brothers in foreign lands or endeavoured to gain colonial possessions. At the outbreak of the Great War, the Powers were still engaged in empire making—or at least in consolidating their empires—almost oblivious of past experiences. Recollections of the great Indian revolt, euphemistically called the Mutiny, were fading; concessions to Indian nationalism were very modest. The violent Chinese rising against Western domination had been put down successfully. Egyptian prosperity had eclipsed Arabi Pasha's aspirations. Subject nationalities outside Europe had scarcely begun to become vociferous.[1] And even in Europe, only in the Balkan Peninsula had empire-breaking on a large scale been successful.

Each of the Great Powers continued to rule some Irredenta. Attempts to stir them up had not been wanting. Russia had used the anti-Austrian animosities in Czechoslovakia and Eastern Galicia very successfully for espionage purposes; she had dangled the ideal of Slavonic brotherhood and of national liberation before the eyes of the various Slavonic peoples under the sway of Austria and Germany. After the outbreak of the War propaganda set in from all sides. Germany appealed to the racial feelings of the Russians of German extraction in the Baltic provinces. Having

---

[1] *Nationality and Subject Races, Report of Conference*, June 28–30, 1910 (London, 1911).

occupied Russian Poland, she advocated a sort of Polish independence. She supported the rising of the intransigent Boers in Cape Colony and of the Sinn Feiners in Ireland. She took the Flemish movement in Belgium under her wing. As the ally of Turkey she propagated the Holy War of all Mohammedans against their infidel European masters.

The British, the Russians, and the French, on the other hand, sought to enlist Polish national sympathies for their own cause. The British conceived the foundation of a great Arab Empire, free from Turkish oppression, and promised the establishment of a Jewish National Home. Slavs and Italians appealed, more or less successfully, to their unredeemed brothers in the Austrian Empire and in the Austrian Army.

But for the entry of the United States into the war, this sort of nationalist propaganda, which had been attempted in former European conflicts, might not have had much influence on the terms of peace.

The United States did not recognize the rights of any national minority in their midst. They had opened the door to immigrants from all parts of the world on the assumption that these members of divergent nationalities would emerge as full-blooded American citizens when thrown into the American melting-pot. The sheltered position of a racially separate, though loyal minority, such as the French held in Canada, was anathema to them. They were not willing to grant such privileges to anybody. The outbreak of the war had showed them how skin-deep assimilation had been after all; large masses of their people openly sympathized with the countries from which they had come. This was considered high treason and a big Americanization campaign was launched, which was to crush such nationalist aspirations completely.

At the same time they became the great apostles of the rights of nationalities abroad. President Wilson's Fourteen

Points became the Bible of modern democratic nationalism.[1] He brushed aside the claim of empire makers that
the Roman peace imposed upon their subjects had given
them safety and prosperity and had benefited them as
partners of their masters' superior civilization; good
government in his view, was no substitute for free government. He would willingly have given up the colonial possessions of the U.S.A.; and he carefully refrained from under-
taking new colonial responsibilities. He recognized that an
immediate withdrawal of all colonial domination would
scarcely be a blessing for the liberated indigenous nations
whose ways of living and of government had been destroyed.
Domination must continue for some time, but it must not
be the domination of a master who exploits his subjects, but
rather the ascendancy of a schoolmaster, whose disciplinarian
teaching fits his pupils for future independence. Colonial
possessions were unevenly divided, a fact which was threatening the peace of the world. There was no need, and no
chance, for complete territorial equality; such far-reaching
reshuffling was neither desirable nor possible. Equality of
opportunity might, however, be established in the colonial
sphere by registering, so to speak, a kind of mortgage for
the benefit of excluded Powers on the various colonial
possessions of the world.

President Wilson's ultimate aims were freedom for the
hitherto subject races and equality for all the nations of the
world. He was a disciple of Cobden and Bright, without
perhaps being aware of it. He had turned their doctrines
into a completely water-tight system. They had been men
of affairs with a strong sense of reality, notwithstanding
their firm faith in principles. He was an intellectual whose
mind delighted in systems, in whose soul burnt red-hot the
passionate flame of bifurcated presbyterian egalitarianism.
He believed in the equality of men and of states, but he
believed too in an Almighty Supreme Power, whose will

[1] Plus the four principles and the five particulars.

was arbitrary law. For the time being, he had delegated his powers to him. He owed it to the Master, who spoke through him, to deal stern justice to those who had broken the covenant. His political philosophy imposed upon the nations of the world what might be called "compulsory Cobdenism." For, unlike his great teachers, who strongly objected to intervention, however attractive it might seem for the moment, he was a great crusader, ready to intervene whenever Providence called out to him. The collapse of the Central Powers had made him the master of the world for a short span of time. He saw his dream of giving it everlasting peace coming true. It was not to be based on brutal force, but on stern justice. He had no selfish ends to serve, for his own country desired no territorial price for its assistance, which had won the war, but a speedy return to the policy of isolation from which his statesmanship had driven it. He did not care overmuch for the details of the peace settlements. He had evolved his scheme during the period of American neutrality, when he had been working for a peace without victory, which would be concluded under his disinterested guidance and would enable him to finish the work of the American Revolution and free all subject races from their masters. But when he was called to the council table, he was one of the victors. He could not make his "associates" swallow his principles and incorporate them in treaties of peace. He could only enforce their application at the expense of the vanquished. He had to be content with lip service from the victors.

II

The Austrian Empire was broken; its nationalities were freed; they either joined their brethren who had been redeemed before the war or set up as new independent states. German Austria, shorn of the provinces, the inhabitants of which she had protected against the Turks and to whom she had given the modicum of modern civilization they enjoyed, was prevented from uniting with Germany, thus remaining both free and fettered.

The Bolshevik régime in Russia had accepted the doctrine of the self-determination of nations. Being sure of an early world revolution which would free all nations from the yoke of capitalism, it saw no reason why it should go on controlling subject nationalities, which would accept the Soviet system of their own free will and become fully-fledged member-states of a Soviet federation. But it could not impose this revolution upon the Baltic States, who were supported by the Allies and ultimately proved unwilling to accept Communism. The entire sea-front from Finland to the German border was torn away from Russia and formed into independent non-Soviet republics. Behind them a new Poland arose, which comprised a good deal more than the regions inhabited by "ethnical Poles." Apart from the Corridor and parts of Upper Silesia, she received a large slice of Ruthenian Eastern Galicia, of Lithuania, and of the Ukraine. Rumania succeeded at the same time in tearing Bessarabia from Russia.

Germany lost some of her border provinces and her colonial possessions. She had to return Alsace-Lorraine to France. A small Danish district was handed back to Denmark. The greater part of the regions taken from Poland in the three partitions of that unhappy country were restored to the resurrected Polish nation. Upper Silesia was divided, against the wish of the majority of its inhabitants. The artificial state of Danzig was created and the Corridor established, in order to make Poland a seafaring nation. The newly made Czech State had to be satisfied with a port on German territory; Austria and Hungary were deprived of their harbours, but Poland and the newly-formed Lithuanian State were endowed with German territory, so as to have ports of their own.

Turkey fared much worse. She almost disappeared from

Europe, but for a small strip of land connecting the Black Sea with the Mediterranean and a very much reduced Constantinople. The Arab revolt had helped to smash the Turkish Empire on the battlefield. But the dreams (and promises) of a mighty Arab Empire, comprising all Arabs, faded out on account of earlier treaties with colonial Powers. Six Arab kingdoms and principalities and four protectorates were formed out of Turkey's Asiatic possessions. France, Italy, and Greece insisted on having large slices of Asia Minor, for Turkey seemed to be the one member of the vanquished nations from whose corpse new colonial empires could easily be carved. Empire-breaking, so it seemed, could not go much farther.

Some subject nationalities who were controlled by the victors had claimed a hearing at the bar of the Peace Conference and had appealed to President Wilson's principles. They did not succeed. Neither the Irish nor the Egyptians, nor the Persians were admitted. They took the matter into their own hands and rebelled. Afghanistan dared to go to war with England and, though thoroughly beaten, gained her independence. Persia, having got rid of the Russian incubus, cut the ties which had made her dependent on England. Egypt, having freed herself from Turkish sovereignty, finally managed to free herself from the shackles of British domination. The newly created mandate states of Syria and Iraq were restive under the mandatory Powers, whose administration was to prepare them for complete independence. The Saudi Empire swallowed up the Hedjaz. And the simmering Arab revolt in Palestine is but another phase of the Arab counter-colonization movement; it is directed as much against the mandatory Power as against the Jewish colonists, the settlements of which the mandatory Power grudgingly admitted.

And last but not least, Turkey rose against the mutilations imposed upon her by the Peace Treaty. She was ready to let depart the alien races which the Ottoman Empire had conquered during its great westward expansion. But she was not willing to sacrifice an inch of the territory which had become the home of the Turkish people. France and Italy coveted rights and spoils in Asia Minor, though they were not prepared to maintain armies of occupation in a far-away land: but Greece was keen on action. She desired to take over the Smyrna region, which had once been the stage of the most brilliant display of Hellenic civilization, and where Greek farmers and traders had maintained the forms, though not perhaps the spirit, of Greek life and Greek language in the midst of Turkish invaders. She was defeated. The withdrawal of her armies enabled the Turks to expel the Greek settlers in Asia Minor from the land on which they had made their home for over two thousand years, and to which they had brought European civilization. But for the League of Nations, which organized an exchange of the Greeks in Asia Minor with the Turkish settlements in Europe, the decolonization of Asia Minor would have ranked with the expulsion of the Moors from Spain as one of the world's most spectacular tragedies.

This political success in uprooting a long-established alien colonization led to a cultural revolt in Turkey and, later on, in Persia. The abolition of the Caliphate had destroyed the rather legendary spiritual empire which had united all Moslems the world over under the green flag flown by the successors of the Prophet. Turkish national consciousness now turned against the alien religion, fit only for desert tribes, which Arab domination had imposed upon the Otto-man nation long ago. The Turkish language, hitherto spelt with Arab characters and interspersed and interlarded with Persian terms, was cleansed of its foreign ingredients and henceforth written in Latin letters. Even the outer signs of this alien religious civilization were to be destroyed. The fez was abolished, and the women had to drop their veils. Turkey flung her Holy Books into the fire and, of her own free will, accepted the technical standards of the West. Her spiritual revolt closely resembled the aggressive anti-Church atheism of the Bolsheviks, both governments seeing in religion an opiate to prevent the people's progress. But there is an even closer parallel with Nazism.[1]

III

The success of these decolonization movements was not so much due to their own innate strength as to the war-tiredness of the great empires. After four years' fighting on far-flung fronts, the glamour of adventure had gone. Even the most reckless spirits had drunk their fill and longed for peace, cleanliness, quiet, and rest. The magic spell of the East had grown stale and pale for those who had experienced it in the relentless desert and who had suffered from its fever-infested swamps. Before aggressive adventures became popular again, fifteen years of a dull, drab peace had to pass, which had deeply disappointed many of those who had fought in the war. A new generation had to arise which could not find jobs in the great economic upheaval accompanying the great depression, and who had learned nothing from war but restlessness and ruthlessness. A great lassitude stopped all colonial ventures. People dimly realized that the Great War had been a failure; they were willing to pay for peace, whenever mere colonial issues were at stake. The English could easily have subjected Ireland had they concentrated all their strength on her. They could have brought her to heel with the help of modern technique and imposed upon her a resettlement, in comparison to which the Cromwellian settlement would have been child's play. But the will to do so was wanting. If those three million people who had been a thorn in the flesh of England for centuries did not want to enjoy the benefits the British Empire offered them, it was not worth while to hold them to it by force. As long as they did not harm Ulster and did not massacre the remnants

[1] See below, p. 180.

of the British garrison in Southern Ireland, they could walk out on their own terms. And if they refrained from advertising their country abroad as an independent republic, they might run her at home as if she were one.

But there was something more than lassitude. The statesmen might talk glibly of the rights of subject nations and free those ruled by the enemy, whilst keeping a hold over those under their own government. They might curse the Imperialism of their former adversaries who had misused their power for low egotistical purposes, and praise the blessings of their own domination. They would not throw off a burden which was profitable to those who carried it and beneficent to those who had to pay for it. But the nations themselves thought quite differently. They had learnt to loathe Imperialism. Their sons and brothers had laid down their lives in order to destroy it and to make the world safe for democracy. They had let their statesmen rearrange it in violation of their principles, but they were not willing to take up arms in defence of a policy which was morally wrong. They had carried the white man's burden under the blazing sun in many a land. They were not prepared to shoulder new responsibilities. It might be their duty to hold on to what they had got and train the subject nations for complete freedom. But if these nations clamoured but loudly enough they were ready to let them go. The democracies of the West had become genuine democracies; they realized the incongruity of vast empires ruled by a democracy. Imperialism, as a missionary creed, did not appeal to the masses any longer. They might be ready to fight for ideas, but not for interests.

The empire-breaking forces in all parts of the globe could count on the active support of the new Russian government. Russia wanted to inflict military punishment on the Western Powers who had invaded her territory, abetted revolutions, or helped her neighbours in Poland, Rumania, or the Baltic states in attack or defence. She wanted to weaken them in order to be safe. She held, moreover, a particular theory of Imperialism.[1] Since the rate of profits must fall in capitalist countries, as the growth of constant capital is reducing the proportion of variable capital (the capital spent on wages, which is the only source of profit), capitalists must transfer their capital to new countries, where labour is cheap and the rate of exploitation not yet limited by high standards of living, labour organization, or legislation. Capitalism must conquer new countries in order to find new human objects for exploitation and additional sources of capital accumulation; otherwise it would soon cease to be profitable. And as the productive capacity of the capitalist system is increasing faster than the purchasing power of the masses at home, new markets have to be found abroad and new consumers have to be raised; this can only be done by the annexation of new territories by a policy of aggressive Imperialism.[2]

Resistance to Imperialism, henceforth, is tantamount to destroying capitalism; it deprives it of its only chance of growth. The capitalist system in most dependent countries represented an alien system of production, implanted by foreign masters, who had either conquered the land and politically subjected its inhabitants or, whilst offering them a kind of spurious independence, had organized their finances, their legal system, and their business life, and had forced them into Western ways. Revolt against it was popular. In these countries the struggle between labour and capital was a struggle between two antagonistic civilizations. It was easy enough to turn the hatred of natives for the machine or the mine, and the unnatural life they were made to lead, into hatred of the capitalist system, which, to them, was embodied in mines and mills. They hated capitalism because it was alien and because it was forced upon them by outside agencies; it strove after purposes they neither

---

[1] See above, p. 35, note.

[2] Rosa Luxemburg, *Die Akkumulation des Kapitals: Ein Beitrag zur ökonomischen Erklärung des Imperialismus*, pp. 328 and 329 seq., 338–9.

understood nor cared for, and employed means abhorrent to their way of thinking. Few of them went as far as Gandhi, who denounced the entire Western system of civilization, of which machines were but the particularly loathsome, soul-destroying embodiment. Most of them were ready to pay lip service to the great technical schemes of progress advocated by Bolshevism, which promised bliss and contentment to the toiling masses after the profit-seeking foreign exploiters had been driven away and prevented from running capitalist plants. Bolshevism furnished a strong leaven to the naïve nationalism of the toiling masses, whose traditional ways of living were threatened by the advent of capitalism. Democratic nationalism might appeal to the educated classes, to whom self-government offered jobs and prospects, besides the hope of resurrecting the national civilization. The masses were not very much interested in an artificial renaissance of their indigenous civilization. They lived in it anyhow and did not have to learn foreign languages. They did not try to pass examinations and aim at getting jobs. They had to do bodily work and make the wheels run. The coming of the foreigner had often raised their standards of living. It had given them legal protection against the exactions of their betters. Health services and the suppression of war had made them spawn, until increased numbers pressed hard against the means of subsistence. They were glad enough to get additional employment in the mills which foreigners had established. But they had to break with their native ways and to work to the beat of a relentless engine, which had no arbitrary whims, but speeded them up all the time. It was quite easy for the Bolsheviks, who idolized machines, to turn the loathing for them and the hatred of those who had imported them and had made natives serve them, into weapons of a native revolt. Amongst the highly skilled, well-organized workers of Western Europe, or of the United States, communist propaganda was not very successful. It strengthened the empire-breaking forces in colonial possessions and in semi-independent countries where capitalist colonization was beginning to take root.[1]

IV

In a world swayed by such ideas empires could no longer be held by force. The United Kingdom was willing to let Ireland go. She granted fiscal autonomy to India and was ready to let this huge composite empire, welded together into a seeming unity by many conquests, of which the British was but the last, grow into a political body determining its own fate. Though she may not be able to satisfy India's national yearnings by teaching her the ways of Western self-government, she is not likely to give her the twenty years of resolute government which more robust Imperialists advocated in similar cases. She receded in China rather than use force. By the Statute of Westminster, she extended to the Dominions self-government far beyond the purely regional self-determination they had enjoyed so far. When the Dominions took their seats in the Assembly Hall of the League of Nations in Geneva, the entire world had to recognize that the British Empire was no longer an empire in the Roman sense of the word, held together by force.

Regional movements all over the world restarted, in which

[1] League Against Imperialism and for National Independence: Resolutions passed at the Session of the General Council held in Brussels on December 9, 10, 11, 1927. This body originally embraced bourgeois as well as proletarian anti-Imperialists, for Lenin had taught his followers that the revolution in *ruling* countries (imperialist countries) must be carried against the bourgeoisie by the workers, whilst in *subject* countries the revolt must be led in the beginning by the nationalist bourgeoisie. (J. Stalin, *Le Marxisme et la Question Nationale et Coloniale*, 1937, pp. 247–53. *Les Tâches de l'Université des Peuples d'Orient a l'égard des Pays d'Orient Coloniaux et Dependants* (written 1925), p. 266 seq. *A propos de la Chine* (written 1927). By the resolutions of the meeting of the Executive Committee in Berlin, June 2, 1931, the bourgeois elements were to be dropped, and the League became "communist." (*The Colonies and Oppressed Nations in the Struggle for Freedom*, p. 5.)

half-forgotten, scarcely known nationalities claimed the
right of self-determination. Some Slavonic remnants in the
Prussian district of Lausitz, of whose existence everybody
but a few philologists had been in happy ignorance, started a
Home Rule movement of their own. Iceland insisted on
separating as a colony from Denmark. Malta discovered
a nationality of her own, over which Italians and Maltese
are fighting bitterly. Albania rose against her Italian pro-
tectors. Cyprus rebelled against the British Government.
Scotland discovered that she was a subject nationality. The
old regional animosities in Spain broke out again, and
Catalonia and the Basque Provinces tried to proclaim their
independence. The Flemish people in Belgium insisted on
equality with the Walloons; the Finns endeavoured to rid
themselves of the cultural dowry their Swedish fellow-citizens
had brought them. The United States have started the
Philippine Islands on the road to independence. The influx
of Western ideas, the aggression of Japan, and the propaganda of Russia have broken up the colonial domination
of China over Manchuria, Tibet, and Mongolia. But for
Japanese pressure Chinese nationalism, on the other hand,
might have turned resolutely against all remnants of Western domination; the repercussions would have greatly
affected all European possessions in Indo-China and Indo-
nesia, especially the French and the Dutch. And but for the
godlessness of the leading independent Islamic States, the
rising of the Mohammedan world might have shaken to
the core the rule of the West over the followers of the Prophet.
Arab unrest may yet assume dangerous proportions. As a
result of relentless persecution in many parts of the world,
the Jews, reputed to be the standard-bearers of modern
universalism, are concentrating their energies on the creation
of a separate Jewish State, the inhabitants of which are supposed to sever the cultural links which bind them to the
various types of Western civilization. Even Switzerland is
affected : the Italian-speaking canton of Tessin is desperately

fighting against the "alien" immigration from German-speaking parts of the Confederation. And since the Lateran Treaty, the Papacy, hitherto the embodiment of a world-wide spiritual universalism, is in danger of becoming once more a national Italian institution.

CHAPTER V

THE ECONOMIC REVOLT

I

UNTIL lately, economic nationalism had not interfered greatly with immigration (apart from Oriental immigration). After the war the great migration movement began to ebb. Ethnical conceptions came to the forefront; immigration policies were no longer directed by economic considerations. The making of a new nation was becoming a "synthetic" process, for which the proper choosing of the constituent elements—by limitation of alien admixtures—was essential. The U.S.A. restricted oversea immigration quantitatively and qualitatively by fixing a quota of 150,000 a year. Most new countries followed their example in some form or other; some of the Dominions interrupted migration even from the mother country.

At the same time, some of the older countries started a "purifying" process of their own by expelling political, racial, or religious "non-conformists." Millions of White Russians fled from the Bolsheviks. The peace treaties provided for the compulsory evacuation from ceded territories of "Optants" who desired to maintain their nationalities. The League of Nations transplanted 1,300,000 Greeks from Asia Minor in exchange for 400,000 Turks. Nazism expelled between 80,000 to 100,000 people from Germany—by no means all non-Aryans—an exodus which has greatly aggravated the Palestine problem.[1]

[1] According to the Committee of International Assistance, the number of refugees dealt with by the Nansen Office and the High Commissioner for Refugees coming from Germany was

Russians 700–800,000
Armenians 240,000

[Continued on next page

The total number of political and racial refugees probably fell short of the mass of immigrants who had rushed annually to North America before the war (Canada and the U.S.A. received in a single year about 1,300,000 people). The difficulties encountered in the settling of these comparatively small groups furnish clear evidence of the strength of disintegrating nationalism.

II

Commercial economic separatism has made gigantic strides. Ever since the American Revolution, economic separatism has permeated commercial policies. Though British statesmanship has succeeded in holding the Dominions within the framework of the Empire and has prevented political separation, their economic separation has proceeded by leaps and bounds. Its objective shifted from the protection of infant industries to the safeguarding of regionally high wages. It had left agriculture to its own devices. Since the prices of exports in world markets could not be protected by purely domestic measures, it attempted a bifurcation of the price-level: agricultural prices were "universal"; industrial prices remained "regional," and above them.

The commercial policy of the Dominions was frequently less considerate of metropolitan interests than that of the great South American Republics, whose protectionist tariff policy became effective only during and after the Great War, while the belligerents, concentrating on the output of war material, had neglected their oversea customers and forced them to industrialization by depriving them of their regular supplies.

Continued from previous page]

Germans	80–100,000
Saar	3–4,000
Assyrians and Assyro-Chaldeans	7,000
Turks	150

See Nansen International Office for Refugees: *Report of the Governing Body*, 1936. The latest estimate for German refugees is 145,000.

The countries who attained statehood after the War insisted on pursuing their most extravagant dreams of nationhood. They tore down the economic structure which had sheltered them and their former masters. They made no use of the possibilities for maintaining established economic connections by some sort of preferential duties. They were at last independent, full-grown, political nations; they must be economically independent too and develop industries of their own, which would make them safe in time of war and give them equality of status in time of peace. They surrounded themselves with high tariff walls and tried to reduce to a minimum the unhampered circulation of men, goods, and capital, which had made their territory, before the war, an important province of a national, as well as of a world-trade, empire.

Russia pursued the same aim. Rapid industrialization, by establishing war industries of her own, was to make her independent of capitalist countries. She had to accumulate "national capital" by a more ruthless exploitation of peasants and workers than any capitalist enterprise had ever dared to undertake. This policy made Russia once more safe and powerful; it greatly strengthened the ranks of the industrial workers who form the main political support of the ruling party. And it withdrew from the activities of the Western business men a large part of the world's yet unexploited resources, which would have provided an almost ideal field for economic colonization.

The anti-colonization features of modern protectionist movements were very much in evidence in countries like China, whose political independence had been precarious, and whose tariffs were kept low by international agreements imposed upon her by Western business interests. Chinese patriots clamoured for the abolition of the capitulations and concessions which, no doubt, were discriminatory, though they gave protection to Chinese, as well as to foreign traders. They vehemently denounced foreign Imperialism,

F

which prevented Chinese patriots from raising tariffs, under the shelter of which Chinese (and foreign capitalists too) could establish branch establishments in China and exploit Chinese consumers. They boycotted the foreign traders who claimed their treaty rights and dared to offer imported manufactured goods at low rates of duties. They demanded the abolition of those iniquities which offended the dignity of the Chinese people, since they had been imposed by force on previous Chinese governments. Half-mature students and partly educated *littérateurs* were the advance guard in this struggle for liberty, the immediate issue of which was not the political freedom of the Chinese people, but the freedom of native and foreign capitalists to exploit them by starting superfluous industries, and the withdrawal of China as far as possible from the world markets. The boycott became a great weapon in the hands of fanatic consumers. Similar events took place in India; India's commercial policy is a revolt, gathering speed all the time, against the industrial domination of the mother country. Whilst her spiritual leaders desire to wean her from the industrial system of the West, her business men endeavour to expand it under the protection of a stiff tariff, directed against the metropolis. In Europe the closest connection between counter-colonization and protection is to be found in Ireland. The new partly emotional, partly commercial nationalism is sometimes expressed in communist terms and supported by communist propaganda.

III

The Agrarian Revolution which followed the Great War put an end to many remnants of feudalism. In countries where landlords and tenants belonged to the same race, for instance in old Rumania, this was a purely domestic issue. In others, however, in Yugoslavia and Czechoslovakia, in Estonia and in Latvia, much of the land belonged to an alien race, whose ancestors had invaded and ruled the country. They had built its cities, established its seats of learning, impressed their culture upon it, and had given it their language. An anti-colonial revolution, which posed as agrarian reform, swept away this alien ascendancy. The expropriation of estates was sometimes preceded by violent occupation, which afterwards had to be legalized; it was sometimes accomplished by regular legislation, which laid down terms and provided for compensation. Since the currencies in which compensation was paid were rapidly depreciating, recipients frequently had not much to choose between it and outright confiscation. The Czechs and Rumanians hated feudalism sufficiently to insist on its complete disappearance, but the prospect of exterminating the representatives of foreign rule gave peculiar zest to their desire for reform. The laws were "general" and not directed explicitly against foreign landlords, but their application was frequently so managed as to hit the alien proprietor harder than the native.

The Peace Treaties dealt specifically with the elimination of alien landowners. The German proprietors in Poland's newly acquired territories had to liquidate their estates within two years and leave for Germany if they wished to retain their German nationality. Those who chose to become Polish citizens were harshly treated. Whilst German landowners in Poznán had owned only 35 per cent of the land, their share of the total expropriations was 51 per cent.[1] And though the Hungarian landowners who had estates in the territories ceded to Czechoslovakia, Yugoslavia, and Rumania were allowed to keep their property under the Peace Treaty, they were subject to expropriation under the new land laws.[2]

Governments had recognized the importance of the land

[1] *Survey of International Affairs*, 1932, p. 352, note 1.
[2] They were compensated by the expropriating Governments. The second Paris Conference made generous provision for them (after an adjournment of the matter by the second Hague Conference) by creating a compensation fund of 219,500,000 gold crowns—value £9,140,000 at par.

question even before revolutionary nationalists. When the Russian Czarist government wanted to russianize the Baltic Provinces, they favoured the indigenous race against their German overlords. The Austrian Government had endeavoured to liberate the Galician peasants; it beat down the rising of the Polish aristocracy with the help of their anti-Polish Ruthenian retainers (1863).

A downtrodden peasantry does not care much for the purely cultural side of nationalism, even after it has become the playground of the intellectuals and the middle classes. Their more ambitious youth are keen on learning the language and sharing the education of the governing race, as this will open new careers to them. In the natural course of events, the native language and, with it, native ways of living and thinking were likely to disappear, if no unwise pressure were put upon the people. But when nationalism appealed to their hunger for land, tenants and labourers flocked to its standards in the hope that the estates which foreign invaders had taken from their ancestors would be returned to them. The agrarian Socialism preached by Michael Davitt, who wanted to nationalize the land of the Anglo-Irish landlords, did not greatly enthuse the Irish tenants. But Parnell's promise of land ownership did. The combination of land ownership and nationalism has dominated Irish affairs ever since. The refusal to pay interest and amortization on the Irish Land Purchase loans, financed by the British government, has been De Valera's most alluring argument for an Irish Republic.

This agrarian revolt was not limited to Europe. Ever since the Spaniards enslaved the Indians and made them work their lands and their mines, native risings have occurred from time to time, especially in Mexico. Probably the first colonial revolt in modern times began amongst Mexican Indians. After independence had been won, the counter-colonization movement continued; it was directed against the heirs of the Conquistadores who represented Spanish traditions. The Spanish aristocracy was ousted politically. A Mexico-born middle class, which included half-breeds and Indians, ruled in its place and developed the country by a kind of secondary colonization. They invited foreign capitalists to invest their money in Mexican railways, mines, and factories. They gave them security and allowed them to exploit the Mexican masses. The wealth the foreigners created enabled the government to run the country by an efficient dictatorship; it enriched it and the middle class which supported it. It kept the mass of the people subject to an agrarian feudalism inherited from the Spaniards and to an industrial feudalism imported from the United States. It broke down with the collapse of Porfirio Diaz. Ever since, the country has gone through a series of social revolutions which culminated in the destruction of agrarian feudalism and in the suppression of the Church as an independent corporative institution, for the Catholic Church, being a great landowner, had benefited from the iniquities of the feudal system. It fettered foreign industrial Capitalism by social legislation and by state-supported trade unionism.[1] An anti-colonial revolution aimed at the overthrow of all things Spanish and at a return to the aboriginal civilization of the native Indian. It vilified the achievements of the conquest—the land system, as well as the alien Church it had imported—and it glorified all things Indian. It has attempted to replace the alien feudal land code by the native Indian system of village communities (ejido).[2] It is quite

[1] Frank Tannenbaum, *Peace by Revolution*, pp. 228–42, 251–8. Harold Nicolson, *Dwight Morrow*, p. 344.
[2] Diaz had decreed the expropriation of ejidos, 1890; 135 million acres were expropriated (like British commons) in favour of 834 people —some of them owning 6 million acres. Of the 17 million people (1910) there were:

Indians	..	.. 6	million—39 per cent
Half-breeds	..	.. 8	million—53 per cent
White	..	.. 1·15	million— 7·5 per cent

Over 3 million were *eones de campo*.—H. Nicolson, *Dwight Morrow*, pp. 318–19. Frank Tannenbaum, *The Mexican Agrarian Revolution*, passim.

ready to sacrifice some of the technical benefits the colonial order brought along with it, if it can but return to a state of affairs in which natives are ruling natives, and Spaniards, foreigners, and half-breeds are deprived of their leading position. It is perhaps the most far-reaching counter-colonization movement of our day. Its centre-piece has been the agrarian revolution, which is giving back to the people the land the colonists had taken from them and is allowing them to work it in the ways they inherited from their ancestors.[1]

IV

The development of most new countries would have been rather slow without financial aid from a metropolis. The richer, industrially more advanced nations have not been content with the capitalist exploitation of their own dependencies; they have developed the natural resources of many a country, which they could not, or would not, control politically. They had established a kind of international consumer's finance business—long before this type of enterprise had become familiar at home. Their export of capital opened up additional markets to their industries, especially to the structural industries, and thus gave employment to their skilled workers and to their administrators; it kept their ships busy. Their promoters made big profits and their investors increased their incomes considerably. In lieu of payment old countries received raw materials they needed for their expanding plants and foodstuffs for the feeding of their growing populations. They assimilated the economic life of their debtors to their own by fashioning these colonial ventures after their national pattern, and by transferring their

[1] In a speech before a gathering of United States diplomatists, consuls, and officials of the State Department at Mexico City, Señor Ramon Beteta, Under-Secretary for Foreign Affairs, reaffirmed the intention of the Mexican Government eventually to eliminate all foreign capital in the country and to aim at a "reconquest of Mexico for the Mexicans."— *The Times*, October 16, 1937.

national types of industrial structure to them. International lending on a very large scale covered the entire world with a network of financial interrelations. It was the most universal of all known forms of inter-state co-operation. It prevented the early breakdown of the established system of exchange of goods by becoming the mainstay of continued economic intercourse after migration had come to a standstill, and when trade barriers had been raised everywhere. Some of the older countries were no longer able to pay for their imports when their foreign customers raised their tariffs and refused their goods; they would have had to reduce their imports or cut down their standards of living, had it not been for the capital investments they had placed earlier in foreign countries.

Nor could countries like the United States have sold their surplus exports to foreign nations, whose goods they were unwilling to accept in return, but for the lending of these surpluses and the re-lending of the interest falling due on them. By these means a somewhat precarious equilibrium in international intercourse was maintained. Whenever it was seriously disturbed, bankruptcy intervened. This had happened in the United States in the 'seventies and 'eighties of the last century, when many of the railways financed by European capitalists went into the hands of the receiver.

The claims of governments and private creditors on other governments have never been properly secured. Few governments can be sued to good purpose in their own courts by their defrauded creditors. The mystical right of being above the law which may belong to rulers by divine grace is exercised by their constitutional successors whenever they have lost borrowed money in financial gambles. They pose as business entrepreneurs when they approach the capital market; but when they should return the money entrusted to them, they discover that their moral duty to their taxpayers prevents them from fulfilling their obligations. They search for some flaw in the original contract, which should justify them in keeping the money which they got by going beyond their constitutional rights, and which they have, on their own showing, illegally wasted. They not only refuse to pay interest; they have no intention whatsoever of returning the capital. The worst sinners in this field have been some of the southern states of the United States, who have defaulted on loans contracted for purposes of business expansion long before the Civil War. They calmly repudiated them, basing their action on various legal quibbles. They could not be made to give redress in their own courts, nor in those of the United States. "An appeal has been made to the sovereign people," said Governor McNutt, of Mississippi, on January 4, 1842, "and their verdict, from which no appeal can be taken, has triumphantly sustained the principles for which I have long contended. . . . This result has gloriously sustained the sacred truth that the toiling millions never shall be burthened with taxes to support the idle few."[1] They have presented the world with some flagrant instances of bad faith and cleared the road for the revolt of debtors which started in the wake of the Great War.

Injured creditors have often mobilized their governments against fraudulent repudiation by smaller states, when a friendly settlement could not be reached. A naval demonstration, a blockade, or the occupation of some port, has ended in an agreement with the recalcitrant debtors. Public opinion tended to disapprove of these coercive methods, which were applied at the expense of the taxpayer in the interest of a comparatively small group of investors and might engender grave political implications. The use of force was limited, moreover, to small countries; nobody would have dared to put pressure on Russia had she defaulted before the War. The doctrine of Calvo and Drago, which

[1] Council of the Corporation of Foreign Bondholders. Sixty-third Annual Report, p. 497.

tended to prohibit coercive collection of foreign debts, generally found favour; as long as profits remain private property, losses should not be nationalized.

An occasional case of bankruptcy or repudiation did not cause far-reaching international dislocations. The solidarity of the creditors blocked the debtors' access to the capital markets of the world. The defaulters soon learnt their lesson: the benefits resulting from non-payments of interest and sinking fund rarely offset the inconvenience of being cut off from further supplies of money. Sooner or later some settlement had to be reached: arrears were compounded or forgiven. Financial reorganization followed, which compensated those who had been able to hold on, for some of the loss they had suffered,[1] and new loans were made at reasonable rates of interest.

Private debtors, too, were sometimes fraudulent, being unwilling, though not unable, to pay and sheltered themselves behind their local jurisdictions. After the American Revolution, American merchants owed considerable sums of money to British creditors. Though various treaty agreements between the two governments had stipulated the faithful execution of properly recognized debts, the greater part of these claims was never met.

V

Until the rise of Communism the various devices of bankruptcy and repudiation had been used in rather a shamefaced, apologetic way. They were the weapons of wasters who did not know how to manage their affairs, and who were called to account when profligacy had led them to the brink of the abyss, from which financial control, in some form or other, would ultimately rescue them, after they had sub-

---

[1] The British Corporation of Foreign Bondholders has been concerned in the settlement of debts aggregating over one milliard pounds. Council of the Corporation of Foreign Bondholders, op. cit., p. 537.

F*

mitted to their creditors and were ready to expiate their financial sins.

The Russian Revolution changed all this. Its repudiation of the pre-war private debts, as well as of government obligations, was not a fortuitous instance of bankruptcy due to inability to pay.[1] It was a declaration of independence of the national proletariat against international Capitalism. Russia was a backward colonial country; many of its foreign loans had been development loans; its creditors were not merely capitalists, they were foreigners. To confiscate their income as well as their investments was not an act of piracy for which apologies were due, and which had to be supported by an array of irrefutable statistical figures, from which the incapacity to pay was clearly evident. It was the opening scene of the great liberation of mankind from the shackles of a body-snatching imperialist horde of alien capitalist exploiters. It was, in fact, part of the colonial revolt. The debtors, who had enjoyed the benefit of the creditors' savings, were justified in confiscating them, for they belonged to colonizing nations, who had used them in order to exercise domination over the less advanced parts of mankind. Peasants and tenants had been in revolt against the alien landholders whom the colonizing Powers had planted as garrisons in their midst. Now debtors were rising against the absentee creditors, who had used their claims for sucking the life-blood of the country and wasting it abroad.

Financial colonization has been resumed after the War, without proper consideration of the changes which had taken place. The confiscation of private property during the War and in the peace treaties had shaken the foundations of the

---

[1] The total principal outstanding on January 1, 1917, including railways and municipal loans, was £945,000,000; £800,000,000 external War loans are not comprised in this figure. The total approximate interest in arrears on all public loans amounts to £1,569,123,307. Council of the Corporation of Foreign Bondholders, op. cit., p. 537.

capitalist system. Contracts were no longer inviolate when their preservation seemed inexpedient to governments desirous of alleviating the burdens of their taxpayers. And inflation had shown a way of defaulting by what seemed to be a perfectly legal method.

The technique of bankruptcy and repudiation has been greatly improved by the growing strength of modern governments, who can control the flow of invisible exports and the flight of capital far more efficiently than their most ruthless predecessors had been able to do, and who have developed, in currency manipulation and exchange control, extraordinarily potent instruments for economic coercion.

New loans were granted somewhat indiscriminately; their proceeds were wasted in industry and agriculture, in raising products for which no additional demand existed. Even the reconstruction loans to Hungary, Greece, and Bulgaria, which the League of Nations had sponsored, and which were secured as a kind of international venture, were rather unsound. The actual spending of these moneys provided employment in the debtor countries; it maintained the export of capital goods from the creditor countries; it did not furnish the additional customers needed, who could have purchased the export surplus. Many creditor countries refused admittance to this additional produce, as they had to protect a farming industry which should have been contracted, but which was artificially expanded. Agricultural prices declined and, with them, the debtor countries' purchasing power. They could neither buy the quantities of manufactured goods they had been accustomed to purchase, except by more borrowing, nor pay the interest on their accumulated debts—except by making new debts. For some time, the world's economic equilibrium was maintained by the prolongation of maturing debts and by renewed borrowing. But when internal disturbances had begun to upset the capital markets, the flow of new loans stopped and the purely artificial balance was thoroughly upset. The debtor countries collapsed. Russia's teachings fell on fertile ground. Capitalism had invaded them and loaded them with a heavy debt. It had bought their governments and made them subservient to its own fell purposes. It was developing the same upstart middle class, which was trying to enslave labour, but which had been destroyed in Russia. Freedom could be won by confiscating the principal the capitalists had originally extorted from their own people. Capitalism in these countries represented foreign domination. The repudiation of debts and the non-payment of interest were as efficient methods of revolt as an appeal to arms. Mexico defaulted against the American—and European—capitalists who had sought to enslave the country, by a repudiation of loans, as well as by the invalidation of concessions. Indian revolutionaries announced their intention of repudiating the debts an alien government had imposed upon them. Turkey, Chile, Brazil, Bulgaria, Greece, Hungary, Rumania, Yugoslavia, and many others either repudiated completely by suspending all payments, or defaulted partially by reducing the interest or by discontinuing amortization. In a few instances they issued funding bonds in lieu of payments. Some governments depreciated the value of their bonds by default, and bought them back cheaply. Control by foreign bondholders was of no avail; such supervision, however much needed, offended national pride and furnished a handy patriotic pretext for financial dishonesty.

Even in the Dominions, angry voices demanded the repudiation of foreign obligations held by the London money market (Australia) or insisted on wild financial experiments (Alberta). Ireland deliberately defaulted on the payments due on the loans with which the British Treasury had financed land purchases and the expropriation of the Anglo-Irish landlords.

After Germany had *de facto* been freed of her reparation debts, the Allied countries defaulted on their payments on the inter-Allied debt to the United States. The doctrine that the world is held in chains by a class of mostly foreign moneylenders swept over all continents, and the somewhat primitive forms into which the economic sages of Nazism had condensed it proved far more attractive than the abstruse Marxian formulas.

Other countries fell back on the time-hallowed method of devaluation. Great Britain's example seemed to justify them. When the greatest creditor country of the world had to defraud her foreign creditors, who had confided in the stability of her currency and in her financial honesty, arbitrary devaluation and exchange control, and even fraudulent repudiation, by financially weak debtor states might well be excused. And when some British statesmen and some economic theorists, instead of apologizing for the default, praised it as the most potent instrument of national recovery and as a courageous exercise of fundamental sovereign rights, the case for a debtors' revolt seemed almost won. It was becoming pretty clear that even the creditor countries no longer cared for the sacredness of contracts and the rights of foreign capitalists.

Devaluation may stimulate exports and diminish imports; but it is of little help as far as debts in foreign currency are concerned. In this respect exchange control is very much more effective. Germany imposed very stringent measures of exchange control on all external transactions. When the flow of foreign loans stopped, political panics survened; credits were withdrawn and the entire banking structure collapsed. She gradually developed the most efficient system of currency and debt manipulation that has yet been devised. The repercussions resulting from her partial bankruptcy led to the desertion of stable currencies by Great Britain, and, later on, by the United States.

Devaluation and exchange control enable a country to reduce its foreign debts without an open breach of its international financial engagements—except in those cases where the rights of foreign creditors are protected by a gold clause.

The United States set it aside. Since no government is willing to give up its fundamental right of defrauding its national creditors by doing what it likes with its currency, it cannot very well except from these remedial measures its foreign creditors, who loom as loan sharks in the popular imagination.[1]

Open repudiation relieved the defaulting government and nobody else. Devaluation can enrich all national debtors —who do not owe foreign currency; and exchange control benefits everybody who owes money abroad. Devaluation can be used for domestic purposes too; if internal prices can be raised by some sort of parallel inflation, the burdens of all debtors are reduced at the expense of national creditors. But internal devaluation is not as profitable as external devaluation, since the sufferers, as well as the beneficiaries, are nationals. It is extremely popular during a depression, when the debtors endeavour to adjust their affairs at the expense of banks, mortgage companies, and moneylenders. Devaluation is "collective bankruptcy," from which all national debtors, the state, corporations, and private individuals profit alike, the greatest gainers being those debtors who are quite able to fulfil their obligations, but who are freed from them at the expense of their foreign creditors. They can pocket these profits and express at the same time sincere regret for having to do so.

The downfall of international finance was greeted with hysterical jubilation not only by Nazi philosophers, but by a crowd of sentimentalists who saw in bankruptcy the end of world economy and the passing of a social order which had been based on freedom and contract.[2] The collapse of the gold standard was to them the doom of the "golden International," that greedy band of Shylocks who had

---

[1] In the nineteenth century such preference was frequently given to foreign creditors.

[2] Christopher Hollis, *The Two Nations*. R. McNair Wilson, *The Defeat of Debt*.

fettered the world in chains of gold. The return to it must not be permitted on any account, not even to a country like Great Britain, in whose empire most gold mines were situated. The freedom of the world and the freedom of national planning were at stake. A gold currency signified the rule of Mammon, greedy, mercenary, arbitrary. It represented the relentless economic automatism behind which capitalism could defy constructive social statesmanship. The stability which it had helped to secure was international; the stability needed was national. For this reason nationalists all over the world hailed the breakdown of the gold standard—especially in countries which owned neither gold stocks, nor gold mines, and which saw in it a badge of serfdom. Even the labour movement in England, whose outlook on world affairs was that of sincere internationalists, voiced such views, for they considered it an obstacle to those monetary dodges which were the planners' handiest instruments.

VI

The anti-colonizing sentiment of the age has found its most uncompromising expression in the theories of Nazi Germany, although, unlike Mexico and Ireland, where the forces of counter-colonization have almost succeeded in destroying the work of the colonizing conquerors, Germany has not been a colony. The Treaty of Versailles, however, had placed Germany very much in the position of a tribute-paying dependency. A large part of her territory was held by an army of occupation; she was burdened by way of reparation with an excessive indemnity. She was disarmed, and an army system foreign to her military traditions was forced upon her, which antagonized even those of her people who had objected to conscription before the War. The fulfilment of the treaty obligations laid upon her was closely supervised. Various schemes of financial and economic control were imposed upon her in order to safeguard the claims of her ex-enemy creditors. Her citizens had to go heavily into debt in order to restore their government's liberty; they had to contract private loans abroad, with which it paid off public claims. This conversion of the reparation debt held by foreign governments into private debts held by foreign bankers and investors transformed Germany's political dependence into a kind of economic bondage by Allied and Neutral creditors. To tax-burdened emotional Nationalists, Germany was an enslaved nation held in shackles by Western capitalist Internationalism, very much as Egypt and Turkey had been held. Turkey had freed herself against great odds. Germany should follow her example and get rid of all limitations on her sovereignty, and first of all of her foreign debt. Russia had repudiated public loans, the proceeds of which she had received, and had spent on her internal development. The loans private German citizens had been compelled to contract were development loans too; but they were only the counterpart of reparation exactions, which had denuded Germany of her own capital. Repudiation in her case would be an act of justice—not the wiping out of a financially fair and equitable obligation, but liberation from political extortion. Bankruptcy meant liberty.

Neither repudiation nor devaluation has played a decisive part in Germany's "liberation" policy. She is paying some of her government obligations in full and she is issuing funding loans in lieu of payment on other bonds. As her foreign debts were contracted mainly in foreign currency, she has refrained from devaluation, and in some respects she benefited from the depreciation of other currencies. She has managed to turn the tables on her creditors by a system of exchange control, preventing the transfer of payments received. They are blocked in Germany. Claimants found it more profitable to leave the money in Germany than to face the loss from its conversion into foreign currencies, which might amount to nearly 80 per cent. By exchange control Germany is getting a forced loan from them at very low rates of interest.[1]

The brilliant technique of her capitalist leaders has enabled Germany to break the debt bondage, which Nazism had denounced, in a respectable bourgeois fashion, which does not offend the tender conscience of bankers, whom downright repudiation would have greatly shocked.

VII

Germany's revolt has gone far beyond denunciation of this purely temporary enslavement. For nearly two centuries the German mind had fought a strenuous battle against foreign cultural domination. German classical literature has successfully freed it from French ascendancy. To achieve this it fell back partly on German national traditions by indulging in a romantic Teutonism, but partly too on an imaginary Greece, from which it drew a Hellenism of its own.[2] Greece, not Rome, was to be Germany's cultural teacher, the source of her humanism and the foundation of her science. She loathed Rome, her Empire, her Church, and her law.

German humanism was the exclusive property of the learned professions, the College men ("Akademiker"), who formed a class by themselves, and who chose to consider themselves the leaders of the nation. They were separated from the people by a kind of spiritual barrier, deporting themselves sometimes with a naïve arrogance, which con-

[1] The Dawes Plan had outlined the mechanism of these forced loans. Under its rule the transfer of German payments in foreign currencies had to stop whenever it was unsettling the German currency. But internal payments had to continue until the particular fund into which they were turned amounted to £250 million. It could be invested in certain securities in Germany. Later on Germany applied this principle on a gigantic scale. It blended harmoniously the foresight of her Reparation creditors with the antipathy of the Nazis for paying foreign debts.

[2] E. M. Butler, *The Tyranny of Greece over Germany*. Ernst Robert Curtius, *Deutscher Geist ist in Gefahr*, p. 11 ff.

trasted sharply with their modest ways of living. The people felt rather envious of the intellectual advantages enjoyed by the College men. They delighted in sending one of their sons to the University, so that he might join their illustrious company. But until the advent of a labour movement which gloated over "scientific socialism," they looked upon their learning as something foreign; it had too often served their masters to their disadvantage. Humanism remained an alien element in German life; it was professional, not national or native; it never became part of the entire nation's spiritual outlook. It was grafted on selected fruit trees in sheltered orchards; those standing on farms and in forests could not be innoculated with it. The fusion of classical culture with the national civilization was never as complete as in the Latin countries, and even in England. Whilst innumerable Latin words have been taken over by their languages and have become "national words" in daily intercourse, the Latin words embodied in German are frequently technical terms used by a learned or would-be learned group, sometimes in its professional work, sometimes in an endeavour to differentiate itself from the less-educated strata. The nationalist philologists who attempted to purify the language by eliminating them represented the people's conscious resentment against foreign influences, which sometimes slumbered, but never died.

The humanist conception of life had once been shared by a struggling middle class, who had been willing to accept the leadership of the College men. But ever since political unity had been accomplished by the sword and not by the word, bringing prosperity along with it, their glamour had been waning. The reign of William II saw the rise of the middle class to economic and political power, and the conversion of the nation from dream-surfeited idealism to scientific and commercial realism. The recognition of the technical high school as the equal of the university was an outward sign of this change. Applied science with its definite outlook on practical objects was gaining on humanism with its somewhat indefinite view of life. The War, this complete, though perhaps not convincing, reversal of everything reasonable and human, discounted thought in contrast to action, however futile the latter's results might be. And the advent of democracy, determined to open all careers to talent, irrespective of origin or surroundings, destroyed the privilege of the College men and drove many of them into opposition to the new order.

At the same time, a generation was coming to the front whose schooling had been defective, but whose disillusionment was complete. Its members had not learned how to think; they felt that they were born to the bitterness of defeat and the futility of hope. Reason to them seemed sterile. It had not prevented a disastrous war, nor a dishonourable peace, nor a distressful crisis. They were faced with the very simple, but very hard problem: How to survive, how to get a job. They ascribed their plight to discordant leadership and dishonest governments, behind which invisible alien powers pulled the wires. Liberalism, Socialism, Capitalism were all the same; they were the masks worn by foreign conspirators, or the rigid moulds they were pressing on the German mind, and in which it was suffocating.

The new generation desired to free Germany from all non-German ideas with which cultural intercourse with the rest of the world had infested the German mind. They fell an easy prey to anti-semitism, partly because the presence of an efficient, ethnographically alien element in their midst frightened them, since, according to their biological materialism, it could never be assimilated. And they objected to the Jews as exponents of those Western concepts to which Nazism is most strongly opposed. They were to them the physical embodiment of hated ideas.

But they hate these ideas wherever they meet them. They look upon their struggle as a kind of continuation of the battle in the Teutoburg Forest, where Herman the Cheruscan annihilated the Roman legions. His victory was but transient. Rome triumphed in the end and retained most of her settlements. She imposed her rule, later her Church, and still later her law, on a large part of Germany. Charlemagne perfected and personified the permeation of Germany with the Roman spirit. His victory over the Saxons who refused to renounce the gods of their fathers, and whom he relentlessly massacred, is a national tragedy to the Nazis. They concentrate their hatred on the alien Church, which looked upon Germany as one of her spiritual provinces and disseminated foreign notions and foreign doctrines amongst the people. Her creed of gentleness and neighbourly love must, if accepted, ultimately sap the fighting strength of a martial nation. This alien Church has survived the first great outburst of German national spiritualism, the Reformation. For the Protestant Churches which arose in Germany not only took over many of the spiritual possessions of the Roman enemy in a purified form; their educated representatives eagerly imbibed the new learning, and ever since have steeped their minds in this foreign humanism. From it shallow intellectualism and insipid liberalism originated. The universalism of Jews and of Roman Catholics and the humanism of the Protestant Church represent ideas alien to the German soul, which craves for emotion. They have made Germany subservient to foreign masters, her spirit as well as her body politic. Germany must remain a kind of cultural colony to the West as long as these powers are allowed to preach their heresies. Their teachings must be eradicated completely and, if needs be, they along with it, if Germany is to be free.

VIII

Nazism and Fascism employ similar methods; their conceptions of the art of government resemble each other.

But they start from opposite points of view: Fascism is based on the classical tradition and its universalist outlook on life. Nazism, on the other hand, is a deliberate revolt against classicism, Latinity, and humanism, and everything they stand for, a revolt of the natives who are not spoilt by an alien education, and of the masses who desire to live an emotional cultural life of their own, and who object to donation, as well as to domination, by alien intellectualism.

Its natural enemy is Bolshevism. Soviet Russia supported anti-capitalist nationalist movements in every corner of the world. She is, at the same time, a great colonizing power. She has imported her theories, her technique, and her organization from the West; she is implanting them by force on many of the backward races, the control of which she has inherited from the Czars. Her colonization of Turkestan is perhaps the most efficient instance of coercive economic colonization yet attempted.[1] Whilst denouncing national capitalist Imperialism, she stands for universal communist Imperialism. Bolshevists are fanatic believers in universalism: they hold that their social system can be fitted in anywhere, regardless of space, time, and race. The methods they employ are those familiar to usurpers of all ages, and they defend their application with the equally time-hallowed assertion that the end justifies the means. They differ from other arbitrary governments in imagining that they have gained, by scientific enquiry, their knowledge of the ends to be pursued, while others have to be content with revelations. For this reason they can afford to be "atheists," whilst other usurpers are in need of some sort of personal God, from whom they can receive their inspiration, and from whom they derive the infallibility they lay claim to. Bolshevism may be a false creed, but notwithstanding its very clever emotional trappings, it is a rational creed. It does not despise reason; it claims a monopoly of it. It is a logical, though erroneous, development of earlier liberal philoso-

[1] Rosita Forbes, *Forbidden Road—From Kabul to Samarkand.*

phies, and more fanatically universalist in its outlook than any of them have been.

Nazi Germany, on the other hand, is the foremost exponent of an anti-universalist conception which is emerging in a world rapidly becoming standardized externally by the forces of science and technique. She may be willing to use the instruments of the machine age and profit from their working; she objects to its deadly levelling influences on the human soul. She hates Bolshevism for glorifying this dumb and dull egalitarianism and for advocating a new fanatic creed of universalism. She popularizes this antagonism by pretending to see in Bolshevism nothing but a nefarious conspiracy to get control of the world, organized by Jews, Freemasons, Roman Catholics, and international gangsters. The Nazis loathe all forms of internationalism; even Rotary, this harmless plaything of self-appointed would-be world-saving Babbitts, had to relinquish Germany!

The central motive of Germany's attitude may be emotional nationalism, but it is strongly reinforced by a fear of world domination by non-Nordic types of civilization. It does not want to impress its own superior culture on other nations, though it advocates and employs coercive methods. It denies the possibility of grafting it successfully on other, less-favoured, races. The Jews may have picked up some of its external trappings; they are quite incapable of ever really understanding it. The Nazis bitterly resent that some of mankind's masterpieces are attributed by a blind and unregenerate world to Jews, and, worst of all, to German Jews. Civilization and culture cannot be taught or learned; they must be inherited. This being so, colonization is really a futile endeavour. A strong nation in need of expansion may wrest contiguous lands from weak neighbours and drive them away so as to find room for its own sons and daughters, the representatives of a higher civilization. But this cannot be done in those overseas countries where the white race depends on native labour. Continental expansion followed by extirpation may be a wise policy for a strong nation; colonization in order to impart one's own civilization to backward peoples is senseless. It can only endanger the purity of the master race.

Nazi philosophy glorifies force, the means by which empires have been won and have been held. But the objects of its policy are anti-universal and anti-imperialist. The German demand for colonies, however sincere it may be, is not based on this philosophy. It signifies much more a craving for equality with other imperial powers than a desire for a colonial empire. It betrays its emotional, non-intellectual origin by overlooking the essential fact that equality—beyond purely formal equality of status—is a thoroughly universalist conception. National equality can neither be measured nor accomplished without universally valid standards of comparison.

The Nazi claim, that all ethnical Germans who live under foreign governments owe allegiance to the Third Reich, irrespective of the origin of their settlement or the treatment they receive at the hand of their rulers, is a thrust at the main principle of empire. It clearly shows that empire breaking rather than empire making is their line. If this demand were to meet with a favourable response from these German fragments, not only those empires and composite states who hold their German population by force would have to face disintegration; it might menace even the Swiss Confederation. And the Germans in foreign states who want to join the motherland could not do so without breaking their framework—since mass repatriation by exchange of population is scarcely a practical policy. Where their settlements are contiguous to Germany more or less violent secession might accomplish their object. Where they are separated by alien populations they must either expel them or rule them.

A reunion of all ethnical Germans would create a mighty super-state, possessing the strength of an empire. It would not be merely united but unified, since in the totalitarian State federative elements are bound to disappear. The "composite" note, the most distinctive feature of empire, would be absent. This vastly expanded, thoroughly centralized and uniformed Third Reich would be very different from the multi-coloured Holy Roman Empire of the German nation. It would be something separate and permanently apart from the rest of the world, free from and inaccessible to foreign influences, a mighty bulwark against all tendencies to universalism.

Western civilization had deeply impressed the rest of the world in the days before the War. Nationalism had been waxing strong, and nationalities had mutually exclusive aspirations. But Western civilization, as such, was universal; it was the only civilization worth having. When the Eastern nations strove for equality, they insisted on the adoption of fundamental Western institutions. All this is changing. The nations of the European West no longer represent the one and indivisible type of Western civilization. Democracies are opposed to dictatorships. Capitalism, Collectivism, and barrack-room Socialism confront one another. Christianity is no longer dominant; it has to fight Atheism in Russia, Tribal Monotheism in Germany, and Indifferentism in even larger parts of the world. Western technique is the only thing which the various cultural, political, and economic types have in common. The film and the broadcast are universal, however national their producers or their beams may be. The makers of guns, aircraft, ammunition, and poison gas represent the only type of enterprise which all the nations of the world are eager to undertake—outside the spiritual island on which Gandhi desires to shelter India from the din of the Western world. Technique apart, neither Turks nor Persians nor Japanese see anything in the Western world they wish to take over or to imitate. The great wave of cultural enthusiasm for Western ways which had swept over the world in the wake of Western colonization seems to have spent its strength for the time being.

CHAPTER VI

AUTARCHY

I

THE tendency toward autarchic nationalism was originally a mighty solvent in the process of the disintegration of world economics. The early advocates of autarchy were opposed to colonial empires and objected to international trade; both were built on force, and both were causing wars and everlasting friction. Complete economic isolation was to ensure peace by breaking up particular national empires, as well as the international trade empire. It does not work in this way at present. It has maintained its pacifist note to some degree, but it is, on the other hand, a pace-maker of economic militarism.

The fear of war and of international friction is driving some of the world's great empires towards a policy of isolation. Two continental empires, Russia and the United States, have taken the lead; their attempts have been favoured by their huge expanse, their infinite resources, and their relatively sparse population.

A sort of economic isolation was forced upon Russia. She wanted to be independent of the technically advanced capitalist countries which she regarded as her sworn enemies, and she desired at the same time to strengthen the collective system, which had to be planned and managed centrally. Isolation favours structural as well as functional planning. More or less far-reaching economic separation is an essential prerequisite for keeping the internal price level independent of external prices, though it may communicate with them at some carefully selected government-controlled intersections. As long as the West is not organized on a collectivist base, points of contact with it must be few. And as the natural resources of Russia are ample, she can do without intensive foreign intercourse, though the accumulation of capital at home has been rather difficult, and its relatively narrow limits may retard a quick rise in national standards of comfort.

The United States are adopting a similar attitude, though for rather different reasons. They had been minimizing their political contacts with the non-American world in order to avoid the moral contamination of the defective European political system. But they wished to sell their surplus agricultural commodities and some particular manufactured specialities, the result of mass production, to oversea consumers. They had repatriated their bonds during the war and had become a creditor country, but they refused to accept return payments in goods, as they would not discard their traditional protectionist policy. By lending and relending to Europe and to South America, they had squared the vicious circle temporarily. They merely increased the total outstanding and postponed a final settlement to a future date. Their debtors' bankruptcy disposed of the issue more or less definitely; it scaled down interest claims and wiped out a large part of the capital.

American investors had been accustomed to domestic defaults on a gigantic scale; their European creditors had frequently been involved in them. But the almost universal repudiation of their foreign debtors shook their faith in world economic solidarity. Though their defective lending methods had been one of the major causes of the collapse of the European credit structure, they saw in it but another proof of Europe's innate wickedness and untrustworthiness, and they wished to withdraw permanently from this vicious connection.

A creditor country looking forward to the regular payment of its claims cannot easily retire into its shell; a complete withdrawal from a wicked world does not involve much heroic self-abnegation when most of them are invalidated anyhow. Bankruptcy shocked a good many would-be internationalists; they became passionate isolationists and stiffened the old-established national protectionist front, which received, at the same time, a kind of spiritual blessing from those enemies of vested interests who wanted to curb the iniquities of the capitalist system by central planning. To plan successfully, the national price-level must be isolated; to isolate it successfully, planning must be resorted to. Planning of imports is fairly easy; tariffs, quota restrictions, and prohibitions universally used by protectionists represent a sort of planless planning. But the scrapping of regular export surpluses which can no longer be paid for by foreign customers must be arranged for by a centralized agency, which has to adjust existing production capacities to home demands. Redundant cotton-fields and superfluous copper-mines cannot be suddenly transformed into rubber plantations or sheep-runs; they may have to be scrapped. Russia's general deficiency in production capacity had to be met by a schedule of preference for her various industries. A wealthy capitalist country, like the United States, has to establish a schedule for scrapping the excess capacity of its various plants, when it wants to withdraw from international markets.

The trend towards autarchy in the United States has lately been strengthened by a new conception of neutrality. For over a century the U.S.A. have insisted on the doctrine of the free seas, which subordinated the rights of the belligerents to those of the peace-loving neutrals. They were not able to enforce it in the Great War against the Allies as well as against the Central Powers. Public opinion has lately persuaded itself that this absence of equality, which made them furnish huge quantities of war material to the Allies, was the main cause which forced them into the war. In order to avoid the recurrence of similar events, the U.S.A. have been overhauling their neutrality policy and, in doing so, are completely reversing it.[1] They now no longer intend

[1] Walter Millis, *Road to War*, Boston and London, 1935. Allen W. Dulles and Hamilton Fish Armstrong, *Can We be Neutral?* New York, 1936. Charles Seymour, *American Neutrality*, 1914–17, New Haven, 1935.

to furnish armaments and war materials to any belligerent. They are even doubtful whether commerce in raw materials and foodstuffs can continue, since belligerents might stretch the concept of contraband very widely. The chief duty of the American Government is to keep the nation out of war; it must not give umbrage to belligerents, nor allow its citizens, who wish to continue a lucrative business, to embroil it with them. Peace comes before profits. The maximum they may concede is the continuation of a normal volume of a regular peace trade. And even in this case, the belligerents must fetch goods in non-American ships at their own risk in United States' harbours and pay cash for them —all forms of credit being taboo.

This new conception of neutrality, based on the duties of neutrals, not on their rights, foreshadows a more or less complete withdrawal of the United States from international trade in time of war. And the prospect of such a policy must greatly affect international economic relations in time of peace. No foreign nation can afford any longer to depend on regular supplies from the United States, if their outflow must cease automatically at the outbreak of war. Nor can the industries of the United States go on producing for foreign markets without grave misgivings, since a declaration of war will close them immediately. A policy of cutting off supplies in time of war involves a policy of shutting them down in time of peace, on the side of importers as well as of exporters. The sea is no longer the world's great neutral highway, which must be kept open against the belligerent Powers—it is a no man's land, which the navies of the belligerents can raid, and from which neutral flags and neutral shipping must disappear.

To make matters worse the United States might impose their conception of neutrality on the Latin-American States. The Latin-American Republics have been, in some ways, the world's great bulwark against inter-imperial autarchy. They have little desire to become self-sufficient and to break

the close economic relations with their customers and
creditors, who take their produce in payment for loans and
in return for manufactured goods, and who will provide
them one of these days with additional capital. They have
gone in for some industrialization, but they do not want to
sacrifice their foreign markets. Nor do the great empires
really desire to break with their Latin-American connections, however much they may favour their own partners
and dependants. They are fostering their own resources at
home, in the Dominions, and in the colonies, but they do
not wish to cut themselves off completely from those centres
of supplies and enterprises which their capital has developed.
They do not mean to give up markets which are at least as
recuperative as their own dependencies, and whose extension may be looked for in the future, when their huge hinter-
land areas will be opened up. Otherwise these republics,
whose independence is no longer menaced by foreign powers,
might become the complementary partners of those European countries which have no dominions or dependencies of
their own, and furnish foodstuffs and raw materials to them.

The foreign policy of the United States would scarcely
favour this development. They would resent any preferential
dealings between an American republic and a European
state, whatever its objects or its basis. They disregard racial,
historic, and economic distinctions and envisage a future,
rather vague, federation of American republics. They assume
a spiritual unity amongst its would-be members, which
scarcely exists. Their constitutions may be more or less
faithful copies of the American original; their politics frequently savour of a rather primitive Fascism. Their adoption
of the new American neutrality policy would close the door
to any inter-continental rapprochement. It would eliminate
the Americas, with the exception of Canada, some West
Indian Islands, and some other colonial remnants, from
economic co-operation in time of peace, as it would be
withdrawn immediately at the outbreak of war.

Since the adoption of protective tariffs, the conclusion of the Ottawa Agreements and the inauguration of the British agricultural quota system, the United Kingdom has been turning towards a policy of inter-imperial isolation. The preferential system agreed upon between the metropolis and the politically independent Dominions liberated the contracting parties from the most-favoured-nation clause, which so far had governed the commercial relations between most independent states. The quota system for agricultural produce is upsetting the division of labour between agricultural Dominions and the industrial metropolis, hitherto in existence; it is reducing the outflow from other (independent) agricultural countries; they must either shift their exports to other markets or reduce their agricultural output and turn towards premature industrialization.

In days gone by, England was willing to pay for the unhampered political control of her far-flung possessions by the grant of free trade with them to her less fortunate rivals. They tolerated her political monopoly, for it guaranteed equality of opportunity to the rest of the world. Her will and her strength to keep intact her political empire may be waning, but her desire to exploit its economic possibilities exclusively is increasing. Her present-day commercial policy is a jumble of more or less fortuitous disconnected measures which are not controlled by a single central conception. And so is her monetary policy. The United Kingdom did not desert the gold standard because she had persuaded herself of the virtues of a manipulated currency. She did not deliberately abandon it—she slipped from it inadvertently, as the result of a series of actions and inactions, few of them purposeful.

But devaluation presented its devotees the great opportunity for managing the internal price level independently, regardless of international relations, as the fullest expression of national economic sovereignty. A government might be allowed to limit its sovereignty by membership of

the League of Nations, by pacts and by disarmament agreements directed towards collective security in the political
field, but it should not be permitted to sacrifice its economic
sovereignty by concluding a pact of economic security. It
must refuse a return to the gold standard or international
stabilization agreements, and insist on maintaining an
absolutely free hand in monetary matters for obtaining
purely egotistical national objectives. Currency manipulation is the most powerful weapon of economic isolation and
centralized planning.[1]

II

The Powers who control dependencies of some sort, or who
possess adequate undeveloped territorial resources within
their frontiers, might shift their demands for American
products to them and endeavour to become more self-
sufficient than they otherwise might have been. Those who
do not own such possessions would try and acquire them.
The old avenues to colonies are closed; they can only be
taken from those *beati possidentes* who, in the views of the less-
favoured nations, hold more than a fair share. This means
war, or warlike pressure, for few colonies can be obtained
by peaceful change. And such wars would not be colonial
wars; they would be decided on the battlefields of the world.

In some ways, they would be futile wars. The value of
colonies to their metropolis is far smaller to-day than it was
in days gone by. The production of independent republics
and dominions and the spread of substitutes are detracting
from it considerably. The limits set to ruthless exploitation
by the growth of a humanitarian anti-imperialist spirit in
the metropolis, and the difficulties in holding colonies in

---

[1] The political theory of currency manipulation as an instrument of
economic nationalism is of German origin. Its grandfathers were Fichte
and the German romanticist, Adam Müller. Professor Knapp made an
admirably reasoned system of it, partially inspired by them. His work,
The State Theory of Money, has been made accessible to the English
reader by the mediation of Mr. J. M. Keynes.

face of the counter-colonization movements are reducing their importance in imperial as well as in international economics. Colonies could never become paying concerns either to the State or to the business men of the country winning them, were they to be charged with the expenditure for a great war.

But colonial problems have never been viewed from this angle only, though the lure of profits has loomed large in men's eyes; they have always played an integral part in the great game of politics, which has never been run under business rules. Politics and wars—at least great wars—have never been conducted as mere profit-yielding enterprises; they caused those huge mal-investments, the national debts, from which peoples seek relief in various forms of bankruptcy.

The philosophy of life of a disgruntled nation is rarely business-like—they despise the attitude of a nation of shop-keepers who build empires for profit; they cannot be expected to take a sober commercial view of a situation which is mainly political and emotional. The withdrawal of neutral reserves from the economic life of the world—as implied in American neutrality policies—would compel them either to aspire to territorial extension regardless of risks, costs, or profits, or to organize their lives on the principles of autarchy within comparatively narrow territorial limits.

The great world empires and, on a smaller scale, some minor colonial empires, might be able to organize a régime of autarchy, without too heavy a charge to their citizens. The sacrifice of economic liberty would be considerable, for adjustments could not be accomplished without centralized planning. Mistakes would be made and serious losses would have to be met. But the ideal of an abundant life need not be given up. The attempt might well be worth while. Trade friction would disappear; territorial claims would be abated. The spectre of foreign wars would vanish and with it the necessity for maintaining powerful navies to keep open the sea lanes in time of war. Armaments could be dispensed with and with them the necessity for organizing the nation's economic forces for such an emergency, a task which might entail an equal amount of planning—though of a less satisfactory type. And if there were war, somewhere neutrals could easily remain neutral—as nobody could interfere with their non-existing trade and nobody could look to them for economic and financial support. Emigration would come to a standstill and with it immigration. No new racial conflicts, the result of such migrations, would arise, and when the older immigrants had died off and their children were assimilated, composite nations would become homogeneous. International lending would cease and with it the attempts to "enslave" foreign communities by putting them in financial bondage. Debtors could free themselves of their obligations without resorting to repudiation, for the creditor nations themselves would insist on cancelling their obligations, which must be settled by importing goods or services. Currencies could be manipulated regardless of foreign exchange; price levels could be raised or lowered internally whenever the position of a particular group needed an adjustment. And as these empires are in possession of unused, or undeveloped natural resources, growth and internal expansion could go on rapidly. Planning and coercion might not be too high a price to pay for peace and progress, if they could but be had on these terms.

They cannot. Only contiguous autarchy could provide all the blessings of peace; disconnected autarchy, the autarchy within an empire whose component parts are separated by the sea, cannot secure them. For autarchy of this type is rather brittle. Federation, as such, does not prevent the shifting of economic strength from one member-state to another. Such changes are accepted with equanimity in a continental empire like the U.S.A. But in an insular empire, like the British Empire, the partners fight one another with economic weapons; they do not even refrain from threats of secession. Their trade with one another must remain a sea-borne trade; it will be subject to the vicissitudes of naval warfare. A thoroughly self-sufficient insular empire could not scrap its navies as long as the dependence of its members on sea-borne trade might incite attacks from less fortunate nations. They really pursue two antagonistic types of autarchy: the autarchy of a composite empire, which implies some sort of imperial federation, and the autarchy of each of the component parts, which necessitates imperial disintegration. The latter type may ultimately develop in the British Empire. In other colonial empires the colonial base is not broad enough. The Belgian Congo, or even the Netherland Indies, cannot aspire to economic self-sufficiency—without sacrificing completely the amenities of so-called progress. They might separate from the empire. They could not set up by themselves.

III

The less-favoured nations will have to move towards a similar goal—the German four-year plan is sufficient evidence. The retrocession of a few colonies would scarcely stop them. For the territories which will be handed over or retroceded to them by peaceful negotiations will not be able to satisfy their wants. They could not make them secure: insular possessions scattered over the oceans cannot provide the strategical self-sufficiency which a continental Power like Germany is in need of. Japan and Italy might hope to control the communications within their insular or quasi-insular empires, since they are far closer to them than any possible enemy. Germany cannot do this. The menace of dependence on foreign supplies, the seriousness of which the Great War has shown, will drive her towards continental isolation rather than towards inter-imperial isolation.

The road to self-sufficiency for less-favoured states who possess no very diversified natural resources, few distinct economic advantages, and no undeveloped spaces for pursuing peaceful internal expansion, is very arduous. Science will come to their aid, and, if prices can be kept high enough, many substitutes may ultimately become commercially successful. But this will cause a considerable rise in the cost of living.

With the disappearance of foreign trade the necessity for considering competitive costs will disappear. As long as the nation can get all the materials needed by it, the price to be paid for them does not matter. It can make good the loss on some commodities by producing others advantageously. It can spread the extra costs over the community. But life will become more expensive than in other, more fortunate states. The nation will have to undergo regimentation on a much larger scale than its neighbours, with whom planning, restricted to production, may be merely corrective. In the case of the poorer nations, planning must begin with consumption, which must be standardized and rationed. Comforts must be curtailed, luxuries must be forbidden. A régime of war economy will envelop the nation's entire life. As goods no longer obtainable abroad will have to be raised under unfavourable conditions, their consumption will be reduced. A relaxation of the tension might be looked for by and by, when navies and other armaments can be scrapped—the former because economic intercourse with other nations need no longer be protected by an up-to-date navy; the latter because saturated states are not likely to disturb the peace.

But this pleasant state of affairs will scarcely ever come to pass. To dissatisfied countries the refusal of colonies and the denial of trade facilities on the part of the great empires does not appear as a movement towards peace, but as an act of war. The withdrawal of the *beati possidentes* from the markets of the world, in order to avoid strife and friction, is to them a deliberate attempt at starving those inconvenient rivals who dare to register claims of their own. Tariffs and other economic policies which make for isolation appear to them as sanctions, the pressure of which is meant to bring them to their knees. They must encounter this veiled blockade by isolating themselves too, and they can only do this by reducing their standards of living, by improving their organization, and by placing the entire nation on some sort of war footing.

The economic isolation of the rich empires would condemn the poorer states permanently to comparative poverty. Their efforts to increase their man-power in order to be politically safe may even lower the vitality of the race: permanent scarcity must either reduce fecundity or affect the physical stamina of a population growing under unfavourable circumstances. They cannot hope to make up for the vast differences in natural opportunities by better organization and by more inventive genius. For organization and invention will not be localized unless intellectual intercourse is completely stopped. And wealthy governments are scarcely likely to take this step, as long as they have to arm. The isolation of the rich implies the isolation of the poor; it will in its turn perpetuate the glaring inequalities under which they chafe. The excluded nations will not stand it. Even if they were met by a united front on the part of the rich nations, they might run the risk. For they see in economic isolation an effort at strangulation and they will fight rather than suffer it. They will not accept the position of permanent inferiority without a last effort.

PART III

EMPIRE MAKING OR EMPIRE BREAKING?

CHAPTER I

INEQUALITY

I

COLONIZATION might have diminished the inequality in extent, strength, and resources which many countries resented. It did nothing of the sort. It raised some and lowered others. It added new problems of its own. Daughter states have matured quickly and demanded self-government; native dependencies under European control have followed their example, though hardly any of them have yet completed this course, for they have, so to speak, been shoved off their lines of development by the might of the conqueror and forced into uncongenial ways.

The peace settlement heralded the end of aggressive expansion. "The day of conquest and aggrandizement has gone by," President Wilson had declared. In future, colonization was to be inadmissible. The administration of existing colonies might continue, though the interests of the subject people must be given equal weight with those of their masters. A new world order was to rise; it was to be based on the equality of all states, advanced and backward alike. All people with well-defined national aspirations should enjoy full sovereignty and join as equals a League comprising all nations.

Vassal states of all sorts, whose governments are controlled by other governments, were not represented in the League. They do not enjoy full sovereignty; the moral right of a nation to its own ways of living does not furnish it, and without sovereignty equality cannot be claimed.[1]

[1] When slavery was a recognized legal institution, equality between master and slave could not exist, though in the eyes of the Divine Ruler a white and a black soul were of the same make. For this reason, theologians have questioned whether coloured slaves could have a soul and have frequently decided they could not. The part of the soul in the relations of men is taken by sovereignty in the relations of states.

The Covenant looked upon dependence as a purely temporary stage in a nation's development. Its originators started from the assertion of the Declaration of Independence that men are created equal. They saw no reason why subject states and nationalities should not mature and be able to assume full statehood by and by. The creation of A and B Mandates laid down the lines for this development. Some of these mandated states have taken or are taking up full statehood by becoming sovereign members of the League, for instance Iraq and Syria. If the League should survive, the day may come when the Philippine Islands, having won complete independence, might choose to become a member and add to the material protection of the United States the formal protection of the Covenant.

In spite of these developments, the number of dependent states is still considerable. The entire African continent, as well as its islands, consists of dependencies, with the exception of the Union of South Africa, Liberia, and Egypt. The West Indian Islands are dependencies, apart from Cuba, Haiti, and San Domingo; so are Burma, Indo-China, and the islands in Australasia. Even if the settlements which have not yet reached Dominion rank are not considered "dependencies"—Southern Rhodesia, for example—the number, size, and population of vassal states in all stages of development is considerable. "Equality of status" does not exist for them, and cannot exist, until they have freed themselves from the control of a dominant power. An undertone, a kind of whisper, of their future emancipation is audible in Wilson's Fourteen Points. For the President, who had an almost mystical faith in the principles of the Declaration of Independence, was looking forward to the day when the Monroe Doctrine could be applied to all colonial possessions and when all nations would be free and equal.

II

The hierarchy of states is tripartite: some governments are subject to the will of another government, some are free, and others control the will of dependent governments:

DIVISION OF STATES

	Subject States (including British India and Ethiopia)	Free States	Ruling States (including China, ruling Mongolia, and Egypt, part ruler of Sudan)
Area (million sq. km.) ..	35	40	50
Population (million) ..	600	350	1,000
Imports (millions $ gold)..	1,500	3,700	7,000
Exports (millions $ gold)..	1,600	4,200	5,700

This hierarchy of states almost reflects the stratification of society into lower, middle, and upper class.

The distinction between ruling and ruled states does not cover all nuances of inequality. The Great Powers once formed the Concert of Europe; their claims have survived in the Covenant; they are, so to speak, born to a seat on the Council, whilst the minor states are only represented on it.

Not all ruling states are Great Powers. Some of the most successful colonizing Powers such as Holland, Portugal, and Belgium, do not aspire to this rank. Germany, on the other hand, is a Great Power though she owns no colonies. The weight and the wealth of the former states would be greatly diminished by the loss of their colonies, whilst Germany's position might be improved by the return of her lost dependencies. Neither loss nor gain, nor the combination of both, would establish equality between them. Great Britain might cease to be a Great Power, were the Dominions to separate from the Empire and the colonies to revolt. But Belgium would scarcely become a Great Power, even if the Central

G*

African possessions of all European countries were handed over to her. The United States would not be deprived of much strength if Hawaii and Porto Rico became independent, and Australia would not lose her status as a Dominion by returning New Guinea to Germany. Modern colonies may be attributes of great power; they are not its source. The demand for "equal status" in the colonial field is political rather than material.

Subject states no doubt sincerely believe in a doctrine of absolute equality of status all round. They desire to get rid of foreign control and become independent. Equality of status is to them the recognition of their claims to national sovereignty. Independent states which insist upon their right to become ruling states claim an equality of status which is exclusive rather than inclusive. They are not asking the other ruling states to abandon their privilege of domination, to liberate the subject nations and to found a society of free and equal nations, which should embrace all states. They do not want to abolish privilege. They wish to share it.

III

Inequality of status and restrictions on full sovereignty are not limited to governments representing backward civilizations. The Statute of Westminster has given the great Dominions complete equality with the mother-country, after their membership of the League of Nations had established their sovereign position; but this newly acquired partnership may imply a kind of diminished sovereignty for each of the self-governing members of the Empire. It certainly does so for the United Kingdom, which can no longer impose its own decisions on its partners, and is hampered by doubts of non-co-operation on their part. The full sovereignty of a federation is vested in its joint collective body, not in its member states. The partners in the Empire are approaching the position of the forty-eight states federated in the United States, each of which is the equal of all the others. But not one of them as a separate unit can claim the status of the negro republic of Haiti in the international field, which enjoys full sovereign rights and is the equal of any other member of the League.

Some native states are under the protectorate of a ruling state, which controls their foreign relations and may even supervise part of their administration. This has been the relation of Egypt to the United Kingdom, which claimed, when renouncing the protectorate, the right to watch over the security of imperial communications, defence against foreign intervention, direct or indirect, and the protection of foreign interests. As long as this claim was maintained, the non-admittance of Egypt to the League of Nations was justified, though self-determination in her case went very much farther than in that of Newfoundland or India.

Other countries have been subject to financial control by foreign creditors, who supervised or even administered the collection of certain revenues, which were pledged as securities for loans. These restrictions of financial autonomy were usually arranged by voluntary agreements, which emanated from the exercise of the controlled state's uncontested unlimited sovereignty. As a matter of fact, they have frequently been instrumental in preserving a country's political independence and maintaining its international status. The several statutes for the protection of the non-Turkish populations, imposed upon Turkey, were designed in such a way as to safeguard the self-respect of the Porte and to maintain her status as an independent power. While such arrangements, financial and otherwise, limit the liberty of action of the governments subjected to them and reduce their political standing below that of other governments, they do not deprive them of legal equality in international affairs. Neither Greece nor China was refused admission to the League of Nations on account of the continuation of some sort of control over its finances. And when financial supervision was imposed upon Germany, Austria, and Hungary, in order to safeguard the claims of their foreign creditors, especially those of the Allied governments, these patent infringements of national financial autonomy were not intended in any way to affect the formal equal status of the countries concerned. Austria especially has been a kind of ward of the League. Her sovereignty is diminished by the clauses of the Peace treaties which forbid her union with Germany. But neither this limitation nor the financial control exercised over her has deprived her of her status as a member of the League. The payment of an indemnity is no doubt a sign of temporary political inferiority, otherwise no country would submit to it and tax its own subjects for the benefit of alien, ex-enemy taxpayers—it is a payment for which the nation receives nothing better than an ignominious peace. The people who are made to pay this debt may see in it the badge of slavery; it not only reduces their standard of living in favour of that of their triumphant masters, but it is a visible sign of political bondage and inequality. But it does not detract from their status of legal equality. On the other hand, a tribute paid by a dependency to its masters implies the recognition of vassalage and of an inferior legal as well as political status; it is frequently exacted as a recognition of such inferiority. From an economic point of view, a tribute does not differ from an indemnity.

All purely one-sided limitations imposed upon the action of an otherwise sovereign or independent government detract from its equality. It does not matter very much whether they are based on a voluntary unilateral act, whether they are the result of free negotiation, or whether they are imposed upon an unwilling partner to a treaty by overwhelming force. The capitulations granted to the European Powers in Oriental states and the clauses in several treaties which guarantee the protection of minorities in certain Western countries, reduce the status of the states bound by them, as long as similar restrictions in favour of their nationals are not reciprocally imposed upon their contracting partners. The application of legal exemptions to countries where individual foreigners and compact permanent minorities enjoy the same civil rights as the natives would scarcely be justified. Since these conditions no longer prevail in many parts of the world, formal equality may have to be secured by a universal system of protection for minorities; though minorities might not profit very much by it in countries where the citizens themselves no longer possess clearly defined rights which their governments are willing to respect.

Disqualifications and inequalities have been frequent enough in the political field. The military clauses of the Treaty of Versailles are but the best-known instance. The obligations binding Turkey not to fortify the Straits and Germany not to fortify Heligoland were of the same type as the imposition on Holland not to close the Scheldt or Russia's earlier undertakings not to fortify the Åland Islands and not to maintain a navy on the Black Sea (1856). A quaint formalism sometimes camouflages these problems: the occupation of Gibraltar by the British is not an infringement of Spanish sovereignty, but if the Rock were to be returned to Spain on condition that she would not fortify it, her sovereignty would undoubtedly be impaired.

Privilege as well as discrimination may sometimes detract from equality of status. The neutrality guaranteed to Belgium in 1839 by the five Powers was supposed to incapacitate her government from concluding a commercial treaty with France, which would have involved a customs union, though it did not prevent her from acquiring a colony later on.[1] Doubts were entertained whether Switzerland's neutrality allowed her government to apply sanctions against Italy decided upon by the League. Even a purely one-sided political declaration like the Monroe Doctrine, which has no legally binding force, is affecting equality.

[1] November 18, 1842. *Memoirs of the Life of Henry Reeve*, vol.i,pp. 158-9.

Under its rule, none of the European countries can interfere in the affairs of Latin America. They are not only
prevented from colonization on the American continent,
a prohibition which is justified by its present social development, but they cannot have any political dealings with
any of these states, either in peace or in war, without the
consent of the United States. The United States exercise a
de facto protectorate over all Latin-American nations in
relation to the rest of the world. It is not recognized as
such by the non-American Powers nor by the Latin-
American states themselves, who are "sovereign"; it is not
even claimed any longer by the United States Government.
But if Haiti were to form a customs union with Denmark,
or if Venezuela should attempt to federate with Spain, the
United States would be sure to interfere. The Monroe
Doctrine imposes a partial inequality not only on the Latin-
American states themselves, but on Europe as well, a state
of affairs which has by now assumed a quasi-legal character.
The will of the United States is the "fiat" on the American
continent. The clauses in the Peace Treaties forbidding
union between Austria and Germany diminish explicitly the
sovereign status of these countries; the Monroe Doctrine
does so implicitly in the case of Latin America.

IV

The line of demarcation between ruling and dependent
states frequently reveals deep-seated factual, physical and
spiritual discrepancies. The ethnical elements which com-
pose the ruling nations of the world differ from those which
form the nations subject to their sway. They are naturally
more advanced in their own particular type of civilization
which, as long as they are in the ascendant, is recognized
as the dominant civilization. Most of them are "old" nations,
whilst the nations formed by offshoots from the mother
country, or conquered and ruled by it, are "young." These

terms are of little value from a biological point of view.[1] Undoubtedly, a long-established civilization may actually decay and die out by the non-reproduction of its members; in most Western countries, Germany included, reproduction rates are below unity; a process of social contraction is well under way, which might end in complete extinction, unless other factors, such as migration, upset the doleful harmony of mathematical forecasts. So far, however, race extinction, as an actual physical process, has been observed only among primitive peoples, who have lost heart when brought in contact with a superior civilization.

From an economic point of view, this distinction is simple and useful. Societies in which the modern capitalist system has been long established, and which have been instrumental in spreading it to other societies are "old." Those which have not yet developed it or are only just beginning to take it over are "young." The rate of industrialization—the percentage of the national population engaged in manufacturing processes—is a useful index of a modern nation's technical and economic development.

The direct offshoots of the old European countries, the dependent, quasi-dependent, and independent daughter states planted by them, are as highly capitalistic as their mother countries. The United States are probably the most capitalistic country of the world, though the pre-capitalist streaks interwoven in their social structure are frequently overlooked. Such countries are old in respect of their social structure and of the national elements they took over from the metropolis, but they are *undeveloped*. Their population is scanty in relation to the natural resources available. They are young in so far as their social system has not yet had time to exploit all opportunities; they are

[1] The late-comers in the colonial field (Germany and Italy) frequently designate themselves as young nations, the proof of their youth being their high (?) birth-rates; at other times they base their claim on a recognition of their achievement as builders of earlier empires.

old in so far as it is completely developed. A country such as Russia is young in both ways. Her natural resources are far less developed than those of Australia or America; and so is the industrial system which is being organized for their exploitation.

V

Some of the smaller, highly civilized, independent states, Switzerland and Denmark for instance, cover an area of between 41,000 and 43,000 square kilometres each; the U.S.S.R. in Europe and Asia, on the other hand, extends over 21,000,000 square kilometres. These huge discrepancies do not disappear when lands capable of production are compared. The United States hold 1,400,000 square kilometres of such land and Denmark 27,000. Denmark and Austria have a similar density of population (83·6 and 80·4 per square kilometre) and a similar structure of population (34·8 and 31·9 per cent respectively being engaged in agriculture); but in the former 60·8 per cent of the total area is arable as against 23·2 per cent in the latter; the percentage of forests and lands not used for agriculture and pasture is 28·8 in the former and 49·4 in the latter.[1] A comparison of some of the raw materials which indicate the natural resources of the several nations makes these discrepancies even more glaring. South Africa produces 47 per cent of the world's gold, Canada 13 per cent, Russia 11 per cent, and the United States 10 per cent; France supplies 27 per cent of the world's iron ores, the United States 21 per cent, and Russia 18 per cent; 34 per cent of the world's coal output comes from the United States, 20 per cent from Great Britain, and 12 per cent from Germany.[2] These visible inequalities by no means tell the whole story. The actual flow of production does not correspond to national reserves. The total reserves of mineral resources may be much more

[1] Carr-Saunders, op. cit., p. 141.
[2] Chatham House, *Raw Materials and Colonies*, p. 22.

important than to-day's output and may ultimately decide the future weight of various countries in world economics. The United States are self-supporting or surplus producers for twelve out of thirty-five important raw materials; Germany is a surplus producer for only two, coal and potash—she has to rely on imports for thirty-three. Japan is self-supporting in three and has a surplus in two commodities, Italy has a surplus in four and is self-sufficient in four. Russia, the United States, and the British Empire are more or less self-sufficient in what have been called "war necessities."[1] The United States and the British Empire combined possess within their territory two-thirds and control three-quarters of the world's mineral reserves.[2]

Geographical situation and climatic conditions complicate matters. The benefits of water-borne traffic are not as great as they were in the days before railways and cars. Men and goods can move to-day over continental areas, irrespective of distance and climate. But the value of natural ports has not vanished; Hungary, Austria, Switzerland, Czecho-slovakia, Afghanistan, and Bolivia, all of which lack access to the sea, are greatly handicapped. They can have mercantile navies of their own—there is no reason why the citizens of a country can hold shares in foreign shipping companies and perhaps control them, and should not be allowed to own ships directly; two Swiss-owned ships are actually crossing the ocean to-day. But the handling of these ships in foreign ports depends on foreign territorial regulations. The demand for access to the sea has been one of the main motives for territorial changes. Poland's desire to become a maritime nation is responsible for the Corridor problem. The Chaco war resulted from the attempt of Bolivia, an inland state, blocked on all sides, to gain an outlet to the Atlantic through the great South American River system.[3]

---

[1] Chatham House, *Raw Materials and Colonies*, p. 29.
[2] Chatham House, *Sanctions*, p. 39.
[3] Y. M. Goblet, *The Twilight of Treaties*, pp. 141–2.

And Russia's need of an ice-free port has been a decisive factor in her policy of expansion. On the other hand, the control of particular favourably situated points, such as the Straits of Gibraltar or of Constantinople, confers specific strategic and economic privileges on their fortunate possessors.

Numbers, wealth, and strength of population ultimately depend on the extent of territory and its permanent resources, though their ethnical qualities count for a good deal in their exploitation. An abstemious, industrious people, like the Italians or the Japanese, can thrive and multiply under economic conditions which would paralyse the energy of Anglo-Saxon settlers. Inequalities in the size of population do not seem quite as glaring as those of territorial extension. The population of the entire British Empire, including India and the Dominions, is 495 million, about a hundred times greater than that of Switzerland; its range, 35,000,000 square kilometres as against 41,000, is nearer a thousand (850) to one.

The correlation of population to area is the simplest (though very clumsy) expression of inequality of opportunity between the inhabitants of the various countries. The density of population of Belgium is 269·8 to the square kilometre, of England and Wales 267·3, of the Netherlands 239·4, of Japan 168·7, of Germany 141·2, of the United States 15·7, of Brazil 5·1, and of Australia 0·8. Some European countries (Sweden and Norway with 13·7 and 8·7 per square kilometre respectively) seem to rank with the new undeveloped countries, but a large part of their surface area is useless for economic purposes. In Sweden only 9·1 per cent and in Norway 2·6 per cent is arable land.[1] The low density in the new countries, on the other hand, indicates natural resources which are as yet undeveloped. Some of these countries appear highly industrialized, as mining enterprises prevail in certain of them; in the United States, Australia, and New Zealand less than 25

[1] Carr-Saunders, op. cit., p. 141.

per cent of the total population is dependent on agriculture. Urbanization and city development is more advanced in some overseas states than in many of the older countries. But the density of their agricultural populations is very low, and extensive systems of farming prevail. Even where free lands are no longer available, closer settlements could absorb a very much greater population if the need for it arose. A national "reserve" against population growth is at hand, such as old settled countries no longer enjoy.

On the other hand, the less developed industrial capitalism is, the greater are the chances of population growth by structural change and industrialization. The growth of China and India must depend on the application of capitalist technique, rather than on the exploitation of undeveloped, untapped resources. While the leading agricultural classes in many a country despised business, they strongly favoured industrialization as a national policy and forced it by tariff protection. It widened the home market for their surplus produce, though it tended to raise the wages of their labourers. It made them independent of foreign manufactures and gave them a feeling of military security. And it satisfied their craving for equality—they were imitating the leading nations of the world, which had built up their economic supremacy on industry; it flattered their pride by raising them above the level of mere yokels. Industrialization was not merely a bait to attract immigrants, a method for keeping people employed and for making a country independent of foreign manufactures, it became a kind of declaration of independence, by which a new country registered its claim to full equality with old-established countries. Artificially accelerated industrialization, due partly to fear of economic dependence in time of war and partly to this craving for equality, is the most important single cause for the disturbances in world economic equilibrium. It accentuates the inequality between old and new countries; it speeds up the transfer of men and of capital to the new countries and enables them to exploit their natural resources at a much more rapid rate. It has shifted population, wealth, and power from the old to the new world.

The United States, Australia, and New Zealand are to-day more highly industrialized than Germany and Switzerland, a mere 22–24 per cent of their population is dependent on agriculture. They forced industrial development by capitalist methods, with almost the same fervour as present-day Russia does by collectivist methods. Only the United Kingdom (6·7 per cent), Belgium (19·3 per cent), and the Netherlands (20·5 per cent) show lower figures. Turkey (81·6 per cent), Russia (85·0 per cent), and Bulgaria (80·9 per cent) head the purely agrarian countries.

VI

The ultimate, tangible aims of all countries striving for equality are wealth, strength, and security. Equalization has not been successful in this respect. None of these objects has been attained. Population aggregates as well as density of population continue to show differences. And so do the estimates of aggregate wealth for the several countries. They vary between £63 milliards for the United States (1928), £12·5 milliards for Germany (1928), £5·9 milliards for Japan (1925), and £3·4 milliards for Italy (1924). The average wealth per head descends from £525 for the United States, £335 (United Kingdom), £195 (Germany) to £100 (Japan) and £85 (Italy).[1] The aggregates indicate the several nations' relative economic strength, whilst the *per capita* figures show the average citizen's individual position. Income figures are equally impressive and somewhat more reliable. In 1928 the United States aggregate income was

---

[1] These figures are not very reliable and therefore not of much use for any detailed economic inquiry; but they illustrate clearly enough the prevalence of economic inequality.

£17·9 milliards against the United Kingdom's £3·8, Germany's £3·6, Italy's £0·9, and Japan's £1·3 (1930). The *per capita* income decreases from £150 for the United States to £82 for the United Kingdom, £56 for Germany to £24 for Italy and £16 for Japan.[1] These great discrepancies help to explain the widespread feeling of injustice which prevails in the poorer countries. It is no use telling an Italian and a Japanese that they must remain satisfied with £24 or £16 a head, when they might be worth £150 a year in the United States, if only they were admitted. Comparisons of aggregate wealth may not convey much to them, but they can understand the meaning of opportunity, expressed in average income figures.

VII

Security is partly geographical—an insular position and an easily defendable frontier are of the utmost importance; but the combination of social and economic factors, of the size and structure of population, its spiritual and physical fitness, may count for more.

Within a given territory, economic security is determined by a compound of skill and of permanently available economic resources. Skill is the result of natural endowment and of adequate industrial training. The regular supply of foodstuffs, raw materials, and manufactured goods, on the other hand, depends on national resources and on international intercourse. Undeveloped countries, which must import their armaments from abroad cannot obtain security, as defence rests on technical skill and industrial organization. The recognition of the needs of national defence and not her craving for large-scale social experiments accounts for the feverish industrialization of Soviet Russia. Only Great Britain, the United States, France, Germany, and perhaps Russia, possess factories capable of large-scale production

[1] Mainly from S. Kuznets in *The Encyclopaedia of Social Sciences*.

of all kinds of heavy guns, ships of war, and artillery ammunition. Nine other countries are exporters of such wares.[1]

Geographical situation may be of greater importance than any other single factor. It cannot be easily modified and the changes resulting from the cutting of a canal, the building of bridges or the excavation of a tunnel, are rarely fundamental. A self-sufficient continental empire is very much safer than an insular empire which possesses a similar economic structure. The former is contiguous and self-supporting in wartime: the latter, being disconnected, is not. Internal communications between the various parts of the former may, even in the age of railways and cars, be more costly, but they are not as much at the mercy of "interruptions" by enemy sea or air-craft, and do not depend on sea-power. A continental empire has problems of its own; if it is vast enough, the tendency to regionalize is sure to be strong.

Such centrifugal forces, however powerful, are certainly weaker than those working for regional economic nationalism in a far-flung insular empire. The sectional spirit in the United States has been very rampant; it has nowhere resulted in the erection of those inter-state barriers which divide the various parts of the British Empire; (the few anti-insect pest regulations which give a mild dose of protection to the fruit growers of one or two states can be ignored). Were the British Dominions as contiguous to England as Scotland and Wales, the Empire as a unit would be much more closely knit than it is to-day; the Dominions might have disappeared as quasi-independent commonwealths, whilst the centre of gravity might long ago have shifted to Ottawa, Canberra, or Pretoria. If, on the other hand, the Mississipi were to widen into a mighty sea and the states lying east of it were torn from the American continent and swept into the mid-Atlantic, without any great destruction of life and property, this new island commonwealth would soon have

[1] Chatham House, *Sanctions*, pp. 30–1.

little free connection with trans-Mississippi America; each would erect high tariffs against the other. The constitution of the United States would scarcely stand the strain, if the continent were to be cut up into island sub-continents.

The massive growth of states has been trans-continental. They grew in the old world by expanding their rule over their neighbours' territory. Overseas colonization came comparatively late, when empty continents were discovered, annexed, and held by sea power; it was originally a substitute, a *pis aller* for European continental expansion. When overland continental communication became relatively easy, the Westward movement gathered speed; sea-coast and riverside colonies were transformed into independent continental republics or quasi-independent daughter states. Power was slowly shifting from an insular metropolis to its continental offshoots.

A nation's dependence on certain classes of foreign supplies determines its *specific vulnerability*. Countries without coal, iron, oil, wood, or water-power are very much more susceptible to foreign pressure than their more fortunate neighbours, who possess ample natural resources. Continental giants like the United States and the U.S.S.R. are fairly well stocked with most of the necessities of war, and so is the British Empire, as long as its communications are not interrupted. Autarchy in an insular empire is *disconnected*, in a continental empire it is *contiguous*. Of the eleven leading industrial states, Germany seems to be the poorest as regards raw materials; even Japan, with a surplus of silk and sulphur and a sufficiency of copper, coal, and graphite, appears to be better off, while Italy has a surplus in mercury, sulphur, silk, and hemp, and is self-sufficient in lead, zinc, and vegetable oils.[1] As a matter of fact, the relatively favourable position of these countries indicates merely a somewhat tardy and incomplete industrial development; it must deteriorate through industrial growth. Seventy-one per cent

[1] Chatham House, *Raw Materials and Colonies*, p. 31.

of Germany's population are engaged in non-agricultural pursuits, against not quite fifty-three per cent in Italy, and scarcely fifty per cent in Japan. The relative importance of various commodities cannot be measured by a general standard. The lack of some relatively cheap and common metal, of which no great quantities are needed, may be decisive at a critical moment, when substitutes are not available.

Human inventiveness and human foresight can diminish these risks. Timber, formerly a sovereign key commodity, has been replaced by coal and iron; oil can be distilled from coal, and the harnessing of water power has somewhat reduced the need for fuel. The use of scrap has diminished dependence on iron ores. Stocks can be accumulated and held in reserve. But countries well supplied by nature with specific goods will always enjoy a great advantage over those which must get them by slow accumulation from abroad, for, after all, even the largest reserve stores are not inexhaustible.

A country's *general vulnerability* is determined by its foreign trade; it is expressed by the relation of the value of its total output and its total consumption to its exports and its imports. The vulnerability of the United States, whose exports are but 7 per cent of its output and whose imports are but 6 per cent of its consumption, is very much less than that of the United Kingdom, who sells 25 per cent of her output abroad and imports 32 per cent of her consumption.[1] The United States need but a few articles from abroad, such as nickel and rubber, in order to keep their system going; they amount to a very small fraction of the entire consumption; if they were not available, the even flow of the country's economic life would be greatly disturbed, but no major catastrophe need occur.

A comparison of aggregate volumes of trade of several

---

[1] E. M. Patterson, *America—World Leader or World Led?* p. 131; C. K. Leith, *World Minerals and World Politics.*

countries does not indicate the true position. The values of British Indian and of Belgian exports in 1935 were nearly identical, and so were those of Japan and Canada. The true position is revealed by *per capita* figures. These rise from 12s. for Russia to £33 for New Zealand, 1929. There are some luxury goods or manufactured goods among them which are imported because they are cheap; they could be replaced by home production. Others again are capital goods, the absence of which might retard the country's development, but need not endanger its existence. When Australia could no longer borrow cheaply, her imports fell from £22 *per capita* to just under £6 (1931). The true measure of a country's general vulnerability might be expressed by its *per capita* imports of raw materials, foodstuffs, and such essential manufactured goods as cannot be produced at home. The large settlement areas of the world are almost invulnerable in respect of foodstuffs. The United States, Canada, Australia, the Argentine, and, in Europe, Russia, Hungary, and Rumania are surplus producers. Some of the older countries are at times self-sufficient; they could remain so, were good harvests always assured, even in wartime, when neither man-power nor traction-power are available for sowing and reaping. Most older countries are dependent on raw materials from abroad. Their strategic position is precarious even if these materials are raised in a dependency, for the safety of communications does not depend on the flag, but on the fleet.

Since imports must either be paid for by exports and by services, or else be offset by previous claims (foreign investments) and promises of future payments (loans), vulnerability might be measured by exports. For when countries are in desperate straights, they can rarely borrow, nor can they in time of great stress rely on payments from their debtors. Exports become the decisive factors. Here again, degrees of vulnerability vary greatly. They run from £11·3 per head (Netherlands), £9·4 (United Kingdom), £6·8

(Germany), £4·5 (France), £1·8 (Italy), to 6s. (U.S.S.R.), and 2s. (China). Germany is fairly low down on the list, while Italy and Japan rank as low as Spain, Hungary, and Egypt. But these figures do not tell the whole story. All depends on the nature of the exported commodities. The only commodity which can always find a market is gold; as long as the leading countries are ready to accept un-limited quantities of it at a fixed price, gold-mining or gold-owning countries can always pay for their imports. No such certainty exists for exports made up by competitive goods. Either other countries can produce them cheaper or a tariff may stop their importation and thus substantially interfere with their producers' means for paying for essential supplies from abroad.

The vulnerability of countries which have to depend on the markets of economically independent states is greater than of those which can sell to dependencies, whose economic policy they control. Sanctions, for instance, can stop all sales to foreign countries, but they do not interfere with the markets of the boycotted country's colonies, if unsupported by an active and effective blockade. In war-time all over-seas communications are threatened, those with colonies even more so than those with neutral countries. Supplies of goods from an overland colony (e.g. Siberia to Russia) or from friendly continental neighbours are far more dependable. Insular empires nowadays seem to be more vulnerable than continental empires.

VIII

Some states are empires, some have been shorn of this glory, others have broken away from empires and have either become separate states or the core of new empires, while others again are simple states, some content with their position and others bent on expanding into empires or becoming great Powers.

A great Power need not be an empire, but an empire

must be a great Power in relation to other states. An empire is a composite state in which a dominant partner exercises control over weaker dependants.[1] Domination and expanse —not mere size—are the attributes of empire. Some empires of the past, like the Athenian Empire, though small when compared with one of the minor states of the present day, ruled a considerable part of the then accessible world and wielded great power over their tributaries.[2]

As domination is based on power, and as power is closely associated with strength of population and natural resources, the latter must be sufficiently impressive to win and hold an empire. Most modern empires are colonial. Their rulers have either annexed semi-vacant spaces in which they planted daughter states, or else they have conquered backward native peoples. Oceans and mountains, floods and deserts, heat and cold, rather than organized fighting resistance made colonial empire building hazardous. The military force needed to win and hold an empire was comparatively small.

An empire stretches over regions the different economic and climatic conditions of which favour the production of different crops. It can easily be conceived as a composite economic unit, inhabited by several nationalities and organized in separate states, each of which is governed by the same superior dominant will and each of which co-operates in some kind of economic self-sufficiency. To assure self-sufficiency and variety of commodities, a vast extension either over contiguous provinces of a continent, or over far-flung islands is necessary.

[1] See above, pp. 33–4.

[2] "The empire of the Athenians consisted of five provinces . . . with a total population of perhaps two million. It formed a complex of islands, peninsulas and estuaries the most remote extremities of which were distant 200 or 250 miles from Athens." . . . "In the age of Pericles, Athens was a city with a population of about 150,000. Attica, the territory of the Athenians, had an approximately equal number of inhabitants. . . . The free and franchised population . . . yielded about 50,000 males of military age."—W. S. Ferguson, *Greek Imperialism*, p. 42.

Empires pass when their dependencies separate from them: their very nature is changed when domination has come to an end and when their former subjects are admitted to federal partnership. The British Empire has not ceased to be an empire, by being transformed into a commonwealth of free nations. Even if it lost its native dependencies, the structure of an imperial federation, embracing various states, races, and resources would remain. Modern Germany, on the other hand, ceased to be an empire when she was deprived of her former colonial dependencies and the continental provinces inhabited by non-German people, over whom she exercised some sort of ethnical domination. She is far more powerful than most of the smaller colonial composite Powers of the day, yet she is no longer an imperial Power. She is homogeneous, not composite. Her anti-Jewish policy is the last stage in a long historical process, by which the German people lost control over foreign continental nationalities. When Bismarck expelled Austria from the German federation, he not only made the new Germany a nearly homogeneous state, which had almost completely shed the composite features characterizing an empire; he unwittingly deprived the German remnant in Austria of the strength needed for the continued exercise of domination over the non-German majorities forming the Habsburg Monarchy. A homogeneous state can be a great Power, stronger than an empire, but it may lack the glamour of an imperial position. Germany's claim for equality has of late centred round the return of some of her colonies; the demand symbolizes her aspiration to imperial rank.[1]

As power is the essence of empire, no empire can nowadays be conceived which does not control a large territory whose resources enable the government to wield permanent domination over others.

[1] See p. 271 seq.

IX

States like the United States and Soviet Russia are not officially called empires. They possess the resources and the population on which power is based, and they control some outlying possessions which may be classed as colonies. Like other empires, they have grown by conquest and annexation; their populations are more composite than those of most countries. The egalitarian philosophies on which their respective political systems are founded denounce the use of force over any component parts of their state population. Both deny the right of domination and renounce its exercise in theory; both have grown by using it and both have attained by it their present imperial status in territorial extent and population. They represent in fact, if not in name, the type of "continental empire" which stretches over huge continuous expanses and harbours a numerous composite populace, the one, U.S.A., covering 7·8 million square kilometres with 127 million inhabitants, the other, Russia, ruling 26 million square kilometres and over 170 million people. Though only 22 per cent of the inhabitants of the United States depend any longer on agriculture, against 85 per cent in Russia, the low density of their population (15·7 and 7·8 respectively) reflects the early stage of development. If the United States were as thickly settled as Belgium, their population would be 2,000 millions. Both are relatively self-sufficient, for, though the entire foreign trade of the United States is considerable, imports and exports are but 6 and 7 per cent of consumption and production, and Russia's exports per head only amount to 12s.

Some of the great dominions, Canada, with an area of 9·5 million square kilometres, and Australia with 7·7 million, are built on an imperial scale in respect of territory; their history reveals elements of imperial domination. They may remain partners in an empire, or they may develop into separate giant states, or they may themselves become empires. Another of the partners in the British Commonwealth, South Africa, possesses even now a highly composite imperial structure. A comparatively small white class not only rules a coloured people directly under its control; it also administers large dependencies inhabited by native races.

Of the former Latin-American dependencies, Brazil exhibits many features of an empire—a truly imperial expansion of 8·5 million square kilometres, a mixed population (40 millions in all), vast unsettled wild areas over which she only exercises nominal, scarcely yet active, domination.

All Latin-American countries are composite states; everywhere some group differing from others in colour, origin, or tradition, exercises some sort of domination over them, in spite of egalitarian principles. Tyranny, as such, does not make an empire, nor does dimension. An empire may be a composite state, but a composite state need not be an empire. A tiny minority, holding an equally inconsiderable majority under its sway, is no more an empire than a small confederation, like the Swiss, which is composed of several nationalities. Dimension and domination combined make an empire. States do not lose their status as states because they are small, but an insignificant empire is inconceivable. Insignificance and power are mutually exclusive.

The greatest continental empire, the Chinese, with 11·1 million square kilometres and 450 million inhabitants, is passing through a phase of temporary disintegration. China has lost nearly all her dependencies; she is at the present moment scarcely able to hold her own against foreign domination. She may break up and be divided into a series of weak states, or she may become partly or entirely dependent on imperial Japan. But as she is only on the threshold of the capitalist age, she may reorganize her forces and become secure, or even dominant once again.

India, once an empire, has become a dependency; she

is on the way to autonomy and may ultimately separate from the British Empire. In respect of size and resources, she is built on an imperial scale, comprising 4·7 million square kilometres, with 353 million inhabitants. Her structure is composite and she may become a federation of equal partners or drift into an empire dominated by powerful groups.

All present day European empires are colonial as well as insular. The British Empire covers an area of 35 million square kilometres with 495 million inhabitants. It is flung across the habitable world and is the most composite state-formation which has ever existed. It is "tripartite." It comprises a co-operative empire, composed of the mother country and the Dominions, whose status is regulated by the Statute of Westminster, with 19 million square kilometres and 32 million inhabitants. The second tier is occupied by a composite unit, India, which, since the granting of fiscal autonomy, has enjoyed economic independence, but which is still controlled politically by Great Britain; the third group is formed by the dependencies proper, comprising 10·7 million square kilometres and 64 million inhabitants. Dominions and dependencies combined cover 34 million square kilometres, with 448 million inhabitants. The character of the British Empire is highly insular. Though a great deal of its trade is inter-imperial, it is not self-sufficient, for its wealth and its very existence depend on world trade. Most of its 3·6 milliard gold dollars imports and 3·2 milliard gold dollars exports are seaborne trade, the proper functioning of which must be protected by sea-power.

The French colonial empire, covering 12 million square kilometres, with 70 million inhabitants, is far less complex. It has no partner states, though assimilation has proceeded quite a long way in Algeria. The empire is partly insular, but the bulk of the dependencies stretch from the Mediterranean coast to the heart of equatorial Africa. The mother country, which is less industrialized and less thickly populated—38·4 per cent of her population depend on agriculture and the density is 75·9 per square kilometre— is far more self-sufficient than the British Empire.

The Dutch, the Portuguese, and the Belgians control insular empires, separated from the mother country by the sea. The Dutch colonial empire covers 2 million square kilometres, with 61 million inhabitants; its exports reach 212 million gold dollars; the Belgian dependencies cover 2·5 million square kilometres, with 13 million inhabitants and 23 million dollars exports; and the Portuguese own 2 million square kilometres with 8 million inhabitants, with exports amounting to 16 million dollars. Belgium, Holland, and Portugal are no longer Imperial Powers, though they hold large native areas by domination. Their dependencies may be called empires, being parts of a composite state ruled by a dominant partner, but the ruling metropolitan Power is never styled so.

Spain, once the mistress of the world's greatest empire, holds but a few remnants of her former greatness in Morocco and along the west coast of Africa—333,000 square kilometres with barely a million inhabitants.

Japan, Italy, and Germany are frequently called the (colonial) Have-not Powers, quite incorrectly as far as Japan and Italy are concerned. Japan's colonial possessions of about 300,000 square kilometres and 30 million inhabitants, constitute nearly half of her entire empire (681,000 square kilometres) and over one-third of her entire population (100 millions). Her colonial trade, excluding Manchuria, amounts to one quarter of her total import and export trade.

Italy's colonial empire covered over 2 million square kilometres before the Ethiopian war; it was thinly populated (2·4 million inhabitants) and had not much trade (10 million dollars exports).

The only real Have-not Power of the three is Germany.

She no longer holds a colonial empire and has been deprived of some of her border provinces. She is the most powerful homogeneous state in the world, but she has no opportunity of exercising power over subject races. Whilst she is deprived of this privilege, a large number of ethnical Germans are living either in separate states such as Austria and Switzerland or under alien domination, in France, Italy, Czechoslovakia, Poland, Hungary, Russia, and the Baltic states. As far as the absence of domination is concerned, her position is not unique. Neither the Scandinavian states, nor Switzerland, Austria, Poland, Hungary, the Baltic and the Balkan states exercise colonial power. Few of these countries desire it, but many of them rule German or other minorities, not always wisely and well.

Some of them are confronted with the same economic problems as Germany. They have to provide employment for a growing population which cannot be settled on the land, as no vacant spaces are available and as their agricultural technique is already fairly advanced. They must industrialize themselves, but to do this they need external markets. The pressure experienced by Germany is felt in Austria, in Switzerland, and in Czecho-slovakia; it will shortly be present in Poland. Economically more backward nations, such as the Balkan and the Baltic states, may not encounter it for some time to come. They can learn to make much better use of their natural resources; the more advanced countries cannot, for they have, so to speak, skimmed the milk long ago. The small countries of Latin America have an even longer breathing-space ahead of them during which they can grow and expand before they will feel cramped. Their populations are scanty, their natural resources scarcely scratched. Most of them are set up on a large scale, compared with Europe. Their people can multiply and wait. And the same holds good of the remaining Asiatic countries whose population is not yet dense enough to make them feel serious pressure in the

H

immediate future, and whose technique and organization can be vastly improved.

Inequality of size and population, of structure and spirit, is the rule and not the exception in the present world system. It is frequently the result of past coercion and earlier conquest; its persistence may lead to the application of similar methods in the near future.

CHAPTER II

EQUALITY

I

THE cry for equality of states originated in the cravings for recognition which animated their rulers. It is far older than the egalitarian philosophies which heralded the advent of democracy. For these rulers, who looked upon the State as their personal patrimony, passionately desired to be the equals of other "state proprietors." Their properties should have the same extension, the same population and the same resources as those of their more favoured rivals; if possible, their financial means and their military establishments should be such as to overawe them. They were frequently dissatisfied with the power and wealth they owned and wished to improve their possessions as well as their positions. They schemed, intrigued, intermarried, and made war for purposes of aggrandizement. They needed strength to do so, but in order to get it they had to expand. Expansion depended on power, but power depended on expansion, and was frequently identified with prestige. Thus princes built royal palaces to vie with Versailles, although they did not care to inhabit them and could not afford to maintain their regal splendour except by squandering their resources. They ran their court life on lines laid down by the "great king," though it may have bored them to desperation. They raised armies which they dared not use and built navies which they did not need. Often enough this striving for greater power led them into policies which did not serve the true interests of their countries. They paid great attention to appearances and equal rank in the princely hierarchy; their ambitions were fired by the hope of outdistancing their equals and of attaining equality with their superiors. These strivings and rivalries underlay the struggles in Italy in the days of the Renaissance; and they account partly for the disintegration of the Holy Roman Empire. But these yearnings for equal rank were not restricted to petty Italian city despots who aimed at turning their sway over a tiny municipality into world domination, nor to German counts who wanted to become emperors, but never got beyond being grand-dukes and kings, if not by right divine, at least by the grace of Napoleon. The outbreak of the Crimean War may have been speeded up by such sentiments. Nicholas I, Emperor by grace divine, deliberately refused equality of standing to Napoleon III, the upstart Emperor, representing a plebiscitarian revolution; he would not call him *"mon cher frère,"* but only *"mon bon ami,"* thereby causing a great deal of resentment.

The advent of democratic forms of government has intensified rather than lessened this cry for equality. It is no longer a question of etiquette; for present-day revolutionary usurpers can scarcely complain of the lack of courtesy shown them by the heads of old established states. They do not need to strive laboriously for recognition and chafe under its denial. But the masses they lead are filled with egalitarian passions and resentments. Even under a democratic régime, the main political conceptions are formed by individual brains. Political issues are never decided collectively, but by a few individuals in the seat of power. They may carry out, interpret or shape the wishes of the masses they represent; they do so by decisions formed in their own minds. No organic conceptions of state or society can alter this fact, though the fluidum emanating from a massed crowd has frequently clouded and clogged the workings of a leader's reasoning. But a man with a magnetic personality, who can pick up a promising idea and who knows how to make and manage a propaganda machine, can easily cast his spell over the masses and make them subservient to his aims and ambitions. Contact with these masses may set his imagination afire, and his powers of persuasion may suggest new ideas to their sluggish minds. The spark is generated individually, not collectively.

The cry for equality of all individual citizens within a democracy can easily be turned into a demand for their "collective equality" with the citizens of other democracies. Trade and transportation have connected millions of men who live under different régimes in various parts of the world. Since printing and broadcasting have come into their own, they possess some knowledge of one another's status and compare it in friendly or unfriendly rivalry with their lot. Few have actual personal contact with their neighbours; few are sufficiently well informed to interpret these experiences in an intelligent manner. They generalize from accidental impressions and see in their own purely individual inferiority or superiority complexes the low or high water-marks of their nation's international standing. International ignorance is stupendous, notwithstanding the Marxian assumption that the members of the same class all over the world have an intuitive facility for interpreting one another's national ways, whilst those of the several classes within each nation are kept apart and deprived of such spiritual unity by class warfare. The masses, as such, are necessarily more ignorant of the ways and means of other nations than were the princes of old, whose jealousies forced them to keep a close watch on one another's doings. They cannot have much direct personal contact. They are at the mercy of those who are better qualified to gather and spread information for them, and they are often enough deliberately misled by their agents for what are supposed to be patriotic purposes. But their yearnings for equal rights for their nation and equal opportunities for themselves have become at least as ardent as were the claims for recognition of their former despotic rulers; they are quite as touchy on questions of rank and probably more inclined to overrate "recognition." "We will fight until the French acknowledge us as having equal rights and position equal to their own . . . and we will crush everyone who calls in question our place as one of the great Powers of Europe," the great German historian, von Sybel, wrote to a friend during the Franco-Prussian War.[1] And very nearly thirty years later (1899), when Germany stood at the height of her power, William II informed his grandmother: "The government of Lord Salisbury must learn to respect and to treat us as equals."[2]

A nation's self-respect is not always the result of deep-seated rational conviction, but occasionally the reflex of some individuals' purely personal experiences. Even those of a few people can play a great part in the awakening of national consciousness. South Africa's policy of excluding the Indians has been a powerful stimulant in the development of Indian nationalism,[3] for it taught Gandhi personally the hopelessness of a policy of real racial co-operation. In many instances, propaganda and mass suggestion are combined. It is much easier to rouse hysterical self-abasement and equally hysterical arrogance than to teach quiet dignity and self-reliance.

Questions of formal recognition and of outward dignity have frequently played an important part in the relations between East and West. The ceremonial to which the Chinese Emperors subjected the ambassadors of European Powers, when receiving them in audience, was intended to impress upon their own subjects, as well as upon the foreigners, the lack of equality between the Chinese and the alien barbarians. The Turks maintained a similar attitude until the year 1832, when Mahmud for the first time received the British ambassador without any of the old degrading formulas.[4] Modern Europe has acted in much

[1] January 9, 1871. *Memoirs of the Life of Henry Reeve*, vol. ii, pp. 193-4.
[2] G. P. Gooch, *Before the War*, p. 214.
[3] "Do not dishonour us. We recognize that there must be distinctions, but do not cast a stigma upon us in the laws of your country." Gandhi to Smuts. S. G. Millin, *General Smuts*, vol. i, p. 243.
[4] Harold Temperley, *The Crimea*, p. 21.

the same way. There may have been some weighty political reasons for not negotiating the Paris peace terms with Germany by the normal diplomatic methods, for these terms were the outcome of extremely precarious compromises, which had frequently been accepted by the several Allies with not too good a grace; direct negotiations with the Central Powers might well have destroyed this hard-won unity. These simple facts were camouflaged by what no doubt seemed a very clever move to its authors at that time —the assertion that Germany was not worthy to be listened to as an equal; she was a criminal, placed in the dock under elaborate police surveillance; she was to be made conscious of her moral inferiority by having to accept the verdict of a court composed of the victors, who assumed the rôle of moral superiors. This deliberate denial of equality of treatment not only had to serve purely material purposes, such as the claim for reparation payments or the spoliation of colonies; it was staged as a kind of moral spectacle, designed to impress ex-enemies and neutrals alike. The German delegation at Versailles was housed in two hotels, connected by the main road; on both sides, a stockade separated the carriage drive from the pavement; the members of the delegation had to walk between the boards along this *via dolorosa*, while the natives could look down on them from their superior moral and structural elevation. The passionate craving for recognition, the demand for a kind of certified equality, which has been playing such an important part in modern Germany's attitude, is but the natural response to these monkey tricks, by which the victors tried to humiliate the vanquished.

The desire for equality for equality's sake is a powerful driving force, even where ulterior motives are absent. The United States' empire is continental, their overseas trade is not as vital to their existence as that of the United Kingdom is to her, though it is of course very important to many of their industries and to the well-being of a considerable section of the population. They need not have insisted on absolute parity of their navy with that of the United Kingdom, the centre of a far-flung insular empire, on whose trade connections depend the standard of living, and probably the very existence of her people; their motive was the desire for equality and equal standing. Similarly, the rise of Fascism and its turning towards colonial expansion is not merely due to an emulation of ancient Rome and its imperial greatness, but to the feeling of national humiliation, from which Italy has long been suffering.[1]

The stronger the internal emotional craving for equality, the more easily can a nation be roused to demand equality with other masses abroad.

At least two separate issues are involved in this insistence on equality in modern politics: on the one hand, a demand for *equal rights* of states, as such, in relation to other states, and, on the other hand, a demand for *equal opportunities* for their citizens with those enjoyed by citizens of other countries.

II

The term *equal rights* (formal equality) may have a quantitative or a qualitative meaning. It implies, on the one hand, the demand for equal rights (equal status) for all sovereign states, ruling states as well as independent states, mighty empires as well as petty principalities, and on the other hand, the right of vassal states or subject principalities to assume full sovereignty and to abolish inequality between master and subject, between ruling and ruled nationalities.

Since the Declaration of Independence, the plea for equal rights has been intimately bound up with the claim for equal rights for all men, from which most modern revolutions have sprung. The notion that all men are equal, as far as they are endowed with human reason or with an

---

[1] Benedetto Croce, *Geschichte Italiens*, pp. 107–9; Giuseppe Carducci, *Canto dell'Italia che va in Campidoglio* in *Giambi ed Epodi*.

immortal soul, implies a system of laws from which privilege and discrimination between any group of individuals must be banned. The political struggle which gave birth to the Declaration of Independence centred round the claims of a limited group of people, who decided after protracted misgivings to set up a separate national government of their own. But if the philosophic principle on which the United States had based their claim held true, the essential equality of all men, severally or collectively, could not be denied within or without the national boundary. All laws emanated from an unwritten law of nature, which bound all mankind and was either embodied in the several national codes of law in force, or overruled them in case of conflict or divergence. Any group of people and any individuals living amongst a population from which they differed in origin, outlook, habit, and language should have access to the national courts and the use of the national codes on equal terms with the majorities among whom they had settled. They were not supposed to apply separate laws of their own and should neither enjoy privileges nor suffer discrimination. As they were created equal, no reason could be adduced why they should either desire or be compelled to live a life different from that of their hosts. Neither the capitulations which exempted the nationals of conquering colonizing European Powers from native law and native jurisdiction, nor anti-alien legislation (such as the anti-Japanese enactments of the United States) comply with this notion of *equal rights*. All members of a state community ought to have the same rights as their fellow-members, and all nationals of one state ought to have the same rights as the nationals of other states in one another's territory. Wherever this conception of equal rights struck root, discrimination was promptly abandoned.

Equality embraced political as well as civil rights. The right to life, liberty, and the pursuit of happiness, which was inalienably invested in every individual, gave him

the status of a citizen, the right to choose his own government and to control the acts of those he put into power,
who were responsible to him. The status of a separate
national or social group and its members (colonies), who
were subject to the will of another separate government,
which they did not control, was inferior to that of those
groups which can control their own government (mother
country); it was a flat contradiction of this principle of
equality. These depressed groups had a right to redress this
grievance if they so desired.

The Declaration of Independence did not lay down the
doctrine of equal rights in order to establish social equality
between all citizens living within the borders of the thirteen
colonies; it did not purport to abolish slavery, nor did it
introduce manhood suffrage in the states which entered the
Union. It was a solemn protest against the absence of
collective equality between the colonies as units and the
mother country as a unit. As the rights of free Britons in
the colonies were not respected by the metropolitan government and as they were taxed by the British Parliament,
in which they were not represented, the colonists renounced
their allegiance to the mother country. By asserting that
men are created equal and had the right, when they so
desired, to "assume among the powers of the earth the
separate and equal station to which the laws of nature
and nature's God entitle them," the Declaration of
Independence became the charter of equal rights, not so
much of all individuals within a state as of all nations
within the world. A new nation could be created any day
by the declaratory act of a separate and distinct group
of men. Vassal states had the right to free themselves by
unilateral action from the rule of the sovereign states which
had controlled them, and subject populations, living within
the borders of a state, had the right to form themselves
into a separate nation, to found a state of their own and
to secede from the parent state in which they had been

incorporated. If all men were created equal, slavery should nowhere be tolerated, nor should any group of people be deprived of their group-liberty. Colonization, i.e. the planting of people and the formation of a new social unit in vacant spaces, was permissible, for the soil had no soul until an occupying nation had instilled one into it, and empty spaces were meant to be settled according to the dispensations of a benign Providence. But the annexation of a country inhabited by a living nation (though not of a primitive native race) was a violation of the equal rights of nations, and so was the maintenance of a colony in a state of dependence against the will of its inhabitants. Later on, the Monroe Doctrine explicitly denounced the application of both methods to the American continent, though it permitted the holding of such colonies as were willing to be held. But the right to counter-colonization, the right of subject races or nations to rebel against their masters and to establish an independent government of their own, capable of exercising unhampered sovereignty, cannot be denied by those who have accepted the principles of the Declaration of Independence.[1]

[1] This did not prevent the Government of the United States from looking upon the secession of the Southern States and the formation of the Confederate States as an act of rebellion.

CHAPTER III

CHANGE

I

INEQUALITY does not much matter when men see in it the outcome of the divine will, which for reasons of its own, unfathomable to the human mind, has made some states strong and others weak, and has given wealth to one nation and withheld it from others. For centuries the material inequality of individuals presented no problems, for it was offset by their absolute spiritual equality before God Almighty, who had endowed the lowest serf and his lordly master with an equally immortal soul. States as well as men were the children of God, so to speak, for he had accorded them sovereignty, and whatever their size or their material resources, they ranked equally high before him.

The preservation and perpetuation of material inequality resulted from men's convictions that stability is a blessing and must not be upset. The human race has ever loathed monotony; it has always been eager to have a few new gadgets to play with. But it abhors fundamental change. Men instinctively turn their faces against the flow of time, as it takes from them all those fleeting moments of happiness to which they cling. They want stability and security, and even if they are not overpleased with things as they are, they infinitely prefer them to things that might be. For experience has taught them that worse is yet to come and that for each of them there is but one definite goal towards which they are relentlessly carried by the flow of time, whether immediate change be for better or for worse— ultimate extinction. In order to free themselves from the fear of death which obsessed their minds, and to get away from that one great certainty, their great religions inverted

values and, by belittling life, have made it a kind of unimportant prelude to a kingdom come, where man's craving
for permanency, stability, and felicity will find satisfaction
in bliss eternal.

But men's religious impulses have never been strong
enough to let them neglect completely this vale of tears,
in which their stay is but a passing phase. Their practical
instincts do not let them submit to such dead certainty;
they turn away from it and endeavour to transform life
into an earthly paradise, where they can enjoy permanent
happiness.

Not all men crave for permanency at all times and in
all places. Change must terrify those who occupy a place
in the sun and are afraid of losing it, but the children of
darkness want to rise from the bottom of the black pit to
which they are chained. They yearn for change which is
to release them from their prison, as all do who long for
the dawn in an endless restless night, regardless of what
the new day may have in store for them.

For many centuries, men's religious doctrines denied the
need for change in the external world. God had created
the world which stood, a monument to his glory, unmoved
and unmovable for all time to come. He had given it a
permanent structure and set the stage for men's actions and
inactions, which they have to accept while they flit across
it in a futile endeavour to remain where they must pass on,
to hold fast where they must let go. This yearning for
stability has coloured the conceptions of natural science,
as well as of social theories. The outer world was rigidly
permanent; it moved, for it was a living, not a dead world,
but it moved within fixed limits. Its movement was not
like a journey into uncharted lands, over hills and dales
and rivers; it was like a daily constitutional, taken in the
park with clockwork regularity between two definitely fixed
points.

Modern natural science has slowly broken down these rigid

conceptions. Physics dissolved heat and light into movement; chemistry transformed matter, turning one element, seemingly permanent and unbreakable, into another, which exhibits quite different properties; geology has recorded the passing of various genera, species, races, and civilizations. And finally, evolution has demonstrated the rise of new types of living things, which are not mere accidental freaks, but the inevitable result of a combination of fixed parental properties imparted to their offspring. The carefully constructed relief of a stable and rigid world has cracked. It had risen ready-made from chaos and has remained unchanged and unchangeable, until the same God who, in his wisdom, had improvised it and made it perfect, might, by the breath of his spirit, put an end to its gyrations and let it sink once more into nothingness. The new world has no longer any hard and fast lines; it is not like a block of stone on to which seas and mountains, rivers and plains have been engraved; it has become a flow which runs through time and silts through space.

The views of political and social stability have completely changed too. The states which formed the political world were an essential part of that universe created by God. Each represented an independent social unit, established by his grace. Their rulers sat on their thrones as vicars and vassals of that eternal power which had made the world and ordained the regular working of its mechanism. But long before the new science revolutionized the physical picture of the world, men had recognized the futility of states and dynasties to which stability was denied. Their span of life was very much longer than that of mortal men, but they too died and decomposed, were born and resurrected. Men had in vain endeavoured to stop the flow of time and tide by binding themselves and their communities in solemn pacts not to destroy one another and not to permit change. By sacred treaties, which were to remain in force for all time to come, their commonwealths had guaranteed to one another the inviolability of their respective territories, the main basis of their statehood life. But eternity was frequently but a short-lived dream. For frontiers were continually altered by war, marriage, or intrigue, and empires crumbled and new empires were born. Men-of-war might conquer forts, and fortresses might control lands, but time sank the fleets and spiked the guns. The balance of power between the several states fluctuated incessantly; change could not be stopped, either abroad or at home.

Each separate state comprised a graduated order of classes with rights and duties in relation to the others. It was based on natural laws, the excellence of which men, being endowed with the divine gift of reason, could easily recognize. Its sacred stability must not be disturbed by their avarice and covetousness. Solemn mutual obligations guaranteed its permanence; constitutions, based on immemorial customs, formed the bulwark against frivolous change. The barons who met in Runnymede did not feel like heralds of a new age clamouring for change; they were intent on maintaining an old order of things, divinely ordained, which a wicked king was bent on upsetting. And even the great written Constitutions of the eighteenth-century revolutions were to guarantee the return to a previous state of affairs, which reckless innovators had destroyed. They were merely forming new moulds after old patterns, in which human society was to be preserved. For they expressed truth eternal, which was to endure for all time. But these rigid constitutions, designed to guarantee stability, were themselves the outcome of social upheaval and of mental disturbance. They had been made in civil war and by armed revolution by men who had uprooted the established order. They may have desired, and honestly desired, to secure a new and better stability than that which they had destroyed. They could not do it. For the huge conflagration they had lit, thawed, as it were, the age-long congelation which had held human society in its icy grip.

The floats were cracking, the frozen blocks were melting, the waters were churning, and ever since they have been running in a mighty flow—the world is no longer a state of affairs; it is a movement.

II

The status of a particular society—either the position of its constituent groups towards one another or its external relations to other societies—can be altered by voluntary agreements (contracts and treaties) between the parties. Or it can be changed by force, the strongest members compelling the others to submit to adjustments desired by them. For centuries such developments, whether peacefully or forcibly brought about, seemed to be purely arbitrary— the act either of an omnipotent God, who suspended his own law, and forced them upon mankind, or who let them happen accidentally without cause or reason. At last Darwinism furnished a scientific *theory of change* which purported to explain the mechanism of qualitative as well as quantitative mutation and disposed finally of all notions regarding biological, social, and historical movements as more or less capricious or fortuitous accidents. It put law and necessity into the place of arbitrariness and chance.

Its concepts contributed greatly to the formation of the theory of social movements outlined by Marx. His predecessors had constructed a system of natural laws which explained the workings of a static society. He outlined a theory of movement. The goal towards which society tended was inherent in the human matter composing it. Science had unravelled the mysteries of history. Cognition of its immutable laws enabled men to intervene more or less successfully in the current of events, but the ultimate objectives as well as the modalities of change were preordained; the Marxist "materialists were Calvinists without God."[1]

[1] Eduard Bernstein, *Die Voraussetzungen des Sozialismus und die Aufgaben der Sozialdemokratie*, p. 4.

Since internal structural alterations in societies were determined by immanent forces, their external movements depended on the reactions emanating from them. They too were subject to laws, the cognition of which was, however, rather difficult, as they resulted from the complicated interplay of many interlaced societies.

Change, internal as well as external, might be peaceful where the contending groups were aware of the laws they had to submit to, and were acting accordingly. Or it might be enforced by people trying either to impede its inexorable course or to deflect it prematurely. In both cases force was bound to fail. And the spread of knowledge was enabling men to bring about fundamental alterations without violent struggles, for if they once held them to be inevitable, it were better to accept them by way of compromise than by the ordeal of battle.

Ignorance of the laws governing the evolution of foreign affairs, due to their great complexity, or passion, prejudice, and short-sighted self-interest over and over again raise new obstacles to peaceful solutions. Even in home affairs force is still playing a considerable part. The Marxian mechanism of social changes works through class-warfare; when the appointed hour has come, it may end in actual civil war before a new order can arise. War as a method of change may survive until the passing of capitalism closes the early history of mankind and inaugurates an age of unrestricted communist bliss: it resembles the rose-coloured dreams of a bourgeois Utopia, but the Russian Revolution has added a few touches of glaring red realism to it.

III

When change has ceased to be taboo, rigid inequality is no longer bearable. Inequality as such is neither a blessing nor need it be a curse. It can be endured, if it merely indicates a set of positions into which men are not born, but for which they compete under relatively fair conditions. This

precludes stability. There is a coming and a going, an incessant rise and an equally incessant fall. The favoured
members (the Haves) in a particular society are fighting
for the maintenance or the expansion of their positions,
and the disinherited (the Have-nots) are endeavouring to
get a share and, when once they have got it, to increase
its size and to prevent its diminution. The same struggle
goes on among states; empires are fighting for further
expansion or defending themselves against disruption;
large states endeavour to found empires of their own and
small states to defend or expand their territory, their population, their wealth, and their strength. Some nations are
saturated. They desire neither change nor the reversal of
inequality; it might threaten their ascendancy, which might
ultimately pass to others. They prefer a *status quo* with
all its inherent frictions, so long as these frictions are not
more dangerous than change. They will consent to changes,
if pressed sufficiently hard, provided they are well equili-
brated and do not upset the relative position of Power
groups—if individual Powers cannot be held down. The
status quo as such is not of much importance, so long
as the balance of power is not disturbed, and no serious
shift from the privileged Powers to possible future rivals
takes place. Others again are well satisfied; they stand for
independence and security, not for growth or annexation.
They are willing to renounce all hope of aggrandizement,
provided they can secure peace and safety. They do not
grudge other nations' emancipation, but they frequently
fear their ambitions. Independence is menaced by empire,
and empire shamed by independence. One group of states
stands for liberty, the other stands for domination; contented, comparatively small civil commonwealths are flanked
by ambitious, expanding military societies. The concept
of a small-scale harmonious civilization represented by
minor states is confronted by the missionary Imperialism
of Great Powers.

Malcontented nations are not much concerned about the maintenance of the *status quo*. It may have its uses as long as it protects them from more powerful rivals; it may be infringed, if it blocks their way to aggrandizement and to the removal of inequality. They do not mind upsetting an existing balance of power, if this is the only way to arrive at another one, in which their own weight will count for more than it did before. They do not worry very much, if, at a given time, they are weaker or poorer than other nations. They can tolerate this while they wait for their chance to redress the position of inferiority which they greatly resent.

The acceptance of the *status quo* implies the renunciation by the smaller states of their claim to equality of opportunity. For, without the acquisition of men, of territory, and of wealth, this claim cannot be made good; if it is insisted upon, the prevailing balance must go. The sacrifice involved in this self-denial is not as great to-day as it would have been a century ago. In the days before universal conscription and mechanized mass warfare, a small, extremely well-drilled and well-led army might successfully wage war against a much larger enemy country, overrun its territory, maintain its strength, and find in its wealth compensation for the dearth of national supplies. The economic and financial strategy of Frederick the Great was based on these considerations. The army carried the war into the enemy country, lived on it, and extorted such contributions as it could and helped to husband the scarce natural resources at home; wars of this sort were profitable, not costly from the point of view of the victorious soldier. Small, aggressive states then had a chance to grow, either by conquering lands from their continental neighbours with their armies, or by settling overseas colonies with the help of their navies. Small defensive states, on the other hand, who could rely on the valour of their citizens, were fairly safe. The spread of universal conscription has given much greater weight to numbers, whilst the new technique of warfare has en-hanced the importance of industrial reserves and natural resources. The position of all small states has deteriorated correspondingly. Being small, they are condemned to remain weak, and being weak, they are condemned to remain small and insecure. Their territorial expansion is blocked; they can never muster sufficient strength for con-tinental annexation, and there are no longer any large empty spaces overseas waiting for occupation. They cannot hope to grow by their own unaided efforts; they can do so by internal structural changes, but external changes, making for greater strength and security, are denied to them. The more pro-gressive small states, like Switzerland or the Scandinavian nations, do not mind this state of affairs. They do not aspire to material equality; they neither strive for territorial aggrandizement nor do they wish to become master states and to rule others. They merely desire security and inde-pendence. But their very independence may be threatened by a collapse of the *status quo*. It may be maintained by a particularly advantageous natural position or as a result of the rivalries of their great neighbours who are bent on preserving the balance of power, or even by alliances with stronger states.

The right of all states to increase their size either pre-supposes never-ending wars and ever-recurrent repartitions of territory, or the existence of a family of nations, run by mutual consent on a kind of communist principle of terri-torial readjustment: to each according to his needs, from each according to his capacity. The corollary of this equality of opportunity would be equality of capacity to make use of opportunities; otherwise a nation which does not know how to exploit the natural resources within its territory and wants to preserve its primitive methods might withhold lands from others. Backward agricultural populations every-where need much more space than more developed farming communities, and very much more than highly industrialized societies. A premium would be put on backwardness. Should the more advanced nations, who can make better use of the opportunities at their disposal, be asked to part with some of them, for the benefit of their less advanced brothers?

IV

Social oscillations incessantly dislocate the economic equilibrium within every nation and disturb the political balance between it and others; but the main forces which undermine the *status quo* are those which originally established it. The existing *status quo* is generally the result of a war, followed frequently by a more or less ignominious peace. The vanquished peoples want to overthrow the existing order, not so much because it cramps their development, as because it perpetuates their defeat; ignominy rather than actual defeat has eaten deep into their souls. A humiliated nation, once it has recovered from the immediate shock of failure, will brood on revenge. The French policy of *revanche* after 1871 was due neither to population pressure nor to irreparable financial and economic losses. It was deflected for over forty years by colonial expansion. France did not need additional wealth and strength, but she needed colonial wars to recover her spiritual equilibrium. The conquest of Algeria and the Crimean War had made her forget Leipzig and Waterloo and the peace forced on her by the victorious Allies. Tunis, Tonkin, Senegal, and Morocco enabled her to wipe off the slate the shame of 1871 and the iniquities of the Second Empire.

The dominant cause of international unrest is the will to grow in strength and wealth, so as to equal one's neighbours at least, if not all the great Powers of the world. The rise of egalitarian fanaticism within a nation has let loose the forces of internal unbridled competition. The modern totalitarian state has curbed them at home; it substitutes external competition between states for internal competition between individuals. This is not a mere by-product of biological factors. Egalitarian fanaticism was quite as prevalent in thinly populated countries like France as in thickly populated Italy, in industrial Germany and in backward Russia. It is not shared by all nations. Neither Switzerland nor the Scandinavian States are in any way desirous of exchanging their relative security for dreams of empire and for unstinted growth. They prefer security to equality. But other small states in Europe and outside Europe are by no means immune from it. They may not be driven by an insane desire for equality with greater states, nor by economic pressure. But they may covet some possession in somebody else's hands, which was either taken from them by force or which they wish to get. Hungary pines for her "natural" national frontiers, Lithuania has not forgotten Vilna, and several Balkan States have not yet accepted quite wholeheartedly their present delimitations. Bolivia wants an outlet to the sea through the Chaco territory and Paraguay seeks expansion and wealth in the same region. The line which divides nations does not run between large and small, between over-populated and under-populated, between advanced and backward, or old and new nations, but between satisfied and unsatisfied nations, between those which want to run risks because they desire change and those which fear risks even more than change.

V

Adjustments in the weight of a state in relation to other states can be accomplished in a threefold way: by transfer of land, by transfer of people and by transfer of goods. These changes are not merely economic, and by no means always peaceful. Predatory economy prevailed for long periods over exchange economy. It revived from time to time in modern aggressive economic policies, which enhance the wealth of one country at the expense of another.

In primitive days most international transfers were effected by force, but conquest counted for little. The invaders did not settle in the conquered territory; they returned to their own land, carrying along with them the cattle, the women and the children of their vanquished enemies. Even under more civilized conditions, these coercive transfers have by no means stopped. The natural growth of population has released modern Governments from the necessity of replenishing their ranks by compulsory importation of aliens; but they peopled their colonial possessions by means of the slave trade and drove undesirables from their homelands when they wanted to offer better conditions of living to their own kith and kin. The expulsion of Jews and Moors from Spain and of Protestants from France was not due to economic motives, but the extirpation of these nonconforming groups, which could not be completely assimilated, was meant to strengthen the country's power. Compulsory inward transfer may have gone for good, but the Nazi programme has endeavoured to justify economically the expulsion of alien groups and to advocate a coercive outward population transfer.[1]

Compulsory transfer of goods too has survived through the ages. Nearly all early empires levied tribute from their dependencies, and early federations frequently groaned under the contribution imposed by the leading state upon the confederates. This tribute was not merely used for the defence of the Empire; it was meant to enable the predominant partner to control his allies.[2] Modern indemnities do not differ much from such tributes; they draw part of the wealth of a vanquished nation into the treasury of the victor.

---

[1] ". . . If it is not possible to feed the entire population of the state, the subjects of foreign states (non-citizens) must be expelled from the Reich." "Only those who are members of the nation can be citizens. Only those who are of German blood, without regard to religion, can be members of the German nation. No Jew can, therefore, be a member of the nation." Arts. 7 and 4.—C. Hoover, *Germany Enters the Third Reich*, Appendix; pp. 229 and 230.

[2] W. S. Ferguson, *Greek Imperialism*, p. 70 seq.

The main volume of population and wealth transfers is no longer compulsory. They are part of a voluntary system of international "exchange." But territory is rarely passed from one nation to another by purely voluntary, peaceful, bi-lateral exchange transactions.

Societies can grow in two ways only—by external expansion, which requires the acquisition of additional territory, or by *social* reorganization, which results in internal structural changes, such as closer settlements, the intensification of agriculture and a turn towards industry. In the absence of undeveloped territory inside the national boundary, territorial (horizontal) expansion must be carried out by voluntary federation, by amicable cession or by war. The scope of federation in the modern world has so far been limited. Federations have succeeded between populations closely related to one another by origin, tradition, history, and outlook. They have greatly increased the influence of their members in relation to other groups. The power of united Germany was very much greater than the combined strength of all her separate states; her wealth was much increased by the abolition of internal customs barriers, by the growth of markets, by concentrated production, and by a better spread distribution. Federation widens the common territory and equalizes the opportunities of its members; it generally contracts those of outsiders. It does not increase the total area nor the total natural resources; it does not offer the partners additional untouched reserves; it merely throws them open to all members and makes their exploitation easier and more profitable. And a predominant partner may see his wealth and strength greatly augmented, sometimes at the expense of his associates. Dublin decayed as a result of the Union, and Berlin flourished at the cost of smaller capitals. The federation of small neighbouring states is bound to raise their strength and their power of resistance against stronger neighbours; it may not always increase economic security. For in many instances their several economic systems are competitive rather than complementary; each country has nearly the same social structure as its neighbours and raises the same commodities; federation does not balance plenty and deficiency; it rather stresses them. The sum total of export surpluses would be increased as well as the sum total of import deficits; dependence on foreign markets and foreign supplies would not be diminished—though internal structural changes would be made much more attractive.

Conquest and occupation have been the main instruments of large-scale territorial expansion. They provided the victors with better frontiers; they gave them additional man-power and additional natural resources. But they saddled them with new political responsibilities, for the changes brought about by force have to be defended by force and can be undone by superior force.

Not all major changes in territorial possessions resulted from war. Peaceful cession, voluntarily agreed upon and not under duress, played a great part when states and nations were considered the private property of their rulers, who often disposed of them in a contractual way, as part of an inheritance, or by incorporating them under a marriage settlement. In the days of the Pope's temporal ascendancy, conquest could easily be disguised as cession. After the Norman Conquest of Ireland, a Papal Act presented Henry II with the country, for the Pope, being the supreme lord of the Western Isles, could easily shift possessions from one liege to another. Louisiana and Alaska changed hands by purchase. Since nationalism has come into its own cession has become difficult, though France got Savoy and Nice from Piedmont as the price for her support of Italy. She was willing to tolerate the unification of Germany on the understanding that she might annex Belgium. Such deals are no longer possible, except in the colonial sphere, where peaceful cessions occurred frequently, before the Covenant extended—

in a limited way—the principle of national self-determination
to primitive peoples.[1]

VI

Change has sometimes lessened inequality and sometimes
increased it. It has occasionally removed it, but more often
caused it. The winning of the West has made the United
States a great power; they have become the paramount
force in the Americas; it has dwarfed their neighbours,
Canada and Mexico. Change is at work all the time. But it is
by no means always dependent on deliberate government
activities. The forces of Nature as well as spontaneous
individual efforts, supported or not by government action,
generate it incessantly.

The *status quo* is a rather formal conception, dealing with
a society's external shape, its boundary; it does not apply
to its internal structure. Frontiers are static and permanently
rigid; the forces of the nation's life which they encom-
pass are dynamic and moving all the time. A country's area
may remain unchanged, but its capacity for carrying population may fluctuate violently, regardless of government
activities or any actions of its inhabitants. The great discoveries of the fifteenth and sixteenth centuries shifted the
centre of gravity from the Mediterranean to the Atlantic;
they prepared the eclipse not only of Genoa and Venice,
but also that of Nuremburg and Augsburg. They ultimately
transferred the world's economic power to Amsterdam,
London, and New York. The cutting of the Isthmus of Suez,
on the other hand, gave new openings to Mediterranean
countries, though it shortened the journey to the East for
all. And the Panama Canal enormously strengthened the
sea-power of the United States, though it shortened the route
to the West Coast of South America for Europe as well as
for them.

Desiccation and soil erosion in the United States and

[1] Cruttwell, *A History of Peaceful Change in the Modern World.*

Canada may attain such dimensions as to limit agricultural production considerably and to reduce the farming population dependent on it. The gold discoveries on the Rand made the Transvaal a rich and potentially powerful state. They resulted in the Boer War and ultimately in the Union of South Africa. They gave her the means to play a part in world affairs, which earlier federation plans could never have secured for her. The discovery of the Thomas-Gilchrist process for making steel from highly phosphoric ores put the German iron and steel industry on a competitive basis (1878). The exhaustion of coal mines in Great Britain's industrial North is throwing the country's economic weight Southward; the depressed areas begin to resemble the ghost cities of California and Nevada when the gold rush had passed.

The advent of the steamship had narrowed the Channel and lessened Great Britain's natural insular security; aircraft and submarines are completing this development. They are depriving her of the peculiar advantages she enjoyed in days gone by over her less mobile continental neighbours, whose slower economic life has, on the other hand, been greatly speeded up by railway and motor transportation, whilst their security has grown proportionately. Under modern war conditions, points of vantage like Gibraltar or Malta might lose their importance, and vast alterations in relative security might follow, even without a change of territorial ownership.

VII

The strongest spontaneous forces making for change are the growth (and decline) of population. Rates of increase or even decrease vary; the movement as such goes on for ever; it incessantly upsets conditions of living in every country and shifts its political, economic, and military weight in relation to other states. Governments have for centuries attempted more or less purposeful population policies;

until lately their results have not been very encouraging. For, short of starting studs for men and women, as suggested by some race purity enthusiasts, they cannot do much by direct action.[1] But indirect action—health services, the widening of economic opportunities, and even premiums and tax exemptions have been fairly effective. The industrialization of an agricultural country by means of tariff protection and the structural changes following it may not raise the birth-rate or lower the death rate, though it has been frequently asserted that industrialization and urbanization reduce the former; but they do keep would-be emigrants at home and attract immigrants from abroad.

Population has grown regularly in nearly all countries—Ireland and France excepted. Until recently, France was the only great country with a fairly stationary population. Hence her conservatism in things social and economic. She experienced no pressure on her social structure and she neither needed emigration on a large scale nor did she depend on widening foreign markets. She had founded a vast colonial empire, not, as the English are supposed to have done, in a fit of absent-mindedness, but by deliberately striving for greatness and glory. She could not fill the comparatively narrow spaces open to white immigration with her own countrymen; Spanish immigrants peopled a large part of Western Algeria, and thousands of Italians settled in Tunis. France herself was an immigration country in a twofold way. The amenities she could offer to foreigners had made her the Mecca of resident wealthy aliens, as well as of money-spending tourists, whilst the needs of her industries have been supplied by masses of alien workers, flocking to her mills and mines. She had become the greatest immigrant country, surpassing the Argentine and the United States. The average yearly immigration for 1922–1924, exceeded 220,000; even from 1929-30 it remained as high as 200,000; in the year 1931, 6·9 per cent of the French population

[1] Carr-Saunders, *World Population*, p. 226 seq.

were aliens. The repatriation, sometimes under pressure, of these people from France in the crisis has increased the great hardship of the countries to which they returned,[1] whilst the absence of the rich money-spending foreign element has paralysed the French luxury trade.

The United Kingdom is rapidly following the French example, though she is not as yet perturbed by the implications this may have for her foreign and imperial policy. The birth-rate is fast declining; the population will soon be stagnant and in a few years may begin to dwindle. Assuming (a) the continuation of present-day tendencies, or (b) the accentuation of these tendencies, or (c) a limited reversion of these tendencies, the population of England and Wales in a hundred years may fall as low as 4,426,000; it will scarcely be higher than 33,585,000.[2]

Italy, Germany, and Japan, less favoured in respect of territory, seem to be in a different position. Their numbers are still increasing rapidly, but limits for each of them are in sight. It is doubtful whether the spurt in marriages and births following the population policy of the new régime

---

[1] Carr-Saunders, p. 159.

[2]   *Future Populations of England and Wales*

Year	A	B	C
	000's	000's	000's
1935	40,563	40,563	40,563
1945	40,876	40,392	42,338
1955	40,207	38,777	43,651
1965	38,504	35,799	43,744
1985	33,106	26,087	41,612
2005	27,090	15,058	38,177
2025	22,121	6,940	35,104
2035	19,969	4,426	33,585

A assumes fertility and mortality rates remain at 1933 level.
B assumes fertility and mortality rates decline at recent rates of decline.
C assumes fertility rates increase to their 1931 level.

Dr. Enid Charles, "The Effect of Present Trends in Fertility and Mortality upon the Future Population of England and Wales and upon its Age Composition," London and Cambridge Economic Service Memorandum No. 40. *Economist*, February 15, 1936.

will gather sufficient speed to stop the decrease in net reproduction which has set in in Germany. 1·4 million births a year are needed to maintain the population on the 1933 level; the figure for 1934 was only 1·18. In Italy, the rate of growth, though fast declining, is still considerable. The net reproduction rate is 1·18 against 0·76 in England and Wales and 0·88 in France.[1] In Japan the annual number of live births seems to be stationary. The tendency of her population is the same as that prevailing in most parts of Western Europe. It may never reach the 100 million level, whilst that of Italy may, by 1961, run to 61 millions, before decline sets in.[2]

The great disparities in densities of population, which range from 468 per square mile in the United Kingdom to three in Canada and two in Australia, are not likely to disappear in the natural course of events. Large-scale migration is diminishing, though the transfer of population might make for greater equalization, and greater equality might lessen tension. Immigration has helped to people the vast new continents and has speeded up their development enormously. Emigration, on the other hand, has nowhere—with the exception of Ireland—reduced population or considerably lessened their rate of increase.

Equalizing tendencies in this direction will not go very far. They presuppose a kind of international spirit on both sides, which does not in fact exist. Even thinly populated immigrant countries have become adverse to indiscriminate immigration and have closed their doors to it. They may have to resume immigration, controlled perhaps, if they want to develop more rapidly, for the net natural reproduction

[1] The *gross* reproduction rate is obtained by measuring the replacement of potential mothers by daughters. It indicates the number of girl children born to every woman between fifteen and fifty. If below unity, population must dwindle. *Net* reproduction accounts for the number of girl babies who die before maturity. Dr. E. Charles in the *Economist*, June 27, 1936. R. Kuczynski, in *The Statist*, December 25, 1937.

[2] Carr-Saunders, op. cit., Table 26, pp. 128–9.

in Australia is but 0·98, in the United States 0·98 and in New Zealand 0·98; only in Canada, thanks to the French Canadians, is it as high as 1·32.[1] In future population gaps in the Dominions are bound to grow wider if they continue to refuse aliens, as they cannot draw the necessary stock from the mother country, whose population is declining.

Emigrant countries do not want to raise and rear their own flesh and blood for the benefit of a foreign power. They will not release them from their allegiance to the old national state. They no longer look upon them as sons and daughters lost to the parent nation, whose ways slowly part from hers; they are to be the vanguards of her expansion. Trade need not follow the flag, but the flag must follow the emigrant. In such circumstances, large-scale immigration is impossible. For peaceful change begun by transfer of population might end in a violent transfer of territory. An Uitlander movement like the one which menaced the independence of the Transvaal might develop; it would result either in wringing a separate territory from a state which had offered hospitality to the peaceful invaders, or in its entire annexation. Union with the parent state would follow, and the erstwhile hosts might consider themselves lucky if they were not subjected to a foreign nation. The Spanish settlers of Texas and California have experienced this fate.

Since mass immigration might finally lead to the formation of new "unredeemed nationalities" and to territorial annexation, it cannot be admitted, especially when the cultural and economic tension between two nations, as between Australia and Japan, is very marked. The nationalists of the empty lands will refuse admission to aliens, mixture with whom is considered undesirable from a social as well as from a biological point of view. Wide spaces will remain empty because governments cannot afford to run the risks

[1] R. Kuczynski, *The Measurement of Population Growth*, p. 213; Carr-Saunders, op. cit., Table 25; R. Kuczynsky in *The Statist*, loc. cit.

of deliberately organizing a social and political symbiosis of a rather delicate nature. Glaring inequality will continue. The peaceful exchange of population (the transfer of Greeks and Turks and Bulgarians and Turks) under the auspices of the League of Nations has been a very great achievement, but it has not equalized economic conditions; it has merely eliminated racial friction.

VIII

The persistence of disparities in density of population (75·9 in France, with a huge colonial empire to exploit, and 139·7 per square kilometre in Germany, with no foreign dominions) gives rise to antagonistic social philosophies. Must ambitious nations, whose numbers increase rapidly, remain content with such openings as might satisfy the needs of a saturated stationary people? Must the Germans, whose birth rate has again risen from 14·7 (1933) to 19·0 (1936) per thousand submit to the standards of the French, whose birth rate has fallen from 18·8 (1926) to 15·2 in 1935? And must the Japanese, whose rate is 31·6 per thousand comply with those of the Australians with a rate of 17·1? Or have Germans and Italians, whose complaints about the scanty territorial home reserves for their existing populations are fairly well founded, the right to claim new lands, which would accommodate all new comers, even if the increase is brought about by propaganda, pressure, and premiums, which make for growth regardless of space? Should a nation whose nationals desire a high standard of living, and whose citizens deliberately restrict the size of their families, perhaps in disregard of their government's activities, renounce part of its territorial reserves, in order that another nation, whose numbers, even without political stimulants, increase very rapidly, may be provided with additional opportunities?

The right to control emigration or immigration is recognized as part of a nation's fundamental sovereignty; its ethnical and social structure may depend on it. Is the right to regulate its natural growth any less fundamental? The restriction of immigration and the withholding of natural resources from foreigners willing to give up their citizenship may appear to growing nations as narrow national egotism, which must retard the development of the restricting country and of the whole universe; it is a kind of dog-in-the-manger policy which puts the supposed future interests of a limited resident group before the pressing and immediate needs of a large part of the world's struggling nations. The stationary nation will insist on its right to plan its national future according to its own standards. *Le bien-être*, the maintenance of traditional comfort regardless of new possibilities of enjoying life, which is so dear to the French people, is quite as respectable a social ideal as the pursuit of restless technical and social innovation by Americans and Germans. To a conservative people, the attempt to stimulate, by premiums and propaganda, the growth of a cramped nation beyond the limits of its territorial resources is an act of overt, almost wanton aggression. The resulting strain may have to be eased by an overflow into foreign dominions; and a mass movement of this sort might greatly depress the standards of living and, in the case of ethnically different races, seriously alter the composition of the resident national population. Social pressure at home might be relieved—the mass exodus from Italy after the 'seventies has undoubtedly done this; wealth might be increased, but not strength. These national fragments, separating from the home country, might ultimately be lost when thoroughly embedded in another statehood, and an irredentist nationalist propaganda might try to save them. Or else a nation must acquire additional territory beyond its frontiers, basing its claims to them on the assumption that a nation which grows faster than its neighbours by greater fertility shows greater virility and has a right to overflow, as fertility is a sign of physical, moral, and spiritual superiority. The interests of the world at large,

I

so it will say, demand that space be found for the expansion of a master race, which might otherwise never come to full fruition, and thus be frustrated if it had to resort to birth control. The weaklings must give way. The romantic "none but the brave deserve the fair" is being democratized, vulgarized, and tribalized.

So-called more advanced peoples, with a declining birth rate, which may be temporarily offset by an even faster declining death rate, will ultimately reach stagnation point; without immigration, their numbers will decline. The nation is ageing; its life force is spent; it is indulging in race suicide. The passing of a great race has begun. The Empire which its ancestors have won is slipping from its feeble hands. But the stationary nations themselves do not by any means take such a despondent view of the state of affairs towards which they are moving. What is "degeneration" to their rivals is social and cultural selection to them. They look upon the faster growing nations as inferior types of human beings, who like rabbits, multiply indiscriminately. But these growing swarms do not behave like meek rabbits. They are not content to remain in their underground burrows; they are strong and aggressive and want to come to the top and spread all over the world. They are fulfilling a divine mission.

If statistics can be relied upon, neither the Germans nor the Italians, nor even the Japanese belong any longer to this group.

IX

Change does not move all the time in one direction; growth and expansion are more than offset by contraction and separation. The modern world is not expanding into a few continually widening empires. It has witnessed the breaking-up of at least four empires and is filled with the strife of separation which is rending others. Present-day expansion is but the shifting of possessions from one power to another. The great international vacant demesne, from which new colonial empires have been carved during the last two hundred years, is all but exhausted. The age of colonization is drawing near its end. The character of the present situation is determined by the absence of any unoccupied, unruled land reserves, on which dissatisfied claimants could draw whenever they felt cramped at home. Some of the colonial powers have large, scarcely opened up reserves at their disposal; these are undeveloped, not unpossessed. Their masters are not willing to share them with their disgruntled neighbours.

Countries which had to feed an increasing population and maintain their standard of living have before endeavoured to do this by structural transformation. They have intensified their methods of agriculture and industry and have turned from agricultural to more industrial pursuits. This change has been peaceful, but it has frequently resulted in serious international repercussions. The intensification of agriculture on the European continent in the years since the war has gravely disturbed the export trade of oversea agrarian countries. The industrialization of agricultural countries, on the other hand, has deranged the export trade of manufacturing nations. The tariffs and premiums which have been used in both cases have strengthened the spirit of nationalism which is breaking up the world economic unity which existed not long ago. Economic policies are once more becoming predatory.[1]

Less favoured nations which attempt to increase their wealth by forcing their exports may have to reduce their standard of living in order to undercut others. But when they are successful, they are excluded from foreign markets by various devices of commercial protection and accused of lowering international standards of living. The Japanese

---

[1] The object of external devaluation is to steal a march on one's commercial rivals. Where it has brought permanent benefit to a country it has done so at the expense of another country.

immigrants were not allowed to enter the Western world, for fear that they would depress its wage standards. When they remained at home and turned their activity to the manufacture of competitive goods for foreign markets, they were penalized, as the comparatively high costs of production of the West had to be protected at all hazards against the rivalry of workers who are content with a different standard of comfort.

CHAPTER IV

EQUALITY OF OPPORTUNITY

I

ECONOMIC equality implies two closely connected, but at the same time different, problems: equal economic opportunities for states as separate collective social units and equal economic opportunities for their citizens.

Governments who demand equal opportunities for their states want to play the same part in world affairs as other governments; for this purpose they need equal strength and equal wealth for the present and equal chances for growth and expansion in the future. This implies equal resources and, since permanent resources which are available all the time are bound up with territorial possessions, a territorial basis which can support an adequate population at a decent standard of living—decent in relation to its own national traditions as well as to those of rival nations—and sufficient territorial reserves to allow for a natural increase in population and a normal rise in comforts.

The connection between the equal opportunities of governments and of their nationals is indirect. By obtaining chances which allow them to rear large families or accumulate riches individual citizens strengthen the power and the wealth of their states. Sometimes this connection is inverted. The chance of making a private fortune may offer prosperity to individuals; it may weaken their states. The great Irish exodus in the famine years, which seriously reduced the Irish population, increased the prosperity of those who went abroad, but it cut the Irish nation into halves. On the other hand legal equality of governments may have little effect on the status or the opportunities of their subjects. The equality of status granted to Ethiopia in 1923 did not give her tribesmen the opportunities which every subject member of the Swiss Confederation enjoys. Since the rise of totalitarian governments, these issues are no longer confined to the dealings of the West with backward Oriental despotism. The newly established totalitarian states have remodelled, and considerably reduced, the civil as well as the political rights of their subjects. Individuals as such no longer count—they have become but straw and bricks, to be used and handled in the raising of a powerful State edifice. They are mere particles of the State, for whose sole benefit they exist. But the older conception of the State as an instrument for improving and increasing the welfare of its citizens has survived in the countries which profess faith in democracy. Thus a very far-reaching spiritual, as well as a material discrepancy between two types of political organization has arisen. This does not prevent egalitarian arrangements between governments as such, though it may sometimes deprive them of practical value.

The Soviet Republic cannot give foreign citizens the right to free enterprise, for its own citizens do not enjoy it.[1] The Russian comrade who goes West, on the other hand, provided his government lets him go abroad, gets opportunities denied to him at home. A commercial treaty, conceived on the lines of the most-favoured-nation treatment of reciprocity, would extend rights of immigration and settlement to Russian subjects—who are not allowed to emigrate, and would present them with equality of opportunity, of which they are not permitted to take advantage. Reciprocity of opportunity of this kind is purely formal. The states which recognize individual rights are supposed to grant them to all; those which do not will withhold them from all. Since totalitarian governments require complete equality of status, they will insist on equal rights and equal opportunities for their individual subjects, as well as for them-

[1] The Russian government has given some specific rights to those foreigners to whom it has granted "concessions."

selves. Indeed, some totalitarian single-party states which limit the rights of those subject to their rule and flatly deny that "men are created equal" have become the most outspoken advocates of equal rights for all states.

Equality of opportunity for the individual citizen may be defined as a state of affairs in which such an individual (not differing very much from other individuals) has the chance of exercising his faculties, such as they are, under fairly equal conditions. As the assertion, "men are created equal" was meant to embrace the citizens of every commonwealth, equality of opportunity is not an issue restricted to home affairs; it implies a claim to equality of opportunity for the nationals of all countries. They should all have the same chance of earning the same income with the same effort and of accumulating an equal amount of property within the same period and with the same sacrifices of "abstinence." If they cannot get equality of opportunity within the confines of their own state, which is often the case in the older societies, where social stratification has long ago hardened into all sorts of class distinctions, they might find it abroad, for instance in the great empty settlement areas of the new world, which offered newcomers from all countries fairly equal chances for acquiring cheap land or for earning high wages, and which invited everybody who was willing to work.

Opportunities in old and new countries varied greatly, though the natural advantages of the latter were frequently offset by lack of capital equipment, by high rates of interest, by high wages and by the dearth of general cultural facilities; this disparity was to be lessened rapidly by giving the inhabitants and the capital of the old countries access to the opportunities of the new.

II

Equal opportunities for all classes and all groups of people never existed in the old-established European countries.

Society was hierarchically stratified, its different layers possessing different duties and rights. The opportunities of the members of one group were circumscribed by their own particular privileges and obligations, as well as by those of groups below or above it. Members of one group might experience diminishing opportunities at a time when those of another would continue to enjoy, quite undisturbed, the limited advantages of their own position. When primogeniture blocked the way to the acquisition of new estates, unrest arose among the land-owning classes of England in the fifteenth and sixteenth centuries, which drove the younger sons to Ireland and overseas as planters. But during the same period, it was often difficult to make members of the lower classes join in these colonial adventures.

The opportunities of one class meant little to another. Transition from one stratum to another was exceptional; only a few stray individuals were affected by it, whose fate did not matter much to their particular groups. The new egalitarian philosophy of the French Revolution designed a society based on liberty, equality, and fraternity. Its votaries smashed the hierarchical *ancien régime* and decreed equal rights for all citizens, regardless of their origin, but the legal equality thus established did not furnish them with equal opportunities for earning an income and for accumulating a fortune. The influence of property, tradition, and education remained overwhelmingly strong. The Have-nots were merely allowed to compete under the same formal conditions as the Haves. This lack of equality of opportunity under a system of legal equality gave rise to the early Socialist doctrines; they might have flooded the densely packed European countries had not the Industrial Revolution and the opening up of the New World held out new hopes. The Industrial Revolution freed men from their single dependence on land and its owners. It offered new ways of attaining wealth and independence to impecunious men endowed with will-power and initiative. And the

American Revolution, followed by the emancipation of Spanish America, finally led to the formation of a series of independent republics among the American peoples. It took a vast continent, whose resources had scarcely been scratched, from the hands of a monopolistic metropolis, and put it, so to speak, at the disposal of all men and women. And it taught Great Britain that she had to abandon colonial exclusiveness, if she meant to retain her remaining or her newly acquired possessions. The American republics contained a very large proportion of the world's open spaces, which Providence had evidently put at the disposal of the European races. To fill them up and to do so as rapidly as possible was their manifest destiny. The native populations inhabiting them were too weak to contest the invading forces; they counted for little in their development. The work of exploitation had to be done by European immigrants, except in the tropical belt, where negro slaves were imported. The vast natural resources attracted a steady stream of immigrants towards this land of Canaan where milk and honey flowed—here was Utopia placed on the map of the world. From 1820 to the present day, 34 million immigrants crossed the ocean to the United States alone. Some of the early comers were inspired by political ideals; they desired to contribute their share to the building up of a free commonwealth. The majority of the men and women who set their faces towards the West were driven by an economic urge. Anybody who had a pair of strong arms and an indomitable will could make a living in the New World and, thanks to the land legislation of the United States government, acquire a farm with very little capital. The effort needed for rising from the ranks of penniless agricultural labour to the ownership of land was but a matter of a few years, given a reasonable amount of good luck. It was equally easy for an industrious man to start a small shop of his own. A kind of classless society sprang up in the American West, fertilized by innumerable streams from all parts of the world.

I*

The master of to-day had been yesterday's labourer, and to-day's labourer might be a master to-morrow. Here the equal opportunities which the eighteenth-century revolutionary dreamers had promised to mankind were offered to all and sundry.

They were not reserved for the citizens of the United States nor for those of the former metropolis. Everybody who was willing to do his or her part was welcome, whatever his origin, creed, or position. "We have," said Abraham Lincoln on July 10, 1858, at the Fourth of July celebrations in Chicago, "besides these men—descended by blood from our ancestors—among us, perhaps half our people who are not descendants at all of those men; they are men who have come from Europe,—German, Irish, French, and Scandinavian,—men that have come from Europe themselves, or whose ancestors have come hither and settled here, finding themselves our equal in all things. . . . They cannot carry themselves back into that glorious epoch and make themselves feel that they are part of us; but when they look through that old Declaration of Independence, they find that those old men say that we 'hold those truths to be self-evident, that all men are created equal', . . . and that they have a right to claim it as though they were blood of the blood, and flesh of the flesh, of the men who wrote that Declaration; and so they are."

The percentage of success was sufficiently high to make people forget the tragic failures and to carry the glad tidings all over the world that equal opportunities were offered to everybody in the new country. The other new countries followed suit and threw their doors wide open to immigrants, on whose influx their rapid development depended. They were not quite as liberal as the United States. The British Dominions naturally endeavoured to attract British people, and as assisted immigration played an important part in their settlement, the British were favoured. And South America had inherited an aristocratic land system which made the rise of the small independent landowners, who had become the backbone of the United States agrarian democracy, rather difficult.

III

THE settlement of these vast new areas in many ways widened and equalized opportunities for residents in other parts of the world. The capital needed for opening them up had to be provided by European investors; they did not have to follow it in person; they could enjoy its fruits by staying quietly at home. Flags and frontiers counted for little in the process. United States bonds and shares were floated on the capital markets of the entire world; the nationals of all countries got a taste of pioneering—in its more comfortable financial aspect at least—by sitting by their firesides and cashing dividend warrants, which were frequently purely imaginary, from the world's rich wide open spaces. The Argentine became a kind of British financial satrapy, whilst it filled up with Italian and Spanish immigrants. Great Britain invested £500–600 million in it,[1] against £540 million in the Dominion of Canada. German capital helped in the building of the Canadian Pacific Railway, which became the backbone of Canadian unity. The gold industry of the Transvaal attracted investors from all parts of the world. The resident capitalists of the new countries frequently enjoyed considerable advantages over their foreign partners, for they were on the spot and familiar with local conditions. They did not mind very much where their new compatriots came from and they did not ask for discriminative legislation against their country of origin.

The huge surplus of foodstuffs and raw materials which resulted from the immigration of men and capital was sent to the old countries, since costs of production had fallen

---

[1] The nominal value of these investments to-day was estimated at £435 million. Mr. Runciman in the House of Commons, May 12, 1936.

rapidly and transportation charges had been reduced. It swamped the European markets and lowered prices everywhere, often to the detriment of resident agriculturalists, but it brought plenty and cheapness. The workers in the European industries could share this plenty almost on equal terms with the inhabitants of the newer world, for, thanks to falling freight charges, the prices of prime necessities in the consuming areas ruled but little higher than in producing countries. European workers participated in nature's bounty as their costs of living fell; they no longer had to expatriate themselves; even if money wages had remained stationary, real wages were rising rapidly. But money wages were rising too. For the demands for manufactured goods on the part of the new producers, settled on the prairies and on the mining fields, had to be satisfied. Markets for such commodities widened, even though protection of local industries dislocated them from time to time. Manufacturers in the old countries got the raw material from overseas on the same terms as their resident competitors or their European rivals. Fall River, Lancashire, and Alsace-Lorraine paid the same price for cotton in Savannah, without national discrimination. The flow of raw materials spread evenly to all parts of the world, wherever people were willing to pay for them; it did not matter whether it rose in dependent colonies or in independent republics. The governments of the new countries or the powers which controlled dependencies made no attempt at securing preference for their own nationals or at favouring the citizens of particular states. A new kind of absenteeism had arisen, the blessings of which were gratefully acknowledged by those who paid, as well as by those who received the rents. Equal opportunities were offered to all. The wealthier countries drew a dividend income from their investments abroad, and the poorer ones shared overseas prosperity by the remittances of their emigrants or the savings of their migratory labourers.

9:::p型型

The meaning of the term "equal opportunity" was rather elastic; it sometimes implied equal opportunity for all the residents of a country and sometimes for foreigners as well as for residents; it sometimes comprised all foreigners, but not foreigners and residents. In other instances again, equality of opportunity for colonial residents and residents of the mother country or some other favoured unit, but not for other foreigners was established. In the matter of imports of manufactured articles, there were frequent restrictions. After the great ardour of the early Cobdenite days had passed, scarcely any new country adhered to free trade. Dominions, as well as independent republics, provided themselves with fairly stiff protective tariffs against foreign manufacturers—including those of the mother country. These tariffs greatly limited the equality of opportunity of foreign mill-owners; those resident in the producing countries were given special favours. But this preference, it was asserted, was justified, since European countries possessed compensating advantages for manufacturing in their old-established industries, their cheap capital, comparatively low wages, and highly skilled labour. The new countries had voluntarily renounced their main advantage (cheap foodstuffs and cheap raw materials) and generously shared their plenty with them on almost equal terms; they had enabled them to keep money wages low, while real wages were rising all the time.

Protection did favour residents; it stimulated the transfer of enterprise from abroad, whatever its national origin, by putting a premium on the establishment of new industries, which were to attract foreign capital and foreign labour. It frequently assisted the inflow of capital goods from the great foreign manufacturing concerns. Big firms were encouraged to found branch establishments behind the new customs barriers; they bought the equipment for them at home. Until a modern preferential régime was instituted in Canada, all non-residents were treated alike in the British Dominions. The most-favoured-nation clause, which was almost universally in force, gave the manufacturers of all foreign countries access to the markets of the new countries under the same terms. Englishmen, Frenchmen, Germans, Italians, and Scandinavians enjoyed equal opportunities in the independent new countries and almost equal opportunities in colonies with responsible governments and dominion status. For quite a long time they could immigrate without restrictions; they could participate freely in capital investments and could share in the supply of foodstuffs and raw materials, and, to a more limited degree, in overseas markets. Their exporters did not enjoy the same opportunities as the residents of the new countries; in all other respects a system of equal opportunities was in being.

IV

This unrestricted international intercourse somewhat softened the glaring inequalities which existed between thinly populated, undeveloped, rich new countries and densely populated old countries, whose natural resources are at best stationary; but it could not wipe them out completely. The free exchange of goods between two neighbouring regions under the rule of the same government will enrich the inhabitants of both regions. But the chances of making a living or of accumulating a fortune in a fertile, not yet densely settled agricultural region are very much greater than in a thickly populated industrial region, with no particular natural resources, however intense internal trade between both may become. The inflow of cheap agricultural products into the poor industrial districts will give its inhabitants some share of the natural plenty of the other area, and the agriculturalists' demand for additional manufactured goods will widen the market for the industrialists' goods and enable them to pay for plenty. Widespread regional inequality of opportunity cannot be completely redressed, except by wholesale migration, when sufficient unappropriated fertile land is available, which the poor immigrants can acquire and work cheaply. The opportunities of distinct groups of people, but not the resources of separate districts, can be equalized by the more or less wholesale transfer of population. Ultimately, the poor districts might become derelict. Something of this sort has happened in the rural areas of New England. Deserted farms dot the hills; the owners have gone West. But here and there immigrants from the poorer parts of Europe have settled upon them, to whom the mean opportunities of these stony parts of New England offer such wealth as they sought in vain in the country from which they came. Under a régime of free migration, populations would move towards those spots which promised them the greatest chances. A complete redistribution of people would result from it; the world would be settled afresh after a purely economic pattern. The physical and psychic properties of the various ethnographic groups called races—their differential efficiencies as well as their powers of adaptation to climatic conditions —would affect this movement considerably. Tendencies of this kind are visible in the United States, where natural wealth is attracting all races to certain favoured spots. Federation has greatly increased the opportunities of the inhabitants of each of the forty-eight States by throwing open to them an enormous Free Trade area, but it has by no means made the forty-eight distinct political regions more equal to one another in strength, wealth, and population. Some of them have declined since federation, by losing people, weight, power, and influence to their more favoured partners. Similarly, the Union of Scotland and England is depopulating the former kingdom. The closest federation of hitherto rival states cannot bring about a rigid equality of opportunity for all their inhabitants, except under an ideal communist régime, where all inequalities are wiped out—a régime which nowhere exists, not even in Russia. But federation can abolish the intense feeling of rival jealousies, which rend a world of independent states, and make them partners in a new commonwealth, even if it equalizes neither the wealth of the states nor the chances of their citizens.

V

Even under the most favoured circumstances the opportunities for nationals and for aliens who live under a foreign flag have nowhere been quite the same. A slight element of discrimination has always been present. The citizens of one country who settle down in another are handicapped by language or habit. Foreign immigrants in English-speaking countries have had a hard time whilst they assimilated themselves linguistically, socially, and politically to their new surroundings, though their lower standards of living frequently enabled them to undercut their more favoured rivals and to offset this handicap to some extent. The "greenhorn" nowhere enjoys equal opportunities with the native born worker, whatever his country of origin. For a time at least he is the natural prey of exploiters. And even when the worst is over he may never get more than a mere pittance. The opportunity to rise above their former status did not come to immigrants until after a fairly lengthy period of tribulation. But the hope of its coming did reconcile them to all sorts of humiliations. The strain did not end completely when the worst was over, for the new country would insist on their shedding part of their national cultural inheritance; it rarely coerced them directly; if they wanted to get on they could not help being assimilated, at least externally, to new conditions of life and language. They, and certainly their children, were lost to the national civilization which had bred them.

Assimilation did not matter much to those European workers who were ready to give up their citizenship. Many of them had disliked the political and social order at home.

They had left, either because they felt too impotent to change it, or because they preferred the chance of a social rise under a foreign flag to stagnation at home. But it did matter to their governments. It depleted their wealth as well as their strength. It may have lessened social tension, but it reduced the number of recruits available for national defence. Most settlement colonies, Anglo-Saxon as well as Iberian, had long ago become independent republics or self-governing dominions. But England had retained the allegiance of great settlement areas which were capable of receiving a large number of immigrants, even after they assumed dominion status. Their ethnical structure had remained fairly British. Over 90 per cent of the population of Australia was of British-Irish stock, and even in Canada with its large, really indigenous, French population (28·2 per cent), nearly 52 per cent were of British-Celtic origin, a little less than in the United States. The Dominions which desired immigrants naturally preferred those of British origin. Only the British could go overseas in large numbers and share in the marvellous opportunities of new vacant lands without having to change their political allegiance or give up their language or their ways of thinking and living. And England alone was able to retain the power and the loyalty of those of her sons whom she had settled in the Dominions. Even those of her emigrants who preferred the United States could enjoy the preference which language and manners gave them over other races.

Equality of opportunity between England and the other European *nations* was evidently non-existent. European governments who let their populations share in the greater opportunities of the new world overseas, had to release them for good from their allegiance, and see them melted down into the citizenship of other countries. They might maintain commercial contacts with the mother country, and even preserve some cultural links. But cultural ties were bound to snap ultimately, even where no pressure was put on the immigrants, for comparatively few amongst the masses had shared to the full the cultural and spiritual accomplishments of the home country. They had not turned to foreign lands with the object of carrying its cultural heritage along with them and propagating its values amongst their hosts; they were bent on participating in their economic and material wealth. In fact, the absence of external pressure seemed to make voluntary assimilation with the people whose hospitality they enjoyed particularly attractive. European-minded nationalist irredentists, who in some immigrant countries looked backward to the country of their fathers, nearly always belonged to the first generation, which could not adapt itself to new surroundings, and to those members of the second generation whom failure had disillusioned.

Some of the great continental countries which owned no overseas settlement areas greatly resented this absence of equal opportunities. The increased social pressure resulting from the growth of population made emigration a grave political issue. They were losing political strength by the transfer of men and women in the prime of their lives, whilst the new countries were growing very much more rapidly in wealth and in political importance. Between 1846 and 1932 Italy lost ten millions by emigration, Austria five millions, Germany five millions, and Spain nearly five millions.[1] In the early days this discrepancy had not mattered very much, but when nationalism began to govern people's minds, and when democracy had transformed the subjects of a despotic government into the members of a self-conscious nation, individuals, as well as their rulers, resented this as a kind of slight. The Germans were easily assimilable; they felt at home in the United States and in many British Dominions. Their political writers had early lamented their loss of nationality and devised more or less fanciful schemes for forming a German State in Texas or within the United

[1] Carr-Saunders, op. cit., p. 49.

States. The people themselves did not mind very much until Germany had become united, strong, and free from outside control. Then it seemed unbearable that a great nation which had come into its own after centuries of impotence should lose by emigration within a single quinquennium (1881–5) over three-quarters of a million men and women, who would help to develop alien nations, but who were lost to their motherland for ever.

Resentment at this grave injustice done to her sons and daughters, who must lose their nationality when they attempted to share in some of the great opportunities which the new countries offered to all, lay behind Germany's early desire for colonies. Why should she be deprived of opportunities which the English nation enjoyed? Her cry was taken up later on by Italy and Japan. It implied a demand for equal rights in the colonial sphere—equal opportunities for governments to acquire colonies and equal opportunities for their subjects to exploit them, without loss of nationality. But the claim was by no means universal. The Scandinavians, the Swiss, and the Austrians were in a similar predicament, and so were countries like Holland and Belgium, who could not keep their people at home and could not find room for them in their tropical colonies. Even Russia lost a great many emigrants, for though immigration into Siberia was successfully organized on a large scale, it took care of the Russian mujik only; it did not provide opportunities for the "alien populations" subject to the rule of the Tsar. The national resentment of so-called Have-not Powers was based on the tacit assumption that nations which were culturally, industrially, and militarily great were entitled to equality in every respect with the leading nations of the world, whilst the minor Powers were not. A great nation had the right to become greater, while the small nation, being small, must remain small.

VI

Emotional arguments of this sort played a great part in the rival activities which culminated in the partition of Africa. They could not evoke those equal opportunities so earnestly desired. For the African and Polynesian lands which were thrown open to colonization were not fit for white mass immigration. Climatic conditions were not responsible for this; they could be mastered by modern hygiene. Moreover, extensive highland areas, which were well adapted for European settlement, were available. The main insurmountable obstacle was the presence of vigorous native populations, who were prepared to work for their European masters, if not efficiently, at least cheaply, and who rapidly grew in numbers after control had stopped tribal warfare and epidemics. As long as they could get cheap and docile native labour, governments as well as settlers would not pay such high wages as would have attracted European workers. Native labour was less efficient, but far more profitable. Three Europeans could do the jobs of five native employees at the rate of twenty shillings a day each, but the natives could be hired, fed, and housed at four shillings a head.[1] European labour, being five times as expensive, had no chance whatsoever. The native, moreover, was not attracted to Trade Unionism, nor bent on setting up as an independent farmer or rival entrepreneur as soon as he had saved enough money. Between workers who must earn twenty shillings a day to feel comfortable and those who can live on four shillings a day equality of opportunity cannot exist. The balance is in favour of the unpretending race, even though the efficiency of its members is low. The communist doctrine, "From each according to his capacity and to each according to his needs", offers better chances to those satisfied with lower standards than to advanced races. This may account (to a

[1] These figures relate to the years 1906–7 in South Africa. The corresponding figures to-day would be nineteen shillings and half a crown.

minor degree) for the great attraction Communism has for backward populations.

The presence of native labour discouraged the inflow of European labour. For reasons of race prestige, white immigrants were carefully safeguarded against falling to the native level by becoming a kind of "white trash." It was difficult enough to prevent the children of white settlers, for whom there were no careers outside land-owning, from sinking in the social scale. The Dutch Bywoners in Cape Colony and the poor whites in the Piedmont regions, or the share-croppers along the Tobacco Road in the United States could not make a decent living from the land on which they were born. They despised its coloured population and prided themselves on their superiority due to their white parentage; but all the time the servile labour of the black men was elevating them from slavery to freedom, whilst the white men's reliance on the services of the black people was slowly dragging them down. Indiscriminate European immigration would have aggravated this evil. The stronger the feeling of racial superiority among the colonizing people and the more intense their wish to plant a new commonwealth in which the national race could reproduce itself under the national flag, the more severe had to be the checks put on immigration. A horde of penniless men flooding the new country, unable to find employment at adequate white wages, would get mixed up with the natives and become the fathers of a low bastard race. The presence of white women, even though fairly numerous, would not solve the problem, as long as the white worker's income was too small to keep a family in decent comfort. Talk about the superiority of the white race and its duty of abstaining from mixture with native women has been pretty general; it has no-where completely prevented miscegenation. For race mix-ture, in whatever stratum of society it may occur, is, after all, not so much due to the absence of white women as to the presence of coloured women.

The survival of the natives and their adaptation to new conditions of life was the real obstacle to mass immigration into the German colonies. Their natural resources were ample; their development was fairly rapid. German administration before the war had reached a pretty high level of prosperous efficiency. The colonies were just beginning to play a useful part in the nation's economic life by offering markets, raw materials, and opportunities for capital enterprise; but they attracted few immigrants. After a quarter of a century of successful development, the total white population of the German colonies was about 24,000, including foreigners, women and children, civil servants and police, as against over fourteen million natives. At that time German emigration had almost come to a standstill; its lowest level was 19,000 a year; its average from 1902–1913 exceeded the entire white population which had been settled in the German colonies within twenty-five years.

The position in other African dependencies was very much the same. After a hundred years of successful domination and expansion, the entire white population of Algeria is but 859,000 against 6,376,000 natives, and the Union of South Africa to-day numbers a white population of 2 millions, while its native population has reached a figure of 7·5 millions, excluding native reservations under the control of the Imperial government. Kenya, with 18,000 whites against 3,013,000 natives, Southern Rhodesia, 55,000 whites and 1,229,000 natives, Northern Rhodesia, 13,800 whites and 1,296,000 natives, and the Congo Free State, 19,000 whites and 9,383,000 natives tell the same story, and so do the Portuguese colonies, notwithstanding the greater adaptability of the Portuguese to tropical conditions and the ease with which they have mixed with natives; 35,000 whites and four million natives live in Mozambique, and 60,000 whites and three million natives in Angola.[1] The same forces have been

[1] R. Kuczynski, *Colonial Population*.

at work in the West Indies and in Mexico for hundreds of years—the slave trade filled the gaps in the ranks of the native population in the islands and even on parts of the Continent, after the indigenous Indian population had become too weak in numbers and strength for the economic burden their white masters had imposed upon them.

The days of "plantation" colonies have gone for good, since all suitable areas have been occupied. Stretches of vacant lands waiting for occupation are still available in the former Latin-American colonies, in the United States and in the Dominions of the British Empire, as well as in Manchuria. The extent of those fit for homestead settlements in the frontier districts of the world has been estimated at three million square miles, from which twelve million homesteads might be carved.[1] But the chances for creating new settlement colonies have gone; they might be revived in limited localities by the wholesale extirpation of native races and by a relentless prohibition of the use of native labour in any form.

Francis Bacon had diagnosed this problem over 300 years ago: "I like a plantation in a pure soil; that is where people are not displanted to the end to plant in others. For else it is rather an extirpation than a plantation."[2]

VII

This process seemed fairly easy at one time. It has been carried out ruthlessly in those parts of the world where weak natives have confronted white settlers and have been driven back from one reservation to another, frequently in disregard of treaties solemnly concluded with them. In the Americas, in Australia, and for a time in New Zealand, a notion grew up among the white settlers that they were carrying out the

[1] Isaiah Bowman, "Prairie Settlement" in *Canadian Frontiers of Settlement*, ed. by W. A. Mackintosh and W. L. G. Joerg, vol. i, p. ix.

[2] Francis Bacon, Essay on Plantation. *Essays*.

decrees of Providence when despoiling the natives of their land and driving them further and further away until they ultimately disappeared from the map, if not from the face of the earth. Later on a curious kind of cheap Darwinism and romantic superman philosophy combined in explaining as evidence of the "struggle for life" the disappearance of an inferior race when brought in contact with a superior one. Its votaries forgot to mention the spread of contagious diseases, the sales of potent spirits and guns, or the destruction of game, on which the native means of livelihood had depended. None of these forces which caused the decimation of the natives were put in operation by the immanent laws of the universe, which the white man, an instrument of God, had unwittingly set in motion; they were let loose by short-sighted greed. Long ago, the Maoris had registered this supposed "law" with the stoic resignation of a doomed race:

> As the Pakéha fly has driven out the Maori fly,
> As the Pakéha grass has killed the Maori grass,
> As the Pakéha rat has slain the Maori rat,
> As the Pakéha clover has starved the Maori fern,
> So will the Pakéha destroy the Maori.[1]

But this doctrine has at no time and nowhere been applied to the African negro. Since the Portuguese had brought to Europe the first African slaves, the white men of all races were quick to appreciate the economic value of the negroes. They did not try to extirpate them in their native haunts, which they looked upon as native breeding-grounds, from where the slave trade might transfer them systematically to all warm countries which needed their labour. Before the mass emigration of the nineteenth century was well under way, the number of negroes transplanted to the Americas

---

[1] Sir Charles Dilke, *Greater Britain*, p. 274. This resignation has ultimately proved to be unfounded. The Maoris have experienced a racial revival and are again increasing in number and status. J. B. Condliffe, *New Zealand in the Making*, p. 84–9.

was probably greater than that of white people.[1] But for the terrible mortality on the middle passage and on the plantations the number of negro settlers to-day would be much greater than it actually is.

In Africa proper regional expulsion, or rather local pushing back, was frequent. The Boer settlements have spread from the comparatively empty Western province of the Cape to the equally empty northern highlands, which the Matabele had laid bare. Wherever they needed additional room, a commando was organized to drive back some native tribes and to clear additional lands from their occupation. But the Boers never dreamed of establishing a purely white settlement, from which all coloured peoples should be excluded. They brought their slaves along with them and settled small remnants of broken tribes on their farms. They established a primitive feudalism wherever they went; their social conceptions were those of a slave-owning aristocracy. And even the most racially minded heralds of white domination in Africa recognized the impossibility of purely white settlements. They advocated the establishment of large estates by a morally superior class of settlers, whose race consciousness would keep them from miscegenation and whose masterful ways would impress the native.[2] They supported the planters' and colonists' opposition to the decrees of a home government which forbade the use of forced labour, as they would greatly increase the costs of exploitation and retard colonial development.

A clearance policy could be enforced by a government willing to pour treasure into the colony in order to create a huge white reserve; it may be less impossible to-day. Governments are accustomed to planning and planning in a new colonial country is very much simpler than in an old-established society. In countries which have adopted the totali-

---

[1] R. Kuczynski, *Population Movements*, pp. 11–22.

[2] Paul Samassa, *Die Besiedlung Deutsch-Ostafrikas*, Leipzig, 1909, p. 128, seq.

tarian philosophy of the state and where social life has become militarized, respect for individual liberty counts for very little. The average young men and women do not value any longer the privilege of making up their own minds; they have become spiritually collectivized and are keen to obey orders. As standards of living at home for the mass of the people have become fairly low and very rigid, they could easily be commandeered to settle overseas in a new country, where the glamour of romance would colour the bareness of the social barrack-room system—somewhat resembling the *phalanstère*—towards which social institutions in many parts of the world are tending. A population trained in labour camps and supported by the highly efficient mechanism at the disposal of modern governments may be able to face problems of colonization from which the pioneers of older days recoiled.

Nor does the fate of the natives complicate matters any longer. If the country's natural resources are not sufficient for all, foreigners must be expelled, runs this modern philosophy—it is, after all, not so very different from the old conception of the rights of the superman. A colony need not be held in trust for the natives, provided it offers a chance to a chosen nation, which may exploit it in its own interest. It would be quite feasible in such circumstances to clear the healthy highlands of all natives, concentrate them in low-lying tropical districts and settle the upland exclusively with white settlers, who must not be allowed to employ coloured labour. The colony would be divided into white and coloured "cantons." As long as native interests do not collide with those of the ruling race, the coloured areas might be administered for the natives' benefit. They could easily be run by means of a benevolent despotism: a government which does not recognize any rights can follow a policy aiming at the welfare of the commonwealth and at nothing else. It need not make concessions to the greed of white traders or give way to the agitation of white planters. Discontent as a political factor has ceased to exist where malcontents are not allowed to voice their dissatisfaction. And where the white people have no political rights and their civil rights are arbitrarily determined by their governments, the natives have no cause to clamour for equality. An intelligent despotism can rule backward natives far more easily than an equally enlightened democracy: a régime of coercion by those who see in it the mainstay of politics is logically unassailable, whereas the rule of force by those who base their creed on the right of self-determination is not.

The government of a totalitarian state could thus easily create a white island among coloured populations, without inflicting too much hardship on the natives; they do not care for cold highlands in any case, and there is still a good deal of room for their expansion. The maintenance of such a bifurcated society would be more difficult than its establishment. The costs of running the experiment would be very high. The exclusive use of white labour would make development as well as production rather expensive. The products raised in the native section of the colony would compete with those from the white section, and a difficult case of internal competition would arise.

It is harder to maintain discipline permanently in a faraway settlement than at home; pioneer surroundings foster a kind of pioneer spirit; the independence needed at the outposts of civilization can scarcely be limited to mere technical objects. White masters will try to get native workers, and white soldiers native women. The sexual appetites of men cannot be regulated by eugenic discussions. The natives are attracted by white civilization; they see in it power, money, influence. They resent it passionately at times; it is a kind of sweet poison to them. Contact and friction with coloured people will somehow ensue, and, as the whites are trained in a spirit of racial arrogance, they may not be very pleasant. Moreover, any experiments of this kind must affect and be affected by neighbouring colonies in which different conditions exist. Native tribes who are expelled from their territory, or who dislike permanent separation, may invade neighbouring countries, so that the inauguration of such experiments might bring about international complications. The "great clearance" cannot be undertaken without complete liberty of action in the international sphere; without it, the space available for white infiltration is comparatively restricted.

The limits are wider for some nations than for others. The Germans have been able to make a living on farms which Englishmen would scarcely look at. The Italians, again, have succeeded in working at a standard of living which other Europeans would have declined. They have, so far, been free from racial arrogance in the social sense of the word. They have done work in the past in the Transvaal which both white and coloured people considered "native work"; Spaniards have done the same in the province of Oran in Algeria.[1] The present régime may have increased their efficiency and not yet counterbalanced it by arousing a feeling of race superiority, such as befits a nation of heroes. But its use of native troops and native labour corps precludes any large experiments in ethnographic separation. And where a régime of co-operation prevails, cohabitation, including commerce and some sort of connubium, can scarcely be prevented. Its presence bars the way to mass immigration. The most which could be done to-day is the foundation of new composite colonies, in which a small number of colonists occupy the upper, and sometimes the middle layers of the society, whilst the half-breeds and the natives fill its main volume.

Societies of this type have been established in Mexico, in Peru, in the West Indies, and in those parts of the United States where the plantation system formerly prevailed. They occupy the northern fringe of Africa and the south-western part of South Africa. The shadow of grave social trouble hangs over them; their future is dark.

[1] M. J. Bonn, *Die Neugestaltung unserer Kolonialen Aufgaben*, p. 23.

VIII

Earlier clearance experiments have been wrecked by the resistance of the colonists, who refused to part with cheap labour; on this rock the great Cromwellian settlement of Ireland foundered completely. Their success depends ultimately on a self-imposed, rigorously maintained self-denial by the colonizing race. Something of this sort is happening in Palestine.

No Jewish national home can be founded without mass immigration; mass immigration is precluded, if the Jews were willing to rely more or less exclusively on Arab labour, for Arab wages are but three-fifths of Jewish wages. Thanks to their enthusiasm, Jewish employers and Jewish employees have been able to develop the country with comparatively expensive Jewish labour and to limit (relatively) the volume of comparatively cheap Arab labour employed. As long as this fervent Jewish fanaticism is aflame and kept at a white heat by an equally fiery Arab national fanaticism, race separation of some sort can continue. If it burned out completely, Palestine might become a composite colony; the top and middle parts might be formed by Jews, the base by Arabs. An upper Jewish stratum, with no overseas mother country to support it, might share the fate of some earlier composite societies and quickly disintegrate. As it is, Arab nationalism has assisted in the formation of a compact Jewish national society; a fairly solid block of 400,000 Jews has been planted amongst 900,000 Arabs. It will grow in strength and extension, even if Arab agitation were to stop further mass immigration. The country's development would be greatly retarded if the immigrant race had to rely exclusively on its natural growth—7,000 a year; the hopes of the Jews in many parts of the world would be dashed to the ground, but the natural increase of the Jews would not come to a standstill, and the compactness of the Jewish society would not be diminished. The only way in which the Arabs could have prevented the rise of a compact Jewish community in their midst was by offering their labour on attractive terms. A conquering country settling a native territory can either establish a composite aristocratic society which offers little room for mass immigration, or it can aim by more or less artificial measures at the formation of a compact immigrant community in the midst of the natives. Palestine is evidently turning to the second alternative. The presence of a strange unassimilated alien body, which in its turn is neither willing nor able to assimilate the natives, must keep passions and strife alive. Social peace in Palestine must be brought about either by far-reaching spiritual and social assimilation, or by a complete separation of the two racial components, though this involves transplantation, somewhat on the lines of the Greco-Turkish settlement. As it is the wrath of the natives against the immigrants has turned against the mandatory power, which is responsible for their political control.

IX

The growth of settlement colonies has been a unique phenomenon in the history of the world. It cannot happen again. No nation can successfully establish new plantations, since the circumstances which favoured their rise have gone for good. Fate has been unfair to some great nations by excluding them from founding and retaining daughter-states such as England and Russia have won and Spain, Portugal, and Holland have won and lost. It may soothe them a little that Spain has forfeited all her dominions, and England the greatest of hers. And the reflection that all settlement colonies, even those which have not yet separated from the mother country, are at liberty to do so whenever they feel so inclined, might mitigate any resentment.

But the essential fact remains: in this field equal opportunities have not been given to all nations, and recent occupation of native territories has not and cannot redress the grievance. Some of the excluded states have become colonial Powers and have gained opportunities to rule or to misrule natives, such as their more favoured rivals had enjoyed for centuries. Neither their governments nor their nationals have reached the parity of opportunity for which they craved. The opportunities of their more favoured rivals may be shrinking. The British Dominions no longer shape their economic policy in the interests of the mother country; over a number of years they have disregarded her needs when regulating their immigration policy. They may frequently have preferred Britons in organized government immigration, but they have by no means refused alien groups who possessed the qualities they desired. The Canadian West abounds with foreign settlements of every description.

Emigration, moreover, was not dependent on the possession of colonies. The main current of immigration did not turn to British Dominions; most emigrants found conditions in the United States and in the Argentine more attractive; these lands became the great receptacles of those who left Europe. Of the 52 million who did so in the last century, 34 million went to the United States, 6 million to the Argentine, 5 million to Canada, and 3 million to Australia. Lately control of colonies or union with dominions has not been of much benefit: in the present emigration crisis, Great Britain has suffered almost as much as other countries. For the Dominions were by no means willing to share their contracting opportunities with home-born Britons. They led the inverted movement. In the years 1931–3 the excess of immigrants over emigrants returning to Great Britain from foreign countries was 36,000, while the numbers of those returning from the British Empire surpassed the outflow by 83,000.

The contraction of opportunities overseas has affected all countries unfavourably. It has not done so evenly. Revival of opportunities, even if it were offered on fair terms, would no longer eliminate tension. For the less fortunate nations are not willing to accept the economic hospitality of a foreign country in settlement of their claims. They look upon their emigrants living under a foreign flag as the ethnical outposts of the great nation at home, in whose interests and under whose orders they work. This attitude will not make them acceptable to foreign hosts who find it easy enough to recruit immigrants among people who do not raise any such pretensions.

CHAPTER V

THE VALUE OF COLONIES

I

Most present-day colonies are native dependencies. The West Indies, Mauritius, the Central African Tableland, and a few others are "composite colonies" in which a smallish white aristocracy and a scarcely more numerous white middle class control native populations. In social structure, certain North African regions, especially Algeria and Tunis, strongly resemble them.[1] Tunis and Morocco rank as native vassal states, whilst Algeria, at least in its three settled departments, is somewhat artificially incorporated in France; it can scarcely be termed a "colony" any longer. India occupies the same status as Australia in the League of Nations. She is enjoying fiscal autonomy—like a dominion— but she is held by an army of occupation; she may be an associate, but she is not yet really autonomous. She might be considered a colony from a political point of view; economically she is nearly independent.

Some native societies have reached a very high cultural level, whilst others are formed of savage tribes who have to be taught by slow administrative pressure the rudiments of economic civilization. A wide social gap separates the pygmies of the Congo State or the leopard men of Kenya from the highly organized ruling races of Nigeria.

The world's native dependencies fall into two distinct groups: those in which economic benefits can be mono-polized by the metropolis and those which are subject to some sort of "open-door" régime. The latter class comprises those dependencies in which the ruling Power voluntarily maintains a system of free trade under which foreigners are

---

[1] South Africa is a Dominion and a composite state.

K

not subject to discrimination—amongst them are the Dutch East Indies, some British Crown Colonies, and a single French colony among the non-assimilated colonies (which are not included within the mother country's tariff system).

To these must be added those colonial countries in which an international régime guarantees "equal opportunities."

The Berlin Conference (November 15, 1884–January 30, 1885) had recognized the International Association of the Congo, the offspring of the International Association for the Exploration and Civilization of Africa, as owner of the Congo Free State; it had stipulated complete freedom of trade for all nations in the Congo Basin. It agreed upon a free-trade line which went far beyond the Free State; it comprised the French Congo, the Cameroons, Portuguese Angola, and British and German East Africa.[1] It guaranteed free imports—the imposition of customs duties up to 10 per cent was later on (1890) conceded to various governments—and free enterprise. But the Free State (Belgian) government evaded these regulations pretty soon by monopolizing enterprise for the state, thus enabling it to restrict private initiative to the people and the companies it favoured.[2] The Convention of St. Germain (September 10, 1919) upheld the régime of the open door in Central Africa by guaranteeing its benefits to its signatories and to the other member-states of the League.

The original conception of the Congo Free State had been very ambiguous. International rivalries were to be overcome by the foundation of an international colony, organized as a private chartered company. Once more groups of private traders were entrusted with economic privileges and with government functions; in the race for new territories they could, without entangling their governments, pursue a policy of unscrupulous expansion from which administrations acting under the control of a European colonial office would have had to refrain. Their formation satisfied, moreover, the

[1] Keltie, *Partition of Africa*, p. 209.   [2] Ibid., p. 220.

anti-bureaucratic, anti-state bias of a liberal age; remembering the monopolistic character of earlier chartered companies, which its great writers had so successfully denounced, it granted them political autonomy but withheld from them economic monopoly.[1] The recognition of an international business corporation (the International Association of the Congo) as an independent state, whose shareholders could come from all countries, whose officials might be selected from all nations, and whose territories were open to the activities of all, would put an end to the rivalries of competing states; it would stop all dangerous friction in Central Africa and bring to the land the blessing of a united European civilization. This dream of international unity dissolved into a Belgian monopoly.[2] But the idea survived. To safeguard equality of opportunities to the nationals of all countries, if not to their governments, seemed an excellent device for buying goodwill, whenever an important part of the formerly neutral or independent international demesne was swallowed up by annexation.

The United States, taking up an English suggestion, formulated what has since been called the "open door" doctrine, when the disintegration of China seemed imminent. They aimed at safeguarding the trading rights of their nationals, but did not wish to share in the partition of China. They asked the Powers acquiring parts of China in any form to bind themselves not "to interfere with any treaty port or vested interest" within their sphere, to maintain the low Chinese tariff against imports, and not to grant preferential harbour dues or railroad charges to their nationals (September 6, 1899).

They succeeded in forcing the recognition of this doctrine on all the Powers interested in China, but had to remind them at times of their engagements. Russia tried to dodge hers almost from the beginning by insisting that Manchuria

[1] Pierre Bonnassieux, *Les grandes compagnies de commerce*, pp. 517–22.
[2] Keltie, op. cit., pp. 128–33.

was not really a part of China, a point of view adopted later on by the Japanese, who openly flouted these obligations by the formation of the State of Manchukuo.

It had become evident fairly soon that the regulations laid down in open-door agreements were easily evaded; a stricter interpretation was attempted when Germany imposed the régime on France in the Morocco negotiations (1909 and 1911). The term "open door" was no longer limited to imports and to the settlement rights of nationals; concessions and contracts were included. The strict observance of "no preference agreements" in respect of tariff duties on cotton goods could easily be enforced. (The Japanese dodge in northern China of encouraging smuggling, and thus favouring their own products while breaking the back of the Chinese customs administration, was not yet known in those days.) But when a mining concession or a railway contract was at issue, a colonial administration could always find ways and means of favouring its own nationals, even if their tenders were high. The terms of the tender could be drawn up in such a fashion as to handicap the foreign competitor, or the national industry could get advance information which enabled it to promise earlier delivery than its foreign rivals. The Morocco treaties were meant to stop such practices. Though their success was doubtful, the faith in a régime establishing a kind of international economic demesne, under whose rule every nation would enjoy the same economic opportunities as the Powers administrating it, survived. The political control was to be entrusted to one Power, whilst the economic exploitation would be open to all.

The Peace Settlement offered a chance for a broad experiment. President Wilson objected to territorial annexations. His allies insisted on annexing the German colonies. A compromise was reached by giving them control over these areas by way of mandates, on which equality of opportunity was imposed. The mandatory power was bound to safeguard equal opportunities for the trade and commerce of all members of the League (Article XXII B). As the United States were not joining the League they had become "outsiders," but they insisted on participating in these rights and detailed them carefully. They claimed equality for all nationals or subjects with those of the mandatory Power in law and fact, in respect of taxation, residence, business profession, concessions, freedom of transit of persons and goods, freedom of communications, trade, navigation, commerce, industrial property, and other economic rights or commercial activities. They specially safeguarded their nationals against the granting of any exclusive economic concession covering the entire territory and against any monopolistic concession relating to any commodity or to any economic privilege subsidiary or essential to the production, development, or exploitation of such a commodity.[1]

These points were incorporated in each of the several mandates of the B type which were given to England, France, and Belgium.[2] A wider, and from a legal point of view,

[1] United States Letter, May 12, 1920, *History of the Peace Conference*, vol. vii, pp. 507–8.

[2] Article relating to equality of opportunity for B Mandates:

"The Mandatory shall secure to all nationals of States Members of the League of Nations the same rights as are enjoyed in the territory by his own nationals in respect of entry into and residence in the territory, the protection afforded to their person and property, the acquisition of property, movable and immovable, and the exercise of their profession or trade, subject only to the requirements of public order, and on condition of compliance with the local law. Further, the Mandatory shall ensure to all nationals of States Members of the League of Nations, on the same footing as to his own nationals, freedom of transit and navigation, and complete economic, commercial, and industrial equality; except that the Mandatory shall be *free to organize essential public works and services* on such terms and conditions as he thinks fit.

"Concessions for the development of the natural resources of the territory shall be granted by the Mandatory without distinction on grounds of nationality between all States Members of the League, but on such conditions as will maintain intact the authority of the local Government.

"Concessions having the character of a general monopoly shall not

almost exhaustive interpretation of the term "equality of opportunity" had thus been laid down. The régime applied to all Germany's equatorial African colonies, but not to South-West Africa or to her Pacific possessions, which, as C mandates, were as good as incorporated in the Union of South Africa, Australia (New Guinea), New Zealand (Samoa), and Japan. Somewhat similar conditions were imposed on the Powers to whom A mandates (Syria, Lebanon, Transjordania, Palestine, and Iraq) were given. In A and B mandates equality of opportunity was established for all members of the League. As long as Germany was not a member she had no share in this equality; during this transition period, her citizens could be evicted from her former colonies; their property could be expropriated. For instance, in November 1924 the plantations in British Cameroons were sold for £224,670, most of the purchasers being German repurchasers. Germany became a partner in a system of equal opportunities only when she joined the League and, like Japan, she lost these privileges by renouncing her membership.[1]

The régime of equal opportunities, guaranteed and *de facto* maintained in favour of all non-residents in a number of colonies, may be infringed in favour of the local residents. This is not of much importance as long as the bulk of the residents are natives whose interests under the Covenant have to be safeguarded by the mandatory. The state of their social development does not justify an attempt at artificial indus-

be granted. This provision does not affect the right of the Mandatory to create monopolies of a purely fiscal character in the interest of the territory under the mandate, and in order to *provide the territory with fiscal resources which seem best suited to the local requirements; or, in certain cases, to carry out the development of natural resources either directly by the State or by a controlled agency, provided that there shall result therefrom no monopoly of the natural resources for the benefit of the Mandatory or his nationals, directly or indirectly, nor any preferential advantage which shall be inconsistent with the economic, commercial, and industrial equality hereinbefore guaranteed."*

[1] Japan did not hand back her mandates and Germany was not *de facto* deprived of her privileges. (Italics in these notes are mine.)

trialization; tariff protection is not in their interest, as it would merely increase the cost of living.

In some colonies subject to the régime there is a smallish nucleus of white settlers demanding self-government; they are filled with a more or less nationalist spirit—however violent their occasional attacks on the mother country may be. Their mere presence affects the régime considerably. Their ways of living are those of the home country; they prefer its national brands. Their personal affiliations are with its trade and with its industries. The foreign settlers living amongst them have to conform to their ways and become, as it were, agents for preferential consumption. British settlers and officials order their goods from the catalogue of the Army and Navy Stores or from Harrods; French officials order theirs from the Magasin du Louvre or the Galeries Lafayette. The partial extirpation of German settlers from Africa and Polynesia has affected imports from Germany, but the tenacious habits of those Germans who managed to hold on explain the comparative importance of the German trade in those regions under present-day conditions.[1] But the British colonial service in Tanganyika cannot be expected to do its shopping in Berlin or Hamburg. The national educational stamp with which the natives are branded favours national teachers, who order national weeklies, national magazines, national school books, and national reproductions of works of art. And while missionaries may disregard national turnpikes in Kingdom Come, their stations order their spiritual as well as their material goods from home. The growing social influence of such groups is materially attenuating the open-door régime. Were

[1] Germany's share (1928) of imports into Mandates and Colonies was as follows:

MANDATES	per cent	COLONIES AND DOMINIONS	per cent
French Cameroons ..	13·6	French West Africa ..	2·5
South-West Africa ..	20·4	Union of South Africa..	7·6
Tanganyika	12·3	Kenya and Uganda ..	3·7

they to get responsible government, their claims for complete self-determination must come into conflict with the international obligations which regulate the economic policy of these regions.

The countries comprised within this liberal (open door) régime cover 5,034,000 square miles, with 117 million inhabitants, an export trade of 397 million gold dollars and an import trade of 384 million gold dollars (1935).

The other, larger group of dependencies is neither subject to international obligations nor administrated voluntarily as a free-trade area. It covers 7,379,000 square miles, with 138 million inhabitants, an import trade of 1,147 million dollars and an export trade of 1,126 million dollars. The metropolis which rules these possessions is free to follow a policy of commercial discrimination, though, as the purchasing power of the natives is insignificant, tariffs are mostly low. But preferential policies prevail in nearly all French colonies, including Tunis and Indo-China, in the Philippine Islands, while they were controlled by the U.S.A., in the Portuguese dependencies, and in quite a number of British possessions. India is not included in this group; she enjoys a particular status of her own—fiscal autonomy; but she is economically far more dependent on the United Kingdom than the Dominions. The C mandates, Samao, New Guinea, and South-West Africa, belong here too, though South-West Africa, with 31,000 white and 328,000 native inhabitants, is a composite colony and not a native dependency.

II

The object of the open-door régime was to secure to the nationals of a nation excluded from political control equal opportunities for selling their wares and for pursuing their occupations. It was a kind of elongation of the most-favoured-nation clause, which otherwise would have lapsed when a hitherto independent or semi-independent territory passed under the control of a metropolis. It was evolved during a period when free trade and free competition seemed to have broken the power of monopoly. It dealt exclusively with imports; it did not settle explicitly the supply of raw materials, for it was tacitly assumed that equal opportunities for selling goods implied equal opportunities for buying them.[1]

The earlier colonial Powers had organized colonial monopolies. The Dutch monopoly of the spice trade, especially the clove trade, was perhaps the most efficient of its kind ever established. Colonies in those days furnished rare commodities which the whole world sought; not only did their owners grow rich by selling them abroad, but the profits from the sales paid for the military and naval forces on which the exercise of their political and economic monopoly depended. To such a régime monopoly or at least an export duty on sales to foreigners seemed an ideal form of taxation. The foreign consumer cannot evade it; he must pay his contribution to an alien exchequer. This situation lasted for quite a time. England exploited it fairly successfully in her struggle against the Continental System, by which Napoleon attempted to stifle her commerce. She concentrated the trade in colonial produce in her own hands by forcing all ships into her ports, and endeavoured to tax the continental consumers for her benefit. Fifty years after Napoleon's fall, the cotton famine accompanying the American civil war showed clearly enough the danger resulting from a colonial monopoly. And at the turn of the century, when the world's rubber output came from primæval tropical forests, the countries controlling these few sources of supply could for a short time fleece the foreign consumers with some measure of success by means of an export tax.

---

[1] Herman Merivale, *Colonization and Colonies*, p. 187: " . . . and yet it is singular to observe how the latter object, that of importation, is overlooked in ordinary reasoning of the subject, as if the only benefit of colonies resulted to our producers."

K*

The development of dependencies into independent republics and dominions has greatly reduced the importance of colonies as sources of oversea foodstuffs and raw materials.

Colonial produce can roughly be divided into six groups: foodstuffs and stimulants, minerals, fuel, fibres, rubber, and oil-seeds, etc.

PERCENTAGE OF TOTAL WORLD OUTPUT CONTRIBUTED BY COLONIES

I Foodstuffs and Stimulants		II Minerals		III Fuel	
Cocoa	74·0	Tin ..	56·9	Petrol .. 3·7	
Tea ..	48·0	Phosphates ..	52·0	Coal .. 0·3	
Cane Sugar	35·9	Graphite ..	46·0		
Bananas ..	30·2	Copper ..	21·3		
Citrus Fruits	9·7	Tungsten Ore	15·6		
Coffee ..	7·6	Manganese ..	13·7		
Tobacco ..	4·8	Bauxite ..	13·1		
Wheat ..	1·9	Chrome ..	12·3		
Beef ..	1·5	Nickel ..	9·0		
Pork ..	1·0	Pyrites ..	3·4		
Butter ..	0·7	Iron Ore ..	3·4		
		Zinc.. ..	1·9		
		Antimony ..	0·7		

IV Textiles		V Rubber	VI Oil-Seeds, etc.	
Hemp	6·2	96·1	Palm Oil ..	98·8
Silk	3·1		Copra	64·4
Cotton	2·5		Ground Nuts ..	28·5
Wool	2·3		Olive Oil ..	12·9
Jute	0·3		Soya	11·4
			Sesame	8·0
			Cotton Seed ..	2·6

Of the thirty-nine commodities included in these six groups, only two (rubber and palm oil) are almost exclusively of colonial origin; four others (cocoa, copra, tin, and phosphates) are mainly so; while six (tea, graphite, cane sugar, bananas, ground nuts, and copper) are so to a considerable degree. Colonial production of bauxite, manganese, chrome and tungsten ores, olive oil, and soya beans accounts for more than one-tenth of the world production. According to the findings of the League of Nations Committee on Raw Materials only 3 per cent of the world's supply of raw materials and foodstuffs come from colonies.

Potential colonial production is no doubt very much greater than these figures indicate. Any country could develop a particular colony by increasing its vegetable production very considerably, if it so desired; and though mining ventures are more dependent on natural conditions than on human decisions, extensive exploration might strike new paying lodes in many a land.

A few colonies, and through them their rulers, do enjoy a kind of monopoly. Forty-six per cent of the world's rubber production comes from British Malaya and another 37 per cent from the Dutch East Indies; 99 per cent of manila hemp is grown in the Philippines. But the monopolistic positions some colonies enjoy are scarcely more marked than similar advantages of other countries. Germany (59 per cent) and France (19 per cent) raise four-fifths of the world's potash output, Japan 78 per cent of its silk, Manchuria 77 per cent of its soya beans, and the United States furnish 59 per cent of the world's petroleum production. The two contiguous continental empires, the United States and Russia, possess much greater natural resources than any other state; they are more secure than equally rich composite, but disconnected, empires. But their colonial possessions are few and not very important.

Ever since Napoleon inaugurated the Continental System, monopolies in colonial commodities have been losing ground. Beet sugar has become a very successful rival to cane; it is grown to-day in many a country which was considered unsuitable for it even less than thirty years ago. Rayon is displacing cotton as well as silk; oil can be derived on a quasi-commercial basis from coal, and wool from casein.

Synthetic indigo has undermined the prosperity of the native indigo grower, synthetic camphor has deprived the Japanese of monopoly profits from Formosa, and the skill of the chemist has freed the lovers of ice cream in the United States from the stranglehold of colonial vanilla producers. The process of manufacturing rubber synthetically (Buna) has been carried far enough for commercial purposes if prices were sufficiently high to make it profitable. A few counterstrokes in favour of colonial production have been made— the manufacture of margarine is based on the production of vegetable oil-seeds or nuts, which have brought prosperity to many parts of West Africa; they have furnished the raw materials for the modern soap industry, though lately new chemical discoveries have been threatening them. But, generally speaking, the tide is running away from colonial monopolies. The length to which it will go is much more a question of prices than of processes. It might certainly be cheaper to turn out rubber and wool by synthetic methods than to pay the cost of a large-scale colonial war and to face its political repercussions. The interest on the debt which Italy will have to pay for the conquest and occupation of Ethiopia might easily cover the cost of all subsidies needed for securing her supplies of synthetic rubber and synthetic wool. If prices were sufficiently attractive, many independent countries, most of them former colonies, could offer any amount of additional tropical commodities. The American experiments of growing rubber in Latin America may not have turned out very well; but had there been scarcity and scarcity prices they would have been successful.

A colony's output is rarely monopolized by the mother country; many foreign customers buy it regularly. The demands of the metropolis, on the other hand, frequently far exceed the supplies from all colonies. The main consumers of rubber are not Great Britain and the Netherlands, though their possessions account for more than 95 per cent of the world's output. And though Great Britain's colonies are the

chief producers of cocoa (59 per cent), she is by no means
the chief importer. Neither Great Britain, France, Holland,
nor Belgium can rely exclusively on cotton from their
dependencies.

Some mother countries have assisted their own colonies
by granting them preferential treatment with regard to
import duties. Their rivals in independent countries or in
foreign colonies may dislike it. The Dutch colonial growers
of cocoa may resent the favours shown to cocoa from French
colonies in the French market; they cannot protest against
them, for preference in the home market is not considered an
infringement of an open-door agreement, or the most-
favoured-nation treatment clause. It may cheapen the supplies of foreign buyers, who are free to bargain or choose
foreign markets, whilst home consumers are charged the
high prices ruling in sheltered markets.[1]

Subsidies might raise the colonial producers' demand for
capital goods, and home consumers might indirectly benefit
from the increase of the colonists' wealth and the growth
of their purchasing power, which will enable them by and by
to dispense with direct subsidies to their revenue from the

[1] The mother country which allows preferential rates on colonial
products provides a sheltered market for colonists. If they can produce
enough or more than enough, they will not get a much better price than
they otherwise would; competition merely shifts. The mother country
will be supplied exclusively by its colonies, which compete among themselves, while foreign countries will have to rely on outside sources. A
slight increase in the total world supply may result from the stimulus
given to preferred colonial production, and world market prices may
fall a little. If the colonies cannot satisfy the entire home demand, notwithstanding the stimulus given to their production, foreign supplies
will continue to come in, but the price the metropolitan consumers have
to pay will rise by the amount of the duties; proceeds from import
duties on foreign materials will go to the customs authorities, whilst
additional profits will accrue to colonial producers. World market prices
may rise, though they will remain below protected prices. Under the
stimulus given by preference, colonial producers will, however, expand
their profitable production to such a degree as to cause a general over-
production, which will result for the time being in declining prices all
round, in the home as well as in the world market.

metropolitan treasury; they might even return some of the advances made to them, though this has never yet happened.[1]

As part of the cost of running the colonial government was usually charged to the mother country, the foreigner really got colonial goods more cheaply than the home consumer. But the preferential system was a convenient cloak for hiding the higher costs of production of commodities grown under the national flag; without it, they might not be raised at all in the colony. To grow one's own colonial produce in one's own colonial backyard is frequently an unfailing method of satisfying the ruling nation's wants as expensively, and those of the foreigner as cheaply as possible.

A number of raw materials and tropical foodstuffs, rubber, palm-oil, copra, phosphates, and tin, are raised in a few spots only, where their owners might monopolize them and fleece the foreign consumers by high prices. But this is quite as difficult as putting political pressure on some foreign government by withholding such materials from it. In both cases, international co-operation is essential, either in the form of world-wide sanctions or of the establishment of an international monopolistic combine.

III

The failure of sanctions against Italy and the slight damage done by them may somewhat weaken the case for colonies. Italy has satisfied her needs for colonial raw materials in spite of a boycott embracing almost all colonial dependencies and in spite of an embargo on her exports in the markets of fifty-two countries, which must have severely curtailed her purchasing power. The danger of relying on supplies from foreign countries had evidently been exaggerated. But a more courageous application of sanctions, which would have drawn a ring round Italy and barred her supply of

[1] Merivale, op. cit., p. 203 seq.

foreign goods more or less completely, would have led to very different results from the half-hearted measures, which, moreover, were in force only for a very short time. It might have been too slow and too loose to save the independence of Ethiopia, but it would have ended in the economic collapse of Italy.

The failure of sanctions has discredited the value of economic pressure; it has probably lessened the fears of a complete blockade; but it has given a certain new aspect to colonial possessions. For the most stringent and universal sanctions would not be applied by the colonies of an offending state. No dependency could be expected to withhold its supplies of raw materials from its mother country or to refuse to accept goods from it by order of the League of Nations, however universal its membership might be. For a colony's connections with the League depend on those of its sovereign metropolis. The writ of the League does not run in colonial territory—except when endorsed by its own metropolitan government. The foundation of a big, self-sufficient colonial empire would enable a recalcitrant state to flout the League of Nations successfully, as long as anti-trading sanctions were not enforced by a universal naval and military blockade, and a ruthless search of all ships carrying goods to the offending state, irrespective of the origin of these goods. A partial blockade, which does not stop supplies on the land frontier as well as on the sea, or does not hold up indirect imports, would merely shift the direction of supplies, without cutting them off. But in this respect the control of a mandate—certainly of a B mandate —would not be a substitute for the possession of a colony. For the League, and not the mandatory power, might exercise sovereignty over a mandated territory. An interesting problem would arise, as to whether the will of the mandatory government or that of the mandatory sovereign should prevail when sanctions against the former were to be applied. Where the mandated areas are economically mixed up with colonies proper, a complete muddle might result.

The menace of a foreign national or international monopoly has frequently been overrated. As monopolists cannot derive profits from commodities which are not sold, they do not attempt to withhold supplies from foreign consumers, though they may try to tax them by raising prices above those charged to national consumers, where it is possible. The Brazilian coffee valorization scheme endeavoured to raise the price of coffee to external consumers; it may have let off the internal consumers more lightly, but it did not discriminate between the several foreign countries and did not deprive them of coffee. Its success, such as it was, was due to the support of foreign banks in coffee-consuming countries, which lent the Brazilian government the money to finance the withholding of the stocks of coffee from the market; otherwise the external prices of Brazilian coffee would have collapsed. The Brazilian planters have reaped benefits from this monopoly; they levied a fine on their fellow-countrymen, who had to pay additional taxes, and they greatly stimulated the planting of coffee in rival countries.

The outcome of the cotton experiment undertaken by the United States' government has not been very different. Internal prices have been raised, and the American cotton manufacturers have had to pay higher prices for their raw materials than their foreign rivals. They can recoup themselves on the protected home market, but they are losing foreign markets. The artificial rise in prices has stimulated cotton production in many parts of the world, especially in Brazil, where costs of production are very much lower than in the United States, and from where cotton is being furnished to foreign manufacturers at very much lower prices than their American rivals have to pay at home. American cotton growers receive a higher total income from a small crop than they formerly did for a larger one, but they are losing their foreign markets and can only regain them by selling at lower prices abroad than at home.

Various other colonial monopolies, such as the several rubber restriction schemes and the tin and copper pools, have been more successful, for a limited time at least. They may continue to be so, as long as they are truly international, embrace all important producing groups, and follow a moderate price policy, which does not stimulate additional outside production. The so-called Stevenson scheme certainly did help the rubber planters of British Malaya for a short time, but it ultimately collapsed, as the Dutch producers, who had reaped very great benefits from it, did not co-operate. It caused much irritation in the United States, though it did not discriminate in favour of the home market, since no manufacturing is carried on in Malaya. It raised the price of export rubber considerably, but indiscriminately, to British, American, and continental manufacturers. The British-owned rubber plantations profited handsomely, and the value of their shares rose rapidly. Any foreigner could come in for some of the spoils by buying these shares at market prices, and the profits were made quite as much at the expense of British consumers as by exploiting foreigners. Modern international monopolies of this type are scrupulously "fair" to all countries; they fleece all customers indiscriminately, regardless of domicile or nationality.

National discrimination by powerful monopolist groups is by no means beyond the range of possibility; it might become very irksome in connection with sanctions. But it is dangerous only in a time of world scarcity. The menace of such a monopoly is by no means limited to colonial produce. Some of the most powerful international monopolies flourish in old established continental industries. Neither the Potash Combine nor the International Steel Cartel is colonial. The latter is organized on a far broader basis than any known colonial monopoly. Its all-embracing internationalism has frequently been hailed by emotional pacifists as evidence of a better world order, but it was by no means inspired by benevolence. It serves to raise prices wherever it can. Its nationalism might be called "introverted." It does not favour home consumers at the expense of foreign consumers by charging the latter high prices; it burdens its own nationals with high home prices in order to gain foreign markets. The internal prices of its syndicated products invariably exceed the external prices in open foreign markets. The trust does not want to benefit foreigners, but its own investors. Its member plants have a production capacity far in excess of consumers' demands—at least at prices which the less efficient plants consider profitable—and these surplus plants must either be scrapped or made profitable at someone else's expense. Exports must be forced; otherwise sales cannot expand beyond the normal purchasing power of inland markets. The high costs of production which result from the insufficient exploitation of over-expanded plants are covered by raising prices at home and by lowering them abroad. No other way of securing yields on the total investment can be found. For monopolists greatly prefer the maintenance of high prices at home and the dumping of surplus products abroad to the scrapping of surplus capacity, the laying off of inefficient plants, and the concentration of production on the most favoured spots and in the most efficient enterprises, where costs are low and low prices are remunerative.[1]

The menace of monopolistic discrimination in colonial produce against a particular country is not very great, as long as present-day economic conditions prevail. For it can be raised in many an independent state as soon as prices promise profits. Monopolistic contraction of coffee in Brazil

---

[1] Since the armament boom some scarcity of iron and steel has been experienced by most countries outside the United States. This is evidently a passing phase.

and of cotton in the United States has resulted in additional coffee-growing in Central America and additional cotton-growing in Brazil. Monopoly prices rapidly stimulate outside competition; and the scope of synthetic production is widening all the time. New scientific substitutes would quickly ward off the threat of monopoly, which is not very serious in time of peace. In fact, monopoly is on the defence; it is safe only as long as it is internationalized, non-discriminatory, and reasonable, and its price policy is not aggressive. A country which can pay for its imports is not very likely to have to go without them, even if it owns no colonies; it can get all the raw materials and foodstuffs it may need at the same prices as its most powerful rivals, as long as peace is maintained. But in time of war and under a system of war economics it may suffer greatly. If the countries producing war materials and foodstuffs are retaining them for their own use, either because they want to handicap their rivals' armaments or because they wish to isolate themselves from international economic intercourse, the picture may change completely. A policy of isolation and planned economy eliminates the automatic functioning of the price system. It cuts off sources of supply as well as means of payment. If in an endeavour to eliminate friction which might result from international commercial intercourse it were adopted by a majority of the countries supplying raw materials, some countries might be cut off as effectively as during a blockade.

IV

States of unequal strength, wealth, and structure cannot enjoy equal economic security in a world rent by international rivalries.

A Power which controls the sea may safely rely on seaborne trade; it need not hold contiguous possessions outside its own territory from which it can obtain additional supplies, for it can conquer and hold oversea colonies. As long as it rules the sea lanes it can be assured of the loyalty of its colonies and can depend on their resources. Trade protected by an invincible fleet is as secure as territory defended by an invincible army. But under modern conditions no country within striking distance of another's sea- or aircraft is safe from trade interruption by submarines, mines, or air attacks, no matter whether its supplies come from foreign or from colonial sources.

Sea-power enables a country to starve its opponents; but it may not secure the uninterrupted flow of goods essential to its national existence and strength. The Great War has shown this quite clearly. The numerically greatly superior Allied navies successfully blockaded Germany and they were supported by a blockade on land, which was broken at a few comparatively unimportant points. Notwithstanding this tremendous pressure the German submarines very nearly starved Great Britain.

The risks involved in international trade are infinitely greater to-day than they have ever been. And the substitution of colonies for neutral countries as main bases of supply would increase rather than diminish them. From a military point of view colonies may be an element of weakness as well as of strength. They may require a large garrison for the control of natives and the support of planters and colonists; the protection of this army against outside naval interference may necessitate the presence of parts of the navy in waters where no ultimate strategic decisions can be taken, and where no pivotal posts have to be held. Colonies may, on the other hand, offer excellent recruiting grounds where warlike native armies can be trained, vantage points from which expeditions into the enemy's dominions can be launched, or a secure basis for wireless and coaling stations, for blockading the great trade routes, or for starting a submarine campaign. The possession of the Philippine Islands can scarcely increase the strength or the security of the United States, but the control of Ethiopia by Italy may affect the safety of the Eastern Mediterranean, the Suez Canal, Egypt, Africa, and India.

But colonies hardly ever increase the economic security of the metropolis directly. They can supply her with goods under a régime of sanctions, when other countries may try to starve her, as long as such sanctions are timidly applied and are not accompanied by some sort of blockade. In war, supplies from colonies will be cut off quite as mercilessly as those from neutral countries, if they have to move upon the same great trade routes. The sea-power of the belligerents and the attitude of neutrals will decide whether, and to what extent, trade will continue. Nearly all raw materials and all foodstuffs are contraband to a belligerent sea Power who feels strong enough to intercept them and to brave the neutrals. It would undoubtedly hold up all colonial supplies destined for the consumption of the mother country, and also stop those for neutral countries, as they yield foreign exchange with which other contraband goods can be bought. How far neutrals' rights will be respected will depend on the neutrals' strength.

For nearly a century and a half the United States have denounced foreign war as a highly immoral enterprise, the repercussions of which must be severely limited to the belligerents; it must in no way affect the neutral nations, who desire to pursue their normal peaceful vocations, in which they do not want to be disturbed by the criminal folly of the belligerents. These neutrals are entitled to pursue their trade with both parties on its pre-war level; they are even justified in making additional profits from the increased demand for their goods and the scarcity created by the belligerents' madness.[1]

During the first part of the Great War, the United States upheld the traditional American doctrine that the trade of

[1] Thomas Jefferson to Livingston, 1801, quoted in *Can We Be Neutral?* A. W. Dulles and H. F. Armstrong, p. 16.

neutrals must not be interfered with. Had this attitude been supported energetically by all neutral Powers who either shipped raw materials and foodstuffs to the belligerents or were in need of goods from them, the doctrine of the free seas might have triumphed, and sea-borne trade might have been placed on a fairly safe foundation. As none of the overseas countries desire to get mixed up in European quarrels, the surplus produce which they can raise could easily satisfy all legitimate demands, even if some sources of supply were closed to one or both belligerents. Such a state of affairs would offer much stronger safeguards for the uninterrupted inflow of goods than the possession of colonies. Neutral trade might go on undisturbed where inter-imperial trade would be stopped. This may happen in a rather small, more or less regionalized war, when neither belligerent is strong enough to lay down the law to neutrals.

But the United States failed to impose the principle of the free seas upon the Allies. They finally entered the war on their side after German submarine retaliation against the infringement of the doctrine of the free seas had caused the loss of American lives; otherwise their government might have gone on protesting against the Allies' violation of international law without taking steps to vindicate it, but they would have demanded penalties for non-observance of their favourite doctrine, and at the close of hostilities would have claimed damages for the loss of trade suffered by their nationals.

The infringement of international law by future belligerents might thus have become expensive, but the financial sacrifices involved would scarcely have been a sufficient deterrent against a more or less one-sided interruption of international trade. The rights of the neutrals to uninterrupted international trade were practically waived. They were made to acquiesce with or without protests in the doctrine of unlimited sea-power. Notwithstanding these disappointments the United States resumed their efforts to secure the recognition of the doctrine of the free seas as a law of the world after the War, until American public opinion, in its strong desire to keep out of war, began to turn away from it. Even if this rather timid attitude might be somewhat modified in a long-drawn-out war by the pressure of profiteering groups, it revolutionizes the conceptions of international intercourse.[1] When the most powerful neutral state no longer insists on the maintenance of its sea-borne foreign trade, the countries depending on oversea supplies from it and from other neutrals can no longer rely on their continuance in wartime under the protection of the neutral flag. If they cannot depend on sea-power they will have to rely on their own resources. And these resources must be within safe reach of their land guns, otherwise the enemy's sea power might cut them off. Colonial supplies are not accessible when the enemy controls the sea, even if the colony is not invaded and not occupied by enemy forces, and if continued production is not disturbed and can be carried on. Reliance on colonies for raw materials and food-stuffs is dangerous when the metropolis is not supreme at sea. As it is very doubtful whether, under modern conditions of warfare, such supremacy can be maintained at all times, it is at least as risky as dependence on international resources. The purchase of goods in colonies is easier than in foreign countries, since credit operations can be arranged more conveniently, even if the colony is poor, but transport is equally, if not more difficult. Economic security during war does not depend on the political control of some territory across the seas, but on naval control of the seas. If the spectre of a major war cannot be laid, reliance on overseas supplies is a gamble, the outcome of which depends on the fortune of war. Neither the possession of colonies nor the goodwill of neutrals can really safeguard them. Economic security depends on sea-power, which may prove utterly precarious. The colonial supply problem is but a minor and compara-

[1] See above, pp. 187–9.

tively insignificant part of the vast problem of international economic security. The United States have recognized its true nature. They are trying to solve it for themselves by making their country self-sufficient in time of peace. By doing this and by withdrawing their support from the doctrine of the freedom of the seas, they are weakening the security of all countries depending on oversea supplies. They are driving them towards self-sufficiency, and those countries whose resources are limited cannot accomplish it without lowering the standards of living of their people. And even if they succeeded in time of peace, they would fail during a lengthy war, when the consumption of war goods is increased a thousandfold, whilst man-power and mechanical power are diverted from producing to fighting. This has strengthened their desire for colonial expansion, for these countries evidently hope somewhat paradoxically that sea-power may save them after all.

V

Raw materials from colonies and goods and services from other countries are paid for by the same methods, except in the rare cases when tribute is levied on a colony. In earlier times valuable commodities had to be furnished gratis to the metropolis. The Spanish government took a share of the gold and silver mined in the new world; the Dutch in the East Indies devised an extremely efficient system of forced cultivation of valuable tropical produce, which the government exacted by way of taxation. And it is only a quarter of a century since the rubber exactions in the Belgian Congo were abolished, whereby the natives had been forced to furnish at regular intervals fixed quantities of rubber, either as a corvée or against infinitesimal pay. Some remnants of systematic exaction may have survived in a few remote spots.[1]

[1] As far as the mechanism of payments is concerned, colonial tributes resemble war indemnities.

Apart from this single exception, raw materials as well as foodstuffs from colonies must be paid for by skilled or unskilled, manual or mental labour, by services or by goods. Loans may have been advanced to the colonies in the form of capital goods for equipment or investment, against which future remittances are expected later on, or they may have obtained a promise for future payments in goods in return for present deliveries of colonial output.[1]

The scope for manual labour in present-day colonies for members of highly advanced Western nations is rather limited, as most of the work is done by indigenous natives or by coloured immigrants. What little room there is, is usually taken up by nationals of the ruling country, whose technical skill is needed—though in many African colonies a sprinkling of foreigners, of Greeks, Italians, Portuguese, and Spaniards, can be found in comparatively low paid positions. The demand for highly skilled experts for government as well as for private enterprise is fairly high. Government appointments naturally go mainly to the nationals of the ruling country, though a few foreign specialists have sometimes been enlisted for particular services (e.g. forestry). The higher managerial posts in private enterprise are a little less nationalized, though even here metropolitans prevail. Salaries are comparatively high; officials, as well as traders and workers, contemplate an early retirement on savings or on a pension; a considerable percentage of the income they are earning in the colony is sent home. It forms part of the colony's exports; it is so to speak "ear-marked," and no metropolitan goods are returned for it. Items of this kind are quite important in the balance-sheet of some colonies; the pensions payable to retired Civil Servants charged to India amounted to about £2,400,000 during the

[1] This case is rather academic, for the colony is rarely in a position to furnish goods without previous or immediate payment. During the war, the Argentine and a few other new countries which are as a rule indebted to Europe advanced commodities to belligerents by way of a loan.

'eighties. Countries which possess no colonies cannot hope to draw large incomes from the activities of their nationals in foreign dependencies; their numbers are inconsiderable, though the employees of the merchant-houses established in some colonies count for something. But some of them have derived a considerable revenue from the labour of their nationals in foreign independent countries. The remittances to the home country of Italian emigrants settled in the United States and the Argentine and the earnings of the 200,000–300,000 seasonal labourers who annually went to South America and to the Continent, have played an important part in the Italian balance of payments; they amounted in 1928 to 2,250–2,340 million lire, in 1929 to 2,300–2,350 million, and even in 1930 to 1,970–2,020 million lire.

Before the present relapse into mutual compensation agreements, international economic activities had never been merely bilateral; they were frequently not even triangular; they might be called multi-angular or polygonal. The savings of the Italian emigrants to the United States were not earmarked for buying American cotton. They formed a claim for Italy which could be drawn upon for buying coal in England, wool in Australia, or rubber in Malaya. It did not matter much where such claims arose, as long as they sufficed to cover an import surplus, which the recipient country could not settle otherwise. The strangling of Italian immigration into the United States to an annual quota of barely 6,000 has greatly reduced Italy's capacity to pay for colonial produce; it has done her much more harm than the absence of such produce in her own possessions; the exclusion of Japanese labourers whose emigration might have relieved the labour markets at home and whose earnings might have increased the national income has not only offended Japan's *amour propre*; it has compelled her to seek means of payment by speeding up industrialization and by entering upon what her rivals call "cut-throat competition."

VI

The most-favoured-nation clause usually covers the right of the foreign entrepreneur to work on equal terms with the nationals of the country with which the treaty has been concluded, including its colonies; in this respect he is frequently put on a par with colonials as well as with citizens of the mother country.

The foreign entrepreneur, the technical expert, the manager, and the merchant, who possess particular skill, knowledge, and capital have benefited from these rights. They have been made welcome in most native dependencies, but not in all. In colonies not subject to the open-door régime, discrimination is not unknown; foreigners and foreign enterprise are excluded from certain branches of business; oil or minerals have sometimes been reserved for national undertakings; the domicile of the concern must be in the mother country, or the majority of the capital, or of the responsible management must be national[1]—either under the most-favoured-nation clause or under the open-door agreements. Even where foreign rights are scrupulously and carefully respected by law, actual discrimination is by no means barred. In a smallish white community, comfort as well as success depends on social intercourse; if the foreigner is not a member of the club or invited to Government House, neither the white community nor the native will look upon him as a desirable citizen, whatever the ramifications of his business or his legal status as a member of his country may be.

On the impersonal side, a foreign Power's participation in the development of native dependencies, the provision of capital and the organization of business, is somewhat different. Metropolitan enterprise is predominant in most dependencies. Most colonial Powers, with the exception of Spain and Portugal, are wealthy. They do not need foreign

[1] Chatham House, *Raw Materials and Colonies*, pp. 47–8.

capital for the exploitation of their demesne. The rate of
interest has always been much lower in Holland, Belgium,
France, and England than in Germany, Italy, and Japan.
The business men of the former countries have the skill and
the experience needed for the exploitation of their possessions; they have been the pioneers in developing the forms
of colonial exploitation which other countries have subsequently imitated—though German merchants have played
an important part in certain trades and regions. Naturally
most of the capital is furnished by the capital markets
of the metropolis. England is supposed to draw about
£150 million a year from her Empire investments. Metropolitan capital markets have frequently been of mutual
assistance to one another; they have rarely had to apply for
outside help. British capital was invested in the Dutch East
Indian tea industry and Dutch capital in many parts of
the British Empire. Where capital is readily available, legal
obstacles can be eluded. Restriction to nationals can be
circumvented by means of subsidiary companies. Producing
companies in an oil field may be national, while a remote
holding company may own their shares and control their
policies. The ownership of shares is rarely restricted to
nationals. In a few cases "voting" shares are nationalized,
but generally any investor who wants to have a fling can
do so in an open market, though often the law may insist
on a national directorate. Anybody can buy Malayan rubber
shares on the London Stock Exchange and profit or suffer
from their rise or fall; and anybody can go in for Katanga
in Brussels or Paris, or for Deli Matschappy in Amsterdam,
without fear of discrimination. The financial predominance
of the metropolis is not so much the result of deliberate
exclusive nationalist policies as of positive facts and natural
conditions.

Most new countries are badly in need of capital; even
violent nationalists are anxious to attract foreign capital to
all sorts of enterprises. Anti-foreign feeling is rarely ever in

evidence when foreign capital is flowing in, though it can
be easily aroused when high profits are made and remitted
abroad, or when difficulties in paying debts have to be
faced. When a foreign company wants to exploit a basic
natural deposit which national firms covet, and which may
be essential to national manufacturing industries or to the
mother country's defence, a bitter anti-foreign feeling will
rapidly arise. Such deposits are frequently wasting assets;
fervent nationalists assert in one breath that these foreigners
want to paralyse national industries by letting them go to
waste and that their life will be prolonged if exploited by
nationals. Hopes and fears of this type are equally misleading, for the government which controls the region in
which the works are situated holds them in the hollow of
its hands, provided it is an efficient government. If it is
not, legal safeguards can easily be circumvented, though
this may be expensive. But an alien shipping company
or a mere trading concern can shift its operating centre
from one port or terminus to another; it can hurt a country
without injuring itself; an enterprise which has to run
immovable plants fixed in a particular spot is at the mercy
of the local government. An honest, intelligent, liberal
policy does not endanger a country which openly admits
foreign capital and foreign enterprise. But even under the
most liberal régime, foreign nationals will rarely enjoy a
large share of the primary profits from capital enterprise
in the dependencies of advanced countries. The metropolis
business men, with but few exceptions, are a match for
their less favoured rivals, even if, being poorer, they may
do things more cheaply. But the others happen to be insiders.
The profits of forming the company and of managing it go
as a rule to the mother country—not because foreigners are
excluded, but because there is no need to approach them,
as they cannot offer better terms than the nationals. The
great gains in colonial affairs are made by those who get
in on the ground floor; though the total amount of those

primary profits may be overrated, they loom large in people's imaginations. The sight of early Rand millionaires, not shareholders, who buy Crown mines at £15 and sell them a few weeks later at £16, made men's mouths water, and thirst for "Eldorado." But this is not a colonial issue; it is part and parcel of the capitalist system.

The regional origin of income from foreign investment does not matter much; it is immaterial in time of peace whether it arises in one's own colony, or in a foreign colony, or in an independent country, provided it is safe and large enough to be of use in paying for necessary imports. If Germany had a steady flow of revenue from South African mining shares, she might pay for coffee from Brazil, oil seeds from Africa, or for tea from Ceylon. An ample regular supply of exchange from foreign investments is more helpful than the possession of some tropical territory which does not yield adequate profits on the metropolitan capital placed in it. But investments in national colonies are safer in one respect than such investments abroad. Neither arbitrary repudiation nor equally arbitrary currency depreciation is likely to injure the metropolitan creditor, as long as his government is in control of the dependency. Even the outbreak of war need not disturb him; his rights will not be confiscated by an enemy government until the war is lost.

The control of colonies, moreover, offers particular opportunities for investment to metropolitan finance. The mother country can raise the money needed for colonial development by internal loans, the proceeds of which will be accepted at par by the national manufacturing firms supplying the capital goods; they can equip the colony without too great a strain. These orders will give additional employment at home. Colonial ventures financed in this way form a unique type of public works; they do not compete with other enterprises and they can be expected to yield profits. The cost of financing their equipment nationally may be high; tenders submitted to foreign competitors might save some money. But this need not be the case. A highly developed metropolitan industry usually has a large margin of unused capacity, every reduction of which will permit of some considerable abatement of price. As long as raw materials raised in colonies can secure a "sheltered" metropolitan price which rules above world market prices, it does not matter very much whether their producers are charged competitive or monopolistic prices for their initial outlay. And as long as the manufactured goods which are made from costly colonial produce can be sold in protected home markets, the high price for raw materials is nobody's concern. For in colonial affairs neither the taxpayer nor the consumer counts for much. The taxpayer must either subsidize exports, or wages and profits must be cut below those prevailing abroad. The loss of exports to foreign parts, due to increased costs of production, may in the last resort reduce the supply of foreign exchange; it will be easily offset by the saving of foreign exchange which results from producing the goods in the colony. The colonial demand for capital equipment will raise the metropolis' output of manufactured goods, which could not have been sold to foreign countries. For these countries can get cheaper credit abroad and can buy their equipment at least equally well in other countries.

VII

Exports from colonies sometimes balance imports into them: for example, in the Japanese colonies (130 million and 136 million gold dollars respectively). In the British colonies (excluding India) and in the French colonies (Algeria included), on the other hand, imports exceed exports (493 and 333 million gold dollars, and 352 and 273 million gold dollars respectively); the same happened in the Portuguese (24·0 and 16·6 million gold dollars) and the Italian possessions (30 and 10 million gold dollars).[1] These countries

[1] Chatham House, *The Colonial Problem*. All figures refer to 1934.

spend more on their colonies than they receive from them, a great deal of this expenditure being on capital account. The exports of the Dutch colonies (212 against 115 million gold dollars), of the Belgian (23 against 10 million gold dollars), and of the American colonies (134 against 99 million gold dollars) greatly surpass their imports. These colonies return a surplus as payment on former capital investments.

The total imports into all colonies amount to 1,378 million dollars; the exports from all metropolitan countries to colonies, their own as well as those of other nations, reach 954 million dollars. The colonies take about 21 per cent of the goods exported from mother countries and 14 per cent of the world's export trade (less exports from colonies). Exports to their own colonies form 10 per cent of the British export trade, 30 per cent of the French, 4 per cent of the Dutch, 1 per cent of the Belgian, and 25 per cent of the Japanese. The total exports of all European countries not possessing colonies (excluding the U.S.S.R.) are 2,348 million dollars,[1] or nearly double the total imports of all colonies. Their exports to colonies are $2\frac{1}{2}$ per cent of all their exports. The colonies' total exports of raw materials and foodstuffs—841 million dollars—were quite insufficient to provide the mother countries with all the produce they need (3,450 million dollars); their imports from colonies proper were 635 million dollars.

Here again it does not much matter whether trade is direct and bilateral, or triangular, or even multi-angular. The so-called Have-not countries could easily pay for their imports from the colonies without sending a single cargo direct to them, if England were willing to take a corresponding quantity of goods from them; this would provide them with the sterling needed. By thus concentrating the colonial trade in her own hands and by becoming the clearing-house for colonial produce, the United Kingdom

---

[1] Of which German exports represented over 40 per cent.

might make an additional profit—this was the object of the old colonial policy—but the supply to the Have-nots would be assured.[1]

As it is, many colonies are still fairly free of access, though recently discrimination under the Ottawa agreements, especially affecting Japan, has been on the increase. But export possibilities from non-colonial Powers to independent states, ruling states as well as free states, are on the wane. This shrinkage is far more serious than the contraction of the colonial import trade. The independent countries overseas are among the great exporters of foodstuffs and raw materials; a closing of their markets to manufactured goods must aggravate the distress of their customers who cannot pay for them by sending commodities. The United States government has recognized that their customers cannot pay for the U.S.A. export surplus of cotton and wheat, if they are not allowed to send in their goods.[2] They are reducing their output and curtailing their available export surplus, and are attempting to balance their own economic system. These measures neither satisfy the customers' needs for goods, the prices of which have been raised, nor do they give them the means of payment. The narrowing of metropolitan markets is even more serious. The new protectionist policy of Great Britain, combined with monetary instability, quotas, and clearing arrangements, is reducing imports and, with it, the supply of devisen with which Have-not countries might finance their purchases of raw materials; this puts a stop to triangular trade; when exports and

[1] Some of the Dominions have recognized this state of affairs. (*a*) Their output of foodstuffs and raw materials surpasses the United Kingdom's purchasing power for these commodities considerably. (*b*) They have reserved their markets for United Kingdom manufactured goods. (*c*) They must send their supplies of raw materials, etc., to foreign countries. (*d*) They cannot receive payment from these countries in manufactured goods, without sacrificing British manufacturing interests. (*e*) But they could sell their surplus goods to foreign countries, if the United Kingdom were willing to receive foreign goods in payment.

[2] Henry Wallace, *America Must Choose.*

imports between two countries are made to balance each other, no surplus for colonial trade is available. The Have-not countries are quite free to buy in colonial markets, but they are handicapped in selling to them and to the metropolis. As they cannot get surplus exchange which is acceptable to the colony elsewhere, they must either reduce their imports or acquire a colony of their own.

Some of the countries which complain about the strained international economic situation are by no means free from blame themselves. They have, so to speak, blockaded themselves; they have stimulated agrarian production at home in order to become self-sufficient and independent of foreign foodstuffs. In some instances they have been fairly successful. They have shifted their internal purchasing power for manufactured goods from workers to farmers and thus raised the costs of living and of production, which handicaps their foreign trade. They are losing ground to rival manufacturing countries which can sell more cheaply; and they have done their best to impoverish their foreign agrarian customers by stimulating additional agricultural home production; this has intensified the fall in world prices of agricultural products. They have given the agrarian countries cause for industrialization and for new protective measures, and pretexts for not paying interest on their foreign debts.

These developments have not much affected colonial dependencies. Colonial products rarely compete directly with metropolitan goods, though butter and margarine fiercely rival each other, and a severe struggle has gone on between colonial and metropolitan producers of sugar in France and the United States. The independence of the Philippines would scarcely have become an object of practical politics, had not continental beetroot sugar interests (highly protectionist) greatly resented insular cane sugar competition. But some sort of compromise between rival groups could always be reached, as most colonial companies are owned and organized by national capitalists, who claim equal protection of their property with home producers and whose lobbying strength is frequently very great.

As long as tropical colonies do not enjoy fiscal autonomy they can be held in a state of agrarian subserviency, though they need not suffer much damage from it. In most cases industrialization would be premature, expensive, socially dangerous, and economically superfluous. The control of a large area which will not be exploited by spoon-fed infant industries is a very great asset to their owners, even if they let outsiders share its prosperity. No sudden turn towards industry will cut down supplies, and no tariff imposed over-night will stop the exchange of manufactured goods in return for raw materials and foodstuffs.

Exports from a colony cannot be increased very rapidly, even if pressure is brought upon it, for success depends on costly development schemes—mere spoliation by brutal exactions defeats its own ends, inasmuch as it quickly reduces productive capacity. But imports from the mother country into a colony can quickly be augmented. The need for private investments is very great, and there is an almost unlimited scope for public works. Both can be financed with loans raised in the metropolitan capital market, the proceeds of which will be spent almost exclusively on orders for national industries.[1] Public works in colonies rarely compete with existing private enterprise, even when they are remunerative. This expenditure on equipment and material will give additional employment at home, whilst a national labour force may be needed on construction work in the colony. The Italians are employing an army of 250,000 on public works in Abyssinia, and plan to triple or quadruple it in the next few years.[2] The wages paid to these labourers are either held back for the support of their dependants, or sent back in return for national consumers' goods. The

---

[1] See above, pp. 318–19, and below, pp. 357–9 and 388.

[2] Corrado Zoli, "Italy's East African Empire." *Foreign Affairs*, October 1937, p. 90.

wage bill of natives recruited locally is comparatively small, and a large part of it will be spent on European consumers' goods, some of them coming from foreign countries. The bulk of the expenditure will find its way to the pockets of national producers. Colonial wars and colonial public enterprises represent a type of public works by which a great number of unemployed can be absorbed. Colonial subsidies have taken the place of colonial tributes; most dependencies rely on metropolitan subventions. They may strain the national budget. But this does not matter very much in an age when unbalanced budgets are the main instruments for fighting depression. And the material losses may be offset by emotional gains; ultimately they may even become remunerative. Colonial governments can be charged with the service of the loans raised for these purposes; they will not be allowed to default in the cavalier way in which independent countries are in the habit of divesting themselves of their obligations.

Many undeveloped new countries, but only a few colonies, have indulged in an orgy of indiscriminate borrowing. They have to earmark part of their exports for debts; the residue has not always been sufficient for the purchase of necessary imports. They must either expand their exports, which is difficult when world prices fall and imports into creditor countries are severely curtailed, or they will have to reduce their imports and suffer serious privation from the absence of essential commodities, or they will have to repudiate their debts. They are not likely to get a loan, for, as long as they cannot meet their old obligations, capitalist countries will be chary of giving them new credits.

Some highly developed manufacturing countries, Germany among them, have found themselves in a similar predicament. They are short of imported raw materials, for their exports are contracting; they can neither pay their old debts nor get a new loan. Their currencies as well as their credits are frozen. They claim that the possession of colonies could save them from import difficulties due to currency troubles.

The disturbances which upset the trade equilibrium between two independent countries can certainly be minimized in the relations between a metropolis and its dependencies. Identity of currencies as such does not matter much. The Latin monetary union, all of whose members had the same standard, could not protect its several partners from currency troubles, and Australian sterling was not saved by having been on a par with British sterling. The currency of India and Kenya differ from that of the mother country, and so did that of East Africa when it was a German colony.

Colonial currency fluctuations will not be allowed to do serious harm to the mother country, for the currency of a dependency, as well as the metropolitan currency, can be manipulated exclusively in the interest of the mother country. The metropolis can either keep it stable, or it can raise, or lower it in relation to its own or to other currencies. At any given moment the relation of two countries' currencies to each other is determined by their total claims and total obligations. Since currency management has become the order of the day, claims can be manipulated by depreciation, which reduces debts, puts a premium on exports and discourages imports. Independent governments have fought one another with these modern weapons of economic warfare; they have nullified, or at least minimized, the results of other governments' efforts. But metropolitan and colonial governments do not fight each other; for ultimately the metropolis must prevail. Motherland and colony can manipulate their currencies harmoniously. Simultaneous and equal manipulation will not disturb their mutual relations, which remain stable, however much their currency may fluctuate abroad. The same move may be profitable to both, as long as rival countries neither follow their example immediately nor retaliate. But their interests need not always be identical. Separate manipulation by mother country and colony might be attractive.

Devaluation of the colonial currency would cheapen colonial exports to the mother country, as well as to foreign countries—Germany profited from the devaluation of the pound in West Africa—but it would raise the cost of goods imported into the colony. A reduction of the metropolitan currency, on the other hand, while the colonial standard remains stable, would cheapen the colony's imports, but might reduce its profits from exports.

Policies and results will turn on the credit, not on the currency situation. A colony which is indebted to the mother country must sell some of its exports without receiving returns. A depreciation of the metropolitan currency would lighten its burdens—as the debt is usually contracted in the mother country's currency; a depreciation of the colonial currency would, on the other hand, increase them, though it might inflate the volume of its trade.

Within the limits of its productive capacity a colony can furnish raw materials to the metropolis, either in return for past advances or in exchange for manufactured goods— which it might get cheaper elsewhere; it can even be made to grant it a loan and to sell it goods on deferred payment. Control, not currency, is the decisive factor. As long as the colony's output is sufficient to cover old debts as well as new purchases the first alternatives present no difficulties, though compulsory exchange manipulation might hurt a colony which could dispose of its produce to better advantage in a foreign market, or get its imports more cheaply elsewhere.

The third alternative involves some internal credit manipulations, for the colony is rarely in a position to wait for future payments for goods sold to the metropolis. It can always be made to accept metropolitan paper currency without a discount; if this currency is depreciated in foreign countries, so much the better for the metropolis. Her goods will be cheapened proportionately in the colonial market, while the colony will be forced to spend its cash in the metropolis rather than in foreign countries, where it would fetch less than in the metropolis. Colonial payments in foreign currencies will become more burdensome, and colonial purchases which must be made abroad in foreign currencies will become more expensive. But the mother country will benefit at the expense of the colony. She will be able to buy colonial produce more cheaply than she could abroad, and she is compelling the colony to spend its money on additional metropolitan purchases, as she cannot use it profitably in foreign countries. A kind of artificial boom in the colony may follow; the flush money in her hands or the large credits at her disposal will enable her to spend freely within her own frontiers and in the mother country. An expansion of colonial industries might take place. But the process of credit expansion must be kept under strict control, otherwise a rise of prices is sure to follow, which will end in catastrophic inflation. The possession of a colonial empire does not safeguard the metropolitan currency; devaluation by Great Britain, Belgium, France, and Holland has shown this clearly enough—in the latter case the plight of the East Indian planters made it inevitable. And it is not an alternative to exchange control. As colonies do not determine the policy of the metropolis, they cannot save her from the consequences of financial and economic extravagance, which will result in a breakdown of the exchanges. It must be met by foreign loans, open bankruptcy, devaluation, or exchange control. When exchange control has been decided upon, it must be extended to the colony, where it must be managed as effectively as at home—though the presence of large migratory native populations and the scarcity of European administrators will make frontier supervision very difficult. Otherwise the colony might become a convenient channel for the flight of metropolitan capital. An account for the colony must be opened in the metropolis, into which all payments due to it from the mother country would be entered in national currency, and on which the colony could draw for purchases, either from the metropolis or, if the account is not blocked, from foreign countries.

Germany's successful dealings with some foreign countries might become the pattern of a settled colonial commercial policy. She bought supplies from Turkey, Yugoslavia, and Greece by offering them rather remunerative prices above those obtainable in other markets. She recompensed herself by forcing them to spend the German marks thus acquired on purchases in Germany. For these marks were blocked; their internal purchasing power was kept above their external value. The goods bought with blocked currency in Germany may have been a little more expensive than those procurable from foreign countries; but the sales of these blocked marks abroad would have entailed tremendous losses, though their foreign holders had made a handsome profit by selling to the German market. The ease with which a great manufacturing country can get goods from foreign countries, however bad its internal economic situation may be, has been clearly demonstrated by Germany's masterly handling of exchange control. She might not have succeeded in a period of great scarcity, but in such circumstances prices would rise very rapidly, a boom would follow and money-mongering tricks would no longer be needed.[1] Each of the countries concerned had its own particular currency; each of them managed its exchange control quite independently of, and by no means in conformity with, Germany. But Germany's greater economic power decided the issue—temporarily—in her favour. A colony can offer wider and more permanent scope for manipulation, for the

[1] The depreciation of the pound has cheapened colonial produce to gold-bloc countries. In this respect Germany has come off best, for France and the Netherlands suffered from the business crisis in their colonies, which had to sell at English prices,

metropolis can exercise pressure on all its economic activities; it can impose upon it a system of planned, or rather coercive, economics, and the colony—unlike an independent state—cannot retaliate. The absence of retaliation which is implied in the control by the metropolis of the colony's material and human resources is what really matters; currency control is but one of several methods of exploitation. It may be a convenient cloak for hiding downright coercive exactions. A colony can always be made to provide the mother country with colonial raw materials on terms which do not upset the latter's balance of payments, within the limits of the colony's productive capacity, but frequently at a very heavy loss.

VIII

No absolute guarantee against the closing of the few remaining open-door areas can be given. The governments administering a dependency, or even a mandate, can always favour the nationals of the metropolis.[1] They can divert colonial production into certain channels and make it subservient to their national industries. They are not prevented by open-door agreements from giving bounties to colonial produce or from granting it preferential treatment at home. The Congo Convention is not infringed by the preferential treatment of Kenya coffee in the United Kingdom. The mandatory cannot be prevented from showing unilateral generosity to mandated areas by free grants and interest-bearing loans to them. This generosity creates ties which bind colonial markets as well as sources of supply closer to the mother country. And even when equality of treatment of goods and men is scrupulously

---

[1] The contract for the Howrah Bridge has been awarded to a British company whose tender was high, as it was feared that political events might prevent foreign companies from delivering to time.

L*

observed, irrespective of their country of origin, discrimination in favour of local residents' interests is almost inevitable. Neither the most-favoured-nation clause as such, nor open-door agreements, oblige a colonial government to grant to foreigners equality of opportunity with residents; they merely bind it to treat all non-residents alike, without abolishing preference for residents. Resident populations in settlement areas, as well as in native dependencies, are rarely inclined to sacrifice the monopoly of natural advantages which they enjoy in an undeveloped country to the abstract obligation of sharing it with people from oversea.

Currency manipulation is an excellent substitute for preferential treatment where open-door agreements or the most-favoured-nation clause block the way to open discrimination. The metropolis's and the colony's internal price level can be arbitrarily adjusted by it, for its own or for the colony's benefit, either by simple devaluation or by the more sophisticated method of exchange control. No change in tariffs or commercial treaties is needed, exports are stimulated and imports—except colonial imports—are reduced; rival countries must either follow suit or see their markets flooded and their exports prohibited. Exchange control may work more clumsily, but it is more effective in this respect. The customary treaty safeguards against discrimination are of no avail.

Tariffs and customs arrangements have rarely been applied in an arbitrary autonomous way. Most governments have been willing to bargain with other governments about tariff positions and to conclude commercial treaties or trade agreements, in which they offered one another equal opportunities under the most-favoured-nation clause. They bound themselves to abstain at least for a number of years from arbitrary changes. Whenever they resorted to one-sided action their object was to get a better bargain; it never was an end in itself. Commercial policies have always aimed at bilateral or multilateral agreements, if possible for a longish period, even when they have been aggressive. Such agreements prevented autonomous action by the parties concerned during a treaty period; no abdication of sovereignty was involved. Concessions were made because the states who made them were sovereign. Since currency manipulation has become popular, some governments have refused to contract such international ties; they have gloried in a kind of selfish sovereignty; they have carried on a *bellum omnium contra omnes* regardless of the principle of collective security, on which they based their foreign policy. The right to handle currency arbitrarily without regard to its neighbour has become the main plank in a modern state's economic Magna Carta. As long as such views prevail neither the open-door nor the most-favoured-nation clause is of much value.[1] And it is quite natural to base the claim for a colony on the benefits which currency manipulation might offer to a mother country which is unable to pay for all the imports she needs; it is an almost instinctive move towards a policy of nationalist economic self-sufficiency, which disregards the risks of economic world anarchy.

The subjects of excluded nations angrily brood over the injustice done to them. They exaggerate the hardships from which they suffer—the lack of colonial possessions—and greatly overrate the advantages of their more successful rivals. The proprietary nations might have easily appeased their resentment by giving economic scope to outsiders, while retaining political control in their own hands. They might have been content to monopolize the political power derived from the possession of dependencies, whilst sharing their economic opportunities with others; they are not doing this any longer. It would be cheaper and, in the end, far more profitable to buy peace by fair and durable economic concessions, and to return to a system of universal equality of opportunity for the nationals of all nations.

[1] See above, p. 173.

But though free economic exchange on a world-wide scale might equalize business opportunities for the inhabitants of all countries, it would not equalize political opportunities, either for individuals or for states.

IX

To begin with colonies offer "jobs." The soldiers who garrison a native dependency and the administrators who rule it are not genuine immigrants. They may spend their entire active life within its borders and even bring their wives along with them; they do not fuse with the native population, but remain an alien element and retire on a pension as soon as their work is done. The merchants who develop the country's trade and the planters who organize its production never take root even where they have raised a white family. A rubber plantation in Malaya is not going to be their children's home; if they own it, they mean to sell it as soon as they have made enough money; if they manage it, they hand over their job to a successor as soon as they can retire. Tremendous and incessant pressure is put on native society to change its ways, but those who wield it are mere transients and pass on: the steam which drives a mighty engine escapes with a low hiss, but all the time new steam is generated in the boiler, and keeps the piston going furiously. Even the sexual relations between planters and native women which are customary in some regions do not make for permanency; the white fathers abandon their mixed brood when they return home, and the only durable sediment deposited by the alien current flowing unintermittently over the native lands is a thin layer of Eurasians.

Colonies of this type offer a few specific opportunities to the inhabitants of the ruling country. Officers obtain a more rapid promotion and soldiers get a change from the tedium of European garrison life. On the borders there may be war—not the filthy business of muddy trenches, where a man is but an infinitely small cog in an impersonal giant machine, easily clogged and broken—but the glorious romantic war of the frontier, where brave men from the West meet brave men from the East. Young clerks get a chance to shoulder responsibilities early in life which they could not take over at home. They find openings which Europe can no longer offer them, and, if they survive, they can save a sufficient competency for a comfortable and uncramped old age. Life is on a large scale; risks are great, but so are opportunities and rewards. The total number of people, however, who can be accommodated in this way is comparatively small. The increment added to the national income is probably infinitesimal, especially when counterbalanced by the burdens which the metropolitan taxpayer has to shoulder in order to develop the colony. The glorious days when the natives could be squeezed for the benefit of the Crown, as well as for the planters' and merchants' profits, are gone for ever. From the budgetary point of view, colonies cost more than they bring in. Tributes have gone out of fashion and subsidies are the rule.

The recruitment of civil servants or of soldiers is not strictly national; foreign legionaries are frequently employed in native countries to conquer or to garrison them. Dutch sugar plantation managers have been in great request in many parts of the world; Swedish, Swiss, and Belgian organizers have been engaged in native communities, as there was no Great Power behind them which could use them as the thin edge of the wedge for peaceful penetration. But broadly speaking, the avenues of success offered by the possession of colonies to the more adventurous spirits of a nation are strictly nationalized. The number of these administrative posts is very small; competition for them is very keen. But this does not matter. The winning numbers in the lottery of life are equally few, and most of the winnings are small. An intelligent appreciation of probabilities would deter anybody from trying his luck at it. But if all start under fairly equal conditions, the glorious "may" which "His Majesty Chance" promises to one and all, not only makes men put their money on all sorts of stakes, but kindles their hopes anew, after countless disappointments.

Life is getting pretty dull in the old countries; no "frontier" is within visible distance. Even in the United States it has almost completely receded. At a time when many old inhibitions have disappeared young men and young women are more restless than they were in the days when outer duty was very stern. There are no openings any longer for them. For the average man romance is limited to films and political parades, by which mass leadership is trying to generate exaltation. But spectacles and mere contemplation offer no genuine outlet for pent-up dreams. The spectators' lusty yell is but a poor substitute for action. The drabness was bearable as long as modern life seemed perfectly organized and every youngster who worked well and was good (or at least appeared to be good) had a chance to get a job, however mean. There was not much fun, but there was at any rate security; there was no prospect of conquering worlds, but there was the certainty of steady advance. Once you had placed your foot firmly on the lowest rung of the ladder, you could not only hold on, you would climb, slowly, of course, but surely. You would ultimately arrive, not at a very elevated position, it is true, but you would probably outdistance some who had started alongside of you. You had won out against them, and that was fairly satisfactory. To do so, you had to discipline yourself thoroughly, and though you might not enjoy this very much, it was rather salutary. It was almost as good as the spiritual exercises practised by more religious members of society; it chastened the flesh; it did not kill the spirit, but it numbed it sufficiently to prevent explosions. It made you grateful for small mercies, and when once you had been thoroughly broken in, you ended, not by being happy perhaps, but at least by being content.

To-day security has gone and, with it, the certainty of ever getting a job. Unemployment is no longer the punishment meted out to those unfortunates who are a little below the standard of average efficiency—it has become a curse of the young, who see no chance of ever getting away from it, however strenuously they may prepare and qualify for work. Its shadow no longer darkens the path of the working-class exclusively; it had been responsible for their peculiar "proletarian" outlook on life, an outlook greatly changed by the dole. In its new phase it has become "bourgeois unemployment," the bugbear of the lower middle class, whose sons are looking in vain for white-collar jobs. It is terrorizing those very elements of society which most fervently believe in stability, sobriety, and security. For very nearly a century their lives had been widening; the older generation was sure to start the next on a very much more advantageous level and help it towards a future rise by somewhat reducing its own enjoyment. Expectations were mounting from generation to generation. Their hopes have been rudely shattered. No "high level" lies ahead of them; an abyss opens before them. But beyond this abyss stretch wide lands, inhabited by feckless teeming natives under the control of foreign Powers. To conquer them, to bring them to heel, is a task worthy of a noble race. The young people have been taught to glory in the past of their nation. The pride of the self-made man who glories in his achievement has given way to boast of ancestry. The claims of the aristocracy to noble descent are democratized, tribalized, and vulgarized. Present-day youth is more ignorant of foreign lands than their predecessors were, for, as modern all-embracing nationalism can ill brook comparisons, detached comparative studies are discouraged, while self-conscious concentration on their own nation's real or imagined grandeur are encouraged. The outer world is merely a stage on which great deeds can be accomplished. They must be supreme on it and wash off the iniquities which victorious and more successful rivals have heaped upon them.

These people have no very clear ideas as to the actual scope afforded by modern colonies. They dream of endless spaces, from which natives can either be driven or on which they can be made to work for a lordly race, where there is room to breathe freely, where unemployment is unknown, and where thousands of industrious peasants can propagate the race, until it has become overwhelmingly strong in numbers and, therefore, great. They know very little about economic facts and care less for economic argument, though poverty and penury have influenced their attitude, sometimes almost unconsciously. They want to assert themselves in a rather primitive way, that is to rule other people and to subject their wills to their own. They themselves have to undergo daily military drill in the labour camp, in the barrack-room, and in the factory. The more impetuous spirits among them may appreciate the value of discipline, but they do not care overmuch for the tedious and meticulous technical methods by which a modern army is trained. They neither want to be a small wheel in the complex war machine of the present day nor to control the slow working of economic forces—they want to rule directly and personally. They are attracted by power, the simple primitive control of man by man. Many are filled with a red-hot egalitarian passion; to them the nation is a living organism, composed of physically and spiritually homogeneous units. Domination by one half over another is incongruous in such a society; one can only enjoy being a master where there are serfs to rule. The strong desire for superiority over others, which has been inculcated into them, can only receive free play if it can be directed against alien races, which by external and internal marks of inferiority are, in their eyes, clearly destined for serfdom. Jew-baiting is a poor substitute for ruling natives.

The leading nations of the world are imperial Powers; the English, French, American, and even the Dutch, Portuguese, and Belgians rule native empires. These countries stress their undying faith in democracy, but they are the born rulers of coloured men, who must obey their will. This boon has until now been denied to the Germans and the Italians, at least on a large scale. The latter ruled a few deserts, covered with sand and rocks. The former smart under the stigma of Versailles, which, by slander and calumny, deprived them of their colonial empire. It is not the economic value of colonies which matters to them, but the status of superiority which their possession has conferred on their owners. Equality really means superiority. The leader of the German people recently proclaimed with passionate sincerity the right of all members of the white race to rule other races.[1] This is but another paraphrase of the "white man's burden" or of the American claim to manifest destiny. It does not pretend to be a true picture of colonial problems and possibilities.

Colonial administrators no longer set out in the hope of enriching themselves by plunder and extortion. Day in and day out, they are faced with grave responsibilities and have to undergo severe personal privations. But, if they understand their tasks and are equal to their opportunities, they can even to-day exercise power in a direct personal way, which might well be the envy of any dictator. In everyday life, administration and responsibility may often seem rather drab, but legends have grown up in books and films which make those who stay at home deliciously conscious of the glories of empire, which they might share through their

[1] Hitler: Speech at Munich, January 1936.

representatives.[1] They yearn, like Kipling's soldier, to be taken

> " . . . somewheres east of Suez, where the best is
> like the worst,
> Where there aren't no Ten Commandments an'
> a man can raise a thirst."

It is not a question of prestige, the outcome of more or less rational covetous reasoning, it is part of the yearning of man for a wider and ampler world to live in.

---

[1] "Sandi the strong,
Sandi the wise,
Maker of law,
Hater of lies."

CHAPTER VI

CONQUEST AND COMMERCE

I

Two disgruntled nations, Japan and Italy, have lately acquired large colonial possessions. They had been among the less-favoured countries so far. Their internal natural resources are scanty, their population dense (355 per square mile in Italy and 469 per square mile in Japan) and their people are industrious, skilful, and frugal; they are content with a comparatively low standard of comfort, but have little room at home for expansion.

Japan's agricultural area is limited; only about one-sixth of her surface is arable land, thus the density of population of 469 per square mile is really misleading. Farms are small and tillage is very intensified, but about 15 per cent of the main staple food, rice, has to be imported from colonies (12 per cent) and foreign countries.[1] The country has no coking coal, no iron, no oil, no wool, and no cotton; its main surplus articles are silk and sulphur. It is dependent on oversea supplies, though it can draw some from Korea or Manchukuo. As Japan's policy is very aggressive, she must have armaments for securing the uninterrupted supply of such commodities should war or sanctions threaten her. These armaments have greatly increased her needs of foreign overseas mineral products, which she cannot yet obtain, at least not in sufficient quantities, from the regions which she controls or is hoping to control. Whilst she wants to draw these supplies in the future from Manchukuo and China, on whose iron and oil she means to rely, her dependence on foreign sources has greatly increased; during a lengthy period of transition her situation is rather

[1] Ryoichi Ishii, *Population Pressure and Economic Life in Japan*, p. 167.

delicate. Guns and dreadnoughts depend on steel; Japan has to import not only iron ores and pig iron, but scrap too, in order to feed her defence industries.[1] The percentage of war key materials which she can control under all circumstances within her insular empire is so small that she must suffer from the strain of a great and long war, though she has stored supplies and can replenish some from the mainland.[2]

Of late her population has been increasing rapidly. It has doubled from 1872 to 1935 (34·8 millions to 69·3 millions) though the rate of increase is not very high—1·4 to 1·5 per cent a year.[3] The birth rate has declined since 1920, when it was 35 per 1,000. The number of births is now almost stationary, fluctuating a little round two millions a year. But the further decline of the death rate is assuring growth for some time to come, though with decreasing fertility its total may never reach the hundred million level. Economic pressure has been in evidence for quite a long time. Agriculture cannot be much expanded or intensified. The country must either export emigrants or industrialize herself and export goods.

Emigration has not gone very far. The world's great immigration areas—the United States, the British Dominions, and South America—have closed their doors to Japanese immigrants or have limited their numbers. Japan started comparatively late in the day, when most settlement areas had passed the stage of acute labour scarcity and had begun to look upon immigration as a social, as well as an economic issue. At the turn of the century the total Japanese population in the United States was but 24,000, and after the "gentlemen's agreement" of 1907, which had been caused by a "mass" influx of labourers, its numbers were but

[1] Sir Thomas Holland, *The Mineral Sanction*, pp. 57–61.

[2] Chatham House, *Sanctions*, p. 39; Dulles and Armstrong, *Can We Be Neutral?*, p. 165.

[3] Ishii, op. cit., pp. 53 and 60.

72,000.[1] In Canada, which concluded a similar agreement with the Japanese Government in 1908, the number of resident Japanese was only 23,000 (1931). Japanese emigration was directed to South America (Brazil), to Hawaii, and to the Japanese possessions, Korea, Formosa, Sakhalin, and the dependency, Manchuria. In each of these countries (with the exception of Sakhalin, which is poor and climatically unattractive) the Japanese are faced with the rivalry of the native population or the competition of other, more adaptable races, such as the Chinese.[2] As a result of it, the Japanese dependencies contain but one million Japanese—half a million in Korea, 230,000 in Formosa, and 280,000 in Sakhalin; their outflow into these dependencies is very heavily counterbalanced by an inflow of Koreans.[3] Another half a million Japanese are settled in foreign countries—about 230,000 in Manchuria, nearly all in Kwantung, and the rest in Hawaii, the United States, and South America. Manchuria has been swamped by Chinese and Koreans; the Japanese infiltration has been merely governmental and commercial. If the forces at work at present are not completely reversed, Japan must seek expansion in exports and not in emigration.[4]

II

The former blatant admiration for Japan and her achievements, so frequently met in Europe, must be rather offensive to Japanese national pride. The "little yellow men" have often been praised in a condescending fashion, as if they were monkeys whose clever tricks of imitating men deserve a pat on the back. When the Germans called the Japanese the Prussians of the East they merely complimented themselves, since the world's admiration for Prussia was by no

[1] Carr-Saunders, *World Population*, p. 187.
[2] The average wage of a Japanese odd job man in Manchuria was 1·91 yen; that of a Chinese, 0·54 yen (1930). Ishii, op. cit., p. 205.
[3] Carr-Saunders, op. cit., p. 268.
[4] Ishii, op. cit., pp. 191, 193, and 197.

means universal. Even the craze for Japanese art rarely implied a thorough sympathetic understanding of its quality and a sincere recognition of equality. The United States had broken down Japan's century-long isolation by the shots of their gunboats and forced her into intercourse with the Western world. Japan had learned her lesson by bitter experience and westernized the outward forms of her life on the pattern of the mighty European and American States. Her warlike, feudal spirit fitted admirably into the modern military machine designed by the West; her efficiency in handling it was shown by her easy defeat of China. Europe was so astonished that she felt compelled to deprive her immediately of the best fruits of that victory. Until the Great War, each of Japan's expansionist moves was met by counter-moves, which were meant to save China from her domination, as well as from her economic exploitation. The non-alienation agreements and the régime of the open door, by which England, the United States, and, to a lesser degree, Germany, endeavoured to forestall the economic—if not the political—partition of China would never have succeeded, had not Japan risked her all and defeated Russia's ambitions for the control of the Far East. To-day these arrangements no longer serve to baulk European encroachments in that part of the world; in so far as they are observed, they hamper Japan's attempts at getting the privileged economic position, to which tradition, racial affinity, and geographical situation entitle her, in her own eyes.

At the Paris Peace Conference, Japan might have been willing to abandon her territorial designs on China had the European Powers been ready to renounce their spheres of influence.[1] But Europe was neither willing to give up her own privileges nor to grant Japan full equality. Japan had entered the war with a double purpose—she meant to establish her claim to full equality as a world Power and she

[1] Ray Stannard Baker, *Woodrow Wilson and World Settlement*, vol. ii, pp. 248 and 260.

wanted to widen the territorial foundation on which it could be based.[1] She did not succeed in wresting from her allies the recognition she eagerly sought for "all alien nationals of States Members of the League, equal and just treatment in every respect, making no distinctions either in law or fact, on account of their race or nationality."[2] When her sons and daughters wanted to go abroad to share in the equal opportunities of richer lands, they were not admitted, even if they did not ask for equal terms with the resident nationals, but with other foreigners only. They were not even turned away in a decent fashion. Japan could not have taken offence at an immigration quota, such as other countries had to submit to at the hands of the United States; it would have been so low—246—as to have no appreciable effect on the formation of the American population.[3] The United States Senate went deliberately out of its way to slight Japan. The Japanese were racially excluded, and the sprinkling of their people who work in the fields of California and Arizona are precluded from acquiring land and citizenship. Full-blooded Indians can sweep in in masses—in 1930, 1,423,000 Mexicans were accounted for in the United States—and even the members of savage tribes of Philippine Islanders are admitted. But civilized Japanese are barred.

Australia's attitude, though less humiliating to Japanese pride, is even more provoking. Large areas of empty land with a climate suitable to their own physique, but rather repellent to the Anglo-Saxon, stare in the face of the Japanese, who see in them a haven of refuge; they are kept vacant; the fields are untilled. Opportunities for settlement in Australia are generally exaggerated. A good deal may be said for the careful handling of the immigration of Oriental races into white settlement areas. The differences in ways of living, in social standards, and in outlook are bound to cause labour friction between races living in daily

[1] Ray Stannard Baker, *Woodrow Wilson and World Settlement*, vol. ii, p. 225.   [2] Ibid., vol. ii, pp. 234, 239–40.   [3] Ishii, op cit., p. 41.

intercourse. Interbreeding cannot be completely stopped, even where the immigrants are accompanied by their womankind. It is by no means proven that such mixture of races must necessarily produce an inferior mongrel type. But such fusion, even if it were desirable, will scarcely ever be complete; it must result in a tripartite society—two groups of supposedly pure-blooded strains at the top and at the bottom and between them one of mixed origin, which again may show many nuances. In composite societies, racial distinctions overlap social class divisions and aggravate them; social tension in such a society is very much greater than in more homogeneous bodies. The rise of a new mixed stratum, which is repelled by the dominant race when claiming equality with it, and which is not meek enough to stand insults calmly, may add to the danger. The separation of groups habituated to intercourse with one another is difficult;[1] it might be wiser to lock the door and to prevent the rise of a composite society and this incomplete melting process, which disorganizes a nation.

The menace of a Japanese invasion, to which white democracies have so frequently given voice, might have been taken as a recognition of their valour by the Japanese, had it not been couched in terms of contumely, which could not fail to rouse a sensitive nation to bitter anger. The insistence on cultural standards must seem offensive to them, as Mexicans, Hawaiians, and Filipinos are admitted without restriction of numbers, or without the application of a genuine cultural test, whilst they are refused even the grudging courtesy of a small quota.

The Western governments, under British leadership, have renounced the privileges and territorial rights which detracted from Japan's equality in her own territory. They

---

[1] The Californians objected to the Chinese because they did not bring their women, and to the Japanese because they did. The former might breed mongrels and the latter additional Japanese. Of 100,000 Japanese in the U.S.A., 39,700 are women. Ishii, op. cit., p. 197.

have been wise enough to recognize Japan's position and release her from capitulations, though their citizens in the West, as well as in the East, are not prepared to follow suit. Some white people living in the East greatly resented the abandonment of the capitulations; they would have much preferred their continuation.

As Japanese migration had never assumed large proportions,[1] the country found it fairly easy to adapt itself to the restrictions imposed upon it. It began to industrialize itself, to draw its people to the mills as they could not go to the fields overseas. Thanks to its efficiency, to the modest standard of living, and to its excellent technical organization, Japanese industry succeeded in conquering markets by cutting costs. But Japan's endeavours to grow by peaceful commercial expansion were baulked by various devices of commercial discrimination, designed for this purpose. These obstacles threw her back to territorial expansion.

III

The Europeans who descended on the Far East and cut slices from the body of the decaying Chinese Empire subjected an alien civilization to their superior military power. As this had been done with little display of force, they calmly deduced from this feat the superiority of their own culture. Japan is conquering China with instruments borrowed from Western civilization, but adapted to her own requirements. Her penetration of China is not the expansion of a superior over an inferior civilization—it is not a colonial movement. It ranks with alternative annexations and disannexations of Alsace-Lorraine, with the partitions of Poland, or rather with the struggle between Prussia and Austria for the leadership of the Germanic world. It is a conflict between two

[1] In the maximum year, 1929, 25,700 Japanese emigrated, 15,600 to Brazil; but in five years of the decade 1921-30, the inward movement exceeded the outward movement.—Carr-Saunders, op. cit., p. 268.

Oriental nations for supremacy and security in the Far East. The Japanese themselves see it sometimes in the light of an anti-colonial movement, designed to break the domination of the West over the East. It is to be a first step in the liberation of Asia from foreign oppressors. At other times, when they pose as Have-nots, they look upon China as a derelict possession which they have a moral right to annex and to exploit. It is much more a struggle for power and ascendancy than one for wealth.

Under modern conditions, wealth and the control of raw materials are essentials of power. The Japanese are eager to get them. But the army which presses on in Manchuria is the enemy of modern industrial capitalist expansion; it is animated by the feudal instincts of lords and tenants, which survive in a peasantry struggling hard for a living and in a military caste which feels menaced by the growth of the modern money power and which will not submit to a decline in social importance. It has been infected with some collectivist germs gathered from a thorough misunderstanding of Marx. A rural population which is passing through a period of great stress is very receptive of primitive communist teachings.[1] Tribalism and Communism are both collective, but they belong to a different economic age. The creed of the army is the creed of a militarist, feudal nation, to which war is the only occupation fit for gentlemen, and the proper means for territorial expansion, which is the natural basis of national growth. The halo of mysticism round the Emperor is but a sophisticated form of tribal totemism, in so far as it is not due to some misunderstood Western spiritual infiltration.

These soldiers have no wish to share in the opportunities of the Western nations; they want to shape their lives on the pattern handed down to them from their fathers. They do not admire the West. It has taught them how to make guns and ships, how to use steam and electricity; it has fulfilled a

[1] Ishii, op. cit., pp. 155 and 157.

useful function by teaching them how to stand up to it. Its mission is ended. They do not share its ideals and do not wish to imitate it. The spiritual prestige it once enjoyed went for good during the Great War, when the gospel of peace, the corner-stone of the Western creed, was drowned in a sea of blood and hate. The Japanese have been a warrior nation. They do not suffer from the spiritual conflict between their moral teaching and their political ambitions, which makes European statecraft so disgusting in the eyes of disillusioned Oriental observers. The merely commercial argument of equal opportunities for all citizens abroad and at home does not appeal to the mass of the people.

The industrial classes, on the other hand, the manufacturers and the workers, are pursuing the path of European civilization. They strain every nerve to keep going an economic organization which is fashioned after that of the West. They recognize the handicaps from which they suffer and attempt to overcome them by efficient organization. If they could get an approach to commercial equality of opportunity they might be satisfied; their satisfaction might spread to other classes and might lessen social tension, which has greatly helped the revival of feudal militarism.

The struggle between the two groups might have gone on for a long time. An Emperor who is a divinity can steer an even course between rival factions, which no other system of government could attempt to maintain. But it is doubtful whether the aggressive militarism, which is bent on territorial expansion, can solve Japan's economic as well as her political problems. It is by no means certain whether the forward movement in which she is engaged will bring the economic security she desires; it certainly cannot do so quickly. Japan has held a colonial empire for some time. Though comparatively small in extent, it is very populous. (Korea and Formosa comprise an area of only 260,000 square kilometres, with a population of over 28 million. She has exploited them commercially—their exports reach about 130 million dollars—but they offer little room for her nationals). She went farther afield to occupy a better place in the sun in Manchuria. Again she was disappointed, for she has not found the outlet for the surplus population she wished to settle within political reach. The climate does not seem to suit her people. In recent years, 30 million sturdy Chinese have inhabited this country, of whom 9 million are supposed to be recent immigrants; 800,000 Koreans had drifted in, but only about 200,000 Japanese. These hold high positions in government, trade, and industry.[1] They may be strong enough to rule the country under the protection of the Kwantung army, but they are not sufficiently numerous to make either Manchukuo or the northern provinces of China into a new Japan. They have failed to make Korea a daughter-state.

Nor is Japan succeeding in getting all the supplies she needs from Manchuria; her imports from this country (1935) were 191 million yen, from China proper 134 million yen, while those from other countries amounted to 2,147 million yen. Manchurian exports will no doubt grow, but so will Japanese needs. The vaster her armaments, the greater will be her dependence on foreign imports, until the time may come when she has sufficiently developed Manchurian supplies to take their place. Manchuria, moreover, by no means suffices as a market for Japanese goods. Japan's exports to Manchuria (1935) amounted to 126 million yen; those to China proper 149 million yen, and those to other countries 2,350 million yen. Her aggressive tendencies compel her to force the industrial development so abhorrent to her military expansionists. She needs ships and armaments, as well as capital equipment, for the exploitation of Manchuria.

[1] By June 1936 their numbers had risen to 362,911. An army of occupation ready to march forward naturally attracts all kinds of national hangers-on. In 1935 only 1·3 per cent of the Japanese in Kwantung were engaged in agriculture. Ishii, op. cit., pp. 204–5 and 193. Kwantung's imports from Japan amounted to 300 million yen, her exports to 25 million yen; her industrial output was 77 million yen.

She must sell goods abroad to pay for the raw materials used for defence and expansion purposes. Even if milk and honey flowed in Manchuria, the cost of building pipe lines conducting them into Japan would be considerable. The raw materials which form a substantial part of these investments must come from abroad and must be paid for by Japanese exports. Japan has scarcely any foreign investments, little revenue from shipping, and no emigrants' remittances to pay for her imports, for her debts, and for the development of Manchuria. She might ease the economic strain by giving concessions to powerful foreign concerns, but that would weaken her political hold. Her financial strength is limited, but by reducing her standard of living, she can accumulate at home some of the capital needed for exploiting her dependencies, though this is equivalent to more and heavier taxation. Her industrial system is skilfully designed and very delicately balanced; it would scarcely function under the rough and ready militarist Socialism to which her feudalists aspire. It needs very careful handling; for a long time to come defence, as well as expansion, will depend on imports. She has to force her exports by all means in order to pay for her imports—this would be a superfluous endeavour if Manchuria could really satisfy all her wants. She irritates her rivals by pressing on foreign markets. They might be willing to stand aside and suffer the competition of a rising industrial Power whose one and only aim is peaceful commercial expansion. They see no reason why they should open their markets to a Power which is bent on using the economic strength it can draw from these opportunities for encroachment on another Power, with a far superior civilization, and which is undermining its rivals' trade position by exclusive territorial expansion and political pressure.

The Western Powers have frequently denied equality of opportunity to Japan.[1] They are not likely to listen to her

[1] Since 1929 the excess of Japanese purchases in Australia has almost doubled; but she is ousting Great Britain in the Australian market; her

demands when her main object is the exploitation of China and the exclusion of all other nations from the opportunities for peaceful economic penentration China is willing to offer them. But for the glut in raw materials, which forces oversea producers to look out for buyers for their wares, Japan's position might have become rather unpleasant; she has no chance of acquiring settlement areas; she can feed her people only by the exploitation of thickly settled native dependencies or by foreign trade. The territorial expansion on which she is engaged in Manchukuo and China depends on her commercial expansion in other parts of the world. And the contraction of this commercial expansion would retard her colonial expansion. It would embitter the temper of her ruling classes and at the same time handicap their strength. As her territorial ambition is not due to purely economic motives, she was unwilling to renounce it, even if, by doing so, she could buy commercial expansion. For commercial expansion might make her rich; it would not give her the domination of the East. She might have peace with China, Russia, and the West, but in an atmosphere of peace and prosperity China would grow, and time and trade are on her side. As an insular empire Japan cannot attain "contiguous self-sufficiency"; the best she can hope for is "disconnected self-sufficiency." To maintain it, she must be dominant and remain dominant in the China sea as well as on the Chinese continent.

As Korea and Manchuria have not solved Japan's economic problems, she is trying to cover up manifest failure in colonisation by conquest on a colossal scale. The war

cotton, rayon, pottery, and china imports are rising rapidly. The new Australian tariff and licensing policy is avowedly pursued in order to help Great Britain against "unfair Japanese competition." Japan has not a bad case. But her commercial policy in Manchuria and North China deprives her of her best arguments (*Economist*, August 29, 1936). Settlement possibilities in Australia are, moreover, exaggerated. If it were as thickly settled as the Western American States, the potential population would be not quite thirty million (Carr-Saunders, op. cit., p. 175).

in China is not a colonial war; it is a bid for a horizontal empire. Japan may not desire to incorporate parts of China, but she must dominate her politically as well as economically. Without domination she cannot fight the boycott, the most efficient weapon China has so far employed against aggressors. She could not prevent the influx of Western capital into Chinese industries and the exploitation of those abundant raw materials (coal, cotton, iron) which she covets, and which she means to monopolize for feeding her own plants. She must at all costs prevent the industrialization of China under Western leadership. She might be able to defeat the West on the Chinese markets, even if she were to maintain the open-door régime. But she could not compete with modern Chinese industries, which could produce very much more cheaply than she does. She can never hope to direct mass immigration into China. China is a Have-not country on a much larger scale than Japan. The growth of her people is not yet arrested by methods of contraception. They are spilling over her borders. Japan has deprived her of the political control of the main emigration field—Manchuria.

By domination Japan can secure many of the raw materials she needs. She may not be able to widen her markets, for her victory will scarcely increase the purchasing power of the Chinese. But when she is in a position to extract raw materials by way of pressure from an economic dependency, she need not pay for them in goods. An army of occupation and the construction of public works for which China must pay will offer employment to many of her people. If she can keep China disarmed for long years to come, postpone a Russian attack indefinitely, and maintain her trade with the Western world, she may throw the burden of the war costs on China and the Chinese, ease the lives of her own people, and keep her precariously poised social system intact. Her present venture bears little semblance to a colonial enterprise—it is a war for annexation and tribute such as conquerors have undertaken at all times. Its failure would herald the approaching end of every sort of colonial ascendancy in the Far East; its success will entail the final collapse of Western imperialist rule east of Singapore.

IV

Modern Italy claims to be heir to the Roman Empire, to the greatest political legacy which ever fell to a nation. Other empires were "singular" and "ephemeral," the Roman Empire was "universal" and "permanent." The Roman sword gave the world outward unity; the Roman law and the universal Roman Church dominated the mind of the Western nations. For centuries this splendid inheritance lay in abeyance, while foreigners controlled Italy's destinies and prevented the formation of a united nation within an independent State. When unity was at last accomplished, it was far from complete. Corsica, with a thoroughly Italian population, is ruled by the French; so are the large Italian settlements in Tunis; the British control Malta and block the passage between Africa and Italy. The Mediterranean was once an Italian sea, and the hope that it might once again become "our sea" (*mare nostro*) has never died. But the keys to it are in foreign hands. Must they always remain so? Not so long ago, almost the entire Appenine peninsula was controlled by foreigners; on land the tables have been gloriously turned. Cannot the colonial splendours of Genoa and Venice be resuscitated in the Adriatic and the Levant, even though the pillars of Hercules may not yet be free?

But some heavy shadows darken the splendour of Italy's achievements. Unity and liberty were not won by Italy's own strength. The proud saying, "*L'Italia farà da se*" is not borne out by historical facts. England's moral support gave Italian nationalism a strong spiritual backing; the French victories at Magenta and Solferino undid the results of the Piedmontese defeats of Custozza (1848) and Novara

(1849); and the Prussian triumphs at Königgrätz and Sedan turned the catastrophes of a second Custozza, of Lissa and Mentana into a final national success. A nation may be grateful to other nations for help given in adversity; it can scarcely glory in their accomplishments. The attitude of the Allied soldiers towards the Italian army after Caporetto did little to make Italy forget those memories of frustrated effort, and the treatment meted out to her representatives at the Paris Peace Conference rankled in the minds of her people. Fascism was really born at Caporetto; its founders wanted to show the world at large that Italy's greatness had not yet gone, that her people were scions of the mighty Roman race. Machiavelli had attempted to temper the souls of his contemporaries so that they would drive out the barbarian invaders; Mussolini has endeavoured to fashion his country-men into an imperial race, embued with *sacro egoismo*. For a long time they have been baulked and they have rarely been treated as equals. When Italy suggested a compensa-tion at the time of the occupation of Bosnia by Austria, a Russian diplomat remarked: "Why should she ask for more land? . . . Has she lost another battle?"[1] Tunis was filched from her by her Latin sister, who had no need whatever for colonial expansion, but who took it—she had pocketed Nice and Savoy earlier as a gratuity for support half-heartedly and incompletely given. She was allowed to con-quer Tripoli and a few islands in the Aegean from Turkey. She had freed the unredeemed Italy from Austrian domina-tion and took along with her a good slice of German-bred, German-speaking Tyrolese. She had revived some of the glories of the Venetian Empire by extending her borders up to Fiume. But the bulk of the old Venetian and Genoese castles and forts have not been returned to her; they are held by Slavs, Greeks, and the mandatory successors to Turkey.

Italy is a poor country; the density of population to the square mile is 355; very nearly half of her people live off

[1] Benedetto Croce, *Geschichte Italiens*, pp. 109 and 307.

M

the land (47·3 per cent) and only 43·5 per cent of the land
is arable, another 20 per cent being under grass of all sorts.[1]
The "economic density" is evidently very high, for her
mineral resources are scanty. By spending 225 million lire
on the battle of the grain and by paying (1932) more than
twice as much for home-grown wheat as for foreign wheat,[2]
she made home supplies suffice in a good year. She is dependent on foreign imports of coal and its derivatives, such as
oil and gas, of cotton, wool, rubber, iron and steel, copper,
tin, and nickel. Apart from sulphur, she holds no surplus
resources of important raw materials. Her vulnerability is
greater than that of any other world Power—for whereas
Japan is geographically paramount in the Japanese sea,
Italy is surrounded by land Powers and floats, so to speak,
in a land-locked sea.

Her population has grown very fast. Since the foundation
of the Kingdom (1870–1), it has risen from 26,801 million
to 42,445. Birth rates have been high, and so have death rates.
But the main factor affecting population has been the huge
volume of emigration. From 1886 to 1933 16·7 millions
had emigrated. In some years (1905, 1906, 1907, and 1913)
emigration more than offset the excess of births. Later on
immigration control in new countries began to stiffen, and
emigration never regained its earlier volume. But in the
three years 1922, 1923, and 1924, net emigration averaged
over 200,000 a year.[3] The American quota legislation reduced
the possible number of Italian immigrants to 3,845.[4] Continental migration came to the rescue; most of it was directed
to France. In each of the years 1929–1931, an average of
140,000 Italians migrated to European countries.[5] The
crisis greatly reduced this movement and though some of
the oversea countries are more liberal to Italians than the

---

[1] Carr-Saunders, op. cit., pp. 140–1.
[2] Chatham House, *The Economic and Financial Position of Italy*, p. 34.
[3] Carr-Saunders, op. cit., p. 199.
[4] Ibid., p. 194; raised later to 5,802.   [5] Ibid., p. 147.

United States, the mass movement has come to a standstill. The birth rate is slowly declining—it fell from 30·8 per 1,000 (1,175,872) in 1922 to 22·2 per 1,000 (955,189) in 1936. But as the net reproduction rate is above unity (1·2–1·18), a steady growth can be expected. Various forecasts estimate a probable strength of the population for 1961 between 47·3 and 60·6 million.[1] Modern immigration legislation, especially in the United States, is almost as offensive to Italian pride as the cruder methods employed in dealing with Japanese. The United States framed their quota system with a view to keeping out Italian immigrants; they object to an increase of the Latin races, who profess the Catholic faith. But whilst they restrict the countrymen of Dante and Cavour to a bare 6,000 a year, they let in Mexicans indiscriminately, whose Latinity is, it is true, diluted by an overwhelming strain of "Indianity" and whose Catholicism is more than semi-pagan.

Frantic efforts are made to widen the agrarian basis by land reclamation. "It is our task," said the Duce in October 1926, "to change beyond all recognition the physical and spiritual face of our country within the space of ten years."[2] The ten years have gone, but notwithstanding magniloquent plans, creditable achievements, and rash spending, Italy was evidently still too small for her leader, if not for her people.

The rise of Fascism may not be the result of a deliberate effort on the part of the Italian people to demonstrate their equality with the rest of the world. But the sores and slights they have suffered from have enabled the new régime to whip up their passions and to start a *Gran conquista ultramar*. The mustard gas which has secured victory in Ethiopia may erase Custozza and Lissa from the memories of the Italian people, if not from the pages of history.

---

[1] Carr-Saunders, op. cit., p. 129.
[2] Carl T. Schmidt, "Land Reclamation in Fascist Italy," *Political Science Quarterly*, vol. lii, p. 345.

V

But Italy's triumph over Ethiopia does not increase her economic security. Even if Abyssinia were rich in all the raw materials Italy needs—and it is doubtful whether this is the case—they have to pass through the Suez Canal after they have been raised. The political animosities arising from her great adventure may more than offset such economic benefits as she may derive from it. The future alone can show whether the political security of a country which is favoured neither by geographical position nor by natural economic resources can be increased by a successful attempt on collective security.

Italy will have to shoulder a great financial burden. Even if she can pacify the country rapidly and is allowed to exploit it monopolistically, profits will come in but slowly. No colonial war has ever been waged with such a total disregard of expense. Since Cortez brought down the Aztec empire with eighteen armoured horsemen and six hundred followers, colonial conquest has depended on the prestige of the conquering race, whose superior valour made up for any inferiority in numbers. A handful of men, fairly well equipped, supported by scanty native levies, have won the great colonial empires of the world. The cost was small; the loot was great; the prestige of the lordly race, so few in number, impressed the natives enormously and gave the new rulers the chance to run the conquered lands at small expense. The Italians have discarded these methods of colonial warfare. They have overwhelmed their adversaries by sheer numbers and by the weight of modern armaments. The steel-clad Spanish riders appeared to the Mexicans, who had never before seen horses, as the representatives of a god-like race, whose advent had been announced by their seers. Will the airmen dropping gas bombs impress the Ethiopian minds in a similar way?

From an economic point of view, the Ethiopian war has

been a kind of public works enterprise on a gigantic scale, on which thousands of men are employed and for which millions of tons of material are used. Public works of this sort need not be remunerative; they give employment to civilians and soldiers as long as they are continued. And as long as Italy can produce the goods needed for their continuation by equipping Ethiopia and by paying for materials imported from abroad, the dumping into Ethiopia can be kept up. In this respect sanctions may have certainly been useful to her. They have contracted the home consumption of external goods, whilst the need for such privation can be attributed to the wickedness of envious foreign nations and not to the country's poverty. Permanent changes in taste as well as in the direction of consumption may follow their application; all measures of prohibition which do not result in immediate surrender bring about a more or less permanent shift in international trade relations; they make people resort to substitutes which may remain in use long after scarcity has passed. It may be that the much-advertised casein experiments will ultimately reduce Italy's imports of wool. This would dislocate her export industries, which would have to look out for other customers. Nor would it increase Ethiopia's economic value. If science can furnish the substitutes for key products from overseas it would be cheaper to spend money on research than on colonial ventures. But the glories of the battlefield are much better political propaganda than the achievements of the laboratory.

Ethiopia will scarcely be able to replace foreign imports to Italy in sufficient quantities within a reasonably short time. The alleged economic object of the conquest will not be reached rapidly. But the vaster the scale of the development and the longer the time needed for it, the greater will be the additional opportunities offered to soldiers, officers, administrators, and adventurers. It is an enormous asset to any government, and especially to a dictatorial government, to be able to offer employment or to hold out hopes of employment to those young hot-heads who have been born into a bourgeois society which seems no longer able to fulfil the promises held out to them at their birth. In this respect, conquest and colonization are merely a particularly expensive and particularly attractive form of unemployment benefit. The salaries of the numerous garrisons and the scarcely less numerous civil servants who have to be recruited are a kind of dole, without some of its usual drawbacks. For while the normal dole deadens the spirit of industry, upon which an industrial society is dependent, this soldier's dole will keep alive the military spirit it is designed to foster. The new Roman legions doubtless prefer payment for training obstreperous natives on African soil to being trained themselves in labour camps. It might have been cheaper to pension off all those eager for service in Ethiopia. But a régime which is assiduously impressing upon its people the beauty and duty of war fares much better by supporting its young men in an army of occupation or, when the time for active service is over, as veterans of the great war overseas, than by charging their maintenance to a social service account.

Italy's capacity to pay for foreign imports will not be raised by her occupation of Ethiopia. The loss of foreign markets which was caused by sanctions may not be permanent, but her balance of payments has become more unfavourable.[1] Her income from tourists and from shipping has temporarily declined. She had to part with a large amount of gold and with her foreign securities, which have been requisitioned and turned into treasury bonds.[2] Had they been converted into profit-yielding capital investments in Ethiopia from which the same income of goods could be drawn which

[1] Imports for the calendar year of 1937 amounted to 13·5 milliard lire and exports to 7·85 milliard lire, as compared with 5·9 and 3·8 milliard lire respectively for 1936.

[2] Reliable figures as to the amount of these securities are not available, but it is known that the Italian Treasury has been taking over everything —even non-valeurs.

formerly came from abroad, she would not be a loser; by shifting sales and purchases from world markets, she might even be a gainer. The Italian shareholders would, so to speak, convert their holdings in foreign railways into cotton fields or construction companies in Abyssinia. But none of these enterprises will yield immediately the same direct or indirect profits a well-established foreign concern would have shown. Their organization will expand Italian exports. The building of roads, of cities, of villages, and the settlement of half a million Italians on the land will keep Italian industries busy for a very long time. Without foreign loans, such works must be paid for with the proceeds of internal borrowings, or, if it comes to the worst, with paper money. If credit is overstrained, an ultimate collapse may be inevitable. An absolutist government can create a kind of war boom by way of colonial exploitation which may last a long time and which may even finally turn into real prosperity, if and when the natural resources of the colony come into full play. It is a gigantic gamble, such as dictatorial governments must indulge in from time to time. But the cost of increased armaments not only burdens the taxpayer. It will put an additional strain on the balance of trade, as it necessitates additional imports of foreign raw materials. The quality of synthetic substitutes will improve by and by, but their large-scale production depends on huge initial capital outlays—which must come from taxes or from loans; and their products will be expensive.

VI

Italy is stirring up black Africa. She is deliberately fostering Arab agitation. The employment of native Moroccan troops in the Spanish Civil War has done the same in the western parts of the continent. Whilst building an empire of her own, she is undermining the foundation of empire. In the last twenty years, subject races in all parts of the world have been rising against their masters. Empires have everywhere been cracking. An age of empire-breaking has followed centuries of empire-making. In black Africa alone, things were comparatively stable. The Boer War had, it is true, lowered the white man's prestige; the Great War shattered it amongst those who saw the seamy side of the white men's life on the battlefield or in the ranks of the labour corps, "of murder, rape, pillage, wholesale pollution, an eroticism as bad as his own . . . and worst of all, he made the acquaintance of the white-slave traffic and found it to his taste."[1] Nationalist negro movements claiming Africa for the Africans have been under way for some time. So far they have not been very dangerous. They originated amongst the negroes of the United States, who live under a constitution of equal rights, but who suffer a great deal of racial discrimination. A certain amount of propaganda has emanated from this American negro world, which has become race-conscious and assumed the leadership of black African liberation.[2] It got some spiritual support from the Bolshevik propagandist's solicitude for the oppressed races. The aborigines in remote parts of Central Africa, who may be suffering from the encroachments of a few white traders or planters, are rarely diligent and intelligent students of Marx's "Capital"; they do not even read the "Communist Manifesto." But they are conversant with a state of affairs in which black men are ruthlessly exploited by white men.

Large-scale capitalist operations on African mining fields have resulted everywhere in a huge concentration of black workers. They are frequently quite well cared for in a patriarchal fashion and get wages which enable them to raise their accustomed standards of life considerably. But they are subjected to an alien discipline; during the terms of their engagement they lead a thoroughly artificial life, which involves at least a temporary break with everything

---

[1] Daniel Thwaite, *The Seething African Pot*, pp. 155–6.
[2] Ibid., pp. 55–6 and 35–7.

they are accustomed to. They are bossed by white foremen, who are rough and ignorant and are not always good specimens of a lordly race, however brutally they may insist on their racial privileges. The natives may not be forced to go to work, but as they are made to pay taxes, which must be earned before they can be met, and as new wants are implanted on their old needs, they are drawn into a vortex of violent, fateful changes which they cannot resist. Education, as such, may not revolutionize their minds, but industrialization, combined with education, does. Westernized intelligence and industrial efficiency cannot be had without some sort of spiritual revolution. Whether this new régime under which the natives are forced to live is called capitalism, feudalism, or communism, does not matter a whit to them. They profit and suffer from it. But when the representatives of a great European Power denounce it as capitalism and proclaim its abolition within their own empire, where a medley of races are said to live in perfect amity and on a basis of complete equality—they do not find it hard to adopt this wonderful creed called "Communism," which their would-be liberators hold out to them.[1]

Up to now this propaganda has not been very successful. Strikes and riots have occurred and, though some Communist agitators may be credited with the merit of having fanned the flames, most of them were decidedly of a pre-Soviet nature. The administration of the great colonial Powers had become fair and just. Occasional encroachments are nearly always caused by unwise planters or traders, who are trying to shift the "white man's burden" on to other people's shoulders and are duly corrected by the administration. British native administration especially has won the confidence of the native.

Now everything will be thrown into the melting-pot. A

[1] S. G. Millin, *General Smuts*, vol. ii, p. 348 seq.; Thwaite, op. cit., p. 157 seq.; George Padmore, *How Britain Rules Africa*, chap. xiv; see above, p. 157.

M*

new Power has arisen, whose subjects the natives in many parts of Africa did not class as white men. Italy's military success is bound to change this appreciation. It has been accomplished by a powerful military machine, such as Africa had never seen before. It was won in the face of Great Britain, who was unable to stop the aggressor, who had broken the Covenant and had disregarded all engagements in respect of the humane conduct of warfare. May not Italy be strong enough to flout Great Britain and all her allies elsewhere? Has a new Power been born, whose will can shape the future of Africa? Or does it merely mean that the whites are a very much overrated race, always fighting one another, whom the blacks, if properly equipped, could easily drive away? After all, the brunt of the fighting in Ethiopia was borne by native troops. A large part of the garrison work will be entrusted to them. Must these natives always fight on the side of the white invaders? Is there no chance of uniting them one day in a free Africa?

Italy may have done more than break the Covenant— she may have undermined the rule of the white man. The Covenant had attempted to put a stop to further colonization by enabling all nations to become partners in security. It did not end colonial control, at least as far as backward Africa was concerned. For the great counter-colonization movement which was sweeping over the rest of the world did not touch Africa—yet; she still needed the guidance of the white man. She was to get it in an altruistic way. Exploitation must cease; moral and material guidance was to take its place, until after a lengthy process of evolution, self-government and independence might be in sight for all. The task could not be accomplished within a few years, or even a few decades; it might take a century or more.

This attitude is completely reversed to-day. The Italians will not be content with running Ethiopia as a native dependency.[1] Since the days of Francesco Crispi, they have dreamed of possessing a great Abyssinian empire and settling it with millions of emigrants.[2] They were to follow the ways of their ancestors, who planted their legions on African soil and created a new African province of the empire. They do not mean to establish a few white planters who run their estates with the help of the natives and form the top layer of a composite society, in which the white strain is numerically weak and into which mass immigration is impossible. They talk of planting half a million men in Ethiopia within a single decade. This is a stupendous task, even if the lands needed for such a purpose are available. But an absolutist government can do many things from which a Liberal or democratic state must recoil. It can plan on a large scale; it can group its legions in military settlements and it can pay them subsidies for garrison work and enable them to farm poor lands and live on them in comparative comfort, by defraying all initial costs and charging them to its own account. It can send their womenkind along with the men and make them breed fast in their new surroundings. The Italians are a fertile race; under colonial conditions the birth rate is apt to be high— it has been so even amongst the French in Algeria—for in a new primitive land, each additional hand is a help and not a hindrance, as it is frequently in old, over-populated countries. But Abyssinia, with her 900,000 square kilometres, her deserts, and her mountains, has no unlimited spaces to offer. Algeria is twice her size.

[1] The country is to be divided into five zones:

1. A zone reserved for Italian tenants, who will ultimately become owners; this is to be a national, racial settlement, evidently excluding native tenants.

2. A zone reserved for small proprietors with modest capital.

3. A mixed zone for industrial settlements, where racial (exclusive) national settlement is impossible.

4. A mixed zone for industrial settlements where immigration is impossible and inopportune.

5. A native zone. *The Times*, June 17, 1936.

[2] Benedetto Croce, op. cit., pp. 175–6.

Under normal conditions, the annual migration of Italians to oversea countries averaged 200,000, most of the emigrants being men. Abyssinia could never receive more than a small percentage of this stream; she can either give sudden relief to population pressure by taking a great quantity all at once —this would block the way for the future—or she can take a few driblets regularly. As "national settlements" are contemplated, the men would have to be accompanied by women, and colonial breeding would quickly fill all available space. Ethiopia will never be able to absorb masses regularly. But even small settlements will relieve pressure at home, especially as they give employment to those remaining in Italy.[1]

But Ethiopia is not an empty country; eight million natives must be reckoned with. They can be cowed in war by poison gas—they cannot be ruled by it when mixed up with white settlements. They can be driven away from lands set apart for white settlements, though such expulsion will be very irritating. They might possibly be separated completely from white populations. If white settlers were forbidden to employ them, room for a fundamentally white society might be found. The settlements thus established would be comparatively small; they would be flanked or surrounded by areas inhabited by coloured tribes, which must be taught the arts of peace if they are to be demilitarized. They would, under an efficient administration, rapidly increase in numbers, as they have done in many parts of the world. And notwithstanding strict segregation and separation, an Afro-Italian race is bound to arise. A sharp-worded decree forbidding sexual intercourse with the natives has been issued,[2] which

[1] 250,000 Italians are engaged in public works and are to be followed by their families; 125,000 of them are enlisted as Militia Labourers. The army of occupation is composed of 20,000 Italians, 40,000 natives, and 5,000 officers.—Corrado Zoli, loc. cit., pp. 87–90.

[2] *The Times*, January 11, 1937. "The prohibition against marriages between Italian citizens and native subjects, recently promulgated, is to be rigidly enforced; for it aims to prevent dangerous cross-breeding

shows that the Roman policy of civilizing the natives by mixing with them has been given up. But neither government control nor race theories are likely to prevent race mixture as long as no deep-seated physical aversion amongst the masses repels the people on both sides of the pale. The Italian peasant who is to settle in these African lands is quite free from racial prejudice. He has no aristocratic leanings and is ignorant of eugenic snobbism. He is attracted by sexual adventures with womenkind of a different race. In fact, in order to popularize the war, the charms of black women have been largely advertised by official propaganda. The Romans always mixed with their subjects, though they may have called them barbarians and did not immediately give them citizen's rights. Even if the government were to ostracize race mixture permanently, it would not achieve much. Settlers in a colonial land are expected to show a good deal of personal initiative; the control of their sexual appetites cannot be carried very far. It merely turns regular and acknowledged unions into illegal, secret connections. The United States are full of "white negroes," many of whom are unrecognizable as such. By no means all of them are the offspring of illicit intercourse in the brothels and slums of the great industrial cities and large ports. The planter aristocracy had no physical aversion to coloured women— its prejudices were social, not racial. It objected to equality, not to sexual privilege. And in the lower strata, where racial antagonism is closely connected with the struggle for jobs, it has never yet prevented illicit intercourse. The dwellers in the slums may favour their own womenkind for marriage, but they often prefer coloured women for illicit intercourse,

and the consequent danger to morality and public order. The interdiction is due partly to a desire to protect the race. An even weightier consideration, however, was the necessity of preserving the personal dignity and prestige of the Italians who take up permanent residence in the Empire. . . . This policy contemplates the harmonious co-existence of two societies—Italian and native."—Corrado Zoli, loc. cit., p. 85.

and whatever their choices and preferences, they take what they can get.[1]

A well-thought-out settlement policy can influence the scale on which race mixtures will take place, the strata which it may affect, and its reactions on future generations. Italy's domination of Ethiopia will not create an aristocratic society on the lines of Rhodesia or Kenya, but it cannot make Ethiopia a white man's colony. She may develop it somewhat along the lines of Mexico, where the indigenous population and the mixed breeds have ultimately triumphed over the imported colonial strain.

A wholesale expulsion of the natives would not be in accordance with Italian tradition; it would not be good business and it certainly would not be good politics. The African natives will not go; they will increase in numbers and, by fusion and education, in strength. They may misjudge the power of their old masters, who were too feeble to defend their brethren against more robust new-comers, and they may hasten to bow their necks to the new Caesar. Or they may turn against all Europeans in a great upheaval, the tremors of which will shake the entire continent. The immediate result will be a reorientation of the colonial policy of all African Powers. They have to face a partner in colonial affairs, to whom power, not wealth, is the essence of colonial domination, who is raising native armies and entrenching himself on his newly won frontier—an endeavour far more easily achieved than the foundation of a new white society or the creation of an economic paradise which will lessen his financial burdens. For some time to come, Italy will be less secure than she was before the war, and scarcely any richer. She has won back her self-respect and she may be willing to run additional risks. The conquest of colonies may not enrich a country; it greatly strengthens the government which accomplished it.

[1] Kipling's well-known stanza ending—
"I've a neater, sweeter maiden in a cleaner, greener land!
On the road to Mandalay,"
can scarcely be looked upon as an incantation to race purity.

CHAPTER VII

SUPER-STATE OR EMPIRE

I

ITALY's conquest of Ethiopia has changed the international colonial situation. Her belated attempt at empire-making may herald the beginning of a glorious era of rejuvenated Imperialism or it may inaugurate the end of the white man's rule in Africa. The world may have to face a new period of colonial wars, which will lead to a redistribution of colonial spoils, though the value of colonies is not what it was and though the rulers' hold on subject populations is everywhere loosening. Or it may experience a speeding up of the counter-colonization movement all over this part of the globe. Colonial armies, recruited from native populations, may become an element of power on European battlefields, for the militarist spirit which is rising amongst aggrieved nations would scarcely be satisfied with mere colonial triumphs, which nowadays can be but by-products of far more serious hostilities. Minds trained in the tradition of ancient Rome will not shrink from transferring native (provincial) levies to conquer enemies of the European motherland. Whilst the anti-imperialist spirit is rising in nearly all dependencies and even spreading in many a mother country, where it weakens the hands which hold colonies, colonial levies are being employed in a European civil war. For nearly a thousand years Spain has used, and sometimes wasted, her strength in driving the Moors from the Iberian Peninsula. The original *Gran conquista ultramar* was an abortive attempt to make the northern coast of Africa subservient to the Cross. To-day Moorish mercenaries are pouring into Spain to uphold the Cross against what is called Bolshevism. And in many lands neither Church nor State seem to understand the ultimate implications of this historical inversion.

Some of these events have greatly strengthened Germany's moral claim to colonies. She is now the only Have-not country left among the Great Powers. Her demand for colonies does not involve the destruction of a hitherto independent State; in making it she is not breaking a solemn engagement. She can present quite a good case, morally as well as economically. In the not too distant past she had been the leading imperial and colonial Power of the world. She had won for Western civilization the eastern marches of Europe, to whose savage tribes her knights, her merchants, and her artisans had brought the elements of a good life. The glory of the Hanseatic towns preceded that of Amsterdam or London; the lofty red-brick castle of Marienburg, which the Teutonic knights erected above the sluggish waters of the Nogat, is a time-honoured monument to colonization on the grandest scale. The Germans have never lost the qualities of steady pioneers, which had endeared their ancestors to foreign kings, who eagerly sought them as colonists in Bohemia, in Hungary, in Poland, and in Russia. Wherever farming communities had to break new ground in the new worlds, German immigrants were among them. They helped to settle Pennsylvania and Wisconsin; they formed a military shelter belt in British Kaffraria; they flocked into South Australia and Saskatchewan. But wherever they went, they had to renounce allegiance to the homeland. At last, late in the day, Germany acquired possessions of her own, which might become a national home for her sons across the sea; their development had filled the nation with new pride, though its hopes of the growth of a daughter-state were disappointed. After a brief spell of possession this new short-lived empire had gone. And with it had gone the illusion that it might become a substitute for the mighty Holy Roman

Empire, to which the German nation had fallen heir in the days of Carolus Magnus. The rulers of Germany had spilled the lives and treasures of their subjects through the centuries for the maintenance of that empire. It had been the will-o'-the-wisp which had led them across the Alps and over the Appenines. Fighting on the battlefields of Lombardy and Apulia for this "greater Germany," which was but the pale shadow of the old universal empire, they undermined the foundations of a smaller, united Germany; they could not restore them when, for a brief spell, the German Emperor, King of Rome and King of Spain, became the master of the world. The discovery of these new worlds had shifted the axis of power from Central Europe and the Apennine peninsula to the shores of the Atlantic, and ultimately to those of the Pacific. The unity of the German people was slowly broken up in many separate state fragments, until the Holy Roman Empire itself expired under the blows of Napoleon. But the hope of reunion never died, and the dream of a glorious resurrection never faded. The nation's yearning for unity was baulked over and over again by the many dynasties which had succeeded in establishing themselves in large and small territories, and by Germany's neighbours, who preferred a multitude of petty jealous states to a single mighty empire. As long as they prevailed the German people counted for little, though they were more numerous than any other continental race. Their efforts at unification were opposed from abroad. England supported Denmark in the Schleswig-Holstein contest. France demanded compensation as a price for tolerating her union. Germany felt that she had never had a fair deal until unity was won on the battlefield.

The new Germany created by Bismarck was a homogenous super-state rather than an empire. She did not wield domination over any of the foreign nations which clustered round the Habsburg throne in South-Eastern Europe. Apart from a relatively small Polish fringe, she had retained no important alien possessions. Her constitution embodied a sort of federal Imperialism, but the member-states which formed the empire were purely German; the national characteristics which distinguished them from one another were regional and dynastic rather than racial. And the various provinces of the bigger states frequently differed from one another much more than neighbouring districts over the border. The control of alien nationalities remained with German Austria. But Austria's expulsion from the German federation put an end to the supremacy of the German nation in the Habsburg Empire; the German remnant was numerically not strong enough to continue the "mission" which the German nation had pursued since the early Middle Ages. Bismarck's triumph ultimately destroyed the imperial structure of Germany, as well as of Austria; but it did not destroy the nation's restless spirit of expansion.

German unity was not complete. Nearly a fifth of the German people stayed with Austria; millions were scattered over the eastern and south-eastern parts of the continent. Outside the small group of Pan-Germans, nobody wanted to incorporate them before the war. No responsible politician desired the annexation of Switzerland or the reunion with German Austria—nor did the russification of the Baltic provinces greatly disturb the national mind. But the nation did want to "grow." And whatever direction she turned towards, she knocked herself against an iron fence. She felt like a gate-crasher who must elbow his way into privileged company and force it to receive him on terms of equality. William II was very sensitive on this point; he wrote plaintively to his grandmother about slights received from her Ministers.[1] For this reason he would have insisted on building a fleet, even if Germany had had no trade to protect and had not felt menaced by English interference; for the fleet was an outward sign of equality to him, as it

[1] See above, p. 230.

had been to the patriots of 1848. "The Sea gives Freedom." "Das Meer macht frei."[1] And so was the possession of colonies to many millions of Germans, not only to the handful of merchants who were doing quite a profitable business under foreign flags, even though they were sometimes irritated by condescending foreign authorities. The acquisition of colonies showed the masses that the centuries of inferiority were over, that Germany had resumed her proper place amongst the ruling nations of the earth. Once again she held an empire of her own, and though it bore no likeness to the Holy Roman Empire of the past—Austria, not Germany, was the heir to what remained of it—it had re-established her status.

II

Germany's colonial empire was full of promise. Its development had taken longer than colonial enthusiasts had expected; it had been disappointing in respect of settlement colonies, for the presence of the natives had prevented a "true plantation." Only in South-West Africa had something like a composite colony been established; its structure resembled that of the Boer communities domiciled in the less fertile parts of the South African tableland. A mixed colony had grown up in Samoa, and white planters were beginning to settle on the East African highlands. The total number of all white settlers in the colonies was insignificant, when measured by the great expectations entertained at the time of acquisition, when they loomed in man's mind as the future home of a mighty German race. These numerically poor results did not prove Germany's frequently alleged incapacity for colonization; they were in keeping with those obtained in Kenya, Fiji, or even the Rhodesias, as the ubiquitous presence of native workers prevented the mass influx of white labour. Industrialization had stopped emigration. Trade development kept the people at home. The colonies

[1] F. Ratzel, *Das Meer als Quelle der Völkergrösse.*

were beginning to be important markets and supply centres of raw materials. Though their imports and exports formed but a small percentage of Germany's total commerce, they had doubled and quadrupled within a few years. The period of apprenticeship was over; a considerable growth of colonial wealth was assured, for so far only the surface had been scratched.

Germany lost these colonies when she lost the war. Her colonial neighbours wished to secure themselves against her future rivalry. From a military point of view, the German colonies had given a good account of themselves. They had been scantily supported by the mother country, for the sea passages were blocked. But the few settlers and the small colonial army in East Africa had put up a heroic fight. The Dominion of South Africa had to put forward her entire strength to defeat this handful of white men who were cut off from all resources and had to rely on the loyalty and fighting spirit of their black subjects. The British Dominions had always objected to Germany's colonial ambitions. The Boers of South Africa had been quite willing to slobber occasionally over their "Low Saxon" cousins, but they sent their best men to conquer them. The Australians and New Zealanders greatly disliked Germany's proximity in Papua (New Guinea) and Samoa. "Any strong power controlling New Guinea," said Mr. Hughes at the Peace Conference, "controlled Australia."[1] The very valour of Germany's resistance in East Africa was an argument for refusing to give her another chance by returning her colonies to her. She might raise a huge native army, as the French had done, and as some colonial enthusiasts had advised her to do before the war.[2] The fear of a U-boat or an aircraft base was an additional inducement for the retention of the colonies by the Allied Powers.[3]

[1] R. S. Baker, *Woodrow Wilson and World Settlement*, vol. i, p. 258.
[2] Ibid., p. 423.
[3] S. G. Millin, *General Smuts*, vol. ii, p. 239.

These arguments, convincing enough from a military point of view, were wrapt up in a coat of moral disquisitions. President Wilson objected to annexations. In deference to his susceptibilities, the German colonies were not annexed—they were ceded to the Allies, who handed them over to an as yet unorganized League of Nations, which in its turn divided them amongst the aspirants in the form of mandates, to be administered for the benefit of their native inhabitants.[1] Those mandates which were near or within striking distance of the Union of South Africa, of Australia, and of New Zealand, were put in a class by themselves, and so were the Pacific Islands, taken by Japan. They were to be treated as contiguous annexes of the mandatory in question; their status did not differ much from uncontested possession by sovereign states. The others were handed to Great Britain, France, and Belgium under a kind of trust.

To make matters worse, the reasons given for depriving Germany of her colonies were not that she had been defeated and must not be allowed to become a dangerous neighbour again. She was said to have forfeited them by such faulty native administration as clearly showed her unworthiness to rank as a great colonial Power.

Some grave mistakes had been committed in German native policy, especially in South-West Africa, the only German possession which might be looked upon as a possible settlement colony. The natives in this part of Africa were few and scattered, outside Ovamboland, which was a semi-tropical native territory. Climatic and economic conditions resembled those in the various parts of the western province of Cape Colony; they favoured large-scale pastoral farms of a rather extensive type. The climate was attractive and the vicinity of the Boers made the country an ideal settlement

[1] The author of the mandate system was not President Wilson, but General Smuts, who had conceived it as a method for managing territories separated from Russia, Austria, and Hungary, but had no desire to apply it to colonies.—R. S. Baker, op. cit., vol. i, pp. 265–6 and 226–7.

ground for a new Germany in the eyes of some noisy colonial romanticists. The German authorities, the central government, as well as the local colonial government, were not very keen on white settlements. Most of the land was in the hands of the natives: Hereros in the north and Hottentots in the south: it was held by a kind of tribal tenure. The German store-keepers in Hereroland were selling goods to them on credit, looking upon the land as a kind of collateral for their claims: When payments fell due the traders succeeded in possessing themselves of native farms, with the connivance of the paramount chief, who did not much mind parting with the lands of his tribesmen, to which he had no title. The colonial government attempted to stop this process of getting the natives into debt and then foreclosing on them; it withstood the great pressure which the representatives of the land-buying traders put on it and on the Imperial government. An ill-conceived measure, which was designed to stop future foreclosures by invalidating debt claims maturing after a certain date, merely speeded up the process of expropriation. The exasperated natives, led by their paramount chief, who got frightened when he had bartered away a considerable part of their patrimony, rose in arms against the settlers. Many of them were murdered: Germany experienced the horrors and brutalities of an agrarian rising of natives against white colonists. Her people were not familiar with native rebellions; nor were the army men sent out to quell it. They greatly underrated the technical difficulties of native warfare and quite misunderstood its nature. After lengthy operations they succeeded in driving the Hereros into the desert where they were to die of thirst and famine. The general in command announced his intention of wiping them out completely: Providence had ordained that inferior races must die out everywhere as a matter of course when brought into contact with superior races; he was merely carrying out a law of nature.

For a short time this policy commended itself to farmers

who had suffered severe losses, or to whom it held out hopes of getting additional land cheaply. It seemed a God-sent opportunity to colonial Pan-Germans for making South-West Africa a white man's country. But the residents' enthusiasm for a racially pure white settlement did not last very long. They might be willing to take land from the natives and prevent them from acquiring or holding it, but they were equally anxious to keep the native workers on it, provided their numbers were no menace to their own safety.

The German people breathed vengeance and demanded extirpation when the first news of the rising reached them: the English had done the same at the beginning of the Indian Mutiny. Under pressure of colonial interests some legislation was passed which disqualified natives from owning land; they were to be turned into a menial class. But public opinion quickly asserted itself. The German people experienced a feeling of horror, which was fully shared by those in authority, when some phases of the Herero and the Hottentot war had come to their knowledge. They approved neither the aims nor the methods of the military's native policy. A considerable number of African white settlers came to share their views. A nation-wide discussion of colonial problems arose, from which a colonial policy finally emerged which was modelled mainly on the best examples of British native policy.[1]

The customary pressure from the representatives of short-sighted planters and farmers, who advocated a so-called "strong native policy," had had its evil effect in other colonies too; friction and mismanagement had resulted from it. The establishment of a colonial service, with a standard of its own, had taken some time; occasionally some misfits had entered its ranks. Some minor colonial scandals were unearthed and angrily discussed, and probably more public

[1] The names of Dernburg and Solf will always be associated with this policy.

washing of dirty linen was done in this way than in countries with longer colonial experience, where the art of keeping such occurrences dark was better understood. Nothing ever happened which could be compared to the cold-blooded mercenary atrocities organized and committed under Leopold II's rule of the Congo Free State. Things were put right by the German government, under popular pressure.

Germany's supposed colonial atrocities were made the pretext for depriving her of her colonial empire. Her colonial policy had been a bad one, Mr. Lloyd George said; in South-West Africa she had deliberately pursued a policy of extermination.[1] The flimsiness of the case was well known to all colonial administrators.[2] They were quite aware of the success of the German colonial reform movement. A few weeks before the outbreak of the World War, an agreement was to be signed between Germany and Great Britain about the future distribution of the Portuguese colonies, should Portugal wish to relinquish them. Germany was to have Angola. This would have extended the boundaries of her South-West African dependency to the frontiers of the Belgian Congo. The highlands of this country were supposed to be very suitable for settlements of the type started in German South-West Africa. Can it be assumed that a Liberal British government, which was cognisant of the continued perpetration of atrocities in the German colonies, was willing to offer new opportunities for committing them by giving Germany additional territory and additional chances for misruling natives?

The incorporation of this colonial libel in the Peace Treaty hurt German national pride, as well as other vicious,

[1] R. S. Baker, op. cit., vol. i, p. 255.

[2] Dr. Schnee in *German Colonization Past and Future*, p. 63, quotes from a meeting at the Royal Colonial Institute on January 13, 1914, at which praise for the excellence of the German colonial administration and the great work it had done was universal. The lecture on German colonial administration, which gave rise to this debate, was delivered by me. (See *United Empire Magazine*, February 1914, p. 126.)

infantile, equally superfluous disquisitions on morality. The few people whose actions might properly have deserved blame would certainly not have minded it very much—to be accused of having acted according to one's principles is not very offensive, though it may be inconvenient. But others, the colonial reformers as well as the colonial enthusiasts, the soldiers who had fought in the colonial wars and the civil servants who had carried on under very difficult circumstances, did resent these strictures. And the mass of the people were cut to the quick; they received no direct and few indirect benefits from colonies; they looked upon them merely as the realization of a century-old dream, which had at last come true, that Germany was once more recognized as the equal of other great nations. Her empire was now taken from her, not by the right of the victor, which is might—a creed they could easily have understood—but by the verdict of a self-appointed court which managed to combine the function of a judge with that of a plaintiff and applied a law which might be valid in days to come, but which was nowhere in force when Germany's alleged crimes were committed. The German people saw in the passing of their colonial empire an attempt at political discrimination and in the motivation given by their former enemies a deliberate moral degradation. To say that Germany must not have colonies because she might become too strong would have been a painful, though complimentary verdict.[1] To say that she did not deserve colonies lowered her moral standing not only below that of Great Britain, France, and Holland, but also of Italy, Spain, Belgium, and Portugal, not to speak of the United States, Australia, New Zealand, and Japan.

The colonial question became an emotional issue in Germany. It was not so much a question of wealth or of strength as of national self-respect. Whenever people talked of raw materials and markets they were really thinking in

---

[1] General Smuts had 114,000 men in East Africa against Germany's 20,000.—S. G. Millin, op. cit., vol. i, p. 142.

terms of equality. A nation which rightly prides itself on the prowess of its chemists, whose laboratories will by and by oust colonial produce by synthetic substitutes and will render colonies rather superfluous, need not have asked for colonial possessions under terms involving heavy political commitments, were it not that colonies mean recognition.

III

The Covenant held out a promise of equality of status and equality of security to all people; it accepted the principle of self-determination for all nations, great and small, advanced and backward. Its fundamental conceptions were as anti-colonial as the Declaration of Independence and the Monroe Doctrine had been; some of its clauses read like a combination of the two, an attempt to apply the Monroe Doctrine to the entire globe. Whilst acknowledging the right of every colonial Power to retain its present possessions (as the Monroe Doctrine does) it endeavoured to stop further colonization. The self-denial implied in the renunciation of force did not seem very important to the members of the League, for nearly all territories which were "suitable" for colonial acquisition had already found a master. The dissolution of Turkey and the eclipse of white domination in China had withdrawn these regions from possible European colonization. Africa had long ago been partitioned. The only country whose social structure made her a possible object of colonization, Ethiopia, had become a member of the League (1923) in order to be made secure against such a fate; it may have been her undoing. Had she remained a legitimate object of colonization, she might have become a ward of the League of Nations under some newly devised form of mandate, and the conflict between those members of the League who put their faith in force and do not feel bound by their own solemn engagements and those who believe in collective security, but are somewhat afraid of the risks involved in it, might never have broken out.

After Italy's success in Ethiopia, Germany's position has become singularly unsatisfactory. She is the only disgruntled Great Power with no outlet for colonizing activities. She cannot concentrate her energies and her ambitions on some half-civilized dependency, and relieve the spiritual as well as the physical tension of her excited masses. For with the collapse of Ethiopia the last independent African country has gone. Germany must aim either at territorial expansion in Europe—which might involve huge upheavals—or at the acquisition of another Power's colonies, or at the return of the colonies taken from her. The only "easy way" is a return of those colonies.

Before the advent of nationalism and democracy, governments exchanged territories easily enough. They had not to consider the wishes of their inhabitants; they could dispose of them as of other pieces of property. This state of affairs continued in the colonial sphere for ever so long; neither feelings of national dignity nor of responsibility towards the natives were considered when the United States acquired Louisiana from the French or Alaska from the Russians. As late as 1911 an exchange of territory between France and Germany was taking place.

But the scope of such exchanges has always been limited; they were bilateral; the new acquirer either had to pay in cash or in services; or he had to give up some of his more or less well established legal claims. The value of the objects which changed hands was never considerable in the eyes of their former owners. But the peaceful transfer of a colonial empire from one owner to another or the cession of a colonial dependency valuable enough to satisfy the ambitions of a disgruntled Power has never yet been envisaged. None of the great colonial Powers would be willing to give up a considerable portion of their possessions in order to satisfy Germany.

But they might be willing to return to her the colonies taken away from her. Germany is dissatisfied with the present status quo, but is willing to return, with some reservations, to pre-war conditions.

Though the Covenant extended the doctrine of self-determination to comparatively backward races, it was not applied to the colonial changes decided upon in the Peace Treaties. Neither the wishes of the German settlers in South-West Africa, East Africa, or Samoa, nor those of the natives in any German dependencies were ascertained. Germany's unworthiness to handle natives apparently dispensed with this necessity, though the handing over of German South-West Africa to the Union of South Africa can hardly be explained in this way. For South-West Africa is quite as much a white man's country as the Union itself; its settlers should have been consulted, even if they were but a white minority. For the Union of South Africa could scarcely pose as the champion of native rights. The German colonies were divided among several Powers and the natives were not even offered a choice of their future masters; they were never asked whether they preferred British, French, Japanese, Australian, or South African domination. East Africa, the Cameroons, and Togo were partitioned. The principle of self-determination emerged only after the spoils had been divided. To-day, Germany's former colonies cannot be redivided without a recourse to the League of Nations, subject to the safeguards forced upon the mandatories. The United Kingdom could cede Kenya or Nigeria to Germany without consulting other Powers; no obligations would be imposed on the new owner beyond those binding the Powers represented at the Berlin and Brussels conferences. Great Britain as sovereign Power could cede her rights without any restrictions or limitations. But the transfer to Germany of one or two of her former colonies in the form of mandates is a much more complicated problem; it has been discussed in quite a friendly spirit, without leading, however, to any decisive proposals. The further the discussions proceeded, the greater the stress that was laid on the obstacles preventing any change. Whilst the willingness to make some concessions was most loudly voiced in Great Britain, the main objections raised were of British origin too.

British native policy, it is said, is based on the equality of all races within the British Empire. Present-day Germany believes in racial exclusiveness. The relegation of the Jews in Germany to an inferior legal and social position on grounds of race, not of civilization, which is contrary to British principles, betrays the spirit which would dominate German colonial administration. Those racial enthusiasts in Germany who justify their anti-Jewish attitude by comparing Jews with negroes and by alluding approvingly to the anti-negro policy of the Southern whites in the United States, or to the native policy of smallish white oligarchies in African dependencies, have done a bad turn to Germany's colonial aspirations. A government which professes such doctrines will scarcely be able to discharge fairly the guardianship over the backward native races, which the Covenant has imposed upon the mandatory Power. The missionary groups, very powerful in native affairs, frown upon a handing over of one or another of their spiritual provinces to a state whose religious concepts differ greatly from their own, and whose political teachings exclude equality of blacks and whites as a matter of principle, though the denial of equality need not be a stumbling-block to fair native administration. The absolutist Spanish governments in South America who denied equality to the Indians have been pretty fair to the inferior race; the settlers, not the royal officials, advocated the white man's supremacy and indulged in ruthless race oppression. The government of a totalitarian state, which controls the will of all subject to its power, can easily ignore the pressure of planters' interests—if it wishes to do so.

And though the British home government, which is controlled by a white democracy, has strongly insisted on equality, not all Dominion governments nor the leading white strata in Crown Colonies are willing to accept this doctrine.

"Whatever may be the position in the British Empire as a whole, in South Africa we are not based on a system of political equality," said General Smuts. "The whole basis of our particular system in South Africa rests on inequality and on recognizing fundamental differences which exist in the structure of our population. We started as a small white colony in a black continent. In the Union, the vast majority of our citizens are black, probably the majority of them are in a semi-barbarous state still, and we never, in our laws, recognize any system of equality."[1] The General is a humanitarian conservative in native affairs; he might be willing to subscribe to Rhodes's formula: "Equal rights for all civilized men, irrespective of races, south of the Zambesi." But the majority of his countrymen deny the possibility of ever equalizing the two separate races; and if this possibility were proven to them, they would resent and regret it bitterly.

The moral obligation of retaining the mandates as a sacred trust is stressed by combining a sincere faith in treaties, in democracy, and in the superior virtues of British emotional (and exploitative) nationalism.

The business interests which have grown up in several former German colonies thoroughly dislike a political transfer. It might affect their situation unfavourably. They could scarcely preserve the privileged position they enjoy under the British flag if their allegiance were changed. A German administration would naturally prefer German ways. It would insist on changes in the economic system: it might prefer cotton-fields to coffee plantations, and though this transition might be very profitable in the end, it would involve inconvenient shiftings. The capital structure which is based on the abundant supply of British capital might be greatly weakened by being severed from it and by having

[1] S. G. Millin, op. cit., vol. i, p. 247. The mining legislation of South Africa deliberately excludes the black and coloured people from skilled occupations in mining. They must remain unskilled helpers, who do not compete with their white bosses.

to rely on Germany's scanty financial resources. The assimilation of the currency to Germany's currency, the need for which plays such a prominent part in many a German plea, might involve a serious destruction of values. The régime of the open door and the obligations of the mandatory system might prove rather weak safeguards.

The transfer of a mandate would not establish the genuine equality on which Germany insists. The mandatory is not complete master in his own house. He is not only bound to run the mandated territory in the interest of the natives; he must offer equal opportunities to all members of the League in pursuance of the mandate constituted under the Covenant. He is subject to League supervision. He could neither tamper with the currency in the interest of the metropolis, nor would he be permitted to introduce those measures of discrimination which would be essential to a genuine nationalist commercial development of the mandated area.

The present mandatory Powers enjoy full colonial sovereignty in their own possessions. In the mandatory areas they have to be satisfied with a lesser kind of delegated sovereignty under the League of Nations. Germany would nowhere enjoy full colonial sovereignty, but only a delegated sovereignty. Her international position would not be the same as that of the other Powers. If all her colonies were returned to her under a mandate, she would be in a very singular position: she would be the only mandatory Power left, at least as far as B mandates are concerned, and, as such, the only colonial Power subject to the international control of the Mandates Commission of the League of Nations. Could she accept such a position as consonant with the claim for equality, the absence of which she so keenly resents? Would she not feel bound to insist on the abolition of the discriminating fetters by which her colonial administration would be hampered, but which would no longer shackle the colonial administration of any other country? She might demand the application of the mandate system to all Central African possessions, thus vesting sovereignty in the League and making all colonial Powers subsidiary agents of a League policy. She could only do so with even the slightest hope of success after her return to the League, and after her acceptance of the egalitarian and liberal principles on which the Covenant's conception of native policies is based. The colonial Powers who are members of the League would scarcely be inclined to part with their mandates, and to subject at the same time their own colonial possessions to an international control, if Germany gave them nothing in exchange. Would they consider her purely opportunist return to the League a sufficient equivalent? There is no other way to satisfy Germany's colonial ambitions. For she could not remain content with the administration of mandated territories in which preferential policies are prohibited, whilst they are admitted in the colonies of other countries. In fact, she could not accomplish her colonial aims if she were hampered permanently by the imposition of a regime of colonial free trade. A collapse of the League of Nations would greatly simplify this and other problems Germany is confronted with.

But the decisive objections against the return of the colonies to Germany are not based on such rather subtle arguments. They are most clearly voiced by the Union of South Africa. The Union is not anti-German; Afrikanders have always had a sneaking affection for Germany, as they have claimed some sort of racial affinity with her. But this sentimental sympathy has never influenced Union policy. She entered the war in order to conquer the German colonies. "There is now the prospect of the Union becoming almost double its present area," said General Smuts. "If we continue on the road to union, our northern borders will not be where they now are, and we shall leave to our children a huge country, in which to develop a type for themselves, and to form a people who will be a true civilizing agency in this dark continent."[1] The Union

[1] S. G. Millin, op. cit., vol. i, p. 327.

means to be the paramount Power of the African continent, at least in its southern half. It wants no neighbours or rivals who might pursue similar ambitions with similar or dissimilar methods. It is a far greater stumbling-block to German colonial aspirations than British Imperialism or pro-native tendencies. It will not hand back German South-West Africa—and the more violent the agitation in that part of the world and the better founded it is on the principle of national self-determination, the less will it be inclined to support, nay to suffer, German claims farther to the north, for instance, in Tanganyika. Had the Germans in South-West Africa been willing to throw in their lot with the Union, it might have been content to trust to its strong attraction as paramount African Power on all scattered white settlements in every part of Africa. As it is, it is proclaiming an African Monroe Doctrine of its own. Its speakers insist that Tanganyika must not be given back; though they declared themselves willing to offer Germany colonial possibilities in other remote regions of Africa.

A minor Power, for example Portugal, might tire of colonial responsibilities and thus provide the territory needed for an equitable settlement. In the days before the war, a fair division of the Portuguese colonies between Germany and England was foreshadowed in such an eventuality. There is no reason to-day why Portugal should be desirous of parting with her possessions. Her financial and economic position is sound. Her colonies are progressing. Her economic structure is fairly simple. Being situated on the outer rim of the European continent, she is less exposed to the dangers of war, starvation, or devastation than almost any other European country. But for her attitude towards Spain, which may involve her in unexpected complications (a small neighbour who has not been neutral may have to face grave dangers), she need not have been afraid of new developments. There is no reason why she should pay a heavy price for a peace she can have anyhow, without

N

any sacrifice of self-respect. She has no powerful colonial neighbours except England. She need not be afraid of being drawn into a future war because her colonies border the belligerents, as long as all of them belong to one group. Moreover, the Dominion of South Africa would certainly not welcome the transfer of contiguous possessions from the gentle hands of Portugal to those of a powerful Germany. She would find it very difficult to retain South-West Africa, were Angola given to Germany and she would greatly fear for her communications, were the choice to fall on Mozambique. South Africa does not look on colonial problems with the eyes of a mother country, whose numerous dependencies are not always essential to her existence. She is a kind of independent African Republic, within the frame of the British Empire, as partnership with this Empire increases her security. She has close affinities with Germany in blood as well as in outlook. She is animated by an intense racial nationalism, which is always on the defensive, and by a resolute opposition to racial equality. She might raise no objections to German rule in Togo or the Cameroons, but she will not suffer any new neighbours anywhere from the Congo to Somaliland. It is bad enough that Italy should be bidding for an African empire. The Union of South Africa wanted to thwart her, for she looks upon herself as the future paramount Power in Africa.

IV

The recovery of all her colonies, it has been said, would not settle Germany's economic problems. The total exports of these colonies was 26·5 million gold dollars (1934). Of this total 2·9 million dollars (11 per cent) went to Germany. If Germany concentrated the entire exports of the mandates in her own hands, her available supplies might be increased by 23·4 million dollars.[1] No doubt the supplies she could

[1] Germany's total imports in this very poor year amounted to 1,045 million gold dollars.

draw from them could be considerably enlarged. By giving preferential treatment to products specially needed (fats, for example) colonial production could be greatly stimulated; if properly developed, it might very well supply the 15 per cent of Germany's total imports of raw materials colonial enthusiasts claim. The financial strain of the transition period might be rather severe. Non-German capital at present invested in the mandates might wish to retire when a new administration came in; whether or not some sort of compensation were to be paid, Germany's foreign debt would increase. If foreign capitalists did not withdraw their participations, a large part of the profits earned by them would go abroad in return for the money invested by them. Whilst Germany might draw her supplies from the colonies, part of the payments made for them would flow to foreign countries. Preferential treatment in German markets would benefit these foreign investors and raise the costs of raw materials to the German producer. The stimulus given to the production of additional goods would inflate the world's supply of raw materials, for world markets are already overstocked; world prices might fall and Germany's commercial rivals would get raw materials more cheaply than she. At the same time, the foreign colonial producers' purchasing power for industrial goods might decline, and with it Germany's foreign trade.

The total imports of the mandates were 19 million gold dollars (1934); of these, 1·5 million (8 per cent) came from Germany. Here again the margin is not very considerable, especially when imports from neighbouring territories are deducted, which German trade would scarcely replace.[1] Germany could easily expand her exports to the mandates by investing money in new enterprises and by enlarging old ones. By financing these additional capital investments and by issuing loans or credits at home, a kind of public-works

[1] Germany's exports in the very worst year (1934) amounted to 979 million gold dollars; in 1929 they had exceeded 3 milliards.

finance, she could considerably enlarge her capital exports—even if she respected existing open-door agreements and did not grant open preference to her nationals. Government enterprise in a colony can always be financed by the taxpayer at home or by the metropolitan capital markets; even under the régime of the open door, the benefits from such expenditure can easily be kept from foreign rivals.[1] The limits of the expansion of a totalitarian state's activities are very elastic. German exports have lately experienced a colonial boom of this sort; German emigrants to Palestine were allowed to take with them some part of their capital, provided it was spent on goods destined for Palestine. Germany's export trade to Palestine has grown from RM. 8 million in 1932 to 21 million in 1935; her imports have remained stationary (RM. 5·4 million in 1932 and 5·1 million in 1935). Expansion of this sort is limited; otherwise internal prices will rise, and with them costs of production; exports would have to be subsidized either by burdening home industries by an internal levy, such as the one raised under the New Plan or by direct subsidies from taxpayers. The direct economic benefits of a return of the colonies to Germany might be rather disappointing, even if the additional opportunities for civil servants, soldiers, and managers were taken into account. The Powers handing back the colonies would scarcely take over the pensions and retiring allowances due to their own civil servants, nor are they likely to relinquish gratuitously government property or moneys advanced by them.[2] Goodwill may sometimes be counted upon when abstract principles and great schemes are under discussion, but scarcely ever when small bills have to be settled.

Neither the transfer of mandates nor the return of colonies would make Germany self-sufficient, as 85 per cent of her

[1] See above, pp. 323 and 329–30.

[2] Free loans and advances by the British Imperial Treasury to Tanganyika amount to £3,135,446 so far.

imports of raw materials must come from abroad. Such self-sufficiency as can be accomplished would be "disconnected." For the ownership of overseas colonies, however well developed they may be, can never result in "contiguous self-sufficiency." The problem of "security" cannot be solved by it. In fact it might even be aggravated. The control and defence of colonies imposes additional burdens on armies and navies, which the strategical value of colonial positions and the opportunity for recruiting native armies may not always offset. The feeling of being cramped economically from which Germany is suffering to-day, and from which she has suffered in the past, would not die down after the recovery of the colonies, since their economic possibilities are not great enough to bring about a complete change in a reasonably short time.[1] After all, Germany was not a very contented country when she had reached the zenith of her development before the war; the deterioration of her position and the many unpleasant experiences she has since under-gone have made her more sensitive and more envious. The Peace Treaties have certainly not improved her temper. Such comparatively slight concessions as the return of Togo or the Cameroons would not soothe it permanently. It would undoubtedly strengthen the government which could bring about a peaceful change of this magnitude. But a government which has achieved a limited success of this sort in the international sphere could not be expected to rest on its laurels.

A possessory Power might point out to Germany that the animosities and fears caused by her claims to colonies, her expansion and her return to the colonial stage would not be offset by the economic benefits she might reap from them. To refuse to part with a colony because it had little

[1] The loss of the China trade—which is bound to follow a victory of her Japanese friends—can scarcely be offset by additional commerce with a colony. Germany's imports into China (1934) amounted to 18·9 million gold dollars; the total imports of her former colonies were 16·6 million gold dollars.

value and because its recovery might strain the newcomer's finances is not an attitude which can be taken by a great colonial Power. The purely economic deduction that colonial possessions are of comparatively little value in the present-day world applies to all colonies. It is an argument for the liquidation of colonial possessions all round, but not for monopolizing them.

Countries which neither own colonies nor desire them can legitimately adduce it. They may object to any large territorial transfer, for the grave discrepancies between the Have and the Have-not groups of states cannot be removed by considering the claim of a single disgruntled Power and by adding one or two new members to the group of the Haves. As no lands are available for providing a colonial estate for every Have-not state which has come of age, or imagines that it has done so, the transfer from one owner to another is a mere shift of preferential benefits between two states; and as changes in colonial ownership have always deprived the outsiders of some advantage, any new arrangements of this sort are bound to limit their opportunities.

Since Japan is providing for herself, and Italy has declared herself satisfied, Germany is the only great Power left out in the cold. She is, however, not likely to remain the only one; other growing states will become dissatisfied with narrowing opportunities. Economic pressure is most severe in an early stage of a nation's development, when agriculture is the predominant occupation, when the land is completely settled, before a considerable part of the people have found their way into industry. Germany passed through this phase in the 'eighties of the last century. Italy and Japan are in the midst of it. Others are following—Poland is beginning to experience the severe strain of social transition; she has already registered her claims to expansion. She is ousting her Jewish population in order to make room for a rising middle class. And other Have-not Powers, which have so far been content with their opportunities, may not always look forward with equanimity to a permanent exclusion from closed empires.

As all-round colonial expansion is no longer possible—at least not on a large scale—commercial expansion is the only alternative for bringing about change by peaceful methods.

V

Germany's international economic position has greatly deteriorated since 1919. The loss of her colonies was but one of the minor consequences of the war and of the peace settlements which followed it.

She was deprived of valuable European regions containing important raw materials (iron ore), the loss of which compelled her to reorganize the structure of many of her industries. She became more dependent on iron imports. Her export capacity declined, while her need for imports increased. She no longer had an income from foreign investments, which had been valued at over $6\frac{1}{2}$ milliard gold dollars[1] before the war. Her own government had taken over some of these; the remainder was confiscated by the Peace Treaties, including those capital investments in neutral countries which the victors could get hold of. German property in the ceded provinces was expropriated and German enterprise in allied countries and colonies was deliberately uprooted in order to reduce her competitive strength. Her mercantile marine was distributed among the victors; her mines and mills were forced to work for them. A systematic disorganization of her industries was contemplated in order to retard her recuperation. The financial obligations from the reparations clauses of the treaty made her a heavily encumbered debtor country. The fantastic claims of earlier settlements had destroyed all hope of obtaining foreign credits and had driven her along the road

[1] Second Report of Experts' Committee on Reparations (McKenna Report), 1924.

of bankruptcy by inflation. Even the comparatively moderate payments assessed upon her by the Dawes and Young Plans were far beyond her capacity. She managed to pay the annuities due during this period by contracting loans abroad for the rationalization of her industry and agriculture. She had to intensify agriculture in order to become self-supporting and to reduce imports, and to intensify industry in order to raise exports and to pay debts. In the end, Germany was saddled with a foreign commercial debt amounting to over 5 billion gold dollars; an annual export surplus of at least 200 million gold dollars, apart from 400 million dollars reparation payments, was needed to defray the claims for interest resulting from it.[1]

The attempt would have failed, even if the markets of the world had been willing to take unlimited quantities of German goods at remunerative prices. But after England had gone off the Gold Standard and competitive international currency depreciation had disorganized the world, a recrudescence of protection contracted all markets.

Before the war, Germany had been the economic metropolis of the Russian Empire, whose semi-colonial structure presented great opportunities for capitalist expansion. Though France and Belgium provided some of the capital needed, the actual organization had fallen to German entrepreneurs, whose activities found wide scope in this enormous territory. The Austrian monarchy offered an allied, extensive and friendly market with great capacity for expansion, in which Germany enjoyed a certain amount of sentimental preference. Turkey, too, looked to her for financial and industrial support, as Germany was the only big country which had no interest in her partition. Germany's predominant position in these countries, all of them from an economic point of view relatively "young countries," to some degree offset the absence of important colonial markets and supplies. These chances have completely gone. The

[1] Wiggin-Layton Report (1931), p. 3.

Austrian and Turkish Empires have collapsed, and though Russian development is progressing rapidly, exploitation by foreign capitalists is no longer possible. The German population has gone on growing, though the rate of increase has been rapidly declining; its density is almost double what it was in the 'eighties, when emigration figures reached their peak. But emigration has been on the decline ever since the early 'eighties. Industrialization has taken care of the surplus population. During the period 1846–1932 Germany ranked fourth among European emigration countries; her total loss was 4·9 million emigrants, a little over that of Spain (4·7 million).[1] But before the war she had become an immigrant country, and she remained an immigrant country, for her eastern agriculture depended on the influx of seasonal labourers from Poland. Though the large pre-war figures for seasonal immigrants (670,000) subsequently declined, the average of 28,000 for the years 1920–24 rose to 125,000 (1927–30). Since 1930 it has almost come to a standstill.[2] German emigration has been hampered some-what by the restrictive legislation of the immigrant countries, but not to the same extent as that of Italy or Japan. The original quota of 68,000 granted her by the United States was reduced to 51,200 (1924) and to 25,900 (1929); it might have been adequate for her needs in ordinary years. Neither the British Dominions nor South Africa discriminate against her.[3] Her rulers do not favour emigration, apart from Jewish emigration, which has amounted to 60,000 in the last few years. They want to keep their people at home.

Germany's grievances resemble those of Italy only super-ficially. Her central problems are quite unlike those of her would-be teacher. She does not need victories in order to recover her self-respect; she has shown the world that she

---

[1] United Kingdom, 18 million; Italy, 10 million; Austria-Hungary, 5 million.—Carr-Saunders, op. cit., p. 49.

[2] Ibid., p. 147. Last year permits for 10,000 immigrants were granted.

[3] Ibid., pp. 193 and 197.

N*

can wage wars and win battles without the aid of powerful allies. Her main political problems are continental, not maritime. An oversea empire may be of great economic assistance to her. But whatever her romantic imperialists may say, her spokesmen, from Bismarck to Hitler, have always looked upon oversea possessions as complementary parts of a continental empire, not as substitutes for one. They may mean a great deal to her emotionally and economically; they are not the main axis of her policy. Governments come and go, but the geographical situation of a country does not change when new actors enter or old ones leave the stage. Germany is a continental state or super-state, and her main problems are continental problems. She does not want to scatter her people, nor does she want to be saddled with the rule of foreign European races.[1] In not too distant a future she hopes to be the centre-piece of Middle European economic federation.

Germany has experienced great economic pressure; she resents it strongly when comparing her lot with that of more fortunate nations. She does not seek relief in a contraction of population. She sees herself surrounded by unfriendly neighbours, who covet, she thinks, her strength and the little wealth she has. She remembers the nightmare from which Prince Bismarck suffered (*Le cauchemar des coalitions*). None of his successors have ever been completely free from it. Her leaders see the population problem from the defence, and not from the wealth point of view; a decline in the birth rate frightens them. It had fallen as low as $14 \cdot 7$ per 1,000 in 1933; it has since risen to 19 per 1,000.[2] The government has stimulated marriages and births by bounties and tax remissions and other favours. But it is not yet clear whether this improvement will continue for any length of time; the net reproduction rate, which

[1] See *Mein Kampf*, passim.
[2] A birth rate of 21 is needed to maintain national efficiency (Bestands-erhaltung der Volkskraft) under present conditions of age composition.

stood at 1·480 in the decade 1901–10 had fallen to 0·924 (1924–26) and to 0·70 (1933).[1] The slight reversion which has since taken place may go on;[2] it will scarcely reach the Italian figures (1·209–1·18), nor the rate of increase which Japan may reckon on. Germany may in time tend towards a more or less stationary stage. Government policy may influence the actions of her nationals, but if it cannot widen economic opportunities, the final results will not be considerable. And the trend towards greater national self-sufficiency, which the hard facts of the general world situation and the conception of the state as a living combination of race and soil impose on the German economic system, will hardly increase economic opportunities, though they may make for greater economic security.

[1] Carr-Saunders, op. cit., Fig. 25, p. 123.
[2] By 1936 it had risen to 0·89, but it was still below the average 0·924 of 1924–26.

CHAPTER VIII

THE MAIN ISSUE: CONQUEST OR FEDERATION

I

THE picture of a world divided between saturated and non-saturated Powers which confront one another, more or less angrily, is scarcely accurate. A largish group of states are content; they have no ambition either to establish or to maintain an empire; they stand between the expansionist Powers of the past who are saturated and the disgruntled late-comers. The ranks of both of these groups grow and diminish, since change is at work uninterruptedly. The central political problem of our time is whether existing boundaries must be moved, and whether this must be done by war. The age of empire-building on the *vertical plane*[1] has gone for good. Primary colonization is no longer possible, since no objects suitable for it are available. The exchange of smallish colonial possessions in a peaceful way is quite feasible, but transactions of this sort are too insignificant to satisfy ambitions and to change the international balance. But empire-making on the *horizontal plane* may go on, by federation or by world-wide wars.

The claim for equality of opportunity, which has played such a strong part in modern world affairs, was explicitly recognized in the Wilsonian system. It was to be satisfied by economic concessions. Frontiers need not be removed, except in those cases where the self-determination of a separate nation was at issue; they must not poison the body-economic of the world; they were to be "sterilized" by trade. Political domination and ownership must no longer be used for the maintenance of national economic privileges of any sort. The flow of international trade should

[1] For the meaning of the terms *horizontal* and *vertical* empire-making see above, pp. 42–3.

be unhampered by national efforts to deflect it for purely sectional purposes.

The alternative to economic nationalism, making for regional or imperial isolation, should be the resumption of a broad measure of international economic intercourse. In this respect, the question of raw materials is of secondary importance. Any country can buy the raw materials it needs, practically at the same prices as its rivals—provided it can pay for them. A few colonial monopolies may look threatening to particular countries; they could perhaps be made innocuous by consumers' representation on their administrative boards. The main question is how to pay for raw materials. It must be settled by lowering the barriers against imports. The maintenance of the open-door régime in colonies and mandates subjected to it, and even its extension to all non-self-governing colonies, is not enough. Sales to colonies proper cannot provide the hitherto handicapped states with the foreign exchange they need for paying for their imports. The leading imperial Powers of the world must be prepared to make much more far-reaching trade concessions, if they wish to satisfy the disgruntled nations economically. The ideal solution would be universal free trade; the abolition of quotas and clearing arrangements and the gradual reduction of tariff barriers leading to it. The acceptance of an international code of economic hospitality regulating the unhampered exercise of foreign activities in national territories would bring about a far greater measure of "equality" than the shuffling and re-shuffling of a few colonial possessions. Unfortunately this is a counsel for perfection. The ruling protectionist obsession is so strong that tariff abatements or the abolition of a quota are looked upon as quixotic concessions which cannot easily be made, since profits might be diminished, wages might be reduced, and unemployment might be increased. Fortunately there is no need to argue with people who take their stand on the assumption that the age of reason is gone anyhow. Their contentions can be accepted at their face value, not because they are convincing, but because they are quite futile. The issue is not whether protection or free trade is more profitable to a particular state, but whether the advent of war economy and of war can be prevented by a more liberal commercial policy. A policy of sacrifice which ensures peace by timely commercial concessions is cheaper than a profitable policy of isolation which leads to war.

A more liberal commercial policy on the part of the possessory Powers may not absolutely ensure peace; an illiberal policy will certainly ensure war. It will prevent close co-operation between the " Liberal States," and split their otherwise overwhelming strength. The former will certainly lessen tension and soothe the feverish irritation prevalent in some of the disgruntled countries.[1] They will no longer see in the trend towards commercial isolation by the richer countries the menace of a veiled blockade, which is meant to break them, and to which they must retort by a kind of Spartan rejection of "the Life abundant" and by relentless preparation for war. They will be able to relax some restrictions and lean more toward foreign supplies—however much this may endanger them *during a war*. They despise the richer countries as peace-loving degenerate *poltrons*, so they need not be frightened of a military attack from them; but they credit them with sinister plans for strangulation. A policy of economic conciliation would raise standards of living a little, and some of the pent-up bitterness would evaporate. An atmosphere might be created in which an economic reorganization of the world could be discussed. Losses to vital industries which

[1] The Commercial Treaty which Cobden negotiated with the Emperor Louis Napoleon, 1860, acted in this manner. "It was and is my opinion that the choice lay between the Cobden Treaty and not the certainty, but the high probability, of a war with France," Mr. Gladstone noted. John Morley, *Life of Gladstone*, vol. ii, p. 23.

could not be obviated by adequate organization might be charged to the National Exchequer. Modern protectionism has resulted everywhere in the nationalization of losses, whilst profits are still private property. It would be preferable to incur losses resulting from an adjustment of industries to the demands of existing markets than from fostering enterprises whose output is not needed. Surely it is wiser to bribe people not to raise unwanted goods than to subsidize them for doing so. Protection has nearly everywhere combated the flooding of the world markets with unsaleable goods by raising additional goods at home and by dumping them abroad whilst refusing imports. Some Protectionists nowadays prefer a cession of territory—especially other nations' territory—to tariff concessions. They even insist that political advantages are no proper compensation for economic concessions.

These destructive currents reached their high-water mark during the period of competitive currency depreciation, which fortunately seems to be drawing to its close. Its object was to swell exports; it raised paper prices at home and depressed gold prices abroad; it led to a war of all against all, by competitive depreciation as well as by exchange control, quotas and anti-dumping duties. It enabled some of the stronger countries to snatch an increased share of a declining world trade, a decline partly caused by their own actions.

A return to saner policies seems in sight. It will have to go a long way before the spiritual, as well as the material deadlock which is gripping the world will be relaxed. And however successful it may be, it cannot bring about complete equality.

The age of indiscriminate mass immigration has gone for good. The new countries will not re-open their gates to a new flood—if in the present stage of population trends there is to be one. Tariffs will not disappear. The fostering of secondary industries in less developed countries will not be given up completely. Even international lending may not resume its old proportions. Since the great creditor countries are attempting to buy a more or less spurious prosperity by artificially cheap money and by indiscriminate national borrowing, the outflow of capital is limited, whilst the hysterics of flight-capital movements are disquieting governments and investors.

An offer of complete free trade and of free economic movements by the possessory Powers would scarcely be accepted whole-heartedly by disgruntled nations.

Population is an asset to them, not a liability. It strengthens their man-power, spartanizes their standards of living, and makes for concentration and subordination. They do not wish to raise the man-power of foreign countries and to lose strength by large-scale emigration. They may resent immigration restrictions directed against them; they do not want to make much use of their removal. The huge population resources of Russia fill them with fear; their aim is the greatest numerical strength at home rather than spreading their nationals all over foreign possessions. They are very keen on snatching as many trade advantages as possible. In this respect they are influenced by purely temporary motives. They cannot complete their armaments without foreign raw materials and foreign capital on the purely military, as well as on the economic side. Permanent isolation implies an expensive technical equipment, partly based on scarce raw materials (to be dispensed with in future) which must come from abroad. Japan is earning the money she means to spend on the exploitation of the natural resources of China by forcing her cotton trade in foreign markets. Italy's position in Ethiopia will become very difficult without foreign loans. Germany's trend towards isolation is apparently less dependent on foreign imports; her hopes of making her defence independent of foreign supplies are less illusory. But during a lengthy period of transition, additional armaments depend on an increased foreign trade.

She must develop it now, in order to do without it later on. The scarcity she is suffering from is mainly due to the accumulation of reserves of foodstuffs and to the huge demand for structural goods and prime materials needed in erecting the giant plants which are to make her self-sufficient in the future. On the assumption that a great war is inevitable, the paradox of forcing intercourse in order to accomplish isolation is reasonable, both from a military and from an economic point of view. But the richer countries might well hesitate before giving the poorer countries those increased trading and credit facilities on which their armaments and, ultimately, their isolation depend.

The risks the rich countries have to face are not the results of a free trade policy, but of fear and suspicion; policies of freer trade might lessen them, but a kind of autarchish blockade would greatly increase them.

The disgruntled countries cannot avail themselves of free trade facilities on too large a scale. They will abolish protection neither of agriculture nor of their national military key industries. They cannot give up their dream of autarchy until the sufferings entailed by it become unbearable. This is not going to happen in the near future. Failure of autarchy and of central planning will not, for a long time to come, lead to a reversal, but rather to an *accentuation* of policy. For in a totalitarian state autarchy is not an opportunist experiment, but an article of faith. The acquisition of a colony will merely widen its basis, whilst its equipment with public works may offer an alternative to a temporarily fading armament boom. A halting policy on their part will keep down their exports, as foreigners will not take goods which they cannot pay for in other goods. They must maintain a system of exchange control for a long time, for its sudden relaxation would facilitate a tremendous flight of capital. Were national frontiers, national discrimination and national prejudices to disappear completely, a re-settlement of the earth's surface might follow. The poorer regions of the globe might ultimately become derelict.[1]

No measure of free international economic intercourse can wipe out the great inequalities in the economic structure of various countries which are due to natural territorial causes. It might even make them more perceptible. It can help to lessen disparities in the wealth, the income, and the standards of living of their inhabitants—it does not affect directly the natural properties of a separate national area. A closer intercourse with another richer area might even sap its strength and its wealth. The decline of Ireland in population and comparative wealth under the Union with Great Britain was not so much due to the wickedness of the predominant partner, as Irish Patriots have contended, as to the unhampered access which a more favoured region with greater natural resources offered to her people. An independent government, with distinct national ideals of its own, will not run the risks of economic desiccation which completely free economic intercourse with more fortunate nations might bring about.

II

The choice lies between conquest and federation, or rather between compulsory and voluntary federation.

Federations either unite partner states (like the United States of America or Russia) or ruling and subject countries—like the colonial empires, the big ones as well as the small ones. The British Empire is a double- or even a triple-bottomed federation: Great Britain, Great Britain and the Dominions, Great Britain and the Colonies; the Dominions themselves are partner-federations as well as ruler-and-subject federations. Germany alone of all great countries

[1] Movements of this sort are taking place in the U.S.A., where people are not rooted to the soil. In older countries, local tenacity is very much stronger, otherwise the transfer from the depressed areas in England and Wales would have assumed much larger proportions. See above, pp. 270–1.

is a kind of super-state, in which scarcely any federal elements are left.

A few federations are complete. Some are politically united and economically disjoined; others again form more or less closely knit economic unions, but possess few common political agencies. The German Zollverein before 1867 was of the latter type; the British Empire belongs to the former, though the beginnings of economic unity are visible. The preferential commercial arrangements which bind its members are no longer limited to the trade relations between the ruling state and its dependencies. The British Commonwealth of Nations to-day is a loosely knit economic federation; the Dominions claim to be independent states and are recognized as such by the League of Nations, but they give preference to one another and to the mother country. By doing so, they have set aside the most-favoured-nation clause, which had hitherto protected the trading rights of other countries.

So far governments who desire to maintain a completely independent political organization have not yet succeeded in forming a united economic system. They have rarely gone beyond preferential treatment or parallel economic action, which is possible in certain circumstances; the Latin monetary union was a conspicuous example of this sort.

From the currency chaos of the last six years similar co-ordinated economic action has arisen. The members of the so-called Sterling Club have practised a kind of parallel currency manipulation, which involved more or less identical premiums on exports and more or less identical currency barriers against imports. The policy of the gold bloc countries presented another parallelism, of much smaller portent, of course, since it was limited to the defence of a rigid status quo. The tripartite stabilization agreements between England, France, and the United States point in the same direction.

In the absence of political unity, economic federations

are rather loose; they do not go beyond a system of preference and discrimination. Currency manipulation has opened a way to preference and discrimination by which one can get round the most-favoured-nation clause, without formally infringing it; and so has exchange control. Germany's policy enabled her to sell manufactured goods at preferential rates to certain foreign countries after she had admitted their raw materials and foodstuffs at preferential prices. All purely bilateral clearing agreements contain germs of preference and discrimination.

Open attempts at "regional preference" have so far been frustrated by Great Britain. She has prevented other countries from making preferential arrangements based on geographical and historical circumstances which were not unlike those of Great Britain and her Dominions. She has killed the low-tariff federation scheme of the Oslo Powers by insisting on the most-favoured-nation clause. She has been unwilling to concede a customs union between Germany and Austria, after having blocked earlier schemes between Austria and Czechoslovakia, though the proposals between the northern countries, or the successor states of the Habsburg monarchy, can be justified by sound historical and geographical arguments. Having vindicated the principle of reciprocal preference by her dealings with the Dominions, she can scarcely refuse its application in future to those states who desire particularly close relations with their neighbours or with their traditional friends.

No system of preference which is not based on permanent co-operation between the several governments concerned is stable. The economic security attempted by such arrangements cannot be depended upon as long as withdrawals have to be reckoned with. It is either a purely opportunist régime or the forerunner of a customs union and of federation.

Federation does not abolish the inequality in territory, population, wealth, and resources which exists between member states; but it can make them politically innocuous.

A separate sovereign state could not allow the shifting of the cotton industries from New England to the Southern States: it would have to fight it with means fair and foul. The United States do not stop the trend; they try and smooth the shock of the transition. Federation can make the violent changes inherent in the system of modern economics bearable and peaceful.

Genuine economic federation necessitates some sacrifice of economic sovereignty, especially in the realm of public finance. It cannot be attempted by governments whose political outlook is irreconcilable. No government can divest itself of a shred of its supreme power in favour of another government from which it differs fundamentally, in respect of the objectives, as well as of the methods, of policy. Governments can co-operate with one another for particular objects in foreign affairs, irrespective of their constitutions and of the political philosophies underlying them. The alliance between the French Republic and the Tsarist Empire accomplished the purpose for which it was concluded—one might say almost too well. For an alliance presupposes a particular common objective and a common attitude towards this objective only. A federation involves a common outlook on the fundamental problems of government. An economic federation might, so it seems, involve less, being limited to definite economic issues. A loosely knit federation, which does not go much beyond some sort of preferential reciprocity, is a half-way house from which the roads lead in opposite directions: towards separation or towards a customs union. The problems of a customs union cannot be dealt with without joint government agencies, which in their turn depend on the general structure of government. Economic issues are, moreover, not mere business questions, which can be settled by a joint meeting of accountants. They centre, to-day, round social philosophies and creeds of governments.

No single system of economics can be devised to-day which

all the world is willing to adopt. The Capitalism of the West, the Communism of the East, and the Barrack-room Socialism of the Centre cannot co-ordinate their economic policies. It is impossible to federate opposed social systems. A minor[1] social-economic issue, the slavery question, rent the first and greatest modern federation, the United States, from top to bottom; it had to be settled by civil war. It showed the world that two antagonistic social and spiritual systems cannot co-operate peacefully and cannot remain permanently within a single "federation." A house divided against itself cannot stand. The lesson was repeated under different circumstances in the Abyssinian conflict. The League is not a federation. It is a far looser body. There is room in it for the most diverse social systems, but even so it cannot work successfully without a certain identity of outlook amongst its members. The League became ridiculous when it allowed Italy to remain an influential member of the Council after she had flouted the Covenant on which it was founded. However desirable from an economic point of view a reunion of the Baltic States with Russia might appear, it cannot be accomplished, as long as the would-be partner states are organized on diametrically opposed social principles.

III

The use of force for social purposes has been an integral part of those philosophical systems to which the strength and power of the collective unit, the State, is the one and all, and to which the individual's welfare means very little. Philosophers, especially German philosophers, have frequently outlined a super-state, a perfect living social organism, not a mere machine, whose component particles, men and women, cannot lead a separate existence of their own, but live and breathe only in and through the com-

---

[1] The issue was a minor one in so far as it centred round a particular form of private property, not round the much wider discrepancies between Capitalism and Communism.

munity which they form. This community is not made by nature, but by men, or rather by their governments, preferably by force, so that its members can live that higher life, which is denied to the so-called citizens of more or less atomized societies. It might stand for peace, once it has been established, but as it is made by force it must glorify force.

Social militarism, as a working social system, was not copied from philosophic textbooks; it was born in the war, when regimentation of the entire social, spiritual, and economic life of the nation had become inevitable. A kind of War Socialism was organized, from which, later on, most schemes for "planning" generated. Though its success, under the prevailing conditions of scarcity, was not overwhelming, it had demonstrated beyond doubt that the sphere of State intervention could be stretched nearly *ad libitum* and that compulsory organization could be carried to almost any length, since man, under the control of a strong government, was more plastic than clay in the hands of the potter. Government was omnipotent. The State respected no bounds. Leviathan had arisen; it cared neither for the rights of man nor the laws of nature. A resolute indomitable will could easily flout the claims of the former or stop the workings of the latter.

War economies left a large band of devotees behind them. Amongst them were the army men, the bureaucrats, the business men, and even the trade unionists who had been associated in running them. Their experiences and their achievements lent themselves easily to the construction of a glorified system of planned economics and of a totalitarian state. Their notions might never have survived peace, had the peace been honest and intelligent. Four years' fighting had convinced the world (what it had doubted before) that democracy can wage war. But six months' peace parleys in Paris proved to it that democracy could not make peace. It had been crusading for high ideals as long as its fate had hung in the balance. But when it had won victory, it thought of nothing but spoils and selfish security. It taught the vanquished that force was a remedy and the only one at that, and that democratic principles were mere trappings devised to capture gullible fools.

Two distinct, but closely allied, concepts were comprised in this Social Militarism. On the one hand, the notion that society could be organized in a more or less arbitrary way was becoming popular. The laws of Nature which were supposed to regulate the structure, growth, and functions of the social organism were discarded. Society was man-made, not God-made; in making it, man need not bother much about immanent laws. And the other held that physical force was the appropriate instrument for forging society according to the whims of man.

The advent of the Soviet régime greatly strengthened these tendencies in both directions. The doctrine of class warfare had idealized revolutionary violence. It denied the prospects of peaceful change when fundamental issues were at stake. Vital conflicts could not be settled by peaceful negotiation among warring classes. Class warfare meant real, not mere metaphorical war.

Orthodox Marxism had always decried British experience.[1] British political intuition had discovered, so it seemed, a method of peaceful change, by which the claims of warring classes could be equitably adjusted. Ever since the passing of the Reform Bill, the conviction had been gaining ground that force was no remedy. In Paris, Brussels, Vienna, and Berlin, barricades had been erected when new social strata insisted on their rights; the only revolutionary structures ever raised in England, since those days, were the soap-boxes in the Park, from which inspired orators, unmolested by the police, spouted forth their feelings and heralded the advent, or non-advent, of some momentous change, which might, or might not, mature into far-reaching Constitu-

[1] Eduard Bernstein, *Zur Geschichte und Theorie des Socialismus*, 1901, pp. 149 and 382.

tional Reform. The use of peaceful methods was not limited to social strife. The Home Rule Bill had recognized the rights of a subject nationality, and though turbulent minorities had temporarily held up its passage, peaceful change was becoming the central article in the creed of British democracy; its wisdom was more than justified by the grant of self-government to the former Boer republics, which turned them into loyal members of the Empire. Doubts were rife as to its general applicability—the United States, after all, had not been able to settle the slave problem without a terrible internecine struggle. And the organization of an Ulster army against Home Rule, with the active blessing of British Conservatism, marked the beginning of those forms of militarized self-help in Europe which have subsequently been called Fascism. The theory of Fascism was evolved in France by the group of the Action Française and Sorelian Syndicalism; its practice was anticipated by Lord Carson and Mr. Bonar Law in Europe; it had always been endemic in the Republics of Latin America.

Notwithstanding these ominous signs, the Western world's faith in peaceful change was growing; it worked hard for its application to foreign affairs. The colonial issues separating England and France were settled by peaceful negotiations; so were those affecting Italy and France, and France and Spain. Even Germany and France adjusted their colonial differences by a series of peaceful transitions; though lengthy periods of strident and bellicose altercations had preceded them, they finally resulted in a peaceful settlement. None of the issues involved, it is true, were vital to the welfare of both parties. But the moderate results so far accomplished gave promise of future success on a wider basis.

Then came the war and the breakdown, at least temporarily, of all hopes of peaceful change.

The Peace concluding the Great War envisaged a system of "peaceful change," which was to undo the harm caused by one-sided arrangements. By guaranteeing the *status quo* through a League of Nations it stabilized the conditions imposed upon the vanquished and perpetuated the unjust changes forced upon them, and attempted to eliminate force as a remedy in the future dealings of the nations. After having dressed up violence in pacifist disguise (and made pacifism suspect in the eyes of the vanquished), it made it attractive to them as the only remedy for redressing their grievances.

The chance for peaceful change in foreign affairs had gone, however, when once the doctrine of violence was accepted in home affairs. One can scarcely expect goodwill amongst nations split up into warring factions who are engaged in permanent internecine class warfare. And the elevation of the class struggle to the position of a central social law will not create an atmosphere favourable to the extermination of international war. The Marxian verbiage is stuffed with military terms, some of them purely figurative, but all of them breathing a militarist, as well as a militant spirit.[1] The word "comrade" has a military ring; it designates the drilled co-operation of platoons and companies as contrasted with the loose associations of citizens gathering at the polls.

The successful application of a militarist doctrine to the making of a new society by the Soviet régime has converted a pale theory into a blood-red practice. It gave a new lease of life to all militarist social theories the world over. The pre-Lenin Marxist philosophy had been determinist; it had assumed the automatic working of forces immanent in the social body, which men's actions might speed up or retard a little, but which could not be deflected by any arbitrary acts of governments from following the lines laid down in the laws of nature. By moving the clutches one might change

---

[1] Engels strongly objected to the mitigation of the Law of Search on the High Seas as agreed upon at the Paris Conference, 1856. He reproached British statesmen with having sacrificed England's best weapon.—Gustav Mayer, *Friedrich Engels*, vol. ii, p. 206.

gear, but not get a new car. Socialism was inevitable when the society preceding it was ripe for its birth. But Soviet Marxism did not wait for this process of maturing and for the silent working of the laws of nature. It devised a huge incubator which speeded up the hatching of the Phoenix by a few centuries, though the bird looked somewhat scraggy when it crept out of its shell.

The most backward amongst the great peoples of the world, which had just crossed the threshold of the capitalist order, had established a communist society, and has kept it going ever since. Violence, terror, and revolution had not been the handmaids of organic development, lending their help at the last moment, by brushing away the feeble resistance of hitherto ruling classes, who refused to recognize the inexorable laws of social change even after the funeral bells had rung the passing of capitalism. They were the makers of change, forcing it brutally on a mass of peasants and small artisans, who but for them would have gone on living peacefully through an extended pre-capitalist age before finally and inevitably fading out. Force had been the main factor in internal social change; in a brief span of time it had fundamentally altered the structure of society. Its success may not have been achieved in strict accordance with the main body of Marxian teaching. But the romantic streak of glorification of barricades and street-fighting which runs through it—the result of Blanquist connections[1]— enabled the Bolsheviks to claim the authority of the master in their passionate altercations with the German Socialists.[2]

[1] E. Bernstein, op. cit., p. 34 seq.

[2] The purges in present-day Russia go a long way to justify the attitude of the Germans. They show that class-consciousness is not a sufficient substitute for industrial efficiency. The ever-recurring complaints about sabotage are but the recognition of the fact that the rapid growth of a modern industrial set-up does not produce an equally rapid change in the workers' minds, on which the success of running it depends. The time lag between the erection of such plants and the consequent transformation of the Russian workers explains the frequent breakdowns which are blamed on "sabotage."

But arguments really counted for little, as compared with the fact that a mighty social revolution had been accomplished by the most violent means imaginable and had successfully disposed of quietist determinism. It freed Socialism from the shackles of the iron laws of necessity. It enabled its devotees to establish a social order in accordance with their own particular concepts and to force development into its proper channels. But it gave its adversaries new hopes in a fight against their impending doom. A process which could be accelerated arbitrarily might as well be retarded, since the laws controlling the natural growth of societies can be tampered with anyhow. If growth could not be stopped, it might be postponed indefinitely, and the ultimate outcome might be considerably changed. The Communists might protest against this reasoning: they were merely anticipating, by a few decades, an order of things, the advent of which was inevitable, since Karl Marx's prophetic genius enabled them to foretell the course of events accurately, whilst reactionary capitalists were blindly groping to hold up the forces of social development at an arbitrarily chosen strategic point. But there was no unanimity in the Marxist camp about the road which has to be travelled, for the sacred books—as sacred books are apt to do—gave conflicting answers to inquiring disciples. If Kautsky was right, Lenin was wrong; if Trotsky saw the light, Stalin was wallowing in utter darkness. The certainty of ultimate salvation might be beyond doubt, but there was vagueness and haziness about how, when, and where to get it. Objective necessity was getting rather blurred; evidence became subjective and conflicting. Events and arguments thus combined and freed the capitalist mind from the fear of its inevitable fate and the certainty of its downfall in the near future. If force, stressing the trend of future development, could bring in Socialism at a moment's notice, it might work equally well in keeping it out. In any case, it was well worth while making an effort. Such reactionary attempts might ultimately prove futile, the laws of social evolution might assert themselves triumphantly over Fascists who were trying to check them. But one did not know for certain, and in any case one might gain time. Men live in time and space, not in eternity. Eternity does not mean much to them whilst they are alive, but the next few years ahead of them do.

Thus a new conception of society was born in which force, physical and spiritual, war, violence, and terror were not merely handy instruments to be used when the occasion arose for attaining a definite object in foreign affairs—a particular form of policy, a mere variation of it, as the great Prussian military philosopher had called it[1]—but rather the central objective towards which all the nation's energies have to be directed. War economy had necessitated the application of military methods to production and consumption; some of its practitioners had evolved from these experiences a philosophy of social militarism. Social militarism meant an organization of society primarily for war purposes, for war, not peace, is the nation's fate and the main objective of its policy. The army is no longer the nation called to the colours; the nation is the army on leave. To such a society territorial expansion by conquest comes naturally; it might prefer *vertical expansion,* which is easier, looks more profitable, and involves a smaller strain on the natural resources; it does depend on sea-power. In the absence of colonial opportunities it will not refrain from *lateral expansion* which may mean war, but holds out the promise of continental and contiguous autarchy.

Communism and so-called Fascism differ greatly in many respects. The arbitrariness of Communism is ephemeral, a mere passing phase, during which the laws of nature are prodded a little, so to speak. After this transition period, when the obstacles to their proper working have been cleared out of the way, they will be restored to their previous

[1] Von Clausewitz, *Vom Kriege.*

position and function unhampered by human greed and stupidity for all days to come.

The Fascist creed is arbitrary as a matter of principle; it does not believe in any preordained order of things; it arranges them in the order it prefers at a given moment.

The final aims of Communism are pacifist. When class war has come to an end by the disappearance of classes, external wars will cease as well, as they are supposed to be the result of capitalist needs for expansion. The rhythm of the dialectical process will become kindly and friendly, assuming that it will go on working.

Fascism, on the other hand, is free from these remnants of sentimental bourgeois Utopianism. It believes in everlasting strife and the need for everlasting forcible self-assertion. Its pacifism is purely intermittent and opportunist.

At present Russia's foreign policy is extremely peaceful. She needs time for developing her vast dominions and for training her backward peoples rather than additional territorial resources. Communism must catch up with the leading capitalist nations before it can outdistance them. And until the working masses have learned how to handle the capitalist mechanism their leaders have little hope of revolutionizing the world. The recognition of these facts is one of the mainstays of peace and the strongest guarantee against Russian aggression; it has made of Russia a champion of the League of Nations, a somewhat quaint product of miscegenation between Wilsonism and Leninism. But the Communist view of life is quite as aggressive and non-pacifist as the Fascist—at least until the day when all nations shall have been converted to its creed. Communism, moreover, is "universal"; far more universal than Capitalism or Liberalism have ever been. It envisages a time when all nations will possess the same standardized institutions, think the same ideas, and experience the same emotions. It completely ignores, not only racial or regional distinctions, but the far more important differences which result from the dissimilar stages of development, which various nations reach at a given moment. It eliminates not only race and space but time as well as essential features in the make-up of human societies.

Fascism and particularly Nazism, on the other hand, are disintegrating creeds. The latter especially revolts against the universalist tradition of the Western world and insists on evolving a particular civilization of its own, which is unique and singular and cannot be shared by other nations, inasmuch as its distinctive qualities are due to every nation's unchangeable physical components. Both hate the League of Nations, not merely for purely political reasons, but as the embodiment of a new and the repository of an old universalism. They would not mind Bolshevism half as much, were it not for its claim to universalism.

The clash between Fascist and Communist conceptions is a clash of ultimate aims, not a conflict of methods. The devotees of both creeds believe in force. To the Communists it is a mere method, to the Fascists an end as well as a means. To both groups the ends justify the means. It might be said with greater justice that the choice of the means determines the nature of the ends. A society which looks towards force as its main instrument cannot be a peaceful society, however sincere for the time being its profession of peace may be. Structure depends far more on means than on ends.[1]

It is quite impossible to bring about a political symbiosis between the adherents of such diametrically opposed creeds.

For the time being—if not perhaps for ever—the dream of world unity has faded. There is a great deal of outward uniformity, due to the relentless working of technical forces. Spiritually the world is rent as it never has been rent before. A revival of universalism could only be attained by a decisive victory, spiritually as well as physically, of one of the warring groups.

This is not likely to happen. The conflict of aims and of

[1] See above, p. 240 seq.

means will not be settled immediately, however perilous the juxtaposition of opposed systems may be. It cannot be obviated by one-sided territorial concessions, be they ever so fair and generous. Since they are too insignificant for solving the difficulties of disgruntled nations, they will only whet their appetites for additional demands. Concessions on such a scale as to remove pressure completely are out of the question. Even if all possessory Powers were ready to contribute to a colonial fund, it would not be large enough for the satisfaction of the needs of all claimants. And in any case, external expansion will not turn them from pursuing their ideal of militarist autarchy; the farther it goes, the wider will be the basis on which the experiment can be tried. Its ultimate success may appear more likely, and the period of dangerous gambling will be prolonged.

Militarist Powers are loudly advertising their conceptions; they ask the nations of the world to adopt them as their own, without reserve. If they succeeded in their endeavour to convert democratic empires into totalitarian super-states they might find themselves in a curious quandary. The triumph of their principle would deprive them of any chance of political success. For the superiority of the human and material resources of the possessory empires is overwhelming. Their conversion to social militarism would not merely secure the *status quo* for them, it would solve their main perplexities. For as things are their position as overlords of a large part of the globe is illogical. The doctrines of democracy and domination are mutually exclusive. Colonial control should be abhorrent to the citizens of a commonwealth who believe in the equality of all men and in the self-determination of all nations. As long as democracies were driven forward by a strong missionary fanaticism and felt the urge of conferring the benefits of their political system upon other nations, if needs be at the point of the bayonet, a compromise was possible. But aggressive democracy is on the wane, its missionary fires are dying down.

A strong feeling of the wickedness of domination, colonial and otherwise, is nowadays pervading the Western mind. For democratic propaganda has done its work well. It has roused a nationalist spirit amongst the subject races and made the holding of colonies very much more difficult. It has, at the same time, destroyed the spiritual foundation on which empire was based. The simple faith that might is right is gone. Economic domination is quite as bad as political domination. An age of empire-breaking is dawning. The pacifist bourgeois anti-Imperialism of the Manchester School is being transformed into the militarist proletarian anti-Imperialism of the Bolsheviks. By adopting the spiritual outlook and the methods of aggression of their opponents, the possessory countries could easily hold and widen their empires. This means a spiritual surrender on their part, the acceptance of values hitherto denied by the great religions of the world. It implies the ultimate defeat of humanism, which has been the centre of Western faith. But it need not happen. The exponents of Western ideas are powerful enough to encounter assertive force with quiet strength if they are but willing to uphold their own faith.

They can easily impress upon their opponents the grave risks which must accompany any attempt at wars of conquest. And they can decrease, at the same time, the causes of tension which are responsible for a good deal of warlike resentment, by offering economic benefits to the subjects of dissatisfied Powers, even if they have to bring sacrifices from which they cannot expect immediate returns.

Totalitarian governments do not depend on the outspoken consent of their subjects to their policy; they need not formally inquire whether they are pleased or not, but they must try equally hard to satisfy them. The greater content-ment of their subjects would strengthen their position. It may make them less keen on desperate adventures; but it will raise their self-esteem. The demand for territorial aggrandisement is an excellent device for diverting the

O

public mind from scarcity and discontentment at home. But greater individual contentment and smaller economic tension do not provide permanent substitutes for unsatisfied territorial ambitions. The greater the share of emotional romanticism in these yearnings, the more difficult is their gratification. The romance of trade does not appeal to those disciplined in labour camps and trained in barrack-rooms.

When dissatisfied nations are arming and, what is more dangerous, preparing for a clash by organizing the State economically and spiritually on a war basis, the pacifist countries have no alternative but to spend their treasure on adequate equipment. But they might very well ask themselves whether economic concessions to excluded nations might not be very much cheaper than moderate armaments even if they did involve some trading losses. Rich nations are quite ready to lend their allies money for armaments which may ultimately be lost. Would it not be wiser to offer a disarmament loan to a nation willing to disarm spiritually as well as materially? A timid nation, which does not know its own mind, cannot take this step, for its readiness to offer concessions would be a threat to peace. Militarist governments do not believe in compromise; for the core of the militarist creed is blind faith in fear and coercion. Only the weak seek a compromise in order to keep part of what they have got; the strong take what they like. Concessions from a weak state—weak in will-power as well as in resources—are to them a kind of ransom. Ransom cannot buy permanent security but only temporary respite. Concessions from a strong state, on the other hand, which stands at the full height of its power might not be misunderstood if they are contingent on the beginning of "like-mindedness" in political outlook. Without a trend towards such like-mindedness, no offer of incipient international partnership can succeed. Nations which have put their economic and social systems on a war footing for some lengthy time cannot easily shift to another basis. For without far-going co-operation from abroad disarmament would mean economic disaster and social collapse, and genuine co-operation is impossible without previous spiritual adjustments: it cannot go beyond purely practical particular and definite objects.

The aggrieved Powers can be allowed to work out their own salvation. Whilst their attempts at autarchy should not be hindered, they need not be facilitated. A government which plans permanent economic isolation should not be interfered with, though its withdrawal from a system of world economy need not be made easy. The re-establishment of such a system among the saturated Powers would furnish the most convincing proof of its superiority over autarchy. These countries could keep the door wide open for the return of the autarchists when they are ready for it. They should not bribe them to give up their seclusion, for as long as autarchy is but an economic symbol for barrack-room socialism, the bribe will be of no avail. Autarchists must find out for themselves that they are worshipping false gods. They cannot do so if the others imitate them in a more or less half-hearted way in order to obtain by pressure trifling trading advantages from them and from their own political sympathizers. A system of correlated world economy which works to the advantage of its partners, and which is ready to accept new members whenever they are prepared to subscribe to its tenets needs no propaganda. It presupposes a far-reaching "like-mindedness" amongst its members.

To assume the presence of like-mindedness because it holds out a hope of permanent peace will lead to disaster. Temporary appeasement by unconditional concessions may offer an excellent chance for gaining time. It will make an ultimate clash almost inevitable. No policy has ever been discarded which has been found fruitful of results and congenial to the temper of those pursuing it. The longer the period over which aggressive methods have been successful, the greater the certainty that they will be continued. The actions of Italy and Japan have proved this. Threats and intimidation will become part and parcel, not only of a nation's policy, but ultimately of its moral fibre. If for purely opportunist reasons it is allowed to travel along the easy path of unopposed violence, it will prove to be a road which has no turning. The incompatibility of outlook which separates the two types of modern states is fundamental— it cannot be charmed away by political Couéism or by any sort of faith-healing. Its existence must be recognized before an effort to overcome it can be made.

The world has reached a point where no more new colonial possessions can be won and where many dependencies are striving for independence. The area and the value of colonial possessions are shrinking. The total available is not large enough to permit a peaceful redistribution, such as could satisfy all ambitions. The "Colonial Age" has gone beyond recall. The belated efforts of hungry Powers at empire-making are strengthening the counter-colonization movement. The pressure on the Jews in Germany and Poland, which accelerated the influx into Palestine, has fanned an Arab revolt in that country, whilst Italy is backing a Pan-Arab movement against her more fortunate rivals. And whatever the outcome of Japanese activities in the Far East may be, they mark the beginning of the decline of Western colonizing domination in the East.

The expansionist energies of the West are flagging. The Frontier, which beckoned to enterprising men, has almost vanished: the lure of adventure it called out to is fading. The pioneer spirit is flickering low. Economic security has disappeared, but social security has come in; risks at home are smaller than they were; chances abroad have dwindled. Jobs may be hard to get, but the dole softens men's misery.

The relentless pressure of population is easing. Almost every country inhabited by European stock is approaching a stationary stage—or even facing an impending decline in numbers. The age composition is changing; the proportion of young people is diminishing. In a few decades the over-

crowded hives from which emigration sallied forth may cry
out for immigrants to fill their emptying cells; space may
clamour for men where men now clamour for space. The
economics of expansion are giving way to the economics of
contraction. And the process of contraction may prove more
difficult, more painful, and certainly less glamorous than
the way of expansion over new worlds has been. These
worlds are withdrawing their unlimited opportunities from
older nations. And the shrinkage is felt most severely by
those countries which have not yet undergone a full measure
of internal adjustment. Though they recognize the immi-
nence of external contraction, they do not want to adapt
their structure to an inglorious process of shrinkage. They
sense the impending doom, but they hope to escape from
it by more or less aggressive policies. They cannot change
fundamental tendencies. The colonial struggle for which
they are girding their loins is very much like the fight for
the body of Patroclus—even a victor cannot revive a corpse.
The inequality of territory and resources which exists between
various states at home, can no longer be corrected by
vertical expansion. But *lateral expansion*, the conquest of adjacent
territories or the voluntary federation of neighbouring states,
can go on.

The day of a federated Central Europe is bound to come.
What really matters is the choice of means by which it shall
be accomplished. Federations have been set up by aggressive
conquerors after they had forced the owners of rich provinces
into an unwilling partnership, in order to draw tributes from
their taxes and profits from the exploitation of their wealth.
Or they have been established by voluntary incorporation,
under which regional and racial rights were scrupulously
respected. Developments of this sort, not colonial shuffles,
will decide the future of the old continent.

The world is faced by a very simple issue: Can the
territorial discrepancies between various states be equalized
by economic co-operation and ultimately by some sort of

federation, at first only between contiguous groups with a common background? Or is a new period of violent territorial redistribution beginning, in which old empires will be broken, whilst new empires will be formed on their ruins?

IV

Peaceful federation can bring about greater equality in two ways. It can lessen the friction between the home territories of the federating states: and it can open the door to some sort of international colonial administration. The present mandate system is not even a system of inspectorates. Its adaptation to other colonies is unlikely. France and England might accept some limitations of their sovereignty in their Central African colonies in order to get peace. Can anybody imagine Italy presenting the League of Nations with the supervision of her Ethiopian Empire? Mere censorship is, moreover, scarcely sufficient.

The tendency to federation which has spread over all continents will not stop in Africa, where states have been cut out in rather an arbitrary way.

In every African colony local questions present a great variety of issues. The contrasts between the several colonies of the same Power are sometimes very much greater than those between certain groups of colonies held by various owners. It is impossible to standardize local administrations nationally, and even more impossible to do so internationally. But certain fundamental problems, trade, native policy, defence, communications, finance, are common to all colonies. They could be dealt with in Africa as well as in other continents by central federal agencies. The local administrations must remain national, but a federal government for those common tasks could be established. The owners of colonies, as well as the hitherto excluded nations, could participate in this federal government by shaping its policies as well as by manning its services. In the end unity in native affairs, in commercial policy, in financial matters and in military policy is essential to the European Powers, if they are to carry out their mission in Africa successfully. This mission implies the *ultimate liquidation of domination*. It may be a task of decades or of centuries. It can only be solved successfully if the ruling Powers present a united front. If some of them are ready to break up their empires peacefully, whilst others are intent on making new empires by war, peace in Europe and overseas cannot be maintained. Colonial co-operation for the purpose of liquidating the white man's burden, honourably and profitably to all concerned, is an aim well worth while striving for. It must be the end, not the beginning. For it presupposes a common policy and a common outlook on political aims and on political methods.

INDEX

Africa—
  colonization of, 28, 70–1, 276, 278
  federation in 422–3
  (*See also* Races)
Agrarian revolts, anti-colonial, 103, 162–6
Agriculture—
  effects of over-stimulation of, 322
  population engaged in, 210–11, 212, 216, 224
  protection of, 190
Algeria, 29, 223, 245, 252, 284, 289
Arabs, 146, 150, 285–6, 359, 420
Argentine, 217, 267, 287
Assimilation—
  of immigrants, 65, 146, 272–3, 274
  of subject races—
    compulsory, 39–40, 41–2, 43–4, 80–1, 82–3
    voluntary, 40–1, 73, 80, 82–3, 109–10
Australia, 67, 122, 210–11, 212, 217, 221, 254, 255, 256, 273, 279, 287, 343, 372, 373
Austria, 28, 30, 38, 43, 45, 81, 133–5, 148–9, 204, 206, 208, 209, 220, 225, 274, 275, 370, 393 note, 404
Autarchy—
  contiguous and disconnected, 193–4, 215
  early conceptions of, 111–12, 126–7
  in closed empires, 86–7, 90–1
  in less favoured countries, 192, 194–6, 400–1, 416, 419
  present tendencies towards, in large empires, 185–91
  scope and results of, 192–3

Bacon, Francis, 19, 20, 67, 279
Balkan States, 29, 137, 145, 171, 172, 225, 246

Baltic States, 137, 149, 153, 162–3, 225, 406
Belgium, 146, 157, 201, 205, 210, 212, 224, 249, 327
Bismarck, 129, 130, 139–40, 220, 369–70, 394
Bolshevism. (*See* Communism *and* Russia)
Brazil, 54, 172, 210, 222, 304, 306–7
British Empire, 90–1, 93–4, 120, 190–1, 193, 209, 210, 220, 223, 319, 402–3

Canada, 121, 146, 160, 208, 217, 221, 250, 251, 254, 255, 267, 273, 287
Capital Export. (*See* Debts)
Capitalism—
  and Communism, 35 note, 58, 154–6, 169–70, 171–2, 411–12
  and Imperialism, 35–7, 72–3, 82, 141–2, 154–6
  spread of, 24–5, 26–7, 53, 59–62, 72–3, 75, 141–2, 154, 166–8, 176, 392–3
Change—
  conceptions of, 236–41
  forces of, spontaneous and deliberate, 243–60
  methods of effecting, peaceful and forcible—
    in foreign affairs, 242–3, 248–50, 409–11
    in internal affairs, 238–42, 259, 408–9, 411–13
China, 28, 29, 30, 33, 57, 60–1, 64, 73, 140, 145, 156, 157, 161–2, 203, 211, 222, 230, 291–2, 339, 340, 341, 342, 345, 346, 348, 350, 351–3, 400

Churches, influence of, 13, 15, 16–17, 22–3, 41, 81, 116–17, 133–4, 158, 180

Cobden and Cobdenism, 118, 129, 140 note, 147–8

Colonies—
composite colonies, 76, 77, 79, 284, 289, 371
relations between natives and ruling races in, 52, 70, 76, 77–80, 81–3
structure of, 76, 77–9
native dependencies, 71, 289, 296
cultural and capitalist colonization in, 72–3, 74–6
open-door régime in, 289–91, 295–6
ruling race in, 72, 332
structure of, 71–5, 289
settlement colonies, 66, 67, 71
character of, 66–8
conditions for founding, 68–71

Colonies, value of—
and economic security, 307–9, 311–12
capital investment, 317–18
employment, 313–14, 323, 332–8
military importance, 308–9
raw materials, 298–303, 306–7, 311–12
trade and currency relations, 319–20, 325–7, 328–9

Colonization—
in Africa, 28, 70–1, 276, 289
in the New World, 50, 51, 66–8, 71, 84–5, 86–7, 89–90
conditions of, 276–80, 281–4
extent and limitations of, 27–8, 101, 279, 286, 396, 420, 421
medieval, 27, 47, 49–50, 51–2
primary (political), 45, 46, 50–1, 52–3, 101
secondary—
cultural and spiritual, 47, 52–3, 55–7, 61, 62–4, 65, 72–3, 81–2

Colonization, secondary—*contd.*
economic, 53, 54, 55, 58–9, 59–62, 72–3, 75–6, 170–2
institutional, 57, 59, 64–5, 72–3

Communism—
aims and methods of, 413–15
and conceptions of social change, 240–1, 408, 410–12
and counter-colonization, 153–6, 360, 361
and imperialism, 35 note
and universalism, 181, 414–15

Congo Free State, 28, 74, 278, 290–1, 376

Contraction, tendencies of, 207, 287–8, 420–1

Counter-Colonization (De-Colonization)—
and Declaration of Independence, 102–3, 234–5, 378
and Democracy, 103–5, 109
and French Revolution, 103, 107–8
and Liberalism, 117–19, 140–1
and Monroe Doctrine, 104–5, 235, 378
and nationalism, 133–5
and present empire-making activities, 420
and religion, 116–17
anti-imperialist propaganda—
communist, 76, 15–36, 360, 361, 417; democratic, 416–17
post-war lassitude of imperialist countries, 152–3
post-war movements against secondary colonization—
cultural, 56, 76, 175, 177–80, 182–3, 184
economic:—agrarian, 162–6; financial, 161, 165–6, 168–75, 176–7; commercial. (*See* Economic Nationalism)
self-determination and the Wilsonian programme, 146–8, 150, 156–8, 199–200

Counter-Colonization (De-Colonization)—*continued*
self-government and Dominion status, 156, 202
Crusades, 47, 49–50
Currency—
devaluation, 173–4, 190, 326
exchange control, 173–4, 176–7, 327–8, 401
gold standard, 95–6, 174–5, 190
manipulation, 111–12, 126–7, 191, 193, 325–7, 328–9, 331, 403
stabilization, 95–6, 403
Czechoslovakia, 145, 149, 162, 163, 209, 225, 404

Darwinism, 112–14, 240, 280, 374
Dawes Plan, 177 note, 392
Debts (Foreign Loans)—
bankruptcy—
pre-war repudiations, 167–9; post-war, 165, 169–70, 171–3, 174–5, 176–7
export of capital—
pre-war, 59–61, 141–2, 166–7, 316–8; post-war, 170–1
(*See also* Devaluation *and* Exchange Control)
Declaration of Independence, 33, 102–3, 107 note, 200, 232–3, 234–5, 378
De-colonization. (*See* Counter-Colonization)
Democracy, 21–3, 23–4, 102–5, 107, 179, 407–8, 416–17
Devaluation. (*See* Currency)
Discrimination, 161–2, 304–7, 315, 329–30, 404
Dissatisfied countries. (*See* Have-not countries)
Dominions—
and immigration, 159, 255, 279, 287
economic nationalism in, 120–2, 160

Dominions—*continued*
status of, 156, 202, 223
structure of, 221–2, 273

East, relations of the, with the West, 14–15, 52, 55–7, 59–61, 63–4, 88, 157, 161–2, 184, 341–2, 346–7
East India Company, 82, 92
Economic hospitality, international code of, 288, 397
Economic nationalism—
colonial, 120, 121–2, 125
continental, 122–5, 136, 161, 400–2
(*See also* Autarchy *and* Protection)
Egalitarianism, 21–3, 81–2, 102–3, 107–8, 116, 232–5, 245–6, 264
Egypt, 29, 57, 60–1, 140, 145, 150, 203, 218
Emigration. (*See* Migration)
Empire—
characteristics of, 33–5, 218–20, 221–4
methods of founding, 38–9
types of—
horizontal (lateral) and vertical, 42–5, 396; insular and continental, 222–4; ancient, 34, 40–1, 219; modern, 223–4
Equality, meanings and early conceptions of—
and Declaration of Independence, 102–3, 200, 232–3, 234–5
and French Revolution, 23, 103–4
and religious teachings, 22–3, 116
of individuals, 23, 229, 232–4, 235
of states, 227–8, 229–33, 234, 235
(*See also* Inequality)

Equality of opportunity—
and open-door régimes, 289–97
and the Wilsonian system, 396–7
in new countries, 265–70, 272–5
of individuals, 229, 232, 261–3,
296–7
of states, 243, 261–2, 402
Equality of status—
factors diminishing—
capitulations, 204–5
financial control, 203–4
limiting clauses of treaties,
204–5
tributes, 204
of individuals, 103, 233
of states, 203–5, 227–33, 234
Ethiopia, 303, 355–9, 362–5, 378,
400
Exchange control. (*See* Currency)
Expansion, commercial, 84–97,
140–2, 292, 345, 347–50,
400
Expansion, territorial
future possibilities of, 258–9, 396,
420–1
horizontal (lateral) and vertical,
43–4

Fascism, 180–1, 232, 355, 409,
413–5
Federation—
conditions and scope of, 38,
202–3, 248–9, 271, 421–3
types and examples of, 402–3,
421
Feudalism, 36–7, 67, 74, 76, 79,
88 note, 122, 140
Financial control, 59–60, 60–1,
203–4
Foreign Loans. (*See* Debts)
France—
and French Empire, 28, 29, 91,
143, 150, 223–4, 245, 296,
319
population tendencies, 224, 252–
3, 254, 257
trade, 123, 218, 292

Free seas, doctrine of the, 187–8,
310–1
Free Trade—
and present situation, 331–2,
397–9, 400–2
growth of, 89, 92–7, 117–19

Gandhi, Mr., 155, 184, 230
Geographical factors—
and equality, 209–10
and security, 214
Germany—
a homogeneous continental
super-state, 183–4, 220, 225,
369–70, 394
anti-universalism, 177–80,182–3,
colonization, medieval and modern, 28, 29, 30, 49, 79, 368,
371–2
emigration, 139–40, 274–5, 393
movement for unity, 108, 123–4,
129, 133–4, 368–70
population, 210, 215–16, 253–4,
256, 394–5
post-war economic position,
175–7, 194, 209, 391–5,
400–1
the colonial question, 183, 194,
224–5, 337, 368, 371–8,
379–81, 382–91, 393–4
trade, 217–18, 295, 328
Gold Standard. (*See* Currency)
Great Britain—
and empire-making, 28, 29, 30,
39, 43, 86–7, 140–1, 143,
152–3
population figures and tendencies, 210, 212, 251, 253, 254
post-war trade and currency
policy, 173, 190, 216, 321
under Free Trade, 117–19,
123–4
Greece, 34, 40–1, 150, 151, 159

Have-not countries—
attitude to *status quo*, 242–6
colonial demands, 275

Have-not countries—*continued*
economic problems of—
  raw materials supplies, 320–2;
    population pressure, 225,
    251–60, 399–400; trade re-
    strictions, 194–6, 259–60,
    321, 396–9, 401–2
meaning of term, 224–5
measures to satisfy: territorial
  or commercial concessions,
  331, 396–9, 416, 418–20
Herero War, 373–5
Holland. (*See* Netherlands)
Hungary, 38, 55, 133, 134–5, 171,
  172, 204, 209, 217, 218, 225

Immigration. (*See* Migration)
Imperialism—
  League Against, 156 note
  meaning of, 33, 35
  methods of, 33–46
  post-war decline of, 152–3
  pre-war revival of, 138–45
  types of—
    capitalist, 35–7, 141–2
    commercial, 34–6, 50, 84–8,
      140–2
    communist, 35–7, 181
    feudal, 36, 50
    propagandist, 37, 39–40, 41–2,
      43–4, 80–1, 82–3
    tolerant, 34, 40–1, 52, 73, 80,
      82–3
India, 46, 56, 73, 110, 145, 156,
  162, 184, 211, 222–3, 230,
  289
Industrial Revolution, 24, 92–3,
  129–30, 264
Industrialization, 120–5, 161, 190,
  211, 213, 252
Inequality—
  and economic security, 213–18
  and geographical situation, 209–
    10, 213, 214–15
  and hierarchy of states, 201–3,
    218–20
  and industrial development, 211

Inequality—*continued*
  and military security, 214
  and "old" and "young" coun-
    tries, 206–7
  and resources and undeveloped
    lands, 208–9, 213, 215
  and size and density of popula-
    tion, 208, 210, 212, 215–16,
    254–7
  and wealth, 212–13
  of individuals, 23, 116, 199,
    236–7, 241–2
  of states, 199, 200–26, 242–6, 250
International Steel Cartel, 305–6
Iraq, 150, 200, 294
Ireland, 30, 43, 48–9, 54, 56, 67,
  76, 81, 103, 110, 146, 150,
  152–3, 162, 164, 172, 261,
  402, 409
Italy
  and empire-making, 28, 29,
    143–4, 150, 353
  and Ethiopia, 323, 355–9, 362–5,
    366–7, 422
  emigration, 274, 314, 354
  population, 216, 224, 253, 254,
    339, 353, 354, 355–6, 394–5
  present economic position of, 209,
    210, 212, 213, 216, 217, 218,
    319, 339, 353–5, 356–9, 400
  unification of, 129, 133–4, 352–3

Japan
  and commercial expansion, 292,
    345, 347–50, 400
  and territorial expansion, 342–3,
    345–6, 350–2, 419, 420
  cultural and institutional rela-
    tions with the West, 59,
    341–2, 346–7
  emigration, 259–60, 274, 314,
    340–1, 343–4, 345, 348
  population, 210, 216, 224, 253,
    254, 255–6, 339, 340
  present economic position, 209,
    212, 213, 215, 216–17, 218,
    339–41, 345, 347–50

Jews, the, 146, 150, 157, 159, 179, 180, 182, 285–6, 420

Latin America, 160, 188–9, 206, 222, 225, 279
League of Nations—
  and dependence and self-determination, 200, 378
  and Mandates, 200, 292–4, 303–4, 383
  and sanctions, 302–4
  and peaceful change, 409–10
Lenin, on Imperialism, 35 note

Machiavelli, 19, 20, 76
Manchuria (Manchukuo), 157, 279, 291–2, 299, 341, 346, 348, 349, 350
Mandates—
  equality of opportunity under, 292–4
  Germany and, 383–4, 387
  the League and, 200, 292–4, 303–4, 373, 383
Mexico, 26, 29, 44, 45, 46, 61–2, 76, 77, 85, 104, 105, 164–6, 172, 250, 279, 284
Migration
  causes and results of—
    population pressure, 251–60;
    increased equality of opportunity, 265–70, 272, 401–2
  emigration figures, 252–3, 287, 354, 393 note
  emigration and the colonial problem, 255, 273–5
  immigration, and figures, 159, 160, 252, 255, 287
  post-war immigration restrictions, 159–60, 255–6, 354, 355, 393, 399
  refugees and population transfer arrangements, 155, 159–60, 256
Monopolies, 297, 299–301, 302, 304–7

Monroe Doctrine, 47, 60 note, 104–5, 205–6, 235, 378
Morocco, 30, 57, 224, 245, 289, 292
Most-favoured nation clause, 94, 270, 296–7, 315, 330, 331, 404
  elimination of—
    by devaluation and exchange control, 330, 331, 404
    by inter-imperial arrangements, 190

Nationalism—
  meaning of, 105–6
  of ruling races, 135–8, 139–40, 142–4
  of subject races, 82–3, 102–4, 128, 133–5, 144–8, 156–8
  types of—
    biological, 112–6
    institutional, 76, 107–8
    linguistic, 109–11
    spiritual, 107, 112
Native races. (See Races)
Nazism, 177, 180–4, 247, 415
Negroes—
  nationalism, 360
  slavery, 80, 116, 280–1
Netherlands, 30, 86, 87, 201, 224, 320, 327
Neutrality—
  and autarchy, 187–8, 192, 309, 311–12
  and free seas, 187, 309–11
New Learning, the, 18–19, 24
New Zealand, 67, 212, 255, 279, 294, 372, 373

"Old" and "young" nations, meanings of term. (See Inequality)
Open-door régime—
  extent of, 289–97
  object of, 296–7
  infringement of, 291–2, 329–30
Ottawa Agreements, 190, 321

Palestine, 150, 159, 285–6, 388, 420
Peace Treaties, 149–50, 163, 204, 205, 231, 391
Persia, 30, 57, 59, 151, 157
Philippines, 29, 143, 157, 200, 296, 322
Poland, 134, 146, 149, 153, 209, 225
Population—
  attitudes of countries with increasing and with stationary populations, 255–8
  birth rates, 256, 394
  density, 208, 210, 224, 254
  occupational structure of, 210–11, 212, 216, 224
  population movements and change, 251–60, 420–1
  reproduction rates, 207, 254, 255, 394–5
  size, 221, 222, 223, 224
Portugal and Portuguese Empire, 30, 71, 84–8, 201, 224, 278, 319, 376, 385–6
Preferential treatment—
  Great Britain's attitude to, 190, 404
  in customs unions, 123–5, 405
  of colonies, 296, 301–2
  of independent states, 404–5
Protection, in various countries, 120–7, 136, 161–2, 321
  present tendencies, 397–9

Races, interrelation of—
  assimilation, 43–6, 80–1
  economic co-operation and friction, 69–76, 276–7
  expulsion and extirpation, 71, 279–80, 281–5
  in Ethiopia, 362–5, 366
  in German South-West Africa, 374–6
  in South Africa, 79, 382
  in the East, 55–7
  separation and exclusion, 78–80, 82, 382

Raw material resources, unequal distribution of, 208–9, 215, 298–301, 302, 322, 339, 354, 397
Reformation, the, 16–17
Restriction schemes, 304–5
Russia—
  and Communism, 35 note, 153–6, 169–70, 172, 176, 181, 410–12, 414
  and economic isolation, 136, 185–6
  and nationalism, 135–7
  autarchy and defence, 58–9, 161
  expansion of, 28–9, 37, 50–1, 210
  voluntary colonization in, 57–9

Sanctions, 302–3, 309
Scandinavian countries, 210, 244, 246, 275
Security, factors affecting, 213–18, 298–300, 302, 307–9, 311–12
Settlement. (See Colonization)
Smuts, General, 382, 384
Social Militarism, 406–8, 413
Socialism, 264, 411, 412
South Africa, 67, 77, 79, 140, 146, 208, 222, 251, 278, 280, 284, 372, 373, 380, 384–5, 386
South America. (See Latin America)
Sovereignty, 199, 202, 204, 205, 206
Spain, 14, 29, 71, 76, 77, 84–90, 103–5, 108, 157, 218, 224, 247, 274, 367–8, 393
Standardization and universalism, 21, 24
State, the—
  medieval, 13–14
  modern, 15–17, 19–20, 25–6: absolutist, 22, 81, 106–7; democratic, 21–2, 23, 107, 228–9
  the totalitarian state, 245–6, 262–3, 281–3, 401, 417–18
  Communism, 35 note, 153–6, 181, 240–1, 360, 361, 408, 410–12, 413–15

State, the—*continued*
Fascism, 180–1, 232, 355, 409, 413–15
Nazism, 177, 180–4, 415
Social Militarism, 406–8, 413
Super-state, conception of, 33–4, 41, 183–4, 369–70, 394, 406–7
Switzerland, 157–8, 205, 208, 209, 210, 225, 244, 246, 275
Syria, 150, 200, 294

Totalitarian governments. (*See* State)
Trade—
trade policies—
Adam Smith, 88 note, 118
List, 123–4, 125
Manchester School, 88 note, 117–19, 140, 142
of old colonial empires, 85–7, 89–91, 297
Physiocrats, 88 note, 92
trade figures, 216, 217–18, 319–20
trading companies, 92, 290–1
(*See also* Free Trade, Monopolies, Most-favoured-nation clause, Open-door régimes)
Turkey, 28, 29, 30, 33, 57, 59, 60–1, 64, 137, 140, 146, 149–52, 172, 203, 205, 212

United States—
and foreign debts, 167–8, 172
and immigration, 146, 160, 265–7, 287, 314, 343, 354–5, 393
and Latin America, 188–9, 205–6
and open-door régime—
in China, 30, 291–2; under mandates, 293

United States—*continued*
dollar diplomacy, 29
influence on counter-colonization, 33, 102–3, 104, 107 note, 146–8, 199–200, 234–5, 378
present neutrality policy, 188–9, 192, 309–12
structure of, 67, 207, 221
tendencies to autarchy, 187–8, 216
territorial expansion, 29–30, 104–5, 143
Universalism—
Bolshevism, Fascism, Nazism and, 181–3, 414–15
medieval, 13–14; break up of, 15–17, 25, 106
spread of modern, 20–1, 25–7, 53, 108, 109; democracy and capitalism as sources of, 24–5
tendencies disintegrating, 109, 184, 415–16;

Versailles, Treaty of. (*See* Peace Treaties)
Vulnerability, specific and general, 215–18

War and war economics, 129–32, 243–4, 398, 407, 413
Wealth—
comparative aggregate and *per capita* figures, 212–13
conceptions of, 88–9
Westminster, Statute of, 156, 202
Wilson, President, and the Wilsonian system, 39, 107 note, 146–8, 199–200, 292, 396–7

Yugoslavia, 162, 163